Islam, Revival, and Reform

Modern Intellectual and Political History of the Middle East
Fred H. Lawson, *Series Editor*

Select titles in Modern Intellectual and Political History of the Middle East

The Autocratic Parliament: Power and Legitimacy in Egypt, 1866–2011
Irene Weipert-Fenner

Figures That Speak: The Vocabulary of Turkish Nationalism
Matthew deTar

Hakibbutz Ha'artzi, Mapam, and the Demise of the Israeli Labor Movement
Tal Elmaliach; Haim Watzman, trans.

Iran's Experiment with Parliamentary Governance: The Second Majles, 1909–1911
Mangol Bayat

National Symbols in Modern Iran: Identity, Ethnicity, and Collective Memory
Menahem Merhavy

Sayyid Qutb: An Intellectual Biography
Giedrė Šabasevičiūtė

Shaykh Yūsuf al-Qaraḍāwī: Spiritual Mentor of Wasaṭī *Salafism*
Sagi Polka

Watermelon Democracy: Egypt's Turbulent Transition
Joshua Stacher

For a full list of titles in this series,
visit https://press.syr.edu/supressbook-series
/modern-intellectual-and-political-history-of-the-middle-east/.

Islam, Revival, and Reform

Redefining Tradition for the Twenty-First Century

Essays Inspired by John O. Voll

Edited by
Natana J. DeLong-Bas

Syracuse University Press

First Edition 2022

22 23 24 25 26 27 6 5 4 3 2 1

∞ The paper used in this publication meets the minimum requirements of the American National Standard for Information Sciences—Permanence of Paper for Printed Library Materials, ANSI Z39.48-1992.

For a listing of books published and distributed by Syracuse University Press, visit https://press.syr.edu.

ISBN: 978-0-8156-3753-0 (hardcover)
978-0-8156-3750-9 (paperback)
978-0-8156-5545-9 (e-book)

Library of Congress Cataloging-in-Publication Data

Names: DeLong-Bas, Natana J., editor.
Title: Islam, revival, and reform : redefining tradition for the twenty-first century / edited by Natana J. DeLong-Bas.
Description: First edition. | Syracuse : Syracuse University Press, 2022. | Series: Modern intellectual and political history of the Middle East | Includes bibliographical references and index. | Summary: "This edited volume examines the 18th century roots of the often-troubled marriage of politics and religion in the Muslim world and their impact on contemporary developments, including the globalization of Islam in the 21st century"— Provided by publisher.
Identifiers: LCCN 2021029935 (print) | LCCN 2021029936 (ebook) | ISBN 9780815637530 (hardcover) | ISBN 9780815637509 (paperback) | ISBN 9780815655459 (ebook)
Subjects: LCSH: Islam and politics—21st century. | Islam and state—21st century.
Classification: LCC BP173.7 .I8554 2022 (print) | LCC BP173.7 (ebook) | DDC 297.2/72—dc23
LC record available at https://lccn.loc.gov/2021029935
LC ebook record available at https://lccn.loc.gov/2021029936

Manufactured in the United States of America

Contents

Preface

In 1982, John O. Voll published his pivotal work *Islam: Continuity and Change in the Modern World*,[1] presenting an overview of Islamic history that showed the dynamism of the Islamic tradition and its integral role as part of world history, both interacting with and being acted upon by other civilizations and cultures. This work was one of the first to apply the world historical approach to the study of Islamic civilization and societies,[2] challenging otherwise Eurocentric narratives and arguing for ongoing developments within the broader Islamic tradition as Muslims sought authenticity and legitimacy in their struggle to connect historical tradition to their current needs and the developments of their surrounding societies. In addition, it took a global view of Islam, moving beyond the Arab world to include other majority-Muslim populations in South and Southeast Asia and Africa.[3]

One of the book's most important contributions was the discussion of the eighteenth-century world, arguing that the more well-known events of the nineteenth and twentieth centuries had their roots in an

1. A second edition of this work followed in 1994 (Voll 1994b).

2. This work built upon the three-volume work by Marshall Hodgson (1974) as a precursor to world history and preceded other world historical approaches such as Ira Lapidus's book *A History of Islamic Societies*, which marked its third edition in 2014.

3. Voll's book stood in contrast to other works more focused on Arab civilizations and cultures, such as Albert Hourani's *A History of the Arab Peoples* (1991), which, although addressing history comprehensively through the examination of multiple disciplines—including politics, economics, society, and religion as well as multiple layers of "notables"—nevertheless remained focused exclusively on the Arab world.

earlier and, in many ways, more remarkable era, particularly where the quest for "authentic" identity came to be rooted in Islam. Rather than focusing exclusively on the standard political-military narratives of the purported decline of the great Muslim empires, Voll's work included attention to religious and social history, highlighting three major themes for the eighteenth century that showed dynamism and activism: (1) the decentralization of political control and the emergence of regional, provincial, and local notables with increasing degrees of autonomy, if not independence; (2) reorientation of the Sufi tradition, neo-Sufism,[4] toward purification and adherence to a more rigorous interpretation of the Islamic tradition; and (3) the emergence of revivalist movements aimed at the sociomoral reconstruction of society (Voll 1994b, 25). Voll used these themes to explore the trends of scholarship that accompanied them, in particular the attention given to the content (*matn*) of hadith rather than to the chain of transmission (*isnad*); movement away from dependence on medieval scholars (*taqlid*) in favor of independent reasoning (*ijtihad*) and direct study of the Qur'an and hadith; and the Islamic tradition's capacity for revival and reform to spark mass movements upon which new states were founded.[5] These themes have continued to motivate Islamic revival and reform movements in the twentieth and twenty-first centuries as the quest for authenticity and legitimacy continues to shape and be shaped by religious and social identity formation and consolidation in a globalized world. They have also shaped and continue to be shaped by a generation of scholars influenced by Voll's work.

This edited collection serves as testimony to the global impact of Voll's world historical framework, methodology, and careful attention

4. This theme built upon an earlier work by Fazlur Rahman (1979) that noted the eighteenth-century trend toward hadith studies in Sufi circles, which he coined "neo-Sufism," and the increased devotion to Muhammad that accompanied it. Voll examined Rahman's theory in greater depth.

5. For information on the foundational interregional hub of these ideas and how they played out in different movements throughout the Islamic world, see Voll 1994b, 51–83.

to the ongoing relevance of religion in global affairs, rooted in the experiences of everyday people. Beginning in the eighteenth and early nineteenth centuries with case studies from rigorous, fundamentalist[6] movements in Arabia and Africa, on the one hand, and trends in neo-Sufism in India, the Maghrib, and the Sudan, on the other, the collection examines both religious and political roots for contemporary developments throughout the Arab world and into Turkey, South Asia, China, Europe, and even cyberspace, with careful attention to the interplays between religious and social movements and developments as well as the contexts in which they are lived and elaborated upon by people from all walks of life.

The collection opens with consideration of several pivotal eighteenth- and early nineteenth-century scholars who founded lasting movements and trends that have ongoing influence. The first study by Natana J. DeLong-Bas engages a comparative study of the role of women as both adherents and active agents in expanding and consolidating the eighteenth-century Wahhabi movement in Arabia and early nineteenth-century Sokoto Caliphate in what is today northern Nigeria and the Sudan. Both movements reflect Voll's central themes of rising notables exercising increasing agency and independence to the point of challenging existing social and political orders, more rigorous interpretations of the Islamic tradition with particular focus on scripture, and attention to the sociomoral reconstruction of society. What is new in this contribution is DeLong-Bas's focus on women's active participation as students, teachers, and guarantors of education for both women and men. She also gives attention to the unique ways in which women contributed to and embodied the broader religious project of adhering to *tawhid* and eliminating *shirk* by eradicating practices associated with popular beliefs and superstitions as well as

6. The term *fundamentalist*, as defined in Voll 1994b, 22, refers to movements that place the scriptures of religions as the basis for establishing a permanent standard by which existing conditions are to be judged. This position stands in contrast to conservative movements that seek to preserve the past in order to maintain continuity.

reappropriating and reinterpreting women's status and roles within their societies. She further argues that restoration of this story to the broader history of Islamic revival and reform movements allows for a more complex and comprehensive understanding of what sociomoral reconstruction of society looks like with clear precedents and role models for contemporary women to follow as they continue to claim, expand, and repurpose their places in public life.

Marcia Hermansen's analysis of Shāh Walī Allāh of Delhi's methodology of hadith studies connects two eighteenth-century themes highlighted by Voll: reorienting the Sufi tradition through a more rigorous interpretation of the foundational sources and moving hadith interpretation beyond strictly legal or formulaic parameters. Hermansen situates Walī Allāh within the broader context of the Islamic religious sciences, highlighting both the importance of his studies in the increasingly cosmopolitan scholarly environment of Mecca and Medina, where he engaged scholars and instructors from the Hijaz, Indian subcontinent, and North Africa, as well as a wide body of materials and influences that expanded his vision of Islamic intellectual history. Hermansen details Walī Allāh's work to combine spiritual lineage with intellectual learning in his quest to synthesize and unify competing methodological currents, connecting the orthodoxy frequently attributed to literalists and legal specialists concerned with externalities of hadith in chains of transmission, frequency, and reliability to the inner meanings of hadith typically associated with Sufism. Rejecting a singular standard approach to hadith, Walī Allāh's complex methodology required flexibility in considering the legal, contextual, and pragmatic parameters of hadith that enabled both compliance with the law and recovery of its spirit and rationale—the wisdom behind the rulings. The end product is a worldview informed by a mystical understanding of the cosmos that nevertheless conforms to the procedure and intellectual traditions of the Islamic religious sciences, incorporating rather than displacing the shari'a disciplines of hadith knowledge and legal sciences within a broad vision of metaphysics.

Following another major theme of Voll's work that moves beyond foundational figures to their expanding influence through groups of followers,[7] Knut S. Vikør examines the emergence of the nineteenth-century Sanūsīya *ṭarīqa* through debates about Sufism, theology, and law as he investigates the formation of a subsidiary *ṭarīqa* from a foundational one and considers what signifiers indicate the distinction between the two. Vikør's main investigation concerns the previously unknown history of a conflict between two of Aḥmad b. Idrīs's students, Muḥammad b. 'Alī al-Sanūsī and Ibrāhīm al-Rashīd, and how other scholars were drawn into the theological disagreements between them, in particular the rejection of *taqlid* of the four law schools, accompanied by charges of excessive *ijtihad* and whether a particular hadith had been abrogated or was being misinterpreted, either in terms of its content or in terms of its application to a nonrelated case. All of this also led to serious questions about the morality of those following al-Rashīd's purported innovation (*bid'a*). Although the dispute occurred between two Sufi leaders, the issues at the center were predominantly legal in nature, highlighting the reorientation of Sufism toward a more rigorous interpretation of the overall tradition. The juridical and theological debates swirling around this particular case also showcase the interconnection of Muslim scholars in different locations—ongoing debates and discussions between them not only about the issues but also about their potential impact on other believers and how and why relative levels of religious authority were determined and either agreed or disagreed upon. As such, this case study provides a rich mosaic of Islamic legal and theological scholarship and the relationships between various Sufi leaders and renowned jurists, many of whom were Sufis. It is particularly notable that these two categories were not mutually exclusive but relational, suggesting bidirectional fluidity between Sufism and law.

Albrecht Hofheinz's richly detailed documentation of the Majādhīb family of Islamic scholars in al-Qaḍārif in the eastern Sudan similarly engages Voll's framework of decentralization of history by examining it through the lens of a particular group of local notables working to

7. See, for example, Voll 1975, 1980, and 1987.

preserve their tradition and socioeconomic position in a time of change and uncertainty rooted in the invasion by Turco-Egyptian forces in the 1820s. Hofheinz situates this family within vast networks of scholarship, transmission, and *ṭarīqa*s, presenting them as bastions of continuity in learning, particularly of the law, at the same time that he records details of the practical, protective roles they were expected to play as *faqih*s for their populations through their powers as "holy men" providing medical aid, political intervention, security, and psychosocial help. He observes that the effectiveness of the *faqih*s was not unidirectional but relational in nature as effectiveness was rooted in the recipient's faith and trust in both God and the method used by the *faqih*, thus disturbing portrayals of religious tradition that focus exclusively on the scholar or leader at the center. This case study of a particular family offers insight into the inner workings of a local community and records interactions with other contending groups, the Turkish authorities, shifting populations, and developments in agriculture and local markets. Here, history is demonstrated as emanating outward from the focal point of this family as active agents of continuity and adjustment rather than as objects simply acted upon from the center, even as they contended with external events that affected family dynamics, including fragmentation from within, such as differences of opinion about responding to the call of the Mahdi in the late nineteenth century.

Having documented and analyzed major trends and developments in religious movements and groups of scholars, the collection then turns to their impact on changing political dynamics in the modern Islamic world and how we study them. Jonathan Wyrtzen uses the complex web of political unrest from Northwest Africa to Central Asia in the aftermath of the Treaty of Sèvres of 1920 as a case study for challenging historical methodologies rooted in nationalism and colonialism. He presses instead for a methodology that expands on the world historical approach and consideration of Islam and the Islamic world as a "special world system"[8] in order to call for explicit attention to methodological

8. Drawn from Voll 1994a.

relationalism that allows for the interconnection and interaction of local, regional, and global entities and trends as a more realistic approach to the complex histories of the time. He observes that the treaty—as a product developed, debated, and signed by external military powers seeking to negotiate, divide, and control other regions from their own centers—actually resolved very little. Wyrtzen contends that the colonial powers, rather than "making the Middle East" and setting it on the presumed linear, chronological path to "modernity" as they prided themselves on doing, really created a volatile situation that required ongoing attention and presence to try to control local populations contending with colonial powers in a mutual struggle for transformation of the greater political project. He recommends methodologically analyzing these events relationally and thus rebalancing each party's and its associated network's capacity to affect and be affected by the other in the quest for a more nuanced understanding of the Great War and the "making of the modern Middle East" than typically occurs with the Eurocentric lens of the Sykes-Picot Standard Narrative. Zooming out to a broader view of the entire hemisphere provides a more complex view of not only the Mediterranean but also its interconnection with Atlantic and Indian Ocean waterways that were host to a series of skirmishes between different European countries that simultaneously struggled to control local populations and produced future heroes of their own. Wyrtzen contends that the surrounding context of constant unrest throughout the entire region dating to 1911 set the stage for the ultimate eruption of the transregional Great War in 1914 and sheds light on the complexity of a war fought in so many different theaters. This context also calls for a different understanding of documents such as the Treaty of Sèvres. He believes the treaty is better understood not as a definitive resolution but as a signpost marking aspirations that over time would be subject to amendment and redefinition as circumstances developed. As such, it is an imagined political future from the eyes of the signatories, not necessarily a view from the ground by the people who would be living out the terms.

York Norman's study of Turkish liberal conceptions of the caliphate also shows the complex interplays involved in the development of representational government, focusing on the powerful symbolism of the caliphate as the nexus for contending visions of religious symbolism and political change in the early twentieth century. Mustafa Kemal Atatürk's abrupt termination of the caliphate and then of the Ottoman monarchy in favor of a radically and comprehensively secular, republican, and ethnic Turkish nationalist state marked an end to the public role of religion in Turkey across the board—culturally, legally, economically, educationally, socially, politically, and even linguistically. This pressure from the urban center toward the rural periphery ignored alternative voices seeking a more moderate response that would retain symbolic ties both to the Ottoman dynasty and to the public role of Islam as an appeal to authenticity and legitimacy intended to prevent a reactionary "return" to an even more absolutist regime. Ultimately, the back-and-forth between the radical secularist nationalists and the liberal constitutional monarchists highlights the complexity of debates about legitimate governments and rulers in the midst of ongoing European colonialism, occupation, and warfare; contending power seekers; and whether past political and cultural identity had to be sacrificed in order to modernize effectively. In the process, Norman highlights the ongoing and persistent appeal of "Islamic unity" discussed by Voll,[9] rooted in the community and personified by the caliphate, that ultimately divided the country at the same time that the British sought to reappropriate the caliphate to further their own agenda of weakening the Ottomans by justifying and empowering Arab separatism. Alongside ethnic and nationalist pride and prestige, the tensions between remembered, reinterpreted, and even imagined historical and religious identities continued to play a central role in political decision making. Norman concludes that these tensions have remained at play in Turkey ever since, helping to explain the ongoing challenge of movements identified with political Islam.

9. Voll also uses the terminology of "pan-Islam" and "nationalizing Islam" in discussing ideas of Turkish identity and broader unity at this time. See Voll 1994b, 190–95.

Shadi Hamid continues the discussion of political Islam in the contemporary era, assessing how religion, more specifically Islam, might be most productively analyzed and debated as a central component of Islamist movements by recognizing its pervasive presence in the public arena yet not engaging in reductionism or assigning it too much causal power. Within that construct, he calls for resisting the urge simply to insist that Islam plays a role in politics without questioning the nature of that role or assuming that it is necessarily and inherently "conservative." In fact, he notes that these Islamist movements have adopted not only Islamic concepts and terms but also in some cases the language of procedural democracy in order to push back against authoritarian regimes, as highlighted by the case of the Egyptian Muslim Brotherhood. This suggests that the Islamic tradition, rather than being inherently authoritarian, contains within it the seeds for defiance and opposition. In an argument rooted in Voll's assessment that the resurgence of Islam visible in the early 1980s was not "simply the last gasp of a dying religious tradition" (Voll 1994b, 2) but rather the entrance into a new phase of its history, Hamid proceeds to reexamine assumptions about modernity and the lack of space for religious belief and motivation in it. He follows in Voll's rejection of simplistic narratives that assert "secularism" as winning over "Islam," noting that looking only at parliamentary or elite politics tends to mask more localized, grassroots expressions of explicitly Islamic and Islamist sentiment. He also draws attention to the use of Islamic idiom by many players, even by purportedly secular parties, and how states have worked to try to control the kind of "Islam" their subjects need either to embrace or to acquiesce to. He notes the durability of Islamism, rooted as it is in religious beliefs that do not require the same level of proven efficacy as secular or other nonreligious ideologies, whose apparent truth must be evidenced in military or material successes or must be disproven by the lack thereof. In the end, Hamid believes that what is needed is a more robust analysis that engages the complex interaction among theology, doctrine, and political context that recognizes the ongoing presence of religion in the public arena and seeks to determine whether, how, and to what extent to accommodate, support, or encourage that presence and what "Islam" means in relation to the nation-state and political legitimacy.

The evolving understanding and accommodation of Islam in the political realm is further examined in Abdullah al-Arian's case study of the Egyptian Muslim Brotherhood, tracing its history from its foundation in 1928 to its electoral victory and ultimate downfall in a military coup in 2013. Al-Arian calls for a reevaluation of the Brotherhood as a movement rather than as a political party, focusing on its ideological core, goals, and modes of operation, as well as for the contextualization of its emergence in Egypt's transitional period from a colonized protectorate to a modern nation-state. He argues that understanding this movement as purely antagonistic, whether toward nation building, modernization processes, or the state itself, or looking only at its provision of social services overlooks its context within both Islamic modernist movements and the Egyptian national movement. Either approach also fails effectively to answer lingering questions about the viability of its Islamist project and its compatibility with modern forms of governance. Like Voll, al-Arian challenges the compartmentalization of "secular" and "religious," arguing instead for a view that encompasses ongoing interaction and mutual influence—for instance, the Brotherhood's internalization of key features of the modern state since the interwar period. Following Voll's argument that it was the traditional centers of religious and political authority rather than "Islam" as a motivating idiom that had declined, al-Arian argues that the critical issue for the Brotherhood was a reinterpretation of what a modern state with a modern legal system and political authority might look like and what the role of Islam might be within it as both the authoritarian state and the Islamic movements struggled to legitimize their claims to religious authority. In the process, populations had to grapple with emerging political, social, and economic orders from which they often felt alienated even as they sought to develop a new understanding of what an authentically Islamic order might look like—an understanding that al-Arian contends included not revolution but rather greater popular agency and modern notions of citizenship working within the existing state structure. Thus, he observes that the events of the Arab Spring resulted in increased participation by Islamist-oriented parties, including both the Muslim Brotherhood and the Salafis, in elections that ultimately maintained the legislature's existing structure and functions.

While much academic and policy attention has focused on political interpretations of Islam in the contemporary era, from the perspective of globalization there are other trends with much larger audiences and impact—namely, the production and dissemination of knowledge; the phenomenon of Islamic preaching via satellite television, books, websites, and social media; and the production and global broadcasting of music with an Islamic message. The reality of a truly globalized world is that all cultures and languages have become open, even if unawarely selectively, to those who choose to pursue them, particularly where education and mass media can play a supportive role. At the same time, the contemporary, technologically savvy, and positive messages of inclusion, participation, and relevance target youth in particular in an effort to engage in revival and reform of Islam as a normal and integrated part of daily life, while rejecting blind adherence (*taqlid*) and obedience to past tradition.

Shuang Wen opens an alternative approach to the study of history through groups of scholars by examining the mutual production of knowledge between Arab and Chinese scholars in Egypt in the twentieth and twenty-first centuries. Building creatively on Voll's twin themes of the emergence of local notables with autonomy and restoring voices far from the center to the historical conversation, she displaces the West in favor of the East and the "other" East, arguing that the domination of Western hegemony in the study of history has resulted in a false assumption that the West is the appropriate reference and vantage point for the study of world history. She painstakingly documents interactions between Chinese and Arab scholars and students, highlighting the importance of education as a mutual endeavor and tracing intellectual impact through both scholarship and translations in both directions, particularly through Arab and Hui modernists. Her contribution is particularly significant for the study of the globalization of Islam and the Arab world because it fills in information that remains largely inaccessible in the West owing to gaps in knowledge of the Arabic and Chinese languages. Yet, as she demonstrates, this small field of contact has expanded today to include language instruction, translation, literary criticism, and political analyses, even as trade with China has expanded throughout the Arab world, particularly in the Persian Gulf countries.

Tuve Buchmann Floden examines the "new brand" of Muslim media preachers through case studies of Amr Khaled of Egypt, Ahmad al-Shugairi of Saudi Arabia, and Tariq al-Suwaidan of Kuwait. Floden argues that their intentional engagement of youth through modern media and a relaxed, informal style—representing revival and reform of a new variety—has shifted authority and legitimacy away from more traditional centers of Islamic learning and preaching, such as al-Azhar University, into the hands of people with formal training in other disciplines, such as accounting, business, and engineering. In the process, the message has shifted from one of strict and rigid doctrines controlled by a religious establishment to one of self-help and community development in which listeners are both active consumers and participants in the implementation of the message. This shift has been particularly important in outreach to youth, providing them with positive steps they can take to improve themselves, their education, and their skill sets so as to compete better in an overly competitive job market at the same time that it demonstrates the ongoing relevance of religion in daily life. All three preachers have further harnessed the power of social media, including Facebook, YouTube, and Twitter, in building global audiences numbering in the tens of millions and in finding ways to build audience participation, whether through contributing ideas for projects or uploading videos for incorporation into shows. This marks a change from past audiences that passively received religious messages to a new audience of customers and players who are actively engaged with the preachers. The participatory nature of the preachers' changed approach to revival and reform intentionally reaches out to different types of people, providing a new sense of belonging to the "global *umma*" as a new kind of mass movement. This kind of relational, collaborative preaching takes the form of a conversation among partners, both women and men, aided by computer graphics, rather than the traditional, hierarchical approach of an expert speaking unidirectionally and exclusively to men in a madrasa-like setting. In the process, not only do these "media *du'a*" position themselves as competitors to traditional religious authorities, but they also stand in marked contrast to jihadists who similarly make use of computer graphics and social media while calling followers to activism; the difference is that the "media *du'a*" proclaim a constructive message about the improvement of society, beginning with oneself, and encourage audiences to embrace Islam, in contrast to the jihadists' angry, destructive message or the traditional, accusatory approach to religion that causes audiences to fear it.

Finally, Sean Foley's study of Lebanese Swedish rhythm-and-blues superstar Maher Zain calls for attention to the new faces of Islam in the music industry, with billions of views from all over the world. Using the traditional religious singing style of *nashid*, singers such as Zain call for both individual and collective action in the contemporary world, guided by faith and driven by values such as love of God, love of neighbor, and personal responsibility that transcend national boundaries and engage a truly global world. Representative of what Voll has identified as "religionization of what is called 'secular' and secularization of what is called 'religious'" (quoted in al-Arian 2018), this rise of "seculigious" forces indicates ongoing exchanges in both directions, suggesting that understanding "Islam" today must look beyond traditional sources, leaders, and adherents to a more expansive vision that encompasses voices from all walks of life, including art and social media, that shape religious culture and opinion. The development of Awakening Music is thus more than the creation of a music label; it marks the creation of a social space for intellectual and musical alternative perspectives to the binaries of Western modernity and authoritarian regimes that have dominated the political realm since September 11, 2001, and the global war on terrorism. The intentionally multicultural musical productions are a synthesis of Eastern and Western musical styles and ways of thinking that bring together international teams of musicians and production experts and their multiple identities to craft music with Islamic themes and global appeal. They are also a potent means of connecting with and influencing youth, a reality that others, including jihadists, have recognized and attempted to capitalize on, albeit for different purposes. In the case of Zain, the message is simple—a sense of individual purpose and dignity through faith in God in the midst of the common challenges of contemporary daily life. Calling upon Muslims to reform themselves rather than to blame others for their problems, Zain's music encourages collective social action that begins with the individual and is based on hope and courage, not violence or destruction. As such, similar to the media *du'a* discussed by Floden, this type of music represents a global social movement of a new kind with a scope well beyond national or even regional concerns or identities. Far removed from the traditional centers of political power and religious authority, the social media vision of Islam is not bound by singular or legal understandings of what is *halal* or *haram* or by particular venues but reaches across boundaries by using multiple formats and new locations to assure accessibility and sensitivity to people from all walks of life and highlights the "glocal" that Voll has long taught affirms the interconnectedness of global and local events.

Moving into the future, Voll's work as arguably the work of the most important living historian of Islam in transhistorical and global perspective continues to call upon scholars and analysts alike to look not only at the centers of power but also at the daily lives of ordinary people to reorient our understandings of authenticity, legitimacy, and "Islam" in a globalized world, even as the writing of history—and herstory—becomes ever more complex, nuanced, and inclusive.

A Note on Transliteration

Just as this volume engages consideration of the impact of a central scholar upon various followers who take what they have learned in different directions, so each author has developed a preference for particular transliteration styles reflective of his or her disciplines and languages and locations of study. Some of the essays in this volume present exact transliterations so that experts can reconstruct the terminology in the original languages, while others limit use of diacritics for ease of reading. There are also instances in which common-use spellings vary in different contexts, often owing to colonial heritage. Each method has its merits and appeals to particular audiences. Our hope is that the inclusion of different systems offers a taste of the diversity of disciplines, approaches to language, and wealth of languages relevant to the study of Islam.

References

Al-Arian, Abdullah. 2018. "Roundtable on Political Islam after the Arab Uprisings." *Maydan: Politics and Society*, May. At https://www.themaydan.com/2018/05/roundtable-political-islam-arab-uprisings/.

Hodgson, Marshall G. S. 1974. *The Venture of Islam*. 3 vols. Chicago: Univ. of Chicago Press.

Hourani, Albert. 1991. *A History of the Arab Peoples*. Cambridge, MA: Belknap Press of Harvard Univ. Press, 1991.

Lapidus, Ira. 2014. *A History of Islamic Societies*. 3rd ed. Cambridge: Cambridge Univ. Press.

Rahman, Fazlur. 1979. *Islam*. Chicago: Univ. of Chicago Press, 1979.

Voll, John O. 1975. "Muḥammad Ḥayyā al-Sindī and Muḥammad ibn 'Abd al-Wahhāb: An Analysis of an Intellectual Group in 18th century Madīna." *Bulletin of the School of Oriental and African Studies* 38:32–39.

———. 1980. "Hadith Scholars and Tariqahs: An Ulama Group in the 18th Century Haramayn and Their Impact on the Islamic World." *Journal of Asian and African Studies* 15, nos. 3–4: 264–73.

———. 1987. "Linking Groups in the Networks of Eighteenth-Century Revivalist Scholars the Mizjaji Family in Yemen." In *Eighteenth-Century Renewal and Reform in Islam*, edited by Nehemiah Levtzion and John O. Voll, 69–93. Syracuse, NY: Syracuse Univ. Press.

———. 1994a. "Islam as a Special World System." *Journal of World History* 5, no. 2: 213–26.

———. 1994b. *Islam: Continuity and Change in the Modern World*. 2nd ed. Syracuse, NY: Syracuse Univ. Press.

Islam, Revival, and Reform

Part One

Revival and Reform in the Eighteenth and Nineteenth Centuries

Setting the Islamic Stage for the Modern World

1

The Role of Women in Solidifying Eighteenth-Century Revival and Reform Initiatives into Ongoing Mass Movements

Natana J. DeLong-Bas

John O. Voll has compellingly demonstrated that the eighteenth century was a time of reorientation of the Islamic tradition as Muslims from various walks of life sought to purify and revitalize their understanding of their faith through a return to the fundamentals of scripture at the same time that they sought the sociomoral reconstruction of society (Voll 1994, 22, 25).[1] This quest for a more "authentic" identity rooted in Islam resulted in an emphasis on education and greater personal agency with respect to religious belief and practice as Muslim individuals sought more intentionally to engage their faith through direct encounters with scripture and a stronger connection to their faith communities. The hallmarks of these movements—attention to the content (*matn*) of hadith rather than to the form through chain of transmission (*isnad*); reduced dependence on medieval scholars (*taqlid*) in favor of direct study of the Qur'an and hadith; use of independent reasoning (*ijtihad*); and revival and reform of the faith tradition as a

An earlier version of this chapter was presented at John O. Voll's retirement gathering at Georgetown University, April 9, 2014.

1. Voll argues that the term *fundamentalist* is appropriately applied to those movements that place the scriptures of religions as the permanent standard by which existing conditions are to be judged.

spark for mass movements upon which new states were founded[2]—have carried across time and space into the twentieth and twenty-first centuries in an ongoing process of religious identity formation, authentication, and legitimation in a globalized world.

Of the various eighteenth-century revival and reform movements identified by Voll, three became particularly famous (or infamous): those led by Shāh Walī Allāh al-Dihlavī (1702–62) of India, Shehu Usman dan Fodio (1754–1817) of what is today northern Nigeria and central Sudan, and Muhammad Ibn 'Abd al-Wahhab (1702/3–1791/2) of Arabia. All three leaders were scholars, and all shared a scholarly connection through their studies in the Haramayn (Two Sacred Places, referring to Mecca and Medina), yet one of them (Shāh Walī Allāh) became known for his scholarly and philosophical contributions that remained an elite phenomenon until the next generation, while the other two (dan Fodio and Ibn 'Abd al-Wahhab) sparked mass movements that led to the creation of new states (Levtzion 1987, 33).[3] Reflecting a broad eighteenth-century trend of bringing about changes through human efforts rather than waiting for eschatological intervention, the latter two movements challenged existing political and religious orders as part of their practical, activist programs (Levtzion and Voll 1987, 10).

Because so much of history tends to focus on powerholders and politics, the history of these latter two movements has long remained exactly that—his story—leaving to the sidelines what might arguably be the most lasting contribution of both: the spread of mass education

2. For information on the foundational interregional hub of these ideas and how they played out in different movements throughout the Islamic world, see Voll 1994, 51–83.

3. For the purposes of this chapter, the most important connection is between dan Fodio and Ibn 'Abd al-Wahhab. Dan Fodio and his brother, Abdallah, studied the hadith collection *Sahih al-Bukhari* with their paternal uncle, Muhammad b. Raj, who during his visit to Medina had studied with Abu al-Hasan al-Sindi, who had studied with Muhammad Hayat al-Sindi, one of Ibn 'Abd al-Wahhab's teachers. Details on Shāh Walī Allāh can be found in Hermansen's chapter in this volume.

as central to the broader project of the sociomoral reconstruction of society, largely enabled and undertaken by women. In keeping with Voll's focus on the rise of notables with increasing levels of autonomy and independence[4] but applying it through the lens of gender, this chapter seeks to restore her story through the examination of key women in both movements, arguing that these women not only were central to the survival of the movements but also helped to expand them to a broader mass audience. Her story is analyzed through three central themes:

1. Women as recipients of the revivalist/reformist message, namely as students
2. Women as guarantors of education for others in their roles as both teachers and practical supporters who supplied provisions and teaching materials
3. Women as active agents in the eradication of false teachings, particularly through engagement with and challenges to the *bori* and Zar cultures

Women as Recipients and Students

Although dan Fodio and Ibn 'Abd al-Wahhab are best known historically for the "jihadist"[5] movements they inspired, neither one considered this to be their most important venture. Rather, they pointed to their written works and efforts to reshape society in greater conformity with their understandings of Islamic thought and practice as their most important legacies. Both asserted a primary position for scholars as guides for the community, although not necessarily as political

4. This is one of the three major eighteenth-century themes outlined in Voll 1994, 25.

5. Although the term *jihad* is best translated as "struggle" and does not inherently carry militant tones, both movements engaged in military campaigns that were sometimes legitimated as jihads. For a fuller explanation of the various parameters of jihad, see DeLong-Bas 2018, 187–213. For the specifics of jihad in the writings of Ibn 'Abd al-Wahhab, see DeLong-Bas 2008, 193–226.

leaders.[6] The main concern for both was the elucidation of the proper practice of Islam to people who were already Muslims, in particular adherence to *tawhid* (the unity and uniqueness of God), the obligations of Sharia, avoidance of "deviant" practices, and the necessity of suppressing, if not eradicating, "satanic innovations and evil customs" (Brenner 1987, 39–42; DeLong-Bas 2008, 61). Both, for example, denounced the practices of sacrificing to or placing objects or requests on trees and stones and engaging in or consulting astrology or divination (Brenner 1987, 51–52; DeLong-Bas 2008, 63, 69–77). Both talked about the importance of faith of the heart, intent, and actions as more important than purely theoretical knowledge (DeLong-Bas 2008, 80–81). Both also sought to provide clear instructions as to how the doctrine of *tawhid*, in particular, was to be lived out in daily life and practice (Brenner 1987, 45; DeLong-Bas 2008, 56–61).[7] Both were especially concerned about the lack of even the most basic religious education among Muslims, especially the rural common people, to the point that very few were reportedly able to properly perform the obligatory prayers and fasts (Jameelah 1978, 8). In keeping with the hadith that says, "The ink of the scholar is more sacred than the blood of the martyr," both therefore emphasized the importance of literacy and education for and by both women and men (DeLong-Bas 2008, 123–24; Mack 2011, 154).[8]

6. Dan Fodio led the jihad only until his caliphate was established, then stepped back into the role of scholar (see Hiskett 1994, esp. 116–33). Ibn 'Abd al-Wahhab considered himself an adviser to the political leader and withdrew from public life altogether when he was dissatisfied with the political direction of the Saudi state after the death of Ibn Saud (see DeLong-Bas 2008, 35–40).

7. One major difference was that Ibn 'Abd al-Wahhab rejected *taqlid*, whereas dan Fodio considered *taqlid* appropriate for "ordinary" Muslims who were not scholars.

8. Beverly Mack (2011) roots dan Fodio's inclusion of women in a combination of Qur'anic teachings about men's and women's equality in the pursuit of knowledge and the movement's connection to the Qadiriyya Sufi *ṭarīqa*, which recognized no difference in the spiritual and intellectual conditions of women and men and encouraged both in scholarly pursuits.

Mass education with the potential for literacy in at least the Qur'an and hadith for both women and men was a hallmark of these two movements. Ibn ‘Abd al-Wahhab had the advantage of working in an Arabic-speaking environment, whereas dan Fodio faced the challenge of a multilingual context. In dan Fodio's region, only the most highly trained scholars knew Arabic; Fulfulde was the language of the elite, and Hausa was the language of the masses. Making his message accessible to a broad audience meant having to incorporate all of these linguistic groups. Dan Fodio particularly emphasized use of the vernacular for instruction, a format already known to his target audience through traditional poets and bards (Levtzion and Voll 1987, 12).[9] Although many of his works were designed for other scholars or state administrators, his daughter, Nana Asma'u (1793–1864), translated them into Hausa and transformed them into more popular form through the use of rhyme and repetition to emphasize the most important points (Mack and Boyd 2000, 38–39).[10] This written material served as a practical guide for individuals at all levels of social status and academic achievement, from illiterate to scholarly, as even those unable to read were still capable of hearing the works spoken (Mack and Boyd 2000, 10).

Coming from a family in which the education of women was a longstanding tradition, dan Fodio considered ignorance worse than gender mixing (Jameelah 1978, 13; Mack 2015, 79).[11] Although some in his movement criticized his permission to women to leave the house and

9. Linguistically, the movement was led by Fulfulde-speaking groups, including Fulbe pastoralists, and by Torodbe and Toronkawa scholars. The scholars studied and wrote in both Fulfulde and Arabic, whereas the masses spoke Hausa. Materials thus had to be translated and adapted to Hausa speakers in order for the movement to have a mass following.

10. For example, Asma'u's rendition of her father's work *Be Sure of God's Truth*, composed in 1831, became one of the most popular pieces written during this period and is still recited today.

11. Mack (2015) notes that although Nana Asma'u became particularly renowned as a scholar, she was preceded by generations of women who had also been notable scholars and had passed instruction down to their children.

attend mixed preaching sessions (Mack 2011, 156),[12] he insisted upon women's inclusion—and the inclusion of people from all classes—as a necessary precondition for lasting and substantive changes to existing political and social institutions (Jameelah 1978, 9–10). The only concession he was willing to make with respect to mixed-gender settings was to assure that the women in attendance were veiled and seated separately (Jameelah 1978, 9–10). At a broader level, women did not serve in political or military positions but instead were encouraged to pursue education and build a sense of community with each other (Mack and Boyd 2000, 33–34).[13] Such goals were perhaps best captured in a poem by Nana Asma'u called "A Warning II," which asserted a strong yet limited public role for women:

> Women, a warning. Leave not your homes without good reason. You may go out to get food or to seek education. In Islam, it is a religious duty to seek knowledge. Women may leave their homes freely for this. Repent and behave like respectable married women, You must obey your husband's lawful demands. You must dress modestly and be God-fearing. Do not imperil yourselves and risk hell-fire. (translated in Mack and Boyd 2000, 83)[14]

In central Arabia, records from the eighteenth century are scarce, but those that do exist trace Najd's growth as a center of learning to the sixteenth century, suggesting that Ibn 'Abd al-Wahhab's movement built on momentum that was already present and bolstered it

12. Mack found that dan Fodio "stated bluntly that any man who did not support his daughter or wife leaving the house for the purpose of education was not practicing Islam correctly" (2011, 156).

13. Although women did not participate in military actions directly, Asma'u worked closely with her brother, Bello, and her husband, Gidado, in strategizing both warfare tactics and reconstruction efforts to repair the fractured social order following jihad. She focused in particular on the education of women and thereby children as the key to rebuilding communities based on a sense of ethics and social responsibility (see Mack 2015, 80–81).

14. This work was written in Hausa to be accessible to the target audience.

with religious justification (Al Juhany 2002, 5). Women are largely absent from the extant records, given the records' focus on military campaigns and state formation, both of which were viewed as male endeavors. The glimpses we have of women's lives are often disjointed vignettes rather than complete pictures or comprehensive visions of what their daily lives were like. Those women who are present in the record tend to belong to one of three categories:

1. Composers of oral poetry that was popular enough to have been memorized and passed down over time
2. Contributors to social and educational work
3. Relatives of the ruling elite, such as wives, mothers, or daughters (al-Harbi 2008, xii)[15]

Like dan Fodio, Ibn 'Abd al-Wahhab asserted the right to education for women as critical to fulfillment of their religious obligations. Part of the power of the original movement was that it brought women into community and conversation with both the divine and each other yet within accepted religious and social parameters. Because women were theoretically entitled to the same level of religious learning as men, families were encouraged to provide religious education to their daughters. Ibn 'Abd al-Wahhab set the example through his own daughter, Fatima (Al-Harbi 2008, 32–33).[16] Some women achieved

15. Of the fifty-two women profiled by Dalal Mukhlid al-Harbi from the eighteenth through the twentieth centuries, ten were princesses from the al-Saud family, four al-Rasheed, two Sudairi, three al-Shaykh (descendants of Ibn 'Abd al-Wahhab), and three al-Mu'ammar. Some of these women played important roles in protecting Ibn 'Abd al-Wahhab's movement and the foundation of the Saudi–Wahhabi alliance. Examples include Aljawharah bint 'Abd Allah ibn Muhammad ibn Mu'ammar, who was aunt of the ruler of al-'Uyaynah, offered protection to Ibn 'Abd al-Wahhab, and ultimately married him in 1741; Aljawharah bint Uthman ibn Hamad ibn Mu'ammar, the daughter of the ruler of al-'Uyayna who married 'Abd al-Aziz ibn Muhammad ibn Saud, the son of the founder of the first Saudi state, and gave birth to his oldest son, Saud, who later became ruler; and Moudi bint Sultan Abu Wahtan, Muhammad ibn Saud's wife, who first brought him and Ibn 'Abd al-Wahhab together (al-Harbi 2008, 3–4, 21–22, 79).

16. Fatima bint Muhammad ibn 'Abd al-Wahhab was taught by her father and known as a teacher of both women and men.

competence in Qur'an memorization, recitation of prayers, and knowledge of at least some hadith, although whether this competence was broadly on a par with men's is not clear from the historical record.

The Wahhabi educational mission was sufficiently successful to be noticed by later Western travelers, although it was, at least in some cases, limited to performing prayers and did not necessarily include reading and writing (Doumato 2000, 74). Reading and writing were strong among the townspeople of northern Najd, and there were many hadith scholars, imams, and judges from this area who had been educated abroad, as noted in 1845 and 1848. Outside observers found the youth of the area better instructed in the doctrines and rituals of Islam as well as in reading and writing than was the case in other Ottoman or Arab towns. Religious scholars were found to have knowledge of the Qur'an, prayer rituals, hadith, the writings of Ahmad ibn Hanbal, and controversies between Wahhabis and other Muslims, although their focus was on jurisprudence rather than on Arabic grammar or literature (Doumato 2000, 76). In the 1860s, visitors to Riyadh, the center of Wahhabi education, found people knowledgeable in the Qur'an, hadith, historical texts, hadith commentaries, literature (especially poetry), and medicine as well as in classic Arabic literature, treatises on law and religion, travel accounts, geographical treatises, and chronicles of the Wahhabis. In addition, more than one hundred years of travel and missionary accounts show a certain degree of literacy, including among some women, for whom the ability to read and write was a source of social recognition and income as well as an opportunity for leadership, such as by reading at group religious ceremonies, serving as prayer leaders for other women, and reciting holy words over the sick (Doumato 2000, 90–91).

Women as Teachers and Supporters of Education

In terms of female teachers and providers of educational material, no woman of the eighteenth and early nineteenth centuries played a more important role that dan Fodio's daughter, Nana Asma'u. A renowned scholar and intellectual in her own right who was in touch with scholars throughout sub-Saharan Africa, she was quadrilingual (in Arabic, Fulfulde, Hausa, and Tamachek), a prolific author, and a popular teacher of both women and men, beginning during the Sokoto jihad (1804–30) and continuing until the end of her life in 1864. She also trained an extensive network of itinerant women instructors known as Yan Taru to extend her father's teachings to otherwise isolated rural women (Mack 2011, 156–57).[17] It was particularly this work of teaching women students and training women teachers that assured the movement's rapid spread and solid mass support base (Mack and Boyd 2000, 2).[18] Women's participation was critical because it provided a means of demonstrating that all people had an equal opportunity—and responsibility—to access salvation and learn Islam, albeit through knowing rather than necessarily through writing (Mack 2011, 156–57).

Asma'u's education, which included Qur'an memorization and study of Islamic philosophical texts on prayer, legal matters, *fiqh*, mysticism, and the central concept of *tawhid*, was overseen by her father (Mack and Boyd 2000, 7). Dan Fodio believed in the necessity and centrality of education for the spirituality of women and men alike (Mack and Boyd 2000, 8). His inclusion of women also likely reflected his own scholarly background, which included learning from female family members, in particular his mother and grandmother, and his membership in the Qadiriyya *ṭarīqa*, a prominent feature of which was the education of women (Mack and Boyd 2000, 19, 34).[19] Asma'u's education was enabled and enhanced by her father's library, which was filled with hundreds of hand-written volumes that she collated and oversaw and to which she added her own writings after his death

17. As women of post-child-bearing years, the members of Yan Taru enjoyed a relative degree of freedom in their daily schedules and were less restricted in their social roles, which enabled them to travel alone to rural villages to teach other women.

18. The most basic instruction was oral in form.

19. The founder of the Qadiriyya order recognized his mother and his aunt as powerful spiritual influences. Many prominent shaykhs of the order included learned women as influences.

(Mack and Boyd 2000, 9, 11).[20] While the men occupied themselves with the community's survival, rebuilding and engaging in active warfare, Asma'u focused on education, writing, and community activism. Her poetic and prose works over the next forty-five years particularly addressed social welfare and education (Mack and Boyd 2000, 11).

Asma'u began organizing women teachers while she was in her early thirties and was well established as the leader of the community's women by the time she was forty. She was known as "Uwar Gari" (Mother of All) for her work in training women of all ages and appointing women to teach the Qur'an, prescribed prayers, and accounts of Sufi women in history (Mack and Boyd 2000, 11). Known as *jaji*s, this cadre of literate, itinerant teachers was responsible for disseminating Asma'u's instructive poems among the masses. *Jaji*s were recognizable to the general public because of the distinctive headgear they wore as a visible sign of their respectability and status as teachers (Mack and Boyd 2000, 79, 89–91).[21] Strong in their connection to other women and the larger community, this educational network of women subtly challenged the concept of seclusion by providing a "legitimate" reason for women to leave the home that no one could argue with under the caliphate's religious order (Mack and Boyd 2000, 91–92).

The education and training of *jaji*s proved particularly critical for rural areas, where only women could have access to other women and the only means for some women to attain any level of education was by learning within their homes. These newly educated women were then able to pass on what they had learned to their children, both boys and girls, assuring that at least baseline education was accessible to all

20. Books were considered so valuable that they were transported to safety by camel or horse anytime the community had to flee.

21. This was also another way of reclaiming symbols from the *bori* cult (to be discussed later). *Bori* practitioners wore distinctive turbans. *Jaji*s wore balloon-shaped hats made of fine, silky grasses and a piece of red cloth signifying their authority. The ceremony for receiving the turban was an important ritual for women. Young girls received Asma'u's blessing.

members of the community. It is important to note that this education was not restricted to religion but also often had a practical dimension, such as teaching women how to sell the thread they spun (Mack and Boyd 2000, 12).[22] The educational network created among rural women by Nana Asma'u and the *jajis* still exists today.

Jajis trained students in memorization, writing, and reading through the use of poetry. Poems were first to be memorized by the students and then explained in greater detail by the teacher. One pivotal text was Asma'u's poem "The Qur'an," written as a mnemonic device to teach the names of the 114 suras (chapters) in thirty couplets.[23] Although some scholars have dismissed this poem as being of "little scholarly interest," careful examination of the text reveals that every chapter is cited, whether directly or in code, thus enabling students to gain a fuller knowledge of the Qur'an and its basic theological premises. *Jajis* used this poem as a guide into the deeper levels of meaning of each verse, placing memorization of at least part of the Qur'an at the center of education. Using the poem for oral transmission of the basic structure of the Qur'an encouraged easier memorization of its content, which could then extend to discussion and understanding of deeper theological meanings (Mack and Boyd 2000, 23–24). At the same time, recitation of the chapter names of the Qur'an was believed to have talismanic qualities, bestowing blessings (*barakah*) on the one reciting it, regardless of whether one understood

22. Nevertheless, this practical dimension was not the main goal. Some contemporary debates about the Yan Taru have tried to shift focus from the content to the form of instruction—oral versus written, personal instruction in the presence of a teacher versus instruction via the internet. Mack argues that this shift in focus misses the driving purpose of the education model: to provide instruction by whatever means is suitable for the audience with the desired goal of teaching ethics and right behavior, not literacy or computer skills, although the latter may be byproducts (2015, 83).

23. The first nine chapters are cited in their Arabic forms in the first two verses of the poem.

all of the poem's complexities. Simply hearing or reciting it constituted a benefit, while deeper understanding enabled a comparison to *wird* (recitation of prayer litanies) (Mack and Boyd 2000, 25).[24]

Asma'u's poetic works were critical to the spread of the movement because of her literary skill, particularly for mnemonic devices that facilitated memorization and for the use of multiple techniques of composition that frequently embedded additional messages in the structure of a poem.[25] One of the hallmarks of Asma'u's poetry was her focus on character and behavior rather than on wealth and power. Much of her poetry, in particular her elegies, shows ordinary people doing ordinary things in an exemplary way, making her work accessible to the average person and seeking to inspire them to greatness through skills they already possessed—in the case of women, heroic virtue, compassion, and positive impact on the community (Mack and Boyd 2000, 21–22).[26] What defined these women was not their

24. These benefits and terminology highlight Asma'u's connection to Sufism.

25. Beverly Mack and Jean Boyd have documented techniques such as acrostic (use of the first letter of each line of the poem to create its own message related to the message of the entire work), *takhmis* (taking an existing two-line couplet by another poet and adding three verses to make it five, while maintaining the original rhyme and meter), panegyric, end rhyme, and the recasting of preexisting prose works into multilayered poems with messages for both beginners and advanced learners. Asma'u, writing in Fulfulde, and Bello, writing in Arabic, used acrostic for their communications. Asma'u's skill in *takhmi* is particularly reflected in her poem "Fear This," originally composed by her father's former student Muhammad Tukur. Asma'u expanded the poem to ninety-nine quintets in the *wa'azi* style of warning people about the effects of sinfulness while reminding them that God can give either prosperity or punishment, thus demonstrating her knowledge of the Qur'an and her ability to teach it. Reciting the poem was believed to provide spiritual benefit. Another example of a simple yet complex composition is the poem "In Praise of Ahmada (Muhammad)," which uses rhyme to engage the beginner and the constant repetition of sacred words to bring the Prophet close to the reciter. See Mack and Boyd 2000, 50–57, for details.

26. For example, Asma'u praises Halima for being a kind neighbor; Zaharatu for attending women in childbirth, teaching religion to the ignorant, and helping wherever she was needed, as in laying out the dead; and Fadima for giving to charities,

relationships to men but how their actions reflected the depth of their character.

Asma'u sometimes added her own material to and edited the works she was translating for someone else. One famous example was her brother Bello's work on Sufi women, *A Book of Good Advice*, which told women to be obedient to their husbands, give up finery, be pious, upright, and frugal, and own only as much as they could carry on horseback. When Bello asked Asma'u to translate it, she reshaped the role of women by omitting the admonitions and threats of divorce and hell in favor of emphasizing the positive aspects of the practical, pious work of both Muhammad's wives and the many Sufi women she added into the script. In the process, she transformed the work into a poem not only about women but for the benefit of women, including the invocation of help from women Sufi saints (Mack and Boyd 2000, 60–61).

Much of Asma'u's writings about pious women, from Muhammad's wives through contemporary figures, were not intended simply to show specific women as role models but also to make the subtler point that women have always been part of the picture of Islamic interpretation and practice and even of the revelatory experience itself. By citing so many examples of women saints and scholars and of women playing different roles in the Prophet's life, Asma'u worked to create a variety of public and spiritual spaces for women that extended beyond the confines of the home and family.[27] Through the examples

feeding strangers and relatives alike, and generously supporting education. She also dedicates two "Lamentations" to her friend Aisha, whom she describes as a wise, virtuous, pious, humble pillar of the community who memorized and recited the Qur'an and engaged in extra prayers, almsgiving, defense of the unjustly treated, and guardianship of orphans and widows.

27. An outstanding example is her poem "Consolation for Blessed Women," which gives the names of thirty-seven women, ranging from the Prophet's wives and daughters to her own contemporaries, and covers a geographic range from the Middle East to North and West Africa. The women are described as having various qualities, with piety, devotion to prayer, charity, and education mentioned most

of ordinary/extraordinary women of the past, contemporary women gained the ability to construct and bolster their own identities—lessons that continue to have contemporary significance.

Although most literature on the Wahhabi movement has focused on the political and military activities of men, education was also one of the hallmarks of Ibn 'Abd al-Wahhab's movement. Women played a critical role in both engaging and spreading education, beginning with Ibn 'Abd al-Wahhab's daughter, Fatima, who set the standard through her own scholarship and teaching career, setting aside marriage in favor of travel to pursue scholarship (al-Harbi 2008, 32–33).[28] Women's ongoing participation is reflected in their establishment of schools in their own homes throughout the nineteenth and twentieth centuries,[29] thus fulfilling a public need that was ultimately overtaken by the state in the mid–twentieth century. In other cases, women

---

frequently. The most extensive discussion is of the eighth-century Sufi mystic and teacher Rabi'a al-'Adawiyya. Each of these women stands on her own merit. Occasional reference is made to a relationship to a husband or father, but only for identification purposes and not to legitimate the woman's actions. Personal accountability, responsibility, and merit are the main themes of the poem.

28. A strict adherent of her father's teachings, Fatima consistently embodied the practice of *tawhid*, such as by refusing to allow offerings to saints on the Hajj.

29. Al-Harbi (2008) includes the following examples: Aljawharah bint Faisal ibn Turki al-Saud, who was the aunt of King Abdulaziz and was charged with educating the women of the palace; Haya bint Salih ibn Nasir al-Sha'ir, who was the daughter of one of the foremost religious scholars in Hail and opened a school, al-Khatibah Hayah, in her home, where she taught the Qur'an and other religious instruction to girls; Nurah bint 'Abd al-Aziz ibn Ibrahim al-Hajji, who, following religious education by her cousin/husband, opened her own school in her home in 1928 to teach reading, writing, the Qur'an, and other religious subjects to young girls; Nurah bint Sulaiman ibn Fahd al-Ruhait, who was taught reading, writing, and religious subjects by her father, opened a school for girls in her home until the state opened schools, and became one of the first official teachers; Turfah bint Muhammad al-Khuraiyef, who received a religious education and opened a school for girls in her home in 1943 and kept it going until the official school for girls was opened in her area and she was permitted to teach there.

simply made their homes available to other scholars for discussion (al-Harbi 2008, 105–6, 131).[30]

Women's support for education was also seen historically through their contribution of books as *awqaf* (charitable foundations) and other means of supporting schools or other public needs. The donation of books as *awqaf* particularly highlights the connection between religion and education, suggesting that acquisition of knowledge qualifies as worthy of productive charitable support and as tacit recognition of the ongoing financial challenges faced by students. Books donated for such purposes often included a dedication page specifying the amount of time for which the scholar was permitted to borrow the work. The book was expected to be either memorized or hand copied, the inscription often including a statement such as "*Whoever changes it after hearing it knows that it is a sin to change it. God is All-Hearing and All-Knowing.*"[31] In other cases, borrowers were admonished to take care of the book to protect it from damage. Those in charge of the collection were instructed not to hold onto the book and prevent anyone else from using it (al-Harbi 2008, 12). Some further prohibited the sale, mortgaging, inheritance, or donation of the book lest it no longer be available for scholarly use.[32] A sampling of books donated as *awqaf*

30. Examples include Sarah bint 'Abd Allah ibn Faisal al-Saud, whose home became a gathering place, and Turfah bint Faisal ibn Turki al-Saud, an educated lady and strong protector of religion whose home was used as a gathering place for prominent figures, including scholars and elders of the al-Saud family.

31. Al-Harbi (2008) includes inscriptions of this variety in books donated by Aljawharah bint Musa'ad ibn Jalawi al-Saud, Aljawharah bint Turki ibn 'Abd Allah al-Saud, Hussah bint Ahmad ibn Muhammad al-Sudairi, and Turaifah bint 'Ubaid ibn Ali ibn Rashid.

32. Al-Harbi (2008) provides numerous examples and notes that several books in Riyadh bear the inscription of Ibn 'Abd al-Wahhab's granddaughter, Sarah bint Ali ibn Muhammad ibn 'Abd al-Wahhab, and that other donated books are thought to be held by individuals or private libraries. I personally have seen many examples of books donated by women as *awqaf* at the King Abdulaziz Foundation for Research and Archives (Darah) in Riyadh, Saudi Arabia, including works in Arabic and Farsi. Not all have been cataloged yet.

in nineteenth-century Najd shows a variety of authors and a mix of reference books, theological treatises, and scholarly commentaries.[33]

Poetry also played an important role among Arabian women as a means of expressing their feelings, addressing family life issues, and encouraging men in warfare. Although no records of eighteenth-century poetry by Najdi women have survived in common memory, there are a few examples from the early nineteenth century that connect to a lengthy history of women's composition and artistry.[34] Mentions of these poems are scarce, but it must be recalled that poetry was intended to be recited and heard rather than read silently and thus was rarely written down. Of those poems that have survived, it is interesting to note that, unlike Nana Asma'u's poetic production, none has a

33. Specific works include three by Ibn Taymiyya, two by Ibn al-Qayyim al-Jawziyya, three by al-Nawawi, one by al-Dhahabi, one by Ibn Rajab al-Hanbali, one by al-Sanani, one by al-Futuhi, one by Ahmad ibn Nasir ibn Uthman, one by 'Abd al-Rahman ibn Hasan ibn Muhammad ibn 'Abd al-Wahhab, al-Shawkani's eight-volume work *Sharh Muntaqa al-Akhbar*, a copy of *Sahih al-Bukhari*, a copy of al-Bukhari's *al-Adab al-mufrad* (Good Behavior Singled Out), and a printed copy of the Arabic dictionary *al-Qamus al-Muhit*. Twentieth-century offerings included two books by Ibn al-Qayyim al-Jawziyyah, one by al-Nawawi, one by al-Mundhiri, one by Shams al-Din Muhammad ibn Muflih al-Hanbali, one by Ibn Qudama, one by al-Zamakhshari, and a collection of *Sahih al-Bukhari*. It is perhaps not surprising that several volumes each for Ibn Taymiyya and Ibn al-Qayyim al-Jawziyyah were given in the nineteenth century, in keeping with the goal of establishing one "correct" interpretation of Islam at that time, as discussed in Commins 2006. It is interesting that none of Ibn Taymiyya's works appear in the twentieth-century offerings. Information on specific authors is gathered from al-Harbi's (2008) biographies.

34. For example, al-Harbi (2008) mentions Fiddah al-Munif al-Murays, born in the early 1800s, who was known for her popular poetry intended to stir the emotions of those participating in war; Aljawharah bint Turki ibn 'Abd Allah al-Saud, born in the 1820s and sister of Imam Faisal ibn Turki, who was both the subject and author of poetry; Ruqaiyah bint 'Abd Allah al-Sa'ad al-Salihi, born in 1829, who was one of the most famous poetesses of the area, writing poetry in response to events in her town, including praise for the political ruler; and Shaqra' bint 'Abd Allah ibn Khuzam al-'Abd Allah, born in 1839, the daughter of a judge in Hail who was known for her poetic compositions.

deliberately religious or didactic theme. They seem to have been written simply for the pleasure of the poetry itself and for the expression of sentiment rather than to fulfill a public or educational need. Thus, although poetic expression was a form common to both the Sokoto Caliphate and Arabia, its purpose and use varied considerably in these two locations. Nana Asma'u's multilingual poetic cleverness apparently had no parallel in Arabia, which seems to have preferred more scholarly expressions of religious messages.

Women as Active Agents in Eradicating "False" Teachings

One of the most controversial aspects of both movements was their concern with the eradication of "false" teachings and interpretations, including through the use of violence if deemed necessary. Dan Fodio determined that the pervasiveness of pagan religious practices justified a military response, resulting in the foundation of a theocratic empire (Voll 1994, 142–43). Ibn 'Abd al-Wahhab's movement ultimately took on militancy as his project for sociomoral reconstruction required political support and protection owing to the opposition his teachings encountered in many places. Although the end result was also a state, it was not a theocratic one (Voll 1994, 54).

Many of the "false" teachings and practices objected to by both movements were related to popular healing practices. Because women have long served as healers in many societies, women's activities came under particular scrutiny, especially where they were in service to other women. Respect for women's skills and knowledge in healing as an extension of their roles as nurturers was tempered by concerns about women's purported emotional weakness and susceptibility to spirit possession, as evidenced in physical and mental health problems. Recognition of the need for women healers, particularly as midwives, resulted in a recasting of healing as a positive and religiously supported role for women in both movements—another example of creating legitimate space for women's contributions to the service of the broader community and giving them a central role at the heart of community health and well-being.

The context into which dan Fodio's movement was introduced was one in which Islamic beliefs and practices existed alongside animist systems that emphasized magical and ritual practices. Muslim clerics and traditional priests often fulfilled similar roles in mosques and traditional shrines as sanctuaries (Levtzion 1987, 21). Because the traditional practices had such deep roots, African rulers were politically unable to eradicate or denounce them in favor of the Islamic message preached by dan Fodio without risking their own positions. Not only did dan Fodio represent a threat to the existing system because of his religious message, but he also took on roles that were previously the preserve of warriors rather than clerics or diviners, particularly in claiming political authority over a community that separated itself from main society in a hijra (departure) to an alternative location and in engaging in military defense of this community (Levtzion 1987, 22).

Traditional religion in Nigeria includes belief in a supreme being (God) as well as in lesser deities, ancestral spirits, and the power of magic and medicine (Kayode and Adelowo 1985, 235). According to traditional belief, spirits reside in trees, and certain special trees are considered sacred abodes. Respect for the spirits requires people to recite prayers and make sacrifices and libations to these trees when passing them. Similar spirits are believed to live in rocks, mountains, hills, forests, bushes, rivers, and waterways (Kayode and Adelowo 1985, 238). Women have been particularly associated with this traditional religion owing to their apparent vulnerability to spirit possession and their roles in treating it.

Dan Fodio's movement directly challenged these long-standing and deeply held popular spiritual practices, which stood in opposition to the renewal and purification of Islam that he preached through the doctrine of *tawhid*. In practical terms, this purification meant displacement not only of popular religious practices but also of women's jurisdiction over them. As with other instances, traditional structures were recrafted with an Islamic interpretation, rooted in Nana Asma'u's example.

Traditionally, the chief was expected to rule alongside his sister, known as the *inna*. The *inna* served not only as coleader of the tribe but also as a mental and physical support for women as the leader of *bori*, a religious healing cult intended to relieve women of their illnesses, including psychological disorders, caused by spirit possession. Asma'u and her brother, Bello, repurposed this model for the caliphate and ruled together, with Bello in charge of political and military affairs and Asma'u in charge of addressing the *bori* cult based on her status as a highly trained Sufi with widely acknowledged powers of *barakah* (Mack and Boyd 2000, 36).

Asma'u's theological writings took the *bori* cult head-on, describing it as akin to witchcraft and the work of Satan and warning of punishment in hell for anyone practicing it. However, rather than just denouncing *bori*, she wrote about alternative solutions for those afflicted by mental or physical illness or disability, focusing on women and babies. Women were seen as particularly vulnerable because they grappled with loneliness and disorientation following the hijra from their ancestral lands to new locations. As a counter to *bori* medicine, Asma'u wrote a book entitled *Medicine of the Prophet* in which she quoted forty-six suras from the Qur'an, five of which dealt with women's concerns: safe delivery in childbirth, protection of pregnant women, the weaning of children, successful conception of a male child, and protection of children from colic. She also addressed other kinds of illnesses affecting both men and women, including migraines, inflamed eyes, boils, wounds, piles, deafness, dysentery, inflamed liver, toothache, and depression. Worries and anxieties about issues such as poverty, safety of valuables, forthcoming journeys, tyranny of those in authority, and debt were also discussed, as was people's general need for reassurance when experiencing insomnia, fear, and dread of witchcraft (Mack and Boyd 2000, 37). The attention to both physical and mental illness and distress in *Medicine of the Prophet* highlights a holistic approach to health and well-being and caring for the whole person rather than a mechanical approach to the body. Asma'u supplemented her work with Bello's ten works on different aspects of healing, including treatises on medicinal herbs and minerals, piles, and eye diseases as well as ones on metaphysical medicine.

Asma'u also addressed other aspects of popular *bori* practice with a community focus, repurposing them in Islamically acceptable ways.

Her "Prayer for Rain," written in the Hausa language of the masses, shifted the belief that drought is the product of spirit possession to the recognition of God as the source of water and blessing.[35] The prayer served the dual purpose of embracing the reality of public need while displacing the popular method of addressing that need in favor of a "correct" practice, all while maintaining a useful public role for women's worship by requesting something from God that would benefit the entire community. Another repurposed activity associated with *bori* was drumming. Rather than prohibiting it altogether, Asma'u outlined "appropriate" uses for it—calling people to meetings, announcing the departure or encampment of the army, calling the times for communal labor, or announcing one's presence when traveling—but declared other uses "sinful," such as accompaniment to dancing at weddings (Mack and Boyd 2000, 41). Even public mourning, typically associated with women's behaviors, had to be defended. Asma'u used her own example as an argument in favor of expressing grief upon the death of a loved one, noting the depth of her pain and sorrow upon the loss of her friend Aisha and arguing that the Prophet himself did not prohibit the shedding of tears, only screaming. Love and pain of loss were deemed acceptable, but excessive public displays of grief were not.[36]

This practical focus in explaining why the old practice was dangerous and what the average person could do instead, particularly where spirit cults and traditional methods of healing were concerned,[37] has a

35. Asma'u work "Water Request" advised Muslims to recognize God as the giver of water and thus to replace the belief in spirit presence in water sources with belief in water as a sign of God.

36. Recorded in her poem "Lamentation for Aisha, II."

37. Both movements fall into Voll's category "fundamentalist" in the sense of insisting "upon a rigorous adherence to the specific and general rules of the faith" and presenting "a critique of existing conditions by calling for a return to the fundamentals of the faith," as opposed to "adaptationist" or "conservative" (Voll 1994, 21–23). These categories are best understood as orientations rather than as separate movements. In addition, Voll specifies that being "fundamentalist" according to this

parallel in works by Ibn 'Abd al-Wahhab, particularly his most famous work, *Kitab al-tawhid* (The Book of Tawhid [Ibn 'Abd al-Wahhab (1398H) 1977–78b]).[38] Ibn 'Abd al-Wahhab's guiding principle was to embrace medical treatment designed to promote healing, such as pharmaceutical preparations, recitation of Qur'an verses, and prayer, provided that they were performed without supplication to any power other than God—a teaching in keeping with his central doctrine of *tawhid* (Doumato 2000, 133–34).[39] Qur'an recitation was believed to be especially effective because curative power was understood to be God's prerogative (Doumato 2000, 136–37). By contrast, sorcery, witchcraft, spirit possession, and exorcism, rooted in belief in the powers of human beings and spirits to manipulate each other, were prohibited because they violated *tawhid* by their very nature (DeLong-Bas 2008, 73–75). Only cures rooted in belief in the power of the divine and requests for divine intervention were deemed acceptable.

Based on this framework, women's activities and popular healing practices came under scrutiny because many of them were deemed to violate *tawhid*. These practices included praying or wailing at graves, making votive offerings, telling fortunes, making spells, divining, wearing amulets, visiting shrines, praying to saints, chanting, and

---

definition is not the same as being "militant activist" (1994, 52), although both of the movements discussed here developed militant aspects.

38. Specific practices identified in *Kitab al-tawhid* as commission of associationism (*shirk*) to be eradicated were those directly engaging spirits or other forms of theurgy: practicing witchcraft (claiming part of God's power for a human being); listening to Satan's voice (rather than to God's); practicing astrology (believing that stars and planets can foretell a future known only to God); conveying false rumors (deceitful manipulation of human relations); telling fortunes and/or seeking the services of a fortune-teller (claiming or desiring to know a future knowable only by God); making a knot and blowing on it while spitting; uttering curses to cause evil (thus attributing God's power to spirits); and using amulets to protect against the evil eye (thus presuming the power of spirits to do harm and the power of something other than God to prevent it). For details, see DeLong-Bas 2008, 73–75.

39. The underlying assumption was that God would have to predetermine the effectiveness of these methods.

dancing (Doumato 2000, 124–25; DeLong-Bas 2008, 56–77).[40] Particularly problematic was the association of some of these activities with the Zar spirit cult, which taught that illness, both physical and psychological, was the product of invisible beings or spirits, whether jinn or Satan, entering into a person's body and possessing that person (Doumato 2000, 131). Treatment consisted of appeasing the Zar by communicating with it to determine what it wanted and temporarily satisfying it—mainly through offerings of food and drink or by music and dance—in order to make it leave the person's body.[41]

Additional popular healing practices that came under scrutiny were those associated with animism, or the idea that the soul or spirit of a person resides in particular body parts, including the heart, blood, hair, teeth, saliva, sweat, tears, and nails. Manipulation of these body parts, such as by touching the hair, spitting, blowing, or wiping blood, was believed to communicate the essence of one person to another, thereby enabling either the expulsion of spirits as a healing mechanism or the manipulation of one person by another, such as by making them fall into or out of love with someone else (Doumato 2000, 160). Because women tended to participate prominently in these rituals and because communicators with the spirits tended to be female, the Zar cult was proliferated by and popularly associated with women (Doumato 2000, 40, 42, 170–71).[42] In turn, this connection led to the popular association of women with sorcery, witchcraft, and the handling of

40. Although it is difficult to know the extent to which the activities were being engaged, historical records outside of Ibn 'Abd al-Wahhab's own writings, such as Ibn Bishr's chronicle, indicate that these practices did exist in eighteenth-century Najd.

41. Eleanor Doumato notes that the Wahhabis tended generally to view these activities with suspicion (2000, 121, 174). The Zar cult simply represented the most popular and prominent manifestation of these problematic behaviors.

42. Doumato (2000) argues for the importance of such rituals for women as spiritual outlets because although women had access to mosques under the Wahhabis, their presence was not required, and in some places they were permitted to attend only on special occasions.

malevolent spirits as well as with the rituals and folk practices related to fertility, marriage, and healing.

Because of their infringement upon *tawhid*, the exclusivity of God, by conflating the human with the divine, these practices overall were denounced as superstitious. Although both men and women were forbidden from participating in these rituals, it seems that the Wahhabi ulama singled out women in particular for criticism, likely because they accounted for the largest numbers of participants and practitioners (Doumato 2000, 182).[43] These women were working outside of formal religious and institutional structures, so the end result of the eradication of these practices was displacement of women from prior positions of social influence and spiritual leadership (Doumato 2000, 1, 121; al-Harbi 2008, 52; al-Rasheed 2013, 45).[44]

At the same time, though, new spaces were created for female leadership in education, and certain activities and healing practices were repurposed to fit within an Islamic framework, although they were often more limited and regulated than the original rituals. As had been the case with Nana Asma'u's network Yan Taru, Ibn 'Abd al-Wahhab recognized the importance of women's full inclusion in the community and the need to recruit women to help eradicate erroneous practices among other women. Within this construct, the socializing, feasting, dancing, and music associated with Zar ceremonies were reframed for wedding celebrations. Ibn 'Abd al-Wahhab's writings in *Kitab al-nikah* (The Book of Marriage [Ibn 'Abd al-Wahhab (1398H) 1977–78a]) assigned women celebrants the specific tasks of playing the tambourine and lending their voices to the feast, including through the recitation of love poetry, while also encouraging socializing in a

43. Per Doumato (2000), some ulama also expressed concern that women were more emotionally susceptible to associationism owing to their purported emotional deficiencies.

44. Doumato notes the success of this prohibition as evidenced by the fact that in the late nineteenth and early twentieth centuries, the Zar cult could be found virtually everywhere in the Arabic-speaking world, including North Africa, except in Najd, the heartland of the Wahhabi movement (2000, 174).

religiously responsible way that included all members of the community, in particular the poor (DeLong-Bas 2008, 164–68). Similarly, some popular healing practices were revised to be more Islamically permissible, bringing together piety and religious knowledge while setting aside what were considered to be superstitions. Thus, practices such as collecting the saliva of pious men after prayer for healing the sick (al-Rasheed 2013, 51)[45] or consuming Qur'an verses for healing purposes (Doumato 2000, 138) or for warding off evil were set aside,[46] but use of Qur'an verses as talismans to ward off jealousy and to address the sting of venomous animals was allowed (DeLong-Bas 2008, 73).[47] Women were also encouraged to recite the Qur'an over sick people and to use their religious knowledge and expertise to provide important community services.[48]

Conclusion

With respect to both dan Fodio's and Ibn 'Abd al-Wahhab's movements, although most scholarly attention has been given to the traditionally male-directed political-military aspects of state formation, consolidation, and expansion of political power and influence, both movements also contain significant public roles for women's leadership and community guidance, rooted in religiously motivated education.

45. Doumato connects this practice to the animistic belief that a person's essence can be transferred through certain bodily emissions (2000, 160).

46. Methods of consuming Qur'an verses included swallowing the saliva of a person who had recited them or writing them on a piece of paper, placing the paper in water, and then drinking the ink-water solution.

47. Although there was no legal consensus (*ijma'*) on these practices, they were permitted in the hadith and so were approved by Ibn 'Abd al-Wahhab.

48. Although female Qur'an reciters did not necessarily have the same socio-religious capital as male reciters who as men held professional religious credentials as judges or imams, women adherents of the Wahhabi movement nevertheless combined the formal training they received in religious texts with their knowledge of popular medicine. Al-Harbi cites Sarah bint 'Abd Allah ibn Faisal al-Saud as one such example (2008, 105–6).

Their emphasis on ethics, community building, and especially the centrality of women's education and participation in public life is particularly urgent today in light of serious challenges to these same elements by terrorist organizations such as Boko Haram and the Taliban, which seek to establish a very different community model based on militancy and denial of education to women.[49] Islam in a globalized world can set forward an alternative example and legacy rooted in eighteenth- and nineteenth-century practices of education, literacy, and community building in which women's participation is critical to the overall health and well-being not only of the *umma* but also of society in general. Just as Nana Asma'u's ongoing legacy is reflected in the perpetuation of the Yan Taru itinerant teaching network, their *jaji* leaders, and the recitation of her poems from North and West Africa through North America, from Qadiriyya Sufi circles to the internet (Mack 2015),[50] so Saudi women are using their pens to engage in outreach to the broader global community and inserting their voices into global conversations.[51] Women's strength, determination, independence, and dedication to the community have lived on in popular memory such

49. Mack takes grave exception to the "misogynistic criminal Boko Haram movement" claim of inspiration from dan Fodio, given that Boko Haram ignores the strong roles for education and women in the original movement (2015, 87).

50. Mack (2015) has traced the North American adoption of the Yan Taru model to Malcolm X's interest in Qadiriyya Sufism following a visit to Sokoto after his Hajj in 1964. His meetings with members of the dan Fodio family and examination of their collection of written documents exposed him to a cultural history of Africa previously denied by the legacy of slavery. The first formal chapter of Yan Taru in North America was established in Pittsburgh in the 1980s. Efforts have been under way since the 1990s to preserve, translate, and disseminate the writings of dan Fodio, Asma'u, and other key figures to broad audiences, including via the internet. Emphasis remains on the key themes of the original movement: education, community development and activism, health and child care, and entrepreneurship.

51. Examples range from academic works highlighting Saudi women's historical contributions to their society and religion, such as Doumato 2000, DeLong-Bas 2008, al-Harbi 2008, and al-Rasheed 2013, to works that provide direct engagement with global literature, the most recent example of which is Alkhayal and Ahmed 2019.

that, today, women do not ask themselves whether they need their husbands' permission to do something but whether their role models from the revivalist, reformist past would have needed permission.[52]

References

Alkhayal, Ieman Abdulrahman, and Nawal Mursi Ahmed. 2019. *Women Writers of Saudi Arabia: Short Stories, Novels, & Poetry*. Surbiton, UK: Medina.

Brenner, Louis. 1987. "Muslim Thought in Eighteenth-Century West Africa: The Case of Shaykh Uthman b. Fudi." In *Eighteenth Century Renewal and Reform in Islam*, edited by Nehemiah Levtzion and John O. Voll, 39–68. Syracuse, NY: Syracuse Univ. Press.

Commins, David. 2006. *The Wahhabi Mission and Saudi Arabia*. London: I. B. Tauris.

DeLong-Bas, Natana J. 2008. *Wahhabi Islam: From Revival and Reform to Global Jihad*. Rev. ed. New York: Oxford Univ. Press.

———. 2018. *Islam: A Living Faith*. Winona, MN: Anselm Academic.

Doumato, Eleanor Abdella. 2000. *Getting God's Ear: Women, Islam, and Healing in Saudi Arabia and the Gulf*. New York: Columbia Univ. Press.

Al-Harbi, Dalal Mukhlid. 2008. *Prominent Women from Central Arabia*. Reading, UK: Ithaca Press.

Hiskett, Mervyn. 1994. *The Sword of Truth: The Life and Times of the Shehu Usuman dan Fodio*. 2nd ed. Evanston, IL: Northwestern Univ. Press.

Ibn 'Abd al-Wahhab, Muhammad. [1398H] 1977–78a. *Kitab al-nikah*. In *Mu'allafat al-Shaykh al-Imam Muhammad Ibn 'Abd al-Wahhab*, 4 vols., 2:226–53. Riyadh: Jamiat al-Imam Muhammad bin Saud al-Islamiyya.

———. [1398H] 1977–78b. *Kitab al-tawhid*. In *Mu'allafat al-Shaykh al-Imam Muhammad Ibn 'Abd al-Wahhab*, 4 vols., 1:7–151. Riyadh: Jamiat al-Imam Muhammad bin Saud al-Islamiyya.

Jameelah, Maryam. 1978. *Shehu Uthman dan Fodio: A Great Mujaddid of West Africa*. Lahore: Khan & Sons.

Al Juhany, Uwaidah M. 2002. *Najd before the Salafi Reform Movement: Social, Political, and Religious Conditions during the Three Centuries Preceding the*

52. Paraphrased from Mack 2011, 155.

Rise of the Saudi State. Reading, UK: Ithaca Press in association with the King Abdul Aziz Foundation for Research and Archives, Saudi Arabia.

Kayode, J. O., and E. Dada Adelowo. 1985. "Religions in Nigeria." In *Nigerian History and Culture*, edited by Richard Olaniyan, 234–48. Essex, UK: Longman Group.

Levtzion, Nehemiah. 1987. "The Eighteenth Century: Background to the Islamic Revolutions in West Africa." In *Eighteenth Century Renewal and Reform in Islam*, edited by Nehemiah Levtzion and John O. Voll, 21–38. Syracuse, NY: Syracuse Univ. Press.

Levtzion, Nehemiah, and John O. Voll. 1987. Introduction to *Eighteenth Century Renewal and Reform in Islam*, edited by Nehemiah Levtzion and John O. Voll, 3–20. Syracuse, NY: Syracuse Univ. Press.

Mack, Beverly. 2011. "Nana Asma'u's Instruction and Poetry for Present-Day American Muslimahs." *History in Africa* 38:153–68.

———. 2015. "Full Circle: Muslim Women's Education from the Maghrib to America and Back." *Journal of North African Studies* 20, no. 1: 78–91.

Mack, Beverly B., and Jean Boyd. 2000. *One Woman's Jihad: Nana Asma'u, Scholar and Scribe*. Bloomington: Indiana Univ. Press.

Al-Rasheed, Madawi. 2013. *A Most Masculine State: Gender, Politics, and Religion in Saudi Arabia*. New York: Cambridge Univ. Press.

Voll, John Obert. 1994. *Islam: Continuity and Change in the Modern World*. 2nd ed. Syracuse, NY: Syracuse Univ. Press.

2

Neo-Sufi Hadith Interpretation in Shāh Walī Allāh of Delhi's *Ḥujjat Allāh al-bāligha (The Conclusive Argument from God)*, Volume 2

Marcia Hermansen

Although Shāh Walī Allāh of Delhi (d. 1762) is considered a polymath, his specialization within the Islamic sciences is usually identified as hadith studies, as reflected in his honorific title "Shāh Walī Allāh *Muḥaddith* Dihlavī." But what was Shāh Walī Allāh's approach to the hadith, and how did he conceive of hadith studies within the broader context of the Islamic religious sciences?

Among Shāh Walī Allāh's many writings,[1] the masterwork is considered to be *Ḥujjat Allāh al-bāligha* (Walī Allāh 1952–53; *The Conclusive Argument from God* [Walī Allāh 1996, trans. Marcia Hermansen]). The first volume of this two-volume work lays out a metaphysical system explaining the purposes behind the divine injunctions of the shari'a. In fact, this genre of the secrets of the religion (*asrār al-dīn*) could be considered a Sufi-oriented answer to the question "What is the purpose of God's rulings for human beings?" In *fiqh* discourse, this issue is sometimes addressed by investigating the *maṣāliḥ* (the beneficial purposes of divine legislation) or the *'illa* (the reason behind

1. For a bibliography of Shāh Walī Allāh's writings, see Hermansen n.d.

something being legislated). Walī Allāh invokes each of these terms—both in their more limited jurisprudential as well as in their more conceptual or philosophical applications. For example, in *Ḥujjat Allāh al-bāligha* he usually uses the term *maṣlāḥa* in contexts where it could be translated as "beneficial purpose." However, in most jurisprudential works, discussion of the causes and benefits for shari'a legislation is confined to specific cases and rulings rather than devoted to broader philosophical and ethical reasoning. Today, Muslim jurists and intellectuals' renewed interest in exploring the *maqāṣid*,[2] or "goals," of shari'a legislation may be understood as contemporary grappling with explaining the meanings of these religious injunctions beyond asserting the need for compliance or analyzing the circumstantial or logical factors that might allow a jurist to derive a general principle from a specific case. It is within this framework of searching for higher purposes that this chapter discusses Walī Allāh's approach to hadith interpretation in *Ḥujjat Allāh al-bāligha*, volume 2.[3]

Biography

Shāh Walī Allāh was a great intellectual figure of eighteenth-century Islam in India and a prolific writer in Arabic and Persian. He was born in 1214H/1703. Biographical material and anecdotes about his life and family may be found in his brief autobiography "Al-Juz' al-laṭīf fi tarjama al-'abd al-ḍa'īf" (A Small Biographical Fragment about My Life) (1912) and in his work *Anfas al-'ārifīn* (Souls of the Gnostics, 1974), which features accounts of his father, uncle, and other spiritual

2. Contemporary works on *maqāṣid* include Auda 2008 and Duderija 2014.

3. John Voll has had a long-standing interest in Shāh Walī Allāh as an eighteenth-century reformer and welcomed my translation of volume 1 of *Ḥujjat Allāh al-bāligha* from Arabic into English some twenty years ago (Walī Allāh 1996). I hope to complete the translation of the second volume as well. This chapter allows me a welcome opportunity to offer some preliminary reflections on some of the methods behind the author's discussion of selected hadith under assorted topics in *Ḥujjat Allāh al-bāligha*, volume 2.

teachers in both India and the Hijaz. His closest disciple and the compiler of a number of his works, Shāh Muḥammad 'Āshiq (d. 1773), prepared a more detailed Persian work, *al-Qawl al-jalī fī ḥayāt al-walī* (A Clear Account of the Life of the Saint), that has only recently become more widely accessible and received some scholarly attention (Hermansen 2012).

Walī Allāh's father, Shāh 'Abd al-Raḥīm (d. 1719), was a noted scholar and mystic who had been engaged for a time to work on the compilation of Ḥanafī legal rulings known as the *Fatāwā 'Ālamgīrī* (Fatwas Compiled at the Bequest of Emperor Aurangzeb [known as "Ruler of the World," 'Ālamgīr]) commissioned by the Mughal ruler Aurangzeb (d. 1707). Shāh 'Abd al-Raḥīm devoted considerable attention to the education of his precocious son. With his father, young Walī Allāh studied hadith works such as *Mishkāt al-maṣābiḥ* (Niche of the Lamps) (al-Tabrīzī 1963) and *Ṣaḥīḥ al-Bukhārī* (Sound Hadiths Compiled by al-Bukhārī) as well as works on Qur'an interpretation, Islamic jurisprudence, and theology. He was further exposed to works on Sufism composed by such masters as Ibn 'Arabī (d. 1240) and 'Abd al-Raḥmān Jāmi (d. 1492). Walī Allāh took over his father's position as head of the Raḥīmiyya madrasa upon his death in 1719.

In about April 1731, Walī Allāh departed India to perform the pilgrimage to Mecca and Medina, where he stayed for some fourteen months, returning home in December 1732. This stay in the Hijaz was an important formative influence on his thought and subsequent life. While in the Hijaz, he studied hadith, *fiqh*, and Sufism with various eminent teachers whom he mentions in the *Anfas al-'ārifīn*, the most important influences being Shaykh Abū Ṭāhir al-Kurdī al-Madanī (d. 1733),[4] Shaykh Wafd Allāh al-Makkī, and Shaykh Tāj al-Dīn al-Qala'ī (d. 1734). These teachers in Mecca exposed Walī Allāh to the

4. Son of the famous hadith scholar and Sufi of the Hijaz, Shaykh Ibrahīm al-Kūrānī (d. 1690). See Johns 1960–2005, 242–43. Walī Allāh composed his biographical notice in *Anfās al-'ārifīn* (1974, 386–89). On al-Kūrānī, see also Knysh 1995.

trend of increased cosmopolitanism in hadith scholarship that began to emerge there in the eighteenth century owing to a blending of the North African, Hijazi, and Indian traditions of study and evaluation. In two seminal articles, John Voll (1975, 1980) explores these networks of hadith scholars from various parts of the Muslim world, who during the eighteenth century converged in the Holy Cities and interacted in the circles of Ibrahīm al-Kūrānī (d. 1690) and later of his son, Abū Ṭāhir al-Kurdī.

As part of his broad interest in hadith studies and his interactions with these learned teachers from diverse legal schools while in the Holy Cities, Walī Allāh developed a particular respect for Mālik's seminal work on hadith, the *Muwaṭṭā'* (Well-Trodden Path), on which he later was to write two commentaries, *Musawwā* (The Rectified) and *Muṣaffā* (The Purified). Ahmad S. Dallal offers a useful contextualization of these two works as part of Walī Allāh's broader project of reconciling inter*madhāhib* tensions through positioning Mālik as an authentic hadith source that all legal schools could draw on. Thus, the goal of these works is not "to idealize Mālik himself but to extract from the *Muwaṭṭā'* a substratum that serves the cause of unity he [Walī Allāh] championed" (Dallal 2018, 257).

Walī Allāh's writing career began in earnest on his return from pilgrimage. Although he composed *Ḥujjat Allāh al-bāligha* during the decade after his return, it seems that the inspiration to undertake this work came to him while on the pilgrimage. At that time, he saw a vision of the grandsons of the Prophet Muhammad, Hasan and Husayn, holding a broken pen out to him, then repairing it, and later bestowing upon him a robe of the Prophet. From this vision, he understood that he had a mission to restore the Islamic sciences through the study of the reports of the Prophet (Walī Allāh 1996, 1:12).[5] Some scholars have associated the revitalization of hadith

5. This vision is recounted in *Fuyūḍ al-Ḥaramayn*, "The Emanations of the Two Sacred Mosques" (Walī Allāh n.d., 65–66), and *al-Tafhīmāt al-Ilāhiyya*, volume 2 (Walī Allāh 1967, 300). See also Baqā' 1979, 39, and Walī Allāh n.d., 180–81.

studies as a discipline with the rise of eighteenth-century Islamic reform movements advocating social and moral reconstruction. The connection of the renewal of hadith studies with certain reformist tendencies that emerged among Sufis during this period was first noted by Fazlur Rahman, who coined the term *neo-Sufism* for such developments (1979, 206). According to Rahman, some aspects of this "new" expression of Sufism included a revival of hadith studies and increased devotional piety centered on the figure of the Prophet Muhammad. In his characterization of neo-Sufism, Rahman indicated that its goals included "the strengthening of faith in dogmatic tenets and the moral purity of the spirit. This type of neo-Sufism, as one may call it, tended to regenerate orthodox activism and reinculcate a positive attitude to this world . . . [instilling in Sufism] a puritanical, moral meaning and an orthodox ethos" (1979, 195).

Subsequently, a scholarly debate continued for some time regarding the nature and novelty of "neo-Sufism" (O'Fahey 1990, 1–9; O'Fahey and Radtke 1993). For example, Rex O'Fahey and Bernd Radtke (1993) criticized elements of the neo-Sufi characterization based on developments in African Sufi traditions, in particular the idea that devotion to the Prophet and his family received a renewed emphasis in later periods. However, as seen in Walī Allāh's work, it seems that South Asian Sufi thought does exhibit some of the "neo-Sufic" tendencies described by both Voll and Rahman. In particular, Voll's survey of the course of the neo-Sufism debate clarifies that although not all scholars use the term *neo-Sufism*, nevertheless their works can be "seen as part of the school of thought that identified a new reformist style of Sufism as an important aspect of Islamic history in the eighteenth and nineteenth centuries" (Voll 1998, x). Voll also responded to critics of the neo-Sufi hypothesis who conflated reformism with Wahhabism, noting that "it has been common at times to assert that any teacher who happened to go to Arabia in the eighteenth century and who returned to his home full of fundamentalist enthusiasm was somehow influenced by the Wahhabis. . . . [M]any of the revivalist movements that emerged by the end of the century did so in the framework of Neo-Sufi thought and organization rather than by following the Wahhabi attitude" (1994, 56).[6]

Voll (2008) points in particular to developments in eighteenth-century Sufism and to the nature of internal Sufi reforms during that period, arguing that it is a mischaracterization to infer that neo-Sufism entailed a full-scale rejection of Ibn 'Arabī's thought in favor of a return to hadith study. Walī Allāh's metaphysical system corroborates this observation because *Ḥujjat Allāh al-bāligha* and even more so his explicitly Sufic treatises draw heavily on the emanationist cosmology of Shaykh al-Akbar,[7] reflecting a heritage of Islamic intellectual history that combines tracing cosmopolitan connections in Islamic thought with studies of Sufism, hadith-transmission networks, and premodern reform movements.

More recently with the print publication of relevant original treatises and with the emergence of detailed academic work on the scholars of the Ḥaramayn during that period, such as Ibrahīm al-Kūrānī and Muḥammad Ḥayāt al-Sindī (Nafi 2002), it has become possible to further trace intellectual connections and gain more complex understandings of how the approaches of literalist and brilliant figures such as Ibn Ḥazm (d. 456/1064) and Ibn Taymiyya (d. 728/1328) were also appreciated within this circle. The fact that earlier reformist ideas were being appropriated by eighteenth-century Sufi-oriented ulama who had been formed within madhhab traditions of *taqlīd* and acceptance of the authority of past methodologies and opinions within the legal schools discloses that some sort of synthesis among competing methodological currents was being undertaken by scholars at this time, which seems very resonant with Rahman's assessment of neo-Sufism.

It is further emblematic of Walī Allāh's project of synthesis and unification that today diverse Islamic religious movements in South

6. Voll notes that he also made this statement in the first edition of *Islam: Continuity and Change in the Modern World*, published in 1982 (as explained in Voll 1998, xi).

7. *Al-shaykh al-akbar*, "the greatest shaykh," is the honorific title bestowed on Ibn 'Arabi by his admirers.

Asia construe him as their intellectual progenitor.[8] In the Indian subcontinent, the Deobandis have perhaps the most direct link to his heritage in combining the Sufi tradition of spiritual lineage with intellectual learning in hadith and legal studies (Metcalf 1982). Those who have a more reformist and puritanical outlook, such as the Ahl al-Ḥadīth movement and even the Jama'at-e Islamī followers of Abū al-'Alā Maudūdī (d. 1978), find in Walī Allāh's elucidation of the shari'a and call for reform a precursor to their own beliefs. However, it is clear from Walī Allāh's legal works, such as *al-Inṣāf fī bayān sabab al-ikhtilāf* (Doing Justice in Explicating the Causes of Juristic Disagreement),[9] that he did not go as far as some of these reformers, who were prepared to completely reject the four legal schools (Baqā' 1979, 35–36).

The third major religious inclination in contemporary South Asia is that of the Barelvis or, as they term themselves, the Ahl-e Sunna wa-l Jamā'a (Sanyal 1999), who are more oriented to popular religious practices within Sufism. They support the Ḥanafī school of law and have particular reverence for Abū Ḥanīfa (d. 767), its founder, as well as for Sufism. This aspect of Walī Allāh's teaching is best exemplified in his cousin, son-in-law, and Sufi disciple Shāh Muḥammad 'Āshiq (d. 1773) (Hermansen 2012).

At the same time, twentieth-century Islamic liberals such as Muhammad Iqbal (d. 1938) and Fazlur Rahman (d. 1988) have seen in Walī Allāh a thinker who responded to the crisis of his time with moderation and a search for the spirit behind the shari'a injunctions (Rahman 1956; Halepota 1974a, 1974b). In addition, several recent academic studies have posited Walī Allāh as pivotal in assessing synthetic and complex trends in Islamic thought on the cusp of modernity, appreciating the potential of his approach for critique within the tradition, and reflecting on the struggle for meaning within classical Islamic thought (Brown 2014; Ahmad 2017; Dallal 2018).

8. See Moosa 2010 for a more detailed discussion of certain currents in the reception of Walī Allāh in South Asia.

9. This treatise is translated by Marcia K. Hermansen in *Shāh Walī Allāh's Treatises on Islamic Law* (Walī Allāh 2011).

Ḥujjat Allāh al-bāligha, Volume 2

At the time that I was preparing my dissertation under Fazlur Rahman at the University of Chicago, he advised me to focus on the first volume of *Ḥujjat Allāh al-bāligha* as the one in which Shāh Walī Allāh lays out the metaphysical underpinnings of his approach to hadith interpretation. It was only recently that I turned to a more detailed consideration of the contents of volume 2. In the remainder of this chapter, I summarize the contents of this second volume and then reflect on what it discloses about Walī Allāh's interpretive approach to hadith.

In his preface to *Ḥujjat Allāh al-bāligha*, Walī Allāh positions the study of hadith as foundational to all of the religious sciences. He delineates a hierarchy of subdisciplines under the general rubric of hadith studies according to which the closest layer to the surface is identifying whether traditions are sound or weak, multiply transmitted or unfamiliar, and so on. Varying expertise is required for scholars working at distinct levels—the surface level is for those with prodigious memories; the next level, which requires more detailed textual analysis, is for those scholars with expertise in Arabic language and literary studies; and the most erudite scholars specialize in the jurisprudential elements of hadith derivations—for example, by determining legal analogies, deductions, and inductions. "Wali Allah's point, therefore is not to make hadith more important than *fiqh* but to establish that the latter, in spite of its higher status, is and should be founded on the former" (Dallal 2018, 260).

At the same time, according to Walī Allāh, the deepest and most subtle level of interpretation probes beyond hadith or legal studies in order to penetrate to the inner meanings (*asrār*) of religion, and it is only through study of this level that a human being can gain insight into what the divine law commands (Walī Allāh 1996, 5; Dallal 2018, 261). Dallal observes how in order "to sanction the science of the inner meanings of religion, Walī Allāh formally ties it to hadith, the most orthodox of all disciplines. He even calls his potentially controversial science the science of the secrets of hadith ('ilm asrār al-ḥadīth) to highlight the formal connection between the two" (2018, 262).

The second volume of the *Ḥujjat Allāh* undertakes the interpretation of specific hadiths topically arranged following the traditional order of the *abwāb*, or chapters, in standard books of hadith and *fiqh*. In other words, the earlier chapters give precedence to the *'ibādāt* (acts of worship), followed by the topics of the *mu'āmalāt* (the various transactions of human life). One of the intellectual achievements of the early hadith scholars was their development of a system of topical arrangement of hadith within the collections so that subsequent researchers could find the hadith reports that might shed light on the prophet's pronouncements relative to that specific subject. In an era before the encyclopedists, when books might not include chapter headings or indexes, such topical organization made interpretation much more accessible and orderly. Hadith collections arranged according to topic are called *musannafāt*, or "topically classified collections," in contrast to the *masānid* (sing. *musnad*), which are based on tracing the reports back to the name of the first transmitter. It is noteworthy that in the treatise *Sharḥ tarājīm abwāb Saḥīḥ al-Bukhārī* (Topical Commentary on the Chapters of al-Bukhārī's *Ṣaḥīḥ* [Walī Allāh 1949]), Walī Allāh recognized the intellectual contribution of al-Bukhārī (d. 855) in organizing his *Ṣaḥīḥ* according to such topical chapters. Dallal's recent study on reform in eighteenth-century Islamic thought observes that Walī Allāh was using this work to illustrate the fact that "there is a deliberate strategy [that] underlies the structure of al-Bukhārī. His *Ṣaḥīḥ*, therefore, is not just a compilation of raw and unprocessed hadiths. Rather, its organization is informed by juristic considerations; to make proper use of it, these considerations need to be inferred and elaborated. Once again, even a most canonical work of hadith cannot dispense with the need for juristic interpretation" (2018, 258–59).

The contents of *Ḥujjat Allāh*, volume 2, generally follow the order of standard hadith and *fiqh* texts, as follows:

Inner dimensions (*asrār*) of what was transmitted from the Prophet (peace be upon him)
Holding fast to the Qur'an and the Sunna
Ritual purity
Prayer

Zakat
Fasting
Hajj
Iḥsān (chapters about Sufism)
Means of livelihood
Gifts
Management of the household
Policies of cities
Hudud crimes
Judgment
Jihad
Lifestyles
Miscellaneous

Although the topics treated in the second volume of *Ḥujjat Allāh al-bāligha* are ordered in this traditional fashion, the book is far from being a compilation of all the hadith reports about specific issues, which would have been inordinately long and complex. Walī Allāh instead seems primarily to have relied on a single hadith digest as a source for selecting the hadith that he discusses under each topic: the *Mishkāt al-maṣābīḥ* of Muḥammad al-Khaṭīb al-Tabrīzī (d. c. 1337). In his brief autobiography "Al-Juz' al-laṭīf," Walī Allāh mentions having studied this book during his fifteenth year (1912, 163). Al-Tabrīzī's *Mishkāt al-maṣābīḥ* is an expanded version of an earlier work, *Maṣābīḥ al-Sunnah* (Lamps of the Prophetic Tradition) by al-Ḥusayn al-Baghawī (d. 1122) (al-Tabrīzī 1963, trans. James Robson). Al-Baghawī's handbook featured 4,434 hadiths, half of them from the *Ṣaḥīḥayn* (hadith collections of al-Bukhārī and Muslim), and al-Tabrīzī added 1,511 hadiths, so the *Mishkāt* thereafter acquired popularity as a textbook for Muslim religious students, especially in India (Brown 2009, 57–58).

In terms of the hadiths chosen for commentary by Walī Allāh, some traditional scholars have criticized his methodology for lacking rigor in not restricting himself to only verifiably "sound" reports. An annotated Urdu translation of *Ḥujjat Allāh* by a well-known Deobandi hadith scholar, the late Sa'īd Aḥmad bin Yūsuf Pālanpūrī (d. 2020), features expanded discussions of the legal implications of many of the hadith cited by Walī Allāh (Walī Allāh 2005). In some cases, the commentary also presents the Ḥanafī juristic perspective on the legal import of specific hadith, noting and critiquing where Walī Allāh has on occasion departed from the Ḥanafī school's position.

A question for the critical intellectual history scholar is why Walī Allāh, after spending so much effort on laying out a system of Sufi-inspired metaphysics in the first volume of the work, reverts to a more traditional approach to hadith in the second volume in dealing with specific topics and hadiths about them. In other words, where is the mysticism in the second volume?

This question points out a significant element of Walī Allāh's approach to hadith studies as reflected in this work. Although it is informed and based on a worldview infused with mystical understandings of the cosmos, it in most cases conforms to the procedures and intellectual traditions of the Islamic religious sciences. As outlined by Dallal, Walī Allāh maintains hadith studies as foundational to all Islamic sciences. Although rational and spiritual dimensions of the interpretation of revealed sources are incorporated and may on occasion be brought to bear in understanding the meaning of hadith reports, they cannot displace or override literal compliance with the law (Dallal 2018, 260–61). Nevertheless, Walī Allāh asserts in the preface to *Ḥujjat Allāh al-bāligha* that most inner and deep sciences of hadith interpretation are those that investigate the wisdom and rationale behind divine rulings (Walī Allāh 1996, 5, and 2011; Dallal 2018, 261).

In addition, there is one section of volume 2 under the title "Iḥsān" ("Righteousness" and by extension "Sufism") that specifically discusses topics in what we might term practical Sufism. Although the topic *iḥsān* is not treated as such in the standard hadith and *fiqh* collections, Walī Allāh's material in these chapters largely concerns the purpose of Sufi practices in acquiring virtues and the pious litanies (*adhkār*) to be recited as part of spiritual practice. Aside from the theory of virtue acquisition, the bulk of the material about supplications and litanies parallels the topics in sections 9 and 10 of the hadith collection *Mishkāt al-maṣābīḥ* dealing with supplications of the Prophet and invoking the divine names. Beyond this, even in treating more mundane topics, Walī Allāh's more esoteric (if not idiosyncratic) views and perspectives occasionally appear in interpretations, but they do not dominate.

Examples of Hadith Interpretations from *Ḥujjat Allāh al-bāligha*, Volume 2

Three translated selections from *Ḥujjat Allāh al-bāligha*, volume 2, demonstrate Shāh Walī Allāh's diverse interpretive strategies.

1. In this first sample from the "Book of Faith," the topic of the cited hadith lends itself to a "spiritual" or symbolic rather than a juristic interpretation.

> The Prophet's, may the peace and blessings of God be upon him, saying, "Adam and Moses were disputing before their Lord."[10]
>
> I interpret the Prophet's saying, "before their Lord" as meaning that the spirit (*rūḥ*) of Moses, peace be upon him, was drawn toward the Sacred Assembly (*ḥaẓīra al-quds*),[11] and there he encountered

10. Abū Hurayra narrated that Allah's Messenger said: "Adam and Moses argued with each other. Moses said to Adam: 'Your sin expelled you from Paradise.' Adam said to him: 'You are Moses whom Allah selected as His messenger and as the one to whom He spoke directly. Yet you blame me for a thing which had already been written in my fate before my Creation?' Allah's Prophet Muhammad said twice, 'So, Adam prevailed over Moses in the argument.'" Because of its deep implications for human destiny, this hadith has provoked and continues to inspire reflection and commentary.

11. The phrase *ḥaẓīra al-quds* refers to a specific element of Walī Allāh's theory (Walī Allāh 1996, 1:47). Walī Allāh uses the Enclave or Precinct (*ḥaẓīrat*) of the Holy to indicate that area of the heavens where the highest angels, joined by a few select human souls, convene to assist the future course of human affairs. The term appears with this usage in Ghazālī's *Mishkāt al-anwār* (Niche for Lights) together with other aspects of Ghazālī's terminology adopted by Walī Allāh, such as the discussion of the Highest and Lower Councils of angels. According to al-Ghazālī, this place is called the "Enclave" (*ḥaẓīrat*) of the Holy because nothing foreign to it can enter. The term

Adam. The inner dimension and secret of this event is that God disclosed to Moses knowledge on the tongue of Adam, may peace be upon both of them, resembling how a dreamer might see an angel or a righteous person in his dream and then he might ask him something and ask him for advice, returning from this [experience] having received information which he didn't know before. Here we have a case of subtle knowledge that had been hidden from Moses, peace be upon him, until Allah revealed it to him through this event.

This [knowledge] is that there are two sides to the story of Adam, may peace be upon him. The first of these is connected with the special property of the soul of Adam, peace be upon him. This is that so long as Adam had not eaten from the tree, neither thirst nor sunlight affected him, so he experienced neither hunger nor nakedness, and he would have been at the level of the angels. But once Adam had eaten from the [forbidden] tree the animalistic side came to predominate while his angelic side became eclipsed,[12] so certainly eating from the tree was a sin that he needed to seek forgiveness for committing.

The second aspect (of the story) is connected to the comprehensive divine management (*tadbīr*)[13] that God, may He be exalted, intended in creating the world and that He inspired to the angels before He created Adam. This is that God, may He be exalted, intended through creating Adam that the human species would be His representative (*khalīfa*) on the earth and that humans would sin and then would seek forgiveness from Him, and He would forgive them, and that being enjoined with the divine law would be actualized for humans, as would the sending of the prophets, reward and

is also found in a hadith in Ibn Hanbal, *Musnad*, 5:257, and is usually simply interpreted as being a high level in paradise.

12. The positioning of the human between an angelic side and an animalistic side is based on al-Ghazālī and features in *Ḥujjat Allāh*, volume 1, chapter 6, "The Inner Dimension of the Imposition of Religious Obligations" (Walī Allāh 1996, 1:57–59).

13. Walī Allāh explains in the first volume of *Ḥujjat Allāh al-bāligha* that there are four distinct processes of Creation, one of which is an ongoing process of divine management (*tadbīr*).

punishment, and the degrees of perfection and misguidance. This in itself constitutes a major purpose (for creating Adam/humanity). His eating from the tree occurred according to what God had intended and in accordance with His divine wisdom. This is the Prophet's saying, may the peace and blessings of God be upon him, "If you do not sin, God will eliminate you and bring some other people who will sin and then seek divine forgiveness so that He can forgive them."[14]

At the time when Adam was first overcome by the animalistic aspect of his nature, the second type of knowledge was veiled for him, while he comprehended [only] the first type, and he deeply regretted his act. Then his sorrow left him, and a gleam of the second kind of knowledge flashed upon him. Then once Adam had transformed to become a member of the Sacred Assembly,[15] he came to understand the situation as clearly as is possible. Moses, peace be upon him, was thinking along the same lines that Adam had until God (also) disclosed to him the second type of knowledge.

We have already mentioned how external events may have interpretations like the interpretation of dreams and that [the divine] commanding and forbidding are not random but rather to each of them there is an innate preparedness (*isti'dād*) that requires this. (Walī Allāh 1995, vol. 2, at 1:309–10, my translation in all instances)[16]

This interpretation by Shāh Walī Allāh is both theological and in some aspects mystical in accordance with his overarching theory of human destiny. In this case, the discussion of divine management and purpose depends heavily on concepts elucidated in the early metaphysical section of *Ḥujjat Allāh al-bāligha*, volume 1.

14. Muslim, in the book of Repentance (*tawba*) (4:2105/6).

15. *Al-malā al-'alā* is a specific aspect of Walī Allāh's theory of the cosmos. This expression from Qur'an 38:69–70 is taken by many commentators to refer to the highest angels, who are closest to God, but Walī Allāh believes that the souls of the Prophets and highly enlightened humans can also be included in this group after their death.

16. In this edition of *Ḥujjat Allāh al-bāligha* (Walī Allāh 1995), the first section of volume 2 is published at the end of the physical volume 1.

2. A brief example of a hadith interpretation from the book of "Ritual Prayer," the section "Things That Are Not Permitted during the Ritual Prayer," is: "His, may the peace and blessings of God be upon him, saying, 'If one of you yawns during the ritual prayer he should try to suppress it as much as possible for the Devil enters his mouth.'[17] I believe that what this means is a fly or something else entering that will distract his thoughts and keep him from properly praying" (Walī Allāh 1952–53, 2:441).

In this case, we see Walī Allāh providing a simple rationalizing explanation for the potentially troublesome expression in the hadith regarding the Devil entering a person's mouth. In some ways, his more mundane and pragmatic approach to the meaning of the hadith suggests the demythologizing approach taken by certain Islamic modernists, such as Sir Syed Ahmad Khan (d. 1898). Clearly, this is case of Walī Allāh providing a rationalizing interpretation.

3. The third and final example of hadith interpretation from *Ḥujjat Allāh al-bāligha*, volume 2, comes from the material on *ḥadd* crimes and punishments, specifically the section on theft.

> You should know that in the divine laws before us there was retributive justice (*qiṣāṣ*) for murder, stoning (as a punishment) for adultery, and cutting [off the hand] for theft. These three were abundantly inherited in the heavenly revealed divine laws, and all of the Prophets and nations agreed on them, and such things should be firmly maintained and never be abandoned. However, the divine law of Muhammad dealt with these things in another way, by setting the deterrent for each one at two levels—one of them being that of utmost severity, which should be applied in the case of the most grievous sin, while the second lesser level would apply in the case of a lesser sin.
>
> In the case of murder: retaliation (*qawad*) and blood money [were established], and the basic principle in this is His, may He be glorified, saying:
>
> "This is a reduction on the part of your Lord" (Qur'an 2:178).

17. Al-Tabrīzī 1963, 1:201.

> Ibn 'Abbās, may God be pleased with him, said: "They [the Jews] used to practice retributive justice (*qiṣāṣ*) but not blood money."
>
> In the case of adultery, [they practiced] flogging, and once the power of the Jews had declined, and they were no longer able to enforce stoning, they innovated by seating someone backward on a mount (*tajbīh*) and blackening the face (*tasḥīm*), and this was a deviation from their divine law.
>
> For us [Muslims], the two [systems of] laws of those who preceded us were combined—that is, the revealed heavenly one and the humanly invented (*ibtidā'iyya*) one—and this represents the utmost extent of the divine mercy upon us. (Walī Allāh 1995, 2:287–88)

The main orientation of Walī Allāh's hadith interpretation in this case is historical and comparative, seeing the development of rules imposed on Muslims as consistent with rulings revealed to previous religious communities, in particular the Jews, acknowledging the specific elements of the Islamic regulations, as well as suggesting a rationale for them. The understanding behind this development of religions in history is an important topic in the first volume of *Ḥujjat Allāh al-bāligha* (see Hermansen 1986; Walī Allāh 1996, 257–70). The suggestion that Islamic injunctions offer more merciful solutions, such as victims or their families accepting compensatory payments, is presented as an example of flexibility in legislation that yet does not compromise the divine injunctions.

In summary, these brief examples of Walī Allāh's hadith commentary present some of his nuanced and varied strategies of going beyond literal meanings in his approach to hadith. These strategies might entail looking for deeper theological or even mystical ramifications of the text, introducing complex perspectives, taking a pragmatic or rationalizing stance, reflecting on the historical context of revelation, and invoking comparative religion.

Conclusion

Much of the scholarship on Shāh Walī Allāh neglects or understates his practice of Sufism and seems to understand him primarily as a reformer of popular custom. This emphasis does not seem to be borne out either in his writings or in his biography but rather is a conflation of his position with tendencies that emerged later, including among some of his descendants, such as his grandson Shāh Ismā'īl Shahīd (d. 1831). A more nuanced understanding of intellectual strategies for reform is therefore required in order to contextualize Walī Allāh's thought, both within his own age and in terms of its continuing relevance for scholarship within and about Islam. Exploring the scope and nature of this reformism is directly relevant to the concept of neo-Sufism from the aspect of undertaking more detailed studies of how later Sufis conceptualized challenges to Islamic unity and interpretation in their age and, in response, formulated and enacted various types of reforms.

Shāh Walī Allāh's approach to hadith is central to his project of reconciling the fissiparous tendencies within Islam during the eighteenth century. He is one of the important reformers of this era yet is distinguished by his commitment to Sufism and his incorporation of Sufi metaphysics into a schema that could inform but not displace the shari'a disciplines of hadith knowledge and legal deductions (*fiqh*).

Considering examples of his discourse and interpretive frameworks, in this case as applied to several specific hadith reports in *Ḥujjat Allāh al-bāligha*, volume 2, demonstrates that Walī Allāh sought to mediate not only disagreements within and across the four schools (madhhabs) of Sunni *fiqh* but also between literalists and rationalists in the field of theology as well as among the proponents of hadith studies versus experts in technical elements of jurisprudence (*fiqh*). Sufism forms part of the metaphysical background to this strategy of understanding how diverse responses and interpretations emerged within the Islamic tradition over time, but it is only one aspect among many. We may conclude that spiritual, moral, and rational strategies for hadith interpretation ultimately inform Shāh Walī Allāh's "orthodox" and literal understandings of the hadith in matters of theology, practice, and jurisprudence rather than displacing them.

References

Ahmad, Irfan. 2017. *Religion as Critique: Islamic Critical Thinking from Mecca to the Marketplace*. Chapel Hill: Univ. of North Carolina Press.

Auda, Jasser. 2008. *Maqasid al-Shari'ah as Philosophy of Islamic Law*. London: International Institute of Islamic Thought.

Baqā', Maẓhar. 1979. *Uṣūl-e-fiqh aur Shāh Walī Allāh*. Islamabad: Idāra Taḥqīqāt-e Islāmī.

Brown, Jonathan. 2009. *Hadith: Muhammad's Legacy in the Medieval and Modern World*. Oxford: Oneworld.

———. 2014. *Misquoting Muhammad: The Challenge and Choices of Interpreting the Prophet's Legacy*. Oxford: Oneworld.

Dallal, Ahmad S. 2018. *Islam without Europe: Traditions of Reform in Eighteenth Century Islamic Thought*. Chapel Hill: Univ. of North Carolina.

Duderija, Adis. 2014. *Maqāṣid al-Sharī'a and Contemporary Reformist Muslim Thought: An Examination*. New York: Palgrave Macmillan.

Halepota, A. I. 1974a. "Affinity of Iqbāl with Shāh Walī Allāh." *Iqbal Review* 15, no. 1: 65–72.

———. 1974b. "Shāh Waliyullah and Iqbal: The Philosophers of the Modern Age." *Islamic Studies* 13:225–34.

Hermansen, Marcia. 1986. "Shah Wali Allah of Delhi's *Ḥujjat Allāh al-baligha*: Tension between the Universal and the Particular in an Eighteenth Century Islamic Theory of Religion." *Studia Islamica* 63:143–57.

———. 2012. "Shāh Muḥammad 'Āshiq: The Closest Disciple of Shāh Walī Allāh of Delhi." *Oriente Moderno* 92, no. 2: 420–36.

———. n.d. "Shāh Walī Allāh Bibliography." At https://www.academia.edu/2163744/Shah_Wali_Allah_Bibliography.

Johns, H. 1981. "Al-Kūrānī, Ibrahīm." In *Encyclopaedia of Islam*, 2nd ed., vol. 5, edited by C. E. Bosworth, E. van Donzel, B. Lewis, and Ch. Pellat, 432–33. Leiden: Brill.

Knysh, Alexander. 1995. "Ibrāhīm al-Kūrānī (d. 1101/1690), an Apologist for Waḥdat al-Wujūd." *Journal of the Royal Asiatic Society* Series 3, 5, no. 1: 39–47.

Metcalf, Barbara Daly. 1982. *Islamic Revival in British India: Deoband, 1860–1900*. Princeton, NJ: Princeton Univ. Press.

Moosa, Ebrahim. 2010. Preface to Marcia Hermansen, *Shah Wali Allah of Delhi's Treatises on Islamic Law*, vii–xxi. Louisville, KY: Fons Vitae.

Nafi, Bashir M. 2002. "Taṣawwuf and Reform in Pre-modern Islamic Culture: In Search of Ibrāhīm al-Kūrānī." *Die Welt des Islams* New Series 42, no. 3: 307–55.

O'Fahey, R. S. 1990. *Enigmatic Saint: Ahmad Ibn Idris and the Idrisi Tradition.* Evanston, IL: Northwestern Univ. Press.

O'Fahey, R. S., and Bernd Radtke. 1993. "Neo-Sufism Reconsidered." *Der Islam* 70, no. 1: 52–87.

Rahman, Fazlur. 1956. "The Thinker of Crisis—Shāh Waliy-Ullah." *Pakistan Quarterly* 6, no. 2: 44–48.

———. 1979. *Islam.* Chicago: Univ. of Chicago Press.

Robson, J. "Al-Baghawī." In *Encyclopaedia of Islam,* 2nd ed., edited by P. Bearman, Th. Bianquis, C. E. Bosworth, E. van Donzel, and W. P. Heinrichs. At http://dx.doi.org/10.1163/1573-3912_islam_SIM_1024.

Sanyal, U. 1999. *Devotional Islam and Politics in British India: Ahmad Riza Khan Barelwi and His Movement, 1870–1920.* 2nd ed. New York: Oxford Univ. Press.

Al-Tabrīzī. 1963. *Mishkāt al-Maṣābīḥ.* Translated by James Robson. Lahore: Ashraf.

Voll, John O. 1975. "Muḥammad Ḥayyā al-Sindī and Muḥammad ibn 'Abd al-Wahhāb: An Analysis of an Intellectual Group in Eighteenth-Century Madina." *Bulletin of the School of Oriental and African Studies* 38, no. 1: 32–39.

———. 1980. "Hadith Scholars and Tarīqahs: An 'Ulema' Group." *Journal of Asian and African Studies* 15, no. 3: 262–73.

———. 1994. *Islam: Continuity and Change in the Modern World.* 2nd rev. ed. Syracuse, NY: Syracuse Univ. Press.

———. 1998. Foreword to J. Spencer Trimingham, *The Sufi Orders in Islam,* 2nd ed., vii–xviii. New York: Oxford Univ. Press.

———. 2008. "Neo-Sufism: Reconsidered Again." *Canadian Journal of African Studies* 42, nos. 2–3: 314–30.

Walī Allāh, Shāh. 1912. "'Al-Juz' al-laṭīf fī-tarjamat al-'abd al-ḍa'īf' with English translation by M. Hidayat Ḥusain." *Journal of the Asiatic Society of Bengal* 14:161–75.

———. 1949. *Sharḥ tarājīm abwāb* Ṣaḥīḥ al-Bukhārī. Hyderabad, India: Osmania Univ.

———. 1952–53. *Ḥujjat Allāh al-bāligha.* Vols. 1 and 2. Cairo: Multazim al-Tab' wa-l-Nashr Dār al-Kutub al-Ḥadīth.

———. 1967. *Al-Tafhīmāt al-ilāhiyya*. 2 vols. In Arabic and Persian. Edited by G. M. Qāsimī. Hyderabad, India: Shāh Walī Allāh Academy.

———. 1974. *Anfas al-'ārifīn*. Urdu translation of the Persian original. Translated by Sayyid Muḥammad Farūqī al-Qādirī. Lahore: Al-Ma'ārif.

———. 1995. *Ḥujjat Allāh al-bāligha*. Vols. 1 and 2. Beirut: Dār al-Kutub al-'Ilmiyya.

———. 1996. *The Conclusive Argument from God: Shāh Walī Allāh's* Ḥujjat Allāh al-bāligha. Vol. 1. Translated by Marcia K. Hermansen. Leiden: Brill.

———. 2005. *Raḥmat Allāh al-wāsi'a sharḥ* Ḥujjat Allāh al-bāligha. 5 vols. Urdu translation and commentary by Sa'īd Aḥmad bin Yūsuf Pālanpūrī. Deoband, India: Maktaba Hijāz.

———. 2011. *Shāh Walī Allāh's Treatises on Islamic Law*. Translated by Marcia K. Hermansen. Louisville, KY: Fons Vitae.

———. n.d. *Fuyūḍ al-Ḥaramayn*. Arabic with Urdu translation. Karachi: Muḥammad Sa'īd.

Part Two

Groups of Scholars, Networks, and Education

Shifts from the Center to Local Agency

3

When Does a *Ṭarīqa* Become a *Ṭarīqa*?

The Story of a Break-up

Knut S. Vikør

Most Sufi orders began as branches of other, older orders. From the Shādhilīya came the Darqāwīya *ṭarīqa*, from the Darqāwīya came the Madanīya. Sometimes they separated themselves completely from the parent order, as the Tijānīya did from the Khalwatīya; more often they retained the link by adding their branch name to the parent name, so they can be known as, for example, the "Naqshbandīya Mujaddidīya Khālidīya" or by names that are even longer, or they used only some of the elements in the chain for their name.

This nomenclature may lead both outsiders and insiders to be unclear about the historicity of such a process: When do the activities of a gifted student change from disseminating his shaykh's *ṭarīqa* to becoming a subsidiary *ṭarīqa* of his own? If the student produces his own prayer formula (*wird*), different from that of his master, then that change or other doctrinal derivations may give us a clue to the formation of a new branch or order. But often that is not the case, or it is hard to determine when such a distinction came about.

A case in point is the development of the nineteenth-century order we know as the Sanūsīya, active in the Sahara (Libya and Chad) and surrounding areas. The Sanūsīya was a branch of the original Shādhilīya order, which was widespread in the Maghreb. There is no doubt that it was established by the scholar Muḥammad b. ʿAlī al-Sanūsī (1787–1859), and there is also no doubt that al-Sanūsī was a devoted student of the Moroccan Sufi teacher Aḥmad b. Idrīs (c. 1749–1837). Ibn Idrīs, however, never formed a brotherhood structure of his own; only his three most prominent students did—al-Sanūsī, Ibn Idrīs's earlier student Muḥammad ʻUthmān al-Mīrghanī (1793–1852), and the younger Ibrāhīm al-Rashīd (1813–74) (O'Fahey 1990; Karrar 1992; Vikør 1995; Sedgwick 2005).[1] Al-Mīrghanī established the Khatmīya brotherhood in the Sudan in the 1820s, while Ibn Idrīs was still alive, and it fairly quickly achieved a clear distinction, although Ibn Idrīs was and is revered in that brotherhood.

The relationship between the other two is, however, less clear. We know that al-Sanūsī was by far the older student of Ibn Idrīs; he was fifty years old and had been a follower of Ibn Idrīs for eleven years when the latter died, while al-Rashīd, at the young age of eighteen, had come to meet with him only about six years before his death. From the sources, it would seem that al-Rashīd first recognized the seniority of al-Sanūsī but that a conflict arose between them that led to al-Rashīd setting out on his own path, resulting in each establishing a brotherhood that came to carry their respective names.

We know of this conflict through a couple of letters from the protagonists, one from al-Sanūsī to al-Rashīd where he calls him to task and to mend his ways and another from al-Rashīd blaming al-Sanūsī for the dispute, but until now we have not had much more detail on what the split was about.

Recently, however, a new source has appeared that fills in at least some of the gaps and gives a useful glimpse into the issues of the conflict that led to the division of the students of Ibn Idrīs and may perhaps also tell us a little more about their thinking. The document came from an unexpected direction. The Sanūsīya brotherhood was famously destroyed during the Libyan anti-Italian war in the 1920s, and although it was revived as an aristocratic order in the 1950s by

1. For these students' writings, see O'Fahey 1994, 123–227. See also John Voll's pioneering work on the subject, in particular his dissertation "A History of the Khatmiyyah Tariqah in the Sudan" (1969).

Libya's king Idrīs—who was also head of the Sanūsī brotherhood—it was crushed even more thoroughly by Colonel Mu'ammar al-Qadhāfī when he came to power in 1969. The brotherhood survived only as a private order for the royal family in exile. That is, until now. In 2017, I had the pleasure and surprise to receive a visit by a Malaysian scholar, Muḥammad Fuad bin Kamaluddin, who has taken it upon himself to revive the Sanūsīya order in Malaysia and apparently has gathered several thousand students.[2] The group has republished a number of works by and on al-Sanūsī and Ibn Idrīs in Arabic or Malay,[3] and the delegation also brought with them a copy of a previously unknown manuscript entitled "Waqā'i' Ibrāhīm al-Rashīd," attributed to al-Sanūsī's grandson, a scholar in his own right, Aḥmad al-Sharīf al-Sanūsī (1867–1933), which gives a fuller description of the conflict.[4]

The Background to the Events

The context of the conflict is discussed in my book *Sufi and Scholar on the Desert Edge* (1995, 164–70) on al-Sanūsī and in Mark Sedgwick's book *Saints and Sons* (2005, 67–68) on the Rashīdīya tradition, but a brief summary may be useful here.

Muḥammad b. 'Alī al-Sanūsī came to Mecca from Morocco in June 1826 at the mature age of thirty-nine and joined the group

2. Not all three thousand were adherents to the Sanūsīya *ṭarīqa*, I was informed.

3. Thus, there are new editions of *al-Manhal al-rāwī al-rā'iq*, *al-Musalsalāt al-'ashr*, and *al-Salsabīl al-mu'īn* by al-Sanūsī; of *al-Anwār al-qudsīya*, *al-Fuyūḍāt al-rabbānīya*, *Fuyūḍāt al-mawāhib al-Makkīya bi'l-Nafaḥāt al-rabbānīya al-muṣṭafawīya* (probably the same work listed in *Arabic Literature of Africa* as *Fawḍat al-mawāhib al-malikiyya bi'l-nafaḥāt al-rabbāniyya al-muṣṭafawiyya*" [O'Fahey 1994, 174]), and *al-Ikhwān al-Sanūsīyūn* (not previously known) by Aḥmad al-Sharīf; and *al-Nafaḥāt al-kubrā* of Ibn Idrīs. The group has also published modern works by Shaykh Muhammad Fuad and others, including *Nubdha 'an al-imām al-Sayyid Aḥmad al-Sharīf*, *al-Yaqūt fī 'l-asānīd al-muḥaddith al-Sayyid Aḥmad b. Idrīs*, and *Menelusuri Sejahrah Agung Tokoh-Tokoh Sanusi*—all published by Sofa Productions in Kuala Lumpur between 2013 and 2015.

4. On the writings of Aḥmad al-Sharīf, see O'Fahey 1994, 173–75.

around Ibn Idrīs, like himself a Maghribī. Just one or two years later, Ibn Idrīs left Mecca for Yemen, settling in the town of Ṣabyā, where he stayed until his death in 1837. Some students followed him there, but many, perhaps the majority, remained behind in Mecca, among them al-Sanūsī. To cater to these students, a house or lodge was built on the hill of Abū Qubays in Mecca, and al-Sanūsī was put in charge of it, thus becoming the leader of the group of Ibn Idrīs's students in Mecca.

Ibrāhīm al-Rashīd al-Duwayḥī was born in the Sudan in 1813, and his father joined the brotherhood disseminated by Ibn Idrīs's elder student Muḥammad al-Mīrghanī three years later.[5] Ibrāhīm left the Sudan for the Hijaz as a very young man in 1831 and eventually joined Ibn Idrīs in Yemen, staying with him there until Ibn Idrīs's death six years later.[6]

Al-Sanūsī's movements following Ibn Idrīs's death are fairly well established. He first went to Ṣabyā for a brief visit before returning to Mecca and Abū Qubays. But he soon decided to head west to the Maghreb, leaving Mecca less than two years later in early 1840, and after some traveling settled in Cyrenaica, now eastern Libya, where he began building his first lodge at al-Bayḍā' in 1841. After that, he gathered followers among the local Bedouin and built a network of lodges there as well as in neighboring regions. In 1846, he returned to Mecca to pursue his scholarly activities and remained there for eight years until 1854, when he returned to Cyrenaica, where he died in 1859.

Al-Rashīd's movements are a bit more diffuse. The most probable chronology seems to be that al-Rashīd also went from Ṣabyā to Mecca sometime after Ibn Idrīs's death. He joined al-Sanūsī and the

5. Later sources say al-Rashīd's father "joined the Khatmīya," but it is not clear that the structure would have had such a separate identity rather than "the way/teachings of Aḥmad ibn Idrīs" as early as 1816.

6. Most sources say that al-Rashīd first went to Mecca and then passed quickly on to Yemen, but in the *Ikhwān al-Sanūsīyūn*, which our Malaysian colleagues have published, it is stated that he went directly from the Sudan to Yemen "with his two paternal cousins," a detail not known earlier (al-Sanūsī 2015, 111; see also Karrar 1992, 104, and Sedgwick 2005, 66).

community at Abū Qubays and remained there at least until al-Sanūsī left in 1840. Then, at some point in the early 1840s, al-Rashīd left Mecca and went to the lodge that Ibn Idrīs had earlier established at Zaynīya near Luxor in Upper Egypt and from there on to his hometown in the Sudan, spreading the *ṭarīqa* throughout that region. He returned to Mecca in 1855 and remained there for the rest of his life.

The Conflict

The sources we have had available until now establish that a conflict arose between al-Sanūsī and al-Rashīd, but with few details on what it was about or when exactly it took place. Al-Sanūsī's letter scolding al-Rashīd refers to a verse in the Qur'an about Adam but does not say what the problem was. Sedgwick hypothesizes that it may have been al-Rashīd's rejection of "millenarianist" tendencies among the Sanūsīs.[7] The new source appearing from Malaysia may give us the details of what the issues in the dispute were—although from an unabashedly one-sided angle, that of the Sanūsīs.

The Document

The new source is a photocopy of a manuscript in a clear hand, written in what appears to be an A4-size notebook. It is seventeen pages long but clearly comes from a larger compilation because it is paginated from page 439 to page 456, and the text in question begins in the middle of the page, with no headline.[8] It is credited to Aḥmad al-Sharīf al-Sanūsī, although neither that name nor the title "Waqā'ī' Ibrāhīm al-Rashīd" is mentioned in the manuscript itself, only on the printed

7. Referring to al-Sanūsī's naming of his elder son, born in 1844, "Muḥammad al-Mahdī" (Sedgwick 2005, 59, 68; cf. Vikør 1995, 154–58).

8. Borders are drawn by hand around the text on each page, apparently on the original photocopy, while the half-page above the text is blank in the photocopy. The text begins in medias res and ends without any particular marker.

cover of the photocopy. It appears thus to be from a recopy in a larger notebook of sources.

Shaykh Fuad indicated that the source—as for other Sanūsi works that his group in Malaysia has published—is the private library of a contemporary member of the Sanūsī family, Nāfi‘ al-‘Arabī al-Sanūsī. As both authorship and provenance are unconfirmed, we must therefore approach the text with caution. As we shall see, however, there are clear indications that the text, whether it was actually compiled by Aḥmad al-Sharīf himself or not, was composed in the later nineteenth or early twentieth century from original sources.

The Text

The text begins by relating that when Ibrāhīm al-Rashīd came to Mecca from Yemen, al-Sanūsī greeted him with the greatest friendliness (*ikrām wa-in‘ām*). He had heard reports about al-Rashīd's claims and activities in Yemen but had given them no heed. When al-Sanūsī decided to leave Mecca for the Maghreb, he gathered the brethren and said, "I have put my son Ibrāhīm in my place: the eyes that you see me with now, see him with them." However, after he left, he began hearing reports about claims al-Rashīd had made, including that he was the *mahdī* and that he denied that the prophets were *ma‘ṣūm* (without sin). The disturbance caused by these claims reached the level where questions had been raised to the ulama requesting fatwas about al-Rashīd's beliefs. Thus, the brethren were divided into two groups, for and against al-Rashīd. Those who were critical wrote to al-Sanūsī in Cyrenaica to make him aware of the situation. At the same time, an Egyptian follower, ‘Alī ‘Abd al-Ḥaqq al-Qūṣī, came on the Hajj to Mecca and joined and supported al-Rashīd.

The *istiftā’* (request) written by one of the Sanūsī brethren, Ḥāmid al-Ṣa‘īdī,[9] sums up the issues that were in question:

9. Ḥāmid b. Muḥammad b. Ghānim al-Khayra al-Ṣa‘īdī, from al-Ṭā’if, was a student of Ibn Idrīs who stayed behind in Mecca but then joined al-Sanūsī there in

What do the honored ulama say about a man who claims that he is the master of a *ṭarīqa* and dresses in the clothes of the people of knowledge and charges the people with claims for himself and presents to them righteousness and that he is a *murshid* and guide toward God Most High and Mighty and awakens a desire in them for the *ṭarīqa* and its people but turns them away from *ʿilm* and its people. And with what the love of the one who comes to him makes possible, he presents to him false beliefs. The ignorant are not able to defend against the errors and the *bidʿa*, so he leads astray the one he leads astray. And God will rescue whoever He wants of his worshippers.

And of all the things he claims is that the disobedience of Abū ʾl-Bashar [Adam] was a true disobedience and that suckling makes one *maḥram* even if the one who suckles is more than thirty or fifty years old, and he orders with it the people of his *madhhab* (group),[10] and he with his women suckled more than thirty men. And when the people of his *madhhab* saw it, they imitated him; it became all who wanted to be with an unrelated woman and could not find a *ḥīla* (legal excuse) that allowed him to look at her, so she suckled him until the corruption of suckling became common.

And he claimed that he had met with the Prophet (ṣ), awake with all his students, and that he could see others in heaven or hell and know their good or bad outcome, and he recognized every one of his followers sitting in heaven.

And he claimed that the disobedient (*ṣāḥib al-maʿṣiya*) is an infidel *kāfir* and argued for it with the hadith of al-Najārī, "the

---

about 1832. He remained in Mecca when al-Sanūsī went to the Maghreb and later became the head of the Abū Qubays lodge, appointed by Muḥammad al-Mahdī, thus after 1859. He died in 1303H/1885–86 (al-Lībī 1966, 39; Vikør 1996, 175; al-Sanūsī 2015, 84–85). Alfred Le Chatelier says he was head of Abū Qubays as well as regional *khalīfa* when al-Sanūsī left (1887, 273), although al-Lībī's chronology is more probable.

10. When italicized in this chapter, *madhhab* can in different contexts have many different meanings besides the conventional "school of law," including literally "way/place to enter" or "group," "method, way of doing things," and so on. When not italicized in this chapter, "madhhab" refers to "school of law."

fornicator who fornicates is not a believer when he fornicates" (to the end of the hadith).[11]

And he orders them to oppose all the four *imāms* (*r*) and argues that for them with His (most High) saying, "What the Prophet gives you, take it, and what he denies for you, avoid it," and He did not order to follow any of the four *imāms*.

So, clarify for us what you determine for the one who has these views. And you will have the reward of the Greatest giver. ("Waqā'ī‘," 439–40)

The following nine pages of the manuscript reproduce the answering fatwas of ten prominent muftis and scholars of Mecca, all condemning the views put forward by al-Rashīd. From the *istiftā'* and the answers, it seems clear that the charges made against him were the following:

- The claim that by accepting the apple in the garden of Eden, Adam committed a sin. This claim goes against the accepted view that all of the Messengers, thus including Adam, were *ma‘ṣūm*, sinless. By making this assertion, al-Rashīd thus denigrated all prophets.
- The most specific issue was that of *raḍā‘*, "suckling." As is well known, being suckled as a baby creates a constructed kinship ("milk relations" or "foster kinship") between the baby, the wetnurse, and other children suckled by the same wetnurse (Schacht and Burton 1995). Thus, all of them become *maḥram* for each other: they cannot marry and are thus free to mix without the distinction of hijab. The problem stems from a hadith given by Muslim[12] concerning Sālim, a slave whom the Companion Abū Ḥudayba had freed. As a freedman, he continued to have access to their house, something Abū Ḥudayba's wife, Umm Salama, disliked because as a free man he was no

11. "Nor is a thief who steals a believer as long as he steals, and no drunkard who drinks wine" (*Ṣaḥīḥ Muslim*, "Imān," 25). The hadith is related from Abū Ḥurayra.

12. *Ṣaḥīḥ Muslim*, "Nikāḥ," 596.

longer *maḥram* to her. She complained to the Prophet, who said, "Suckle him (so that he may become your foster child)!" and thus *maḥram*, which Umm Salama did. The issue was the topic of considerable debate among the scholars, not least because the Prophet's wife, ʿĀ'isha, was claimed to have supported this view, but the consensus among the madhhabs is that it does not have legal effect because it contradicts the rule that the "suckling period" is two years after the birth of the child and no more. The *istiftā'* claimed that not only did al-Rashīd claim the hadith was valid but also that he and some his followers had practiced it, with evident danger of impropriety.[13]

- The second hadith, "the fornicator who fornicates," implies that he who commits a grave sin is not a Muslim. This implication is opposed by the more common view that grave sin does not constitute apostasy but is reminiscent of the doctrine of *walāya wa-barā'a* (closeness and exclusion), as claimed by various Khārijī currents, although reviled by Sunni Islam (Hoffman 2012, 156–211).
- Like al-Sanūsī, Ibn Idrīs, and others of the *ṭarīqa Muḥammadīya*, al-Rashīd said he had meetings with the Prophet while he was "awake"—that is, not just in a dream. Unlike the others, however, the *istiftā'* asserted, al-Rashīd claimed that in those meetings he had seen who of his fellow Muslims were destined for heaven and who for hell (and that his followers were in the latter group).
- And, finally, al-Rashīd rejected all four madhhabs and claimed that he was able to create doctrine by himself by reading the hadith directly because the madhhabs were not instituted by God or the Prophet.

13. Implied in this claim could also be a charge of being excessively literal in reading the hadith, either for convenience or out of ignorance, and thus misinterpreting the Prophet's intended meaning, a complaint that foreshadows later discussions of Salafism.

The Fatwas

The document then provides the text of ten fatwas given by the most learned men of Mecca. They vary in length, some clearly referring to each other and merely stating their agreement to the general condemnation, while others take up different aspects of the claimed transgressions. The ten are:

- Muḥammad b. Ḥusayn al-Kutubī, Ḥanafī mufti of Mecca,[14] focuses on *raḍāʿ*, "one of the most despicable situations." Knowledge of the afterlife is "blocked for the Seeker of the path, and calling an opponent a *kāfir* because of the external [uninterpreted] meaning of the hadith means denying him his place in the *ahl al-sunna wa'l-jamāʿ*. *Taqlīd* (following) of the four *imāms* (of the four madhhabs) is required.
- Ḥusayn b. Ibrāhīm, Mālikī mufti,[15] states that *raḍāʿ* is for only two years and that to claim that a fifty-year-old can become *maḥram* in this way is against the *ijmāʿ* of the *mujtahids*. This man knows nothing about (the context of) the hadith. As for the views on sin, that is the view of the Khawārij, as is the rejection of *taqlīd* of one of the four madhhabs.

14. Probably Muḥammad b. Ḥasan al-Kutubī al-Makkī. ʿAbd al-Ḥayy al-Kattānī calls him "shaykh al-islām fī 'l-Makka." He taught *fiqh* to Aḥmad Zaynī Daḥlān, one of the other scholars, and thus seems to be older than him; he was at least active in 1845 and 1860. He was also a Sufi follower of Aḥmad al-Ṣāwī. See al-Kattānī 1982–86, 481, 107, 135, 390.

15. Ḥusayn b. Ibrāhīm al-Mālikī (1807–75), commonly known as al-Azharī, was close to the famous Egyptian scholar Muḥammad al-Amīr al-Kabīr and a student of al-ʿĀbid al-Sindī. Originally from Tripolitania, he went from Egypt to Mecca after 1824. He was also close to *sharīf* Muḥammad b. ʿAwn, who made him *khaṭīb* and imam of the Ḥaram mosque and mufti in 1262H/1846 (al-Kattānī 1982–86, 692; al-Ziriklī 1984, 1:71). ʿUmar Riḍā Kaḥḥāla calls him "*qāḍī* of Mecca" (1957, 1:95). He knew al-Sanūsī and "took" knowledge from him (al-Kattānī 1982–86, 1042).

- Ṣadīq b. ʿAbd al-Raḥmān Kamāl al-Ḥanafī,[16] teacher at the Masjid al-Ḥarām, supports the former fatwas; this is what the *ahl al-sunna wa'l-jamāʿa* are agreed on.
- Aḥmad b. Zaynī Daḥlān al-Shāfiʿī,[17] teacher at the Ḥaram al-Sharīf of Mecca, also considers the previous statements of the imams of religion to be correct. This despicable thing must be torn out.
- Aḥmad b. ʿAbd al-Raḥmān al-Naḥrāwī[18] gives a longer fatwa, where he discusses the points in more detail. All prophets are *maʿṣūm* in both small and large things, and nothing in the Qur'an contradicts that. *Raḍāʿ* is for only two years; both al-Tirmidhī and al-Bayḥaqī confirm this, and it is based on the Qur'anic verse (2:23), "and the mothers suckle their children two full years." Anything after that is not *sharʿī* suckling and has no legal effect—although there are arguments in favor of five years, but that is a minority view. As for the hadith in Muslim, it was either *makhṣūṣ*—that is, a specific solution for Sālim's case—or it was abrogated as a general rule.[19] If this person continues to claim these things after the correct view has now been pointed out, he is *fāsid*, corrupt.

16. Possibly Ṣadīq b. Muḥammad Kamāl, a Ḥanafī scholar who taught many of the same people as Aḥmad Dahlān and Muḥammad al-Kutubī (al-Kattānī 1982–86, 107, 686, 753).

17. The historian and scholar (1817–86), known from, inter alia, Christiaan Snouck Hurgronje's work *Mekka in the Latter Part of the 19th Century* (1931). He later became mufti of Mecca but must have been around twenty-five when the events discussed here took place (Brockelmann 1937–49, 2:499, supplement 2:810; al-Kattānī 1982–86, 390–92; al-Ziriklī 1984, 1:129–30). Al-Kattānī mentions him in many places as teacher alongside Jamāl b. ʿUmar, Ibrāhīm al-Fatta, and Muḥammad al-Kutubī in the group discussed in this chapter.

18. Probably the Aḥmad al-Naḥrāwī who is mentioned alongside Jamāl b. ʿUmar as teacher for a student born in 1845 (al-Kattānī 1982–86, 107; see also Snouck Hurgronje 1931, 263).

19. For more on these arguments, see Schacht and Burton 1995, 362.

- Jamāl b. ʿAbd Allāh ʿUmar al-Ḥanafī[20] says that to oppose the madhhabs of the *ahl al-sunna wa'l-jamāʿa* is the work of the Khawārij and the Rāfiḍa (Shīʿīs). Whoever opposes the *ijmāʿ* on suckling commits a *bidʿa*. Only one man, Imām al-Najārī, holds that view, but everyone knows the *ijmāʿ* is against it. Such *zandaqa* (heresy) must be opposed.
- The Shāfiʿī mufti, Muḥammad al-Ḥibshī,[21] supports what "these knowledgeable sayyids" have said—thus, he has seen more than one of the other fatwas.
- Ibrāhīm b. Muḥammad Saʿīd "al-Fatta"[22] also refers to the other ulama and condemns opposing the *ijmāʿ*. God has stated that the unseen cannot be known, citing Qur'an 34:41. All prophets are sinless, before their prophethood and after. Suckling after its ascribed period is *ḥarām* unless it is necessary to save someone's life. This claim is made only in order to rip aside the hijab and reach the *muḥrimāt* (secluded women). The

20. Known as Jamāl b. ʿUmar or Ibn al-Shaykh ʿUmar, Ḥanafī mufti of Mecca (d. 1867), *wāʿiẓ* and *muḥaddith*, head of the teachers of Mecca, and writer of several books (Kaḥḥāla 1957, 3:154; al-Kattānī 1982–86, 176, 556, 840, 1042; al-Ziriklī 1984, 2:134). He had a connection to al-Sanūsī and is mentioned in Sanūsī sources as someone who "listened" to al-Sanūsī and took knowledge from him.

21. Muḥammad b. Ḥusayn al-Ḥibshī al-Bāʿalawī was the son of the Shāfiʿī mufti of Mecca, and his son, Ḥusayn (b. 1842), took the position after him. The family connection seems to be to Ḥaḍramawt, but clearly the family also had a base in Mecca. He was a Sufi of the ʿAlawīya order and initiated, among others, ʿĀbid al-Sindī into that order. Both al-Daḥlān and Muḥammad b. ʿAlī al-Shawkānī (d. 1834) "took" from him; thus, he may have been among the elder scholars in this group (al-Kattānī 1982–86, 320, 204, 390, 698; on the son, see Kaḥḥāla 1957, 4:49, and al-Ziriklī 1984, 2:258).

22. Ibrāhīm b. Muḥammad Saʿīd al-Fatta (1790–1873) was *qāḍī* of Mecca from 1866 and wrote a number of books. A student of ʿĀbid al-Sindī, he is mentioned as a teacher alongside Aḥmad Daḥlān (Kaḥḥāla 1957, 1:85; al-Kattānī 1982–86, 692; al-Ziriklī 1984, 1:71). It is worth remarking here that the kind of analysis I try here to identify some of the more obscure persons who are part of the story draws much from the network analysis of Meccan scholars that John Voll is so famous for, including in Voll 1975, 1980, 1987, and elsewhere.

walī al-amr (authorities) must do with such a person what the shari'a demands as punishment.

- 'Abd Allāh b. Muṣṭafā Faqīh[23] supports that it is for the *walī al-amr* to handle this situation and stop the corruption.
- The tenth and last fatwa is from Yūsuf al-Sinlāwaynī (?),[24] a teacher in al-Ḥaram al-Sharīf. He points to the speaker presenting himself as a man of knowledge, while he is actually professing *shirk* (idolatry) controlled by Satan. He must be prevented by the authorities and expelled from the place he is at. How can he claim that Adam was a sinner, when Adam's act caused the events that followed, such as the existence of prophets and scholars? To believe that Adam was a rebel against God is *ridda* (apostasy). As for his view on suckling, that is just folly not supported by the revealed texts. To claim to know the destiny of men after their death is merely superstition. To point to the hadith of al-Bukhārī in support of calling believers "non-Muslims" (*takfīr*) is simply ignorance. The statement "What the Prophet gives you, take it" is a general statement, which is specified in the *ijtihād* of the four *imām* founders of the schools of law.

Al-Sanūsī's Response

At this barrage of condemnations, including threats to kill al-Rashīd, the *sharīf* Muḥammad 'Awn (r. 1827–51 and 1856–58), the "king of Hijaz," exclaimed, "I will not allow them to kill anyone in absence of their *ustadh*, and I am his *wakīl* (representative)."[25] So the scholars

23. Not identified.

24. This scholar's *nisba* is given in the "Waqā'ī'" document both as "al-S.nlāw.ynī" and "Isb.lāw.ynī." He is not identified.

25. Aḥmad al-Sharīf confirms in *al-Ikhwān al-Sanūsīyūn* that Muḥammad b. 'Awn was a student and consistent supporter of al-Sanūsī both before Ibn 'Awn came to power and afterward and that he looked after the interests of the order as *wakīl* (al-Sanūsī 2015, 108–9). This assertion may have some elements of name-dropping

asked for a meeting with 'Alī 'Abd al-Ḥaqq al-Qūṣī, who apparently represented the Abū Qubays community. They gathered in the presence of the *sharīf*, and al-Qūṣī confirmed that al-Rashīd maintained the views at issue.

Al-Sanūsī was then informed about this situation and wrote back a letter asking "them" to come to him.[26] He wrote, "If I were present, I would be the first to ask about a fatwa to kill you; your penance (*tawba*) can be accepted only in the madhhab of al-Shāfi'ī, and you have thrown off the ties of Islam from your necks. . . . So cleanse yourselves and renew your Islam and renew the contracts with your wives."[27] On receiving this letter, al-Qūṣī took statements from the brethren, in which they confirmed the sinlessness of Adam and rejected "the beliefs of Ibrāhīm al-Rashīd al-Shāfi'ī."[28] This *shahāda* was then witnessed by Ḥusayn b. Ibrāhīm and Muḥammad al-Kutubī, the Mālikī and Ḥanafī muftis mentioned earlier.

Al-Rashīd did not respond, so al-Sanūsī wrote a new letter, which is also included in the "Waqā'ī'." This is the same letter that Muḥammad al-Ashhab published in *al-Sanūsī al-kabīr* (n.d. [c. 1956], 144–49) and that I discuss in my book *Sufi and Scholar* (Vikør 1995, 165–70), but some passages in it now come into a new light.

After deploring the need to have a quarrel, al-Sanūsī confirms that all prophets without exception are sinless before their prophethood

because Ibn 'Awn came to power in 1827, just a few months after al-Sanūsī arrived in Mecca.

26. It is not clear who "them" refers to, but it may introduce the subsequent passage about al-Qūṣī turning up in Cyrenaica and being condemned there.

27. Because a Muslim woman cannot be married to a non-Muslim man, after leaving but then returning to Islam one would need to remarry one's Muslim wife/wives. We must take this statement about remarriage to be a rhetorical emphasis regarding the severity of the brotherhood members' mistakes.

28. The statement reproduced in the "Waqā'ī'" was signed by Ismā'īl b. Ramaḍān al-Ṣa'īdī, Ibrāhīm b. Aḥmad al-Dunqulāwī, Muḥammad Ḥabīb b. Aḥmad b. al-Jittī al-Jayratī, Muḥammad b. Ḥasan al-Zahranī, and 'Abd Allāh b. Zayn. It is not clear if these five were the only ones who signed such a statement or whether their signatures were only meant as an example (*ṣura*).

and afterward and that they must be followed in all matters. This has been established by the earlier scholars, and Ibn Idrīs himself referred to it. And yet "you have no need for all of that." The brethren complained about 'Alī 'Abd al-Ḥaqq after he ['Alī] came to Cyrenaica, but he excused himself, saying that he only followed the order of al-Rashīd and that al-Rashīd had claimed that this was according to al-Sanūsī's wishes. "Where did you hear that? Never, and far away." So al-Sanūsī repeats several times that al-Rashīd should come to him in Cyrenaica to sort out these questions.

He does not go into the particulars of any other issue than the sinlessness of Adam but does state generally that "it is reported from you many matters that contradict the path," both indirectly and directly in al-Rashīd's own writings. "And we pardoned you, until there appeared from you the abominable matter that almost eradicates the path by its root." When Ibn Idrīs died and when al-Sanūsī led the *ṭarīqa* for two years after that,[29] the *ṭarīqa* and its members had no enemies in all of Hijaz. Only when al-Rashīd began disagreeing with al-Sanūsī did the criticism begin, with slander and talk of them being "Khawārij" and a fifth school of law. This constitutes a break with al-Sanūsī's doctrine: "We are in one place, and you are in one place."

Al-Sanūsī ends on a more conciliatory note, saying that the teacher who does not scold his student deceives him, and he expects only the loftiest matters from al-Rashīd. His request for al-Rashīd to come to him is apparently seriously meant because he suggests the route al-Rashīd should take on his travel from Mecca over Jedda to Cyrenaica, passing by the grave of Abū 'l-Ḥasan al-Shādhilī, the founder of their paternal order, in the eastern Egyptian desert, a visit that al-Sanūsī had often desired for himself and that al-Rashīd now could accomplish in his place.[30]

29. The phrase "and we stayed two years and a bit more after him" is not in the Ashhab (n.d. [c. 1956]) version of the letter.

30. This last paragraph about the route and travel is not in the Ashhab (n.d. [c. 1956]) version.

Al-Rashīd's Version of Events

We get al-Rashīd's reply in a letter he wrote some years later. It clearly puts the matter in a completely different light but again does not delve into the content of the dispute.[31] However, it shows that the conflict simmered on for a number of years and flared up again later after al-Rashīd had settled in Egypt. The letter was written in response to a complaint that a number of Sanūsī brethren had brought to Egypt, accusing al-Rashīd and a local Ibn Idrīs student in Zaynīya, Zaydān b. Muḥammad, of spreading *fitna* (disruption) (O'Fahey 1990, 55; Sedgwick 2005, 67). Al-Sanūsī had then repeated these accusations in a letter to 'Alī 'Abd al-Ḥaqq al-Qūṣī, who was with al-Rashīd in Egypt. A council of scholars and notables was thus convened in the town of Asyūṭ in the presence of the local pasha to study the charges made. They completely cleared al-Rashīd of the charges, and he thus wrote the letter we have in order to ask al-Sanūsī to desist from making further trouble in al-Rashīd's land.

The parallels between the two stories are evident: the letter to al-Qūṣī, the gathering of scholars, the presence of the local political power, *sharīf* or pasha. But if both sources are historically accurate, they do refer to two different events because al-Rashīd in the same letter also refers, albeit obliquely, to the former dispute. He begins his letter by citing hadith against slander or calling a Muslim an infidel. Then he reminds al-Sanūsī of their time together: they met in the presence of Ibn Idrīs in Yemen and then in Mecca, where they were happily together for two years spreading the *ṭarīqa* of Ibn Idrīs. Only then did al-Rashīd begin to suspect that al-Sanūsī followed a way at odds with that of Ibn Idrīs. "And what happened from our separation in Mecca until the time of our meeting in the west, then in the Jabal al-Akhḍar and what happened in that region, is not unknown to

31. Misc., no number given, separate untitled item, but paginated as pp. 45–52, National Records Office (NRO), Khartoum. The letter is not dated, and the copy by Muḥammad al-Tihāmī al-Ḥasan is dated April 5, 1963. I am grateful to Dr. 'Alī Ṣāliḥ Karrār for providing this copy from the NRO collections.

you."[32] That phrase would appear to refer to the Meccan conflict but also shows that al-Rashīd did in fact go to visit al-Sanūsī in Cyrenaica, so all bridges were not broken then—in spite of the strong language used in al-Sanūsī's letter, exhorting al-Rashīd to come to him.

If that meeting had been meant to mend broken links, it clearly failed if Sanūsī followers at what must have been a number of years later had gone to Egypt to try to warn people away from al-Rashīd's path. Al-Rashīd's letter does not mention any names of his scholars or notables, but placing the meeting in Asyūṭ makes it clear that he is referring to a group of Egyptian, not Meccan, scholars.

Both protagonists returned to Mecca later on in life. Al-Sanūsī stayed there for eight years, between 1846 and 1854, primarily to continue his scholarly activities, and al-Rashīd came there in 1855, a few months after al-Sanūsī's departure. Al-Rashīd built his own *zāwiya* at Abū Qubays, not far from the building that al-Sanūsī had constructed for the Ibn Idrīs community thirty years earlier and that later became a lodge for his own order. However, Sedgwick notes that the area had a number of lodges of various orders (2005, 71),[33] so the proximity between the two brethren turned rivals was probably not seen as particularly provocative.

The Historicity of the Source

So far I have presented the text of the sources. But how credible are they?

It is clear that the "Waqā'ī'" is a compilation of three elements: (1) at the beginning and after the fatwas is a description of the events

32. Misc., no number given, separate untitled item, 50, NRO. This corrects my earlier reading "after we left Mecca" for *min iftirāqinā* (Vikør 1995, 169); it was Sanūsī's leaving Mecca in 1840 that was the "separation."

33. Based on Snouck Hurgronje (1931, 206). Snouck remarks on the importance of the Sanūsī center, in particular its feast on 12 Rajab celebrating al-Sanūsī's death (actually his birthday) but notes that the center was "until a few decades ago as unknown as the Zâwiyah building itself" (1931, 55). See further references to the Abū Qubays hill in Snouck Hurgronje 1931, passim.

written by a Sanūsī scholar based on memory or tradition; (2) in extenso the texts of the *istiftā'* and the fatwas; and (3) the long letter by al-Sanūsī to al-Rashīd.

Of the three, the letter has the best pedigree. It was first published in a biography of al-Sanūsī by the Libyan historian Muḥammad al-Ṭayyib al-Ashhab, who had access to the royal library collections and clear approval by the king, who was also head of the order (see al-Ashhab n.d. [c. 1956], 144–49). With the new sources from Malaysia, we now have three versions of this letter: the one published by al-Ashhab in 1956, the one in the "Waqā'ī'" manuscript, and a third version that is cited under the entry "Ibrāhīm al-Rashīd" in *al-Ikhwān al-Sanūsīyūn*, also attributed to Aḥmad al-Sharīf al-Sanūsī and published by the same Malaysian group in 2015 (al-Sanūsī 2015, 112–14).

All three show variations from each other. Both the Ashhab and "Waqā'ī'" versions include shorter elements not present in the other one, typically a sentence or two that mostly do not affect the meaning of the text. Thus, some words that Ashhab left as unreadable are spelled out in the "Waqā'ī'," and in one place Ashhab refers to a commentary by "al-Tūnisī," whereas the "Waqā'ī'" correctly gives the name as "al-Yūsī." However, Ashhab's text also includes some elements missing in the "Waqā'ī'." Thus, the two are independent, but on balance the "Waqā'ī'" appears to be the superior source of the two.

The third version of the letter, included in *al-Ikhwān al-Sanūsīyūn*, is shorter and contains only about the first half of the text, including the comments about Adam and the warnings against quarreling but excluding much of the more detailed criticisms that follow. It is clearly independent of the one in "Waqā'ī'" in that it both inserts and deletes words missing in the other, but the *Ikhwān* version follows the "Waqā'ī'" more closely than the Ashhab version and includes the elements omitted by Ashhab.[34] All of this supports the conclusion that

34. The third version, however, includes the opening salutation phrases omitted in "Waqā'ī'." Like that document, though, it correctly names al-Yūsī.

the letter part of the "Waqā'ī'" manuscript is genuine and probably copied before Ashhab's widely distributed book appeared in 1956.

The *istiftā'* and the fatwas are also clearly connected to each other in that all of the fatwas refer to one or another of the complaints in the *istiftā'*. None of them, however, mentions al-Rashīd by name, and it is not clear from the text that the scholars based their knowledge on any direct information about al-Rashīd and his group beyond what was charged in the request. Thus, the link between the fatwas and al-Rashīd is technically only through the claims of the person who asked for the fatwas, the Meccan Abū Qubays brother Ḥāmid al-Ṣa'īdī.

It is noteworthy that in the source we consider secure, al-Sanūsī's letter, he refers to only one single charge, which concerns the sinlessness of Adam,[35] although he refers to "many matters" that came up and in particular an unspecified one that was "despicable." Although most of the fatwas discuss in particular the issue of *raḍā'*, suckling, it is not mentioned explicitly by al-Sanūsī but could be the "despicable" one. But if the Abū Qubays community really had been committing practices that al-Sanūsī would have considered immoral or disreputable, it is surprising that he did not explicitly request al-Qūṣī to put a stop to them. Thus, although the issue of Adam does link the fatwas to issues that al-Sanūsī rebuked al-Rashīd for, we cannot exclude the notion that part of the *istiftā'* and the responses based on it were either slander or exaggerations to elicit the desired amount of condemnation from the ulama.

As for the surrounding "story" elements of the "Waqā'ī'" that describe the events but are not copies of earlier documents, we must of course proceed with greater caution. They most likely represent the memory as recalled and retold by Sanūsī brethren perhaps sixty or seventy years later and represent if not *the* impartial and verifiable history

35. And the same charge is the only one specified in the *shahāda* that some brethren signed in front of the two muftis. Possibly it is the one item that could be construed as *kufr* in denying the status of the prophets.

of the al-Rashīd conflict, then at least *a* version that was established in the Sanūsī brotherhood.

The Date of the Conflict

As mentioned, the chronology of the relationship is murky. Did al-Sanūsī in 1840 appoint al-Rashīd to head the Abū Qubays community? Not surprisingly, al-Rashīd makes no reference at all to having been appointed to anything by al-Sanūsī. Sanūsī sources say yes but are not consistent regarding how this came about. The "Waqā'ī'" describes al-Sanūsī presenting "his son" al-Rashīd to the community and making him his representative. However, the Sanūsī historian 'Abd al-Malik al-Lībī gives a different and more detailed version of the events. On his departure, al-Sanūsī appointed one of his earliest and trusted students, the Algerian 'Abd Allāh al-Tuwātī, as his *khalīfa* and head of Abū Qubays (al-Lībī 1966, 48–49).[36] But on the way westward in Egypt in the summer of 1840, al-Sanūsī fell ill and asked al-Tuwātī to join him. It was only at this point that he asked al-Rashīd to stand in as leader of the lodge. Al-Tuwātī continued westward with al-Sanūsī to Cyrenaica but returned to Mecca to take up his position again in 1842.

The outside time limits for the Mecca conflict are thus 1840, when al-Sanūsī left Mecca, and 1846, when he returned there.[37] However, if we understand al-Rashīd's "events" in Mecca to be the fatwa conflict, then the conflict occurred before he went to Cyrenaica, which again was before he settled in the "Rīf" (Nile Valley). If so, the events must have taken place fairly soon after al-Sanūsī's departure because al-Rashīd was in place in Egypt not far into the 1840s. The most likely dating of the conflict would thus be around 1841–42, just before or after al-Tuwātī returned to head Abū Qubays (although no source links that return to the conflict with al-Rashīd).

36. See also al-Ashhab 1947, 138, and Vikør 1995, 132–34. Ashhab also mentions yet another Sanūsī student, Muḥammad al-Khālidī, as possible head of the lodge.

37. Al-Sanūsī also appears to refer to the dispute in another letter to one of his students, dated 1265H/1849 (Ashhab n.d. [c. 1956], 152–53).

In *Sufi and Scholar* (1995), I placed the dispute a bit later because I assumed that it occurred after al-Rashīd had settled in Upper Egypt. The sources we now have indicate that al-Rashīd was in Mecca when the fatwas against him were made. In particular, the discovered last paragraph of al-Sanūsī's letter, telling al-Rashīd to come to Cyrenaica over Jedda, specifies this. Nevertheless, it is remarkable that in the context story in "Waqā'ī'," it is not al-Rashīd but his spokesman, 'Ali 'Abd al-Ḥaqq al-Qūṣī, who is summoned to the *sharīf* Muḥammad b. 'Awn. Could al-Rashīd still at this point have been in Egypt and al-Qūṣī (who came from Upper Egypt) have been sent there to confirm al-Rashīd's view and act as his spokesman? If so, the conflict may have been more drawn out, with al-Rashīd sometimes in Mecca and sometimes on travel while the exchanges took place.

The Issues of Debate

The charges made in the *istiftā'* were harsh, and there are no other indications that al-Rashīd actually either practiced or espoused, for example, the "suckling" view. It is perfectly believable that it may have referred to an oblique statement that the *mustaftī*, clearly in an antagonistic stance, exaggerated to get the response he wanted from the scholars.

Only one of the topics refers to Sufi practices: al-Rashīd's vision of the Prophet. However, it is noteworthy that none of the ulama, many of whom were Sufis, rejected the idea of seeing the Prophet while one is awake, which is a core belief in the *ṭarīqa Muḥammadīya*. They rejected only that al-Rashīd in this vision could have seen the outcome of his followers and other Muslims, a claim that neither al-Sanūsī nor Ibn Idrīs had made.

However, all of the other issues relate to law and stem from one thing: al-Rashīd's excessive claim to *ijtihād*. On point after point, the problem is that, according to the accusation, the person in question had found the "exterior" text of a Qur'anic verse or a hadith to be at variance with the *ijmā'* accepted among the four madhhabs and that he had then preferred the direct reading of the *naṣṣ*, or an interpretation of his own, over the *ijmāʿ*. This is the criticism on the issue of the sinless Adam, who disobeyed God over the apple, which is still to this day a logical conundrum discussed among Muslims (and Christians); it is the core of al-Rashīd's *raḍāʿ* claim, which was based on the clear statement by the Prophet in the *Ṣaḥīḥ* of Muslim. The view that "the fornicating sinner is not a Muslim" is similar. All this leads up to the summarizing charge that al-Rashīd opposed "the madhhabs."

That is clearly why the *mustaftī* went to the muftis of all the three large madhhabs, so that it could not be said that al-Rashīd simply preferred one madhhab over the others. They all rejected him.[38]

This interchange then deepens our understanding of the issue of *ijtihād* in this community because both al-Sanūsī and Ibn Idrīs are well known to have supported opening the gates to *ijtihād* and denounced *taqlīd*, "blind imitation." They opposed *taʿaṣṣub al-madhhab*, "madhhab fanaticism," and favored exactly the reading of the revealed text over any scholarly consensus that opposed the divine text. Thus, al-Rashīd's view should be right in the middle of the views shared by both al-Sanūsī and the Ibn Idrīs community. Nevertheless, al-Sanūsī joined the established scholars and condemned al-Rashīd. Was this dispute thus only a turf war over the leadership of the Ibn Idrīs community, does it represent a divergence between the views of Ibn Idrīs (in that case followed by al-Rashīd) and al-Sanūsī, or does it reflect a finer distinction in the doctrine?

First, it must be noted that the scholars who wrote the fatwas do not appear to belong to any anti-Sanūsī grouping. Several of them are known from Sanūsī sources as his companions or colleagues who "took knowledge from him" when he was in Mecca, although we do not know whether that was before or after the present dispute—al-Sanūsī was,

38. Or almost all of them did. Surprisingly, none of the ten scholars is identified as a Ḥanbalī, although two are still unidentified. The Ḥanbalī mufti Muḥammad b. ʿAbd Allāh b. Ḥamīd al-Shargī al-ʿĀmirī (1820–78) was close to al-Sanūsī but was too young to have been a mufti already in 1842 (al-Kattānī 1982–86, 1042; al-Ziriklī 1984, 6:243).

of course, a more established scholar in the later period. Several of the fatwas do emphasize the necessity of *taqlīd* of the four madhhabs, but their main charge is that an *ijmāʿ* between the four schools is binding and that the young al-Rashīd did not have sufficient knowledge to know the argumentation for the *ijmāʿ*. What is crucial, however, is his general (claimed) statement that one needs not follow rules made by the school founders, the *imāms* who hold the highest authority in each school. And this is a view that both al-Sanūsī and Ibn Idrīs clearly shared: the authority of the revealed text must be higher even than that of the school founders.

In spite of this, al-Sanūsī does specify in his letter that al-Rashīd was a Shāfiʿī and had to stay within that school. This is in fact in line with al-Sanūsī's own writings, where he never denies his identification with his native Mālikī madhhab. The opposition to "madhhab fanaticism" is exactly against fanaticism, or putting a *madhhab* view over all other concerns and ignoring the views of other schools or of a better understanding of the *naṣṣ*. But the condition is of course that the scholar has sufficient knowledge to know that. The practice of *ijtihād* is not a free-for-all to read your own text any way you like.

As for a divergence between Ibn Idrīs and al-Sanūsī on this question, Bernd Radtke suggested this earlier (Radtke et al. 2000, 3, 81–94), although it must be said that al-Sanūsī's main theoretical work on *ijtihād* to a large degree integrates the text on the same topic in Ibn Idrīs's *Risālat al-radd*, which was possibly put into writing in Ibn Idrīs's name by al-Sanūsī himself. (Ibn Idrīs does not seem to have actually penned any works.) That issue could link the debate discussed here to an earlier disputed moment in Ibn Idrīs's life—his sudden departure from Mecca in 1827. Some sources claim that he left because of a dispute with scholars in Mecca (e.g., O'Fahey 1990, 78).[39] Ibn Idrīs himself, however, says only that he left because of the unrest

39. Le Chatelier argues primarily that Ibn Idrīs was "expelled" from Mecca after a majlis of scholars made that decision (1887, 9, 13).

in Mecca that year. There had been a conflict between two *sharīfī* families—the Dhawū Zayd, who had held power in Mecca for a century and a half, and the Dhawū 'Awn (the ancestors of the Hāshimī royal family of Jordan). Ibn Idrīs is claimed to have had the Dhawū Zayd *sharīf* as his patron and therefore found it best to leave when the incumbent was forced from office in 1827 (al-Amr 1978, 52–54; Hofheinz 1996, 189–92).

However, in the "Waqā'ī'" manuscript we find that it is the rival *sharīf*, Muḥammad b. 'Awn, who is lauded as a close companion, indeed *wakīl*, of al-Sanūsī. Muḥammad b. 'Awn had been installed as ruler of Mecca in 1827 but was called away to Egypt by Muḥammad 'Alī in 1836 and returned in 1840—that is, at the same time or shortly after al-Sanūsī left Mecca. It is not inconceivable that al-Sanūsī had, in fact, made contact with the *sharīf* while he was Ibn Idrīs's *khalīfa* before 1836 because Muḥammad b. 'Awn was, like al-Sanūsī, working actively among the Bedouin in the region around Mecca. It is, however, equally likely that Ibn 'Awn's appearance in the story is merely a matter of name-dropping.

Nevertheless, it strengthens the impression that Ibn Idrīs and the Abū Qubays community did not have any strong preference in the Dhawū Zayd/Dhawū 'Awn rivalry and simply had cordial relations with whoever was in power. It is therefore also possible that the story of a conflict between Ibn Idrīs and the scholars of Mecca actually refers to the fatwa dispute we have here, transferred in memory from al-Rashīd to his earlier master Ibn Idrīs and pushed backward in time to explain Ibn Idrīs's sudden departure in 1827. If this is so, then Ibn Idrīs had probably simply left Mecca to get away from the unruly political situation in the town.

That interpretation conforms with the passage in al-Sanūsī's letter that "no one in Mecca said anything bad about Ibn Idrīs or about me," which rejects the idea that al-Rashīd's views were a continuation of Ibn Idrīs's. The fact that the Abū Qubays community was split and that the *mustaftī* was an established member of it and former student of Ibn Idrīs shows that certainly not all at Abū Qubays saw al-Rashīd's views as those of Ibn Idrīs. But some of them did clearly follow al-Rashīd.

The Role of 'Alī 'Abd al-Ḥaqq al-Qūṣī

One who here is said to have followed al-Rashīd and an enigmatic figure in this story was the Egyptian scholar 'Alī 'Abd al-Ḥaqq al-Qūṣī, who appears first as both a follower of and a spokesman for al-Rashīd but then who, on being taken to task by al-Sanūsī, makes amends and joins al-Sanūsī instead. He merits a somewhat closer scrutiny.

Al-Qūṣī was born in Upper Egypt in 1788 and was thus close in age to al-Sanūsī and far older than al-Rashīd. Having studied with Muḥammad al-Amīr al-Kabīr at al-Azhar, he met Ibn Idrīs in Upper Egypt and went with him to Hijaz. He joined al-Sanūsī either in Mecca or in Cairo when al-Sanūsī came through on his journey west. According to some Sanūsī sources, al-Qūṣī then went with al-Sanūsī to Cyrenaica and stayed with him there for five years before going back to Egypt, traveling the Middle East for some years, and finally settling in Upper Egypt.

The "Waqā'ī'" gives a different chronology for the period in question. It states that as the trouble was brewing in the Abū Qubays community, al-Qūṣī came for a Hajj and was caught up in the events. Siding with al-Rashīd, he became his spokesman in the debate with the *sharīf* Muḥammad b. 'Awn. In the "Waqā'ī'" story line, it was al-Sanūsī's first letter that made al-Qūṣī come to heel, and he then took statements of rejection to al-Rashīd from the brethren at Abū Qubays. In al-Sanūsī's second letter, al-Qūṣī is shunned by the Sanūsī brethren after his arrival in Cyrenaica later on and then excuses himself by saying that he had only been following al-Rashīd's commands (and thus accepting the younger man's authority). In al-Rashīd's description of the events in Egypt, al-Qūṣī again is an important go-between (al-Rashīd calls him al-Sanūsī's "most dear companion [*a'azz aṣḥābikum*]") to whom al-Sanūsī addresses his letter condemning al-Rashīd and asking al-Qūṣī to stay away from the miscreant.

Interestingly, it is through al-Qūṣī that we may find the only independent reference to this conflict. In his history of Egyptian ulama, Gilbert Delanoue (1982) writes that al-Qūṣī rejected *taqlīd* and supported *ijtihād*. For this reason, he came into conflict with orthodox scholars, among them Muḥammad al-Kutubī.[40] As we have seen, al-Kutubī is the scholar who wrote the first fatwa against al-Rashīd and who witnessed the *shahādas* collected by al-Qūṣī. Although Delanoue thus makes al-Qūṣī, not al-Rashīd, the mufti's opponent, it is no great leap to assume that we are talking about the same conflict and the fatwa presented here.

The most likely resolution of al-Qūṣī's role is that his main allegiance was always to Ibn Idrīs and his family; he later kept close connections to Ibn Idrīs's younger son, who had stayed first with al-Sanūsī in Cyrenaica, and then took him to Zaynīya (O'Fahey 1990, 126–27). Al-Qūṣī strongly supported the Idrīs tradition's view on opening the gates to *ijtihād* and rejecting *taqlīd*, a position he took that is remembered in outside sources. In the conflict that ensued between al-Sanūsī and al-Rashīd, however, he seems to have hesitated in taking sides. When al-Sanūsī appointed al-Rashīd to head Abū Qubays in 1840, al-Qūṣī accepted this decision, even though he himself was a mature and well-established scholar, about fifty-one years old to al-Rashīd's twenty-six, and clearly recognized the spiritual stature that al-Rashīd had gained from his long stay with Ibn Idrīs.[41] Thus, if we take the letters from al-Sanūsī and al-Rashīd at face value, al-Qūṣī accepted al-Rashīd's leadership in doctrinal matters when al-Rashīd was the head of Abū Qubays, then bowed to al-Sanūsī's greater authority when the teacher found the need to douse the forest fire that al-Rashīd had set in Mecca.

However, even though al-Qūṣī then took al-Sanūsī's side, it is probably incorrect to call him "a Sanūsī" or a member of al-Sanūsī's

40. Gilbert Delanoue (1982) wavers a bit about al-Kutubī's madhhab—calling him a Mālikī on page 129 and a Ḥanafī on page 190—but identifies the two as the same person. Delanoue places him only at al-Azhar in Egypt, but it is clear the person he refers to is "our" Kutubī because the Meccan mufti was also an Egyptian and a student of al-Amīr. See Delanoue 1982, 129 n. 64a, 190 n. 3.

41. Al-Qūṣī was fond of traveling and may not have wanted to be tied down in Mecca.

organization. He did not settle in a Sanūsī *zāwiya* or hold a position in al-Sanūsī's structure. Instead, he traveled and made his native Upper Egypt his base. He must therefore rather be called throughout his life an "Ibn Idrīs follower" who maintained relations with the other Ibn Idrīs followers, including al-Sanūsī, whose scholarly position al-Qūṣī clearly appreciated. That is probably also the view al-Qūṣī held during the conflicts we discuss here.

Summing Up: The Creation of a Separate Sanūsīya

From all of this, we may then return to our initial question: When did the Sanūsīya become something different from the "community of Ibn Idrīs students"? It is not far-fetched to see the conflict between al-Rashīd and al-Sanūsī as the beginning of this separation and formation of a distinct Sanūsī identity. The Sanūsīya never called themselves "Sanūsīya"; their leaders always referred to their method as the "Muḥammadan Way," the "*ṭarīqa Muḥammadīya*," a generic name used by many other Sufis and by al-Rashīd as well. It was outsiders who came to call their brotherhoods the Sanūsīya and the Rashīdīya, respectively, the latter later morphing into derivative names such as the "Dandarawīya" and the "Ṣāliḥiya." The Sanūsī name survived because their brotherhood had a stronger structure in Cyrenaica built around their integration with the Bedouin there, as described by many authors (e.g., Evans-Pritchard 1949; Ziadeh 1958; Peters 1990, 10–28). Thus, the foundation of the first Cyrenaican lodge at al-Bayḍā' in 1841 could be as likely a candidate as any for the date the Sanūsīya came into being.

However, the conflict described here shows that this identity did not appear suddenly along with the physical construction of a lodge. It is reasonably clear that al-Rashīd never saw himself as part of a Sanūsīya structure, even when he and al-Sanūsī were together at Abū Qubays before 1840. He bowed to the greater seniority of al-Sanūsī and to his leadership of Abū Qubays because it had been Ibn Idrīs's decision to make al-Sanūsī the leader. The "difference" from the *ṭarīq* of Ibn

Idrīs that al-Rashīd began to find in al-Sanūsī, as he writes, was thus that al-Sanūsī's organization began developing its own identity. So in al-Rashīd's letter of a few years later, he emphasizes his own role as the true continuation of Ibn Idrīs's tradition as opposed to the "splitter" al-Sanūsī, who had created his own thing. Thus, the 1840s were most likely a longer period of transformation of al-Sanūsī's group of students from *ṭarīq* Ibn Idrīs to *ṭarīqa* Sanūsīya. But al-Qūṣī could hope to remain on good terms and in intimate contact with both al-Sanūsī and al-Rashīd, keeping his main emphasis on Ibn Idrīs rather than on Ibn Idrīs's two heirs.

The Ibn Idrīs students who had stayed with al-Sanūsī at Abū Qubays through the 1830s, however, must have considered him the natural authority among the Ibn Idrīs followers and have seen al-Rashīd as a young upstart who tried to upset the order that Ibn Idrīs himself had instituted. If al-Rashīd really made careless remarks about freeing himself from the *ijmāʿ* of the madhhabs, it could have caused a concern among the students that it would make even those ulama who were positively inclined to Ibn Idrīs's Sufism but less enthusiastic about his views on *fiqh* turn against the community. Or the ruckus could simply have been a way of targeting al-Rashīd's leadership in the eyes of the overall leader, al-Sanūsī, and of using the Meccan ulama as a weapon.

The dispute in question could also have been an actual doctrinal disagreement about what "opening the gates" to *ijtihād* really meant. For al-Sanūsī, it did not mean to destroy the madhhab structure but to make gaps in the walls between madhhabs, which was controversial but not threatening to the ulama who were or became his colleagues. The brash statements ascribed to al-Rashīd, in contrast, were taken as being close to the *takfīrī* views of the hated Wahhābīs, who had only recently been expelled from the Hijaz. Thus, the critics responded with threats to "expel," "fight," or "kill" a person who made such wild claims. The *istiftāʾ* was thus both an appeal to the learned authorities against al-Rashīd but also a way to safeguard the community from the wrath of those scholarly authorities. Al-Sanūsī came down on the side of caution, and so al-Rashīd left Mecca but returned a decade later without causing problems.

The charges made against Ibrāhīm al-Rashīd were probably exaggerated, possibly from a lack of nuance in his statements about *ijtihād* and the authority of the madhhabs but primarily as a stage in the transformation of Ibn Idrīs's legacy from a *ṭarīq*, "path," to more than one *ṭarīqa*, "brotherhood." It was not the single turning point because the relations between al-Rashīd and al-Sanūsī were not immediately broken, and it was possible for al-Qūṣī to maintain good relations with both. But it was a dramatic moment in the process and an illustrative example of *ṭarīqa* identification.

References

Al-Amr, Saleh Muhammad. 1978. *The Hijaz under Ottoman Rule, 1869–1914: Ottoman Vali, the Sharif of Mecca, and the Growth of British Influence.* Riyadh: Riyadh Univ. Publications.

Al-Ashhab, Muḥammad al-Ṭayyib. 1947. *Barqa al-'arabīya ams wa'l -yawm.* Cairo: Maṭba'at al-Hawārī.

———. n.d. [c. 1956]. *Al-Sanūsī al-kabīr: 'Arḍ wa-taḥlīl li-di'āmat ḥarakat al-iṣlāḥ al-Sanūsī.* Cairo: Dār al-Qāhira.

Brockelmann, Carl. 1937–49. *Geschichte der Arabischen Litteratur.* 5 vols. Leiden: E. J. Brill.

Delanoue, Gilbert. 1982. *Moralistes et politiques musulmans dans l'Égypte du XIXe siècle (1789–1882).* Cairo: Institut français d'archéologie orientale.

Evans-Pritchard, E. E. 1949. *The Sanusi of Cyrenaica.* Oxford: Clarendon Press.

Hoffman, Valerie. 2012. *The Essentials of Ibāḍī Islam.* Syracuse, NY: Syracuse Univ. Press.

Hofheinz, Albrecht. 1996. "Internalising Islam: Shaykh Muḥammad Majdhūb, Scriptural Islam, and Local Context in the Early Nineteenth-Century Sudan." PhD diss., Univ. of Bergen.

Kaḥḥāla, 'Umar Riḍā. 1957. *Mu'jam al-mu'allifīn.* 14 vols. Beirut: Dār Iḥyā' al-Turāth al-'Arabī.

Karrar, Ali Salih. 1992. *The Sufi Brotherhoods in the Sudan.* London: Hurst.

Al-Kattānī, 'Abd al-Ḥayy b. 'Abd al-Kabīr. 1982–86. *Fihris al-fahāris wa'l -athbāt.* Beirut: Dār al-Gharb al-Islāmī.

Le Chatelier, A. [Alfred]. 1887. Les Confréries musulmanes du Hedjaz. Paris: Ernest Leroux.

Al-Lībī, ʻAbd al-Malik. 1966. *Al-Fawāʼid al-jalīya fī taʼrīkh al-ʻāʼila al-Sanūsīya al-ḥākima fī Lībīya*. Damascus: Maṭbaʻat Dār al-Jazāʼir al-ʻArabīya.

Muslim b. al-Ḥajjāj, Abū al-Ḥusayn. n.d. *Jāmiʻ al-Ṣaḥīḥ*. 2 vols. Cairo: ʻĪsā al-Bābī al-Ḥalabī.

O'Fahey, R. S. 1990. *Enigmatic Saint: Ahmad Ibn Idris and the Idrisi Tradition*. London: Hurst.

———, ed. 1994. *Arabic Literature of Africa*. Vol. 1: *The Writings of Eastern Sudanic Africa to c. 1900*. Leiden: Brill.

Peters, Emrys L. 1990. *The Bedouin of Cyrenaica: Studies in Personal and Corporate Power*. Cambridge: Cambridge Univ. Press.

Radtke, Bernd, John O'Kane, Knut S. Vikør, and R. S. O'Fahey. 2000. *The Exoteric Aḥmad Ibn Idrīs: A Sufi's Critique of the Madhāhib and the Wahhābīs*. Leiden: Brill.

Al-Sanūsī, Aḥmad al-Sharīf. 2015. *Al-Ikhwān al-Sanūsīyūn*. Kuala Lumpur: Dār al-Sanūsī lil-Turāth al-Islāmī (SOFA Production).

Schacht, Joseph, and John Burton. 1995. "Raḍāʻ." In *Encyclopaedia of Islam*, new ed., vol. 8, 361–62. Leiden: Brill.

Sedgwick, Mark. 2005. *Saints and Sons: The Making and Remaking of the Rashīdi Aḥmadi Sufi Order, 1799–2000*. Leiden: Brill.

Snouck Hurgronje, Christiaan. 1931. *Mekka in the Latter Part of the 19th Century: Daily Life, Customs, and Learning*. Leiden: E. J. Brill.

Vikør, Knut S. 1995. *Sufi and Scholar on the Desert Edge: Muḥammad b. ʻAlī al-Sanūsī and His Brotherhood*. London: Hurst.

———. 1996. *Sources for Sanūsī Studies*. Bergen: Centre for Middle Eastern and Islamic Studies, Univ. of Bergen.

Voll, John O. 1969. "A History of the Khatmiyyah Tariqah in the Sudan." PhD diss., Harvard Univ.

———. 1975. "Muḥammad Ḥayyā al-Sindī and Muḥammad ibn ʻAbd al-Wahhāb: An Analysis of an Intellectual Group in 18th Century Madīna." *Bulletin of the School of Oriental and African Studies* 38:32–39.

———. 1980. "Hadith Scholars and Tariqahs: An Ulama Group in the 18th Century Haramayn and Their Impact on the Islamic World." *Journal of Asian and African Studies* 15, nos. 3–4: 264–73.

———. 1987. "Linking Groups in the Networks of Eighteenth-Century Revivalist Scholars the Mizjaji Family in Yemen." In *Eighteenth-Century*

Renewal and Reform in Islam, edited by Nehemiah Levtzion and John O. Voll, 69–93. Syracuse, NY: Syracuse Univ. Press.

Ziadeh, Nicola A. 1958. *Sanūsīyah: A Study of a Revivalist Movement in Islam.* Leiden: E. J. Brill.

Al-Ziriklī, Khayr al-Dīn. 1984. Al-'Alām. 8 vols. 6th ed. Beirut: Dar al-'Ilm li'l-Malāyīn.

4

A Flame of Learning in the Winds of Change

Notes on the History of the Majādhīb of al-Qaḍārif

Albrecht Hofheinz

"Continuity and change" is the theme that John Voll (1982) placed at the center of attention in one of his most influential books on Islam in the modern world. The present piece investigates elements of this theme as it unfolded in the country where John Voll did his first fieldwork: the Sudan, in particular the eastern parts of it. Rather than painting a broad picture, however, it attempts to preserve what has come down to us of the local history of a particular group of people during the nineteenth century, a time and place where religious leaders who may be characterized as conservative representatives of Islam sought to preserve both their tradition and their social position in the face of dramatically changing circumstances. Highlighting local microhistory should serve to redress a perspective on Sudanese history that is still all too often focused on the center, the capital. Attention to regional nuances and diversity has always characterized Voll's work, even in his masterly attempts at a synthesis. This chapter also pays homage to another field where John Voll has done pioneering research: the reconstruction of scholarly networks that connected individual religious specialists with a wider world of learning both through direct contact and through their introduction to a shared scholarly corpus that was held to be authoritative in understanding and defining Islam

(Voll 1975, 1980, 2002). My contribution is based largely on oral and manuscript material that I collected during fieldwork in the Sudan in 1986–88 but that was not included in my doctoral dissertation (Hofheinz 1996), which focused on one particular reformer rather than chronicling the history of his family, the Majādhīb, over four centuries.

Much has been written over the past decades on eighteenth- and nineteenth-century Islamic reform movements (including my own work, Hofheinz 2018, with further references there). The people I foreground here are, in a way, less "spectacular"; they were not attempting to reform but rather to uphold a religious tradition threatened by the winds of change. Studying and teaching, reading and traveling, migrating and resettling into new geographical and sociopolitical spaces, they pursued and sought to transmit a world of learning that to many was no less influential than the conscious attempts at reforming this tradition that some of their contemporaries engaged in. A full understanding of Islamic history therefore needs to pay attention to these local, conservative figures alongside those with a more radical agenda.

In the course of the eighteenth century, the Majādhīb of al-Dāmar acquired a reputation as the foremost religious specialists among the Ja'aliyyīn of the northern riverain Sudan. Partly outshining older centers such as al-Ghubush (near Berber) and Nōrī (near Karīma), al-Dāmar emerged as a center of learning under the leadership of *Fakī* Ḥamad w. Muḥammad al-Majdhūb (1105–90H: 1694/3–1776/7) and some of his sons, most notably 'Abd Allāh al-Naqar (1145–1228H: 1733–1813) and Aḥmad Ab Jadarī (b. 1159H: 1747/6, d. between 1804 and 1808).[1] The Swiss explorer Johann Ludwig Burckhardt, who spent

1. The year of death, "c. 1823," given for Aḥmad Ab Jadarī in O'Fahey 1994, 244, needs to be amended because it has been confused with that of his son, Muḥammad Ab Ṣurra, who fell in the fight against the Turco-Egyptian forces suppressing the Ja'alī rebellion. For dates, if both Hijrī and Christian dates are given, they are separated by a colon, with the Hijri date/range coming first. In names of persons, the "original" individual's name appears without cognomina; the names of others who are named after this "original" individual are set in quotation marks. The abbreviation "b." stands for the Arabic *ibn* (son of); "w." for the equivalent Sudanese colloquial

a week in al-Dāmar in 1814, reports that "the whole town of Damer has acquired great reputation. Here are several schools, to which young men repair from Darfour, Sennaar, Kordofan, and other parts of Soudan, in order to acquire a proficiency in the law, sufficient to enable them to make a figure as great Fakys in their own countries" (1819, 266).

While 'Abd Allāh al-Naqar established his own school during his father's lifetime, Aḥmad Ab Jadarī became *Fakī* Ḥamad's official successor (*khalīfa*) and passed this position on to his son Muḥammad Ab Ṣurra (d. 1823). Two of Ab Jadarī's other sons, the full brothers *al-Ḥājj* 'Alī and Muḥammad "al-Azraq" (1201–89H: 1787/6–1872/3),[2] became the best-known teachers in al-Dāmar in the early nineteenth century. *Al-Ḥājj* 'Alī had studied Qur'ān with the Awlād Jābir in the Shāyqiyya country before teaching it in al-Dāmar.[3] His brother, Muḥammad "al-Azraq,"[4] had memorized the Qur'ān in al-Dāmar before leaving

---

wadd (which if spelled out is rendered here as *wad* in deference to dominant practice in the literature).

2. Their mother was Kulthūm bt. Ḥāshimī (of al-Zaydāb), whose mother was Āmna bt. 'Umar (of al-Shā'addīnāb), whose mother was bt. Asad (of the 'Umarāb, the descendants of *Shaykh* 'Umar w. Bilāl *rājil Muṭmir* (religious leaders of the Jabal Umm 'Alī area between al-Dāmar and Shendī). Before or after 'Umar al-Shā'adīnābi, bt. Asad was also married to *Fakī* Ḥamad. Majādhīb oral and written genealogies frequently list both parents and group children of the same father according to whether they have the same mother, too. As is common in the Sudan and elsewhere, individuals are thereby linked to specific families and clans, and marriage ties serve to establish and uphold these bonds. None of the women mentioned in this chapter is on record to have played another role.

3. The Awlād Jābir were the most prominent religious teachers in the Shāyqiyya area in the latter part of the sixteenth century. Some of their descendants later founded schools in other parts of the Sudan. The "original" school evidently maintained some reputation throughout the eighteenth century. See Holt 1967b.

4. Muḥammad "al-Azraq" was named after his uncle, "al-Azraq" b. *Fakī* Ḥamad. The latter may have been named after Muḥammad al-Azraq b. al-Zayn b. Ṣigheyrūn (d. 1696/7), a famous *fiqh* teacher at al-Fijeyja / Qōz al-Muṭraq / "Qōz al-'Ilm," just south of Shendi (Muḥammad al-Nūr b. Ḍayf Allāh 1970, 356–57). Ultimately, the Sudanese use of the name points back to Abū Ya'qūb Yūsuf b. 'Amr al-Azraq

to study *fiqh* at Kutrānj with the famous Azhar-trained Mālikī scholar Aḥmad w. 'Īsā (c. 1737–1826) and the latter's student Muḥammad b. Aḥmad wad al-Jibeyl (d. 1824).[5] When Aḥmad al-Ṭayyib w. al-Bashīr (1742/3–1824) visited Wad 'Īsā's school in the 1790s, Muḥammad "al-Azraq" followed his teacher Wad 'Īsā in taking the Sammāniyya; reputedly, he received a written *ijāza* from al-Ṭayyib.[6] He did not practice this *ṭarīqa*, however, and did not pass it on to his descendants.[7] Because of his training, "al-Azraq" was considered a specialist in *'ilm* (the sciences of deriving normative rules from the canonical sources), while his brother *al-Ḥājj* 'Alī was in charge of the Qur'ān lessons.

(d. around 850), the most important transmitter of the Qur'ānic "reading" (*qirā'a*) of Warsh (d. 813/2) (*'an* Nāfi' [d. 785/6]), which is dominant in all of Mālikī North Africa (interview, 'Abd Allāh al-Ṭayyib, Feb. 18, 1988, 1; the interviews I conducted are listed in the references, and the parenthetical citations to them in the notes include page numbers for my field notebooks); Nöldeke 1909–38, 3:176, 186–87).

5. Interviews, Wad al-Naqar, Mar. 15, 1987, 11, and Mar. 18, 1987, 1–2; interview, Muḥammad al-Azraq Aḥmad al-Ḥājj 'Alī, Mar. 21, 1987, 1–2. Aḥmad w. 'Īsā, known as *rājil Sinnār*, was the most important member of the Āl 'Īsā al-Anṣārī, "famous as teachers from the seventeenth century onwards at their mosque-school at Kutrānj . . . on the Blue Nile south of Khartoum"; he became "an extremely influential teacher with a wide circle of students from the Gezira to Darfur" (O'Fahey 1994, 15). Muḥammad b. Aḥmad wad al-Jibeyl hailed from the 'Umarāb of Jabal Umm 'Alī near Shendī, where he memorized the Qur'ān before studying *'ilm* with Aḥmad w. 'Īsā first in Ḥillat Khōjalī, then in Sinnār. Aḥmad w. 'Īsā gave him one of his daughters in marriage and set him up as a teacher of *'ilm* in Ḥillat Khōjalī. Toward the end of his life, he moved to Kutrānj, where he died on 5 Sha'bān 1239H: April 4 or 5, 1824 (al-Qindīl 1982, 21, 118; the editors of al-Qindīl 1982 miscalculated the Gregorian equivalent of wad al-Jibeyl's date of death). His name appears among the adjudicators in several Fūnj documents published in Abū Salīm 1967, 29, 108–10, 123, 128.

6. Aḥmad *al-Ṭayyib* w. al-Bashīr introduced the Sammāniyya in the Sudan after having taken it from its founder, Muḥammad b. 'Abd al-Karīm al-Sammān (1130–89H: 1718–75), in the Ḥijāz, where he had lived for more than two decades (O'Fahey 1994, 91–97).

7. 'Abd Allāh al-Ṭayyib 1980, 85; 'Abd al-Maḥmūd b. Nūr al-Dā'im b. Aḥmad al-Ṭayyib w. al-Bashīr 1973, 67–68, 241, 338; interview, 'Uthmān 'Abd al-Raḥmān al-Azraq, Mar. 18, 1987, 1–2.

The flourishing of education in al-Dāmar was cut short, however, by catastrophe. The Turco-Egyptian troops advancing up the Nile in 1821 apparently had bypassed the town as they moved west of the river toward the political center of the Ja'aliyyīn at al-Matamma and Shendī. Reports of a few skirmishes notwithstanding, most Sudanese leaders learned from the heavy defeat of the Shāyqiyya in November 1820 and chose to avoid confrontation with the superior intruder. A year later, however, faced with the new rulers' crushing tax demands, the Ja'aliyyīn rose in revolt. On November 3, 1822, their leader, Makk Nimr w. Muḥammad w. Nimr (c. 1780/85–1846), ruler of the Ja'aliyyīn on the east bank of the Nile since 1216H: 1801/2, burned the commander-in-chief of the Turkish army, Muḥammad 'Alī's son Ismā'īl Pāşā (b. c. 1795), to death. The Turks suppressed the revolt in a brutal campaign that destroyed many settlements along the Nile and disrupted the livelihoods of the population there. A series of clashes, most heavily in early 1823 but continuing into 1824, witnessed the victory of modern firepower over old-fashioned lances and swords; in the vicinity of al-Dāmar, tradition has kept alive memory of the battles of al-Kiweyb (on the Atbara–Nile confluence), Qōz al-Ḥalaq (on the Atbara east of al-Dāmar), and Thāqib (or Abū Sileym, on the west bank of the Nile opposite al-Dāmar, slightly upstream) ('Abd Allāh al-Ṭayyib [1412H] 1992, preface, 25; Muḥammad 'Abd al-Raḥīm [1371H] 1953, 110).

Along with an untold number of its residents, some of al-Dāmar's leaders, including the *khalīfa* Muḥammad Ab Ṣurra, perished in these confrontations; the town was ruined, and many or most of its remaining inhabitants joined the exodus of Ja'alī cultivators from the Nile to areas in the east that lay outside the immediate sway of the Turco-Egyptian forces for the time being. Some moved only as far as was necessary to reach safety from the Turkish soldiers and began to return as little as two years later, when the government assured them of amnesty.[8] Others followed Makk Nimr and his sons (the Nimrāb)

8. The reversal of the harsh policies of the Turkish authorities toward the Ja'aliyyīn has often been attributed to the more lenient approach pursued by Maḥw Bey, interim commander in chief between September 1825 and June 1826 (Holt

in retreating farther away to the Abyssinian borderlands, where some of them remained for decades and others settled for good.

Among the people who tried to escape the Turkish oppression were some of the Majādhīb from al-Dāmar. We do not know how many fled or exactly where they went at first. Preserved are only the names of those whose descendants remained in the east instead of returning to al-Dāmar when the amnesty was granted. The core of this group consisted of *Fakī* al-Makkī (the youngest son of *Fakī* Ḥamad w. al-Majdhūb, also called "wad Niyya" after his mother, a slave) and a number of his nephews, sons of Aḥmad Ab Jadarī: *al-Ḥājj* 'Abd al-Raḥmān al-Fāris; the two teachers (and full brothers) Muḥammad "al-Azraq" and *al-Ḥājj* 'Alī; and the twins Bābikr and 'Abd al-Raḥmān.[9] These Majādhīb did not cross the Buṭāna as Makk Nimr had done but moved up the River Atbara. They lived in various places in the eastern marches, but, according to oral accounts, they eventually joined the Nimrāb in Ghabṭa (Cafta/Kafta), where the Nimrāb had been allowed to settle by the Abyssinian authorities and which served as a market for goods traded between Abyssinia and the Sudan as well as Sawākin.[10]

1967a, 48–49). The Majādhīb, however, were granted a written amnesty on May 1, 1825, issued by then deputy commander in chief 'O̱smān Āğā Ḫarpūṭlı. For details, see Hofheinz 1996, 279–81.

9. Interviews, Wad al-Naqar, Mar. 15, 1987, 11, and Mar. 16, 1987, 7. 'Abd al-Raḥmān al-Fāris is buried in Ḥajar al-Maktūb near Ḥumära on the Abyssinian border; he left two sons and a daughter. One of his grandsons, Muḥammad Majdhūb b. al-Azraq b. al-Makkī b. 'Abd al-Raḥmān (d. 1963), founded Ḥillat al-Makkī in Wad Madanī. The twin brothers Bābikr and 'Abd al-Raḥmān fathered children in the east but died relatively young (between 1841 and 1857) and are buried in al-Ṣūfī al-Makkī ("al-Shaykh" Muḥammad Majdhūb b. al-Ṭāhir b. al-Ṭayyib b. Qamar al-Dīn al-Majdhūb, "Tanāsul al-buṭūn wa'l-shu'ūb min āl al-faqīh Muḥammad al-Majdhūb," [1338] 1920, MS, Bergen 506, Hofheinz Collection, Centre for Middle Eastern and Islamic Studies, University of Bergen).

10. Cf. Shuqayr 1967, 511. Cafta/Kafta (the name of the place on modern maps) lies at 14°10'00"N and 36°54'00"E. Parkyns (who traveled through Cafta in late 1845) mentions horses and slaves (both of inferior quality) and a well-known cotton cloth as the principal commodities sold here; salt from Sawākin was one of the goods

After the Turks had conquered the eastern Sudanese province of Tāka in 1840/41, they increased their pressure on the Ja'aliyyīn led by Makk Nimr. Nimr himself did not surrender, but in 1841[11] some of the Ja'aliyyīn accepted an amnesty granted by the governor-general, Aḥmad Pāşā. Among them were the Majādhīb refugees from al-Dāmar. Like other Ja'aliyyīn, they were ordered to settle and were given land on the Atbara, south of Tōmāt, on the frontier of Egyptian-held territory in the country of the Ḍabāyna, an Arab tribe allied to the Shukriyya under Aḥmad Bey Abū Sinn (1790/89–1869/70) and loyal to the Egyptian government.[12] It may be that at least some of the Majādhīb moved there already before the amnesty in 1841; a manuscript kept in

---

offered in exchange (Parkyns 1966, 2:441). Aḥmad Ḥamad al-Naqar is said to have sold there the cotton he grew in Wad al-Naqar in exchange for slaves (two *'idlas* of cotton for one *farkha* and one *khādim*). A *'idla* is "either of the two balanced halves of a load carried by a beast of burden" (Wehr and Cowan 1976, s.v. *'idla*), or about 100 kilograms (220 pounds) according to my informant in Wad al-Naqar. A *farkha* is a young slave girl, a *khādim* a grown-up male slave.

11. In Jumādà I 1257H: July–June 1841, Governor-General Aḥmad Pāşā (d. 1843) led a brief expedition against the Nimrāb in Walad 'Awaḍ and Jabal Qabṭa (Ghabṭa?). Nimr himself fled, eventually establishing himself on a hill thirty-five kilometers (twenty-one miles) farther to the west at Mai Gova (13°58'45"N and 36°51'3"E), but some of the Ja'aliyyīn, including one of Makk Nimr's sons (Aḥmad), surrendered. Aḥmad Pāşā ordered them "to settle in the region of al-Ṣūfiyya" (Holt's translation of the Nottingham manuscript of the Funj Chronicle, *Sudan of the Three Niles* 1999, 116–17).

12. At the end of the Turkiyya, the Ḍabāyna (also called Ḍabāniya) were estimated to number fifty thousand people, the Shukriyya five hundred thousand (al-Qaddāl 1973, 15; 'Uthmān [b.] Ḥamad Allāh [1965] 1966, 13). Aḥmad Bey Abū Sinn was a famous Shukrī leader who through his skillful balancing of government and tribal interests became one of the most important Sudanese personalities of the nineteenth century. He succeeded in attracting many of the Ja'alī refugees to his realm after 1824; they helped him to consolidate the town of al-Rufā'a and establish the market center of al-Qaḍārif (originally known as Sūq Abū Sinn). This process was encouraged by a Turco-Egyptian government keen on developing the rain-fed savannahs between the Rahad and Atbara Rivers into sources of grain for commercial exploitation, relying chiefly on slave labor. See Reichmuth 1990a and 1990b, 40.

al-Qaḍārif states that "al-Azraq" left Abyssinia thirty-six years after fleeing from al-Dāmar—that is, in 1254H: 1838/9.[13]

The largest settlement of the Ja'aliyyīn was established at al-Ṣūfī, on the west side of the Atbara–Setīt confluence about twenty kilometers (thirteen miles) from Tōmāt.[14] The previous history of this place remains somewhat obscure; it may have been a settlement of religious teachers claiming *sharīfī* origin.[15] The Ja'alī village established after the amnesty lay immediately to the south of an older settlement; it became also known as "Ḥillat al-Fuqahā',"[16] a designation common in the Sudan for places just outside older settlements where a group of *fakī*s had established themselves. The Majādhīb became chiefs of this new village. Mansfield Parkyns, who passed through al-Ṣūfī in late 1845, calls al-Makkī its "principal man" and *al-Ḥājj* 'Alī its "civil chief" and mentions al-Azraq as the third leading figure (Parkyns 1966, 2:395).[17] In Arabic, al-Makkī is known as *rājil al-Ṣūfī*, pointing to his leading position there. The learned men are said to have "lit the fire of the Qur'ān" in al-Ṣūfī. Their most prominent student there is said to have been Muḥammad al-Ḍikeyr 'Abdallāh Khōjalī

13. Muḥammad Aḥmad b. 'Abd Allāh, "Nubdha min akhbār al-faqih [*sic*] al-Azraq al-kabīr," manuscript 1 in the appendix.

14. "12 miles" (Baker 1867, 140).

15. The tombs of one "Ḥamad al-Ṣūfī" and one "*al-sharīf* Abū Diqn" lie north of the present settlement (field notes, Mar. 16, 1987, 21; photographed Mar. 17, 1987, 12). According to Richard Hill, al-Ṣūfī had been the first center of Makk Nimr's rebel "state" (1967, 295). The most likely source for this opinion is Baker 1867, 140, but Samuel White Baker's account of Makk Nimr is not very precise, and he completely ignores the Ja'alī settlement in al-Ṣūfī after the amnesty. Therefore, I hesitate to consider this information reliable.

16. "Hellet el Foukha" (Parkyns 1966, 2:391). The name is usually pronounced "Ḥillat al-Fuqarā."

17. Majdhūbī oral tradition still refers to the place as "al-Ṣūfī al-Makkī" after its elder *fakī*; to others, the place is generally known as "al-Ṣūfī al-Bashīr" after its Mahdist *amīr*, 'Abd al-Qādir w. al-Bashīr, a Ja'alī originally from al-Mukābrāb (south of al-Dāmar) whose task it was to concentrate all the eastern Ja'aliyyīn there (interview, Majdhūb al-Naqar, Nov. 19, 1986; interviews, Wad al-Naqar, Mar. 16, 1987, 1).

(d. 1307H: 1890/89) of al-Ghubush, who later gained fame as teacher of Muḥammad Aḥmad, the future Mahdī, and subsequently renamed "Muḥammad al-Kheyr" as commander of the Mahdist troops in the Berber area.[18]

Apart from teaching, our *fakīs* also had to fulfill another important function: to protect the population from a range of dangers, protection rooted in the extraordinary powers such "holymen" often were attributed in the Sudan. Parkyns reports that al-Makkī

> was universally believed to offer up the sunset prayer in his own house at Soufi, and the "Assha" (an hour and a half after) at Mecca, which is distant some hundreds of miles, and on the other side of the Red Sea. It is said that a pilgrim from his own village once saw him there, and was cautioned by the saint not to reveal what he had seen to any one, on pain of death. The pilgrim returned and remained for some time in Soufi, but, dying suddenly, his brother confessed that he had divulged the secret only a few minutes before he was taken ill. (1996, 2:395)

The *fakīs*' powers, the common people hoped, should help to protect them from illness, wild animals (lions, crocodiles, hippopotami, and many other species lived in abundance in these tracts at the time), robbers, and not least the extractions by their overlords. As Parkyns prepared to leave, he received "a charm from each of the three 'fouckha'; one was against robbers, wild beasts, &c., another against fevers and other maladies, and the third was to make me agreeable to great men, kings, &c." (1966, 2:400). It is important to recall that this kind of support against threats otherwise unmanageable by the individual was and often continues to be an essential function of religious

18. O'Fahey 1994, 245. In the absence of further biographical information about Muḥammad al-Ḍikeyr, we are left to speculate: Perhaps he was taken to the east as a child by his family as they fled from the Turks and spent his young years among the Ja'aliyyīn in the borderlands before returning to his native al-Ghubush?

specialists in the Sudan. It is equally important to note that the *fakīs* generally provided this support—medical aid, political intervention, and what may be seen as psychosocial help—with the recognition both that its effectiveness depended on the recipients' belief in the method used and that ultimately their charms were but a supplication because it was God Almighty who solely had the power to provide relief.[19]

On the economic side, the Majādhīb engaged in grain cultivation and animal husbandry on a large scale. They were given land along the Atbara between al-Muqaṭṭaʿ and Tamarqū (west of the Atbara–Baḥr al-Salām confluence), land that allegedly was tax exempted—a measure also used elsewhere by the Turkish authorities to attract cultivators to return to the territories controlled by Khartoum and to stimulate the development of the rain-fed savannahs between the Rahad and Atbara Rivers into sources of grain for commercial exploitation (an expansion relying on the raiding for slaves in the Abyssinian borderlands and their exploitation for farming).[20]

The population of the new village soon surpassed that of its older neighbor; in 1853, there were an estimated five hundred huts with 2,500 Jaʿalī inhabitants.[21] This growth eventually led to problems—and perhaps clashes—with the local Ḍabāyna, who apparently felt threatened by the Jaʿalī expansion. The situation was further complicated by the continuing struggle between the Nimrāb and the Turkish authorities. Ḍabāyna fighters supported Egyptian regulars and irregulars against the Nimrāb. The Jaʿaliyyīn, in contrast, though paying tribute to the Egyptians, acted as spies and informed Nimr of the Egyptian movements and in particular the localities where the Ḍabāyna and Shukriyya kept their herds. During the dry season (starting October/November), the Nimrāb were able to cross the Atbara, drive away the cattle, and retreat to the mountainous hinterland. In retaliation, the

19. For a further discussion of *ruqya*, see Hofheinz 1996, 445–58.

20. Interviews, Wad al-Naqar, Mar. 17, 1987, 3; Holt 1988, 253; Ewald 1989, 74–75.

21. Constantin Reitz (1817–53), quoted on the map in Hassenstein 1861.

Egyptians used to burn the villages deserted by the Ja'aliyyīn—no great loss because the straw huts could easily be rebuilt.[22]

In 1857, when Muḥammad Sa'īd Pāşā (*wālī* of Egypt, r. 1854–63) visited the Sudan, he offered, among other far-reaching decrees aiming at a reorganization of Egyptian rule, a new amnesty to the Nimrāb. Before news of this reached them, however, they had already attacked the government customs post at Dōka. Following this attack, the Egyptians again resorted to force; and in the wake of these events, in 1274H: 1858/7,[23] al-Ṣūfī was sacked and burned. Its Ja'alī inhabitants were dispersed for the time being, leaving the Ḍabāyna[24] in sole control. In 1861, al-Ṣūfī had been reduced to just about thirty straw huts; the local shaykh was Ḥasan be'l-Qādir ('Abd al-Qādir?) (Baker 1867, 140, 143–44).

After the leveling of al-Ṣūfī, its Ja'alī inhabitants were brought under closer government control by moving them to al-Qaḍārif, the newly emerging market center formerly known as "Sūq Abū Sinn."[25] Al-Qaḍārif was a cluster of about forty villages with two markets, and the Ja'aliyyīn built a new settlement there next to the wells of Khōr Farakha. They called it "al-Ṣūfī al-Jadīd" (the New Ṣūfī) after the

22. Baker 1867, 278–80. Very little research has been done on the fate of Makk Nimr's descendants in the East. For an account based on oral traditions, see Sudan Archive at Durham SAD.110/2/123–163: "An account of McNimr and his sons on the Abyssinian Frontier."

23. This date is inferred from Muḥammad Aḥmad b. 'Abd Allāh, "Nubdha min akhbār al-faqih [*sic*] al-Azraq al-kabīr," manuscript 1 in the appendix; it fits perfectly with all other information at my disposal.

24. The residence of the Ḍabāyna leadership was Tōmāt. Their shaykh, 'Adlān [w. 'Īsā?] w. Zāyid, died relatively young of a fever in September 1861 while on a visit to Aḥmad Bey Abū Sinn; he was succeeded by his brother Maḥmūd [w. 'Īsā?] w. Zāyid (d. 1310H: 1893/2 or August 1896) (Baker 1867, 143, 227, 278; 'Uthmān [b.] Ḥamad Allāh [1965] 1966, 13; al-Qaddāl 1973, 15, 24, 117; interviews, Wad al-Naqar, Mar. 17, 1987, 8).

25. According to oral information, the Ja'aliyyīn benefited from the intervention of the powerful Shukrī leader Aḥmad Bey Abū Sinn (1790–1870), who was loyal to the Turkish government. See also note 12.

settlement they had had to abandon.[26] Over time, it came to be known as "al-Ṣūfī al-Azraq" because its leaders were the "Azāriqa": none other than the brothers Muḥammad "al-Azraq" and *al-Ḥājj* 'Alī (their uncle, *Fakī* al-Makkī, leader of the "old" al-Ṣūfī, had died before the move).

Having been prominent teachers already in al-Dāmar before 1823, these two "Azāriqa" brothers were the main pillars upholding the family's learned tradition after the destruction of their hometown, first in the original al-Ṣūfī, then in the "new" al-Ṣūfī in al-Qaḍārif. In their new home, they and their offspring became influential religious leaders, and it became not unusual for the Majādhīb of al-Dāmar to turn to their cousins in al-Qaḍārif for more advanced education.[27] "Al-Azraq"'s grandson Muḥammad (al-Azraq) al-Aṣghar "al-Diqnāwī" (d. 1937/8) founded what became al-Qaḍārif's main mosque, the Jāmi' al-Sūq (also called "the Old Mosque"), in addition to the mosque that the Azāriqa had already established before the Mahdiyya.[28] *Al-Ḥājj* 'Alī's great-grandson, Majdhūb al-Ḥājj 'Alī Aḥmad (b. c. 1937, d. Feb. 5, 2019), was for many years imam of this mosque (as well as a teacher of Arabic at the Gedaref Secondary High School); later, he became president of the Fatwa Department of the Sudan Scholars Corporation (Hay'at 'Ulamā' al-Sūdān) in al-Qaḍārif State (Ri'āsat al-Jumhūriyya 2019). His brother Aḥmad (b. 1938) obtained a doctorate from al-Azhar and taught for some years at the Islamic University of Medina before becoming professor of *uṣūl al-dīn* at Omdurman Islamic University; another brother, al-Ṭayyib, was professor of biology at the University of Khartoum.

26. Guillaume Lejean passed through the village in April 1860 (1865, 21). Oral information suggests that the Majādhīb first found refuge in Abbāyō (on the east–southeast side of al-Qaḍārif), perhaps with the local religious leaders there, before building their own mosque in al-Ṣūfī al-Azraq (interview, 'Uthmān 'Abd al-Raḥmān al-Azraq, Mar. 20, 1988) (see also note 47).

27. For example, *Fakī* 'Abdallāh "al-Naqar" al-Ṣaghīr b. Aḥmad b. Jalāl al-Dīn (1847–1935) (interview, Muḥammad Aḥmad b. 'Uthmān al-Hawwārī, Mar. 1, 1988, 4).

28. On "al-Diqnāwī," see note 31.

Prior to the twentieth century, however, the most renowned scion of the Azāriqa was *al-Ḥājj* ʻAlī's son Aḥmad, who became famous as "the Medina scholar" (*ʻālim al-Madīna*). It is to him we shall now turn as he illustrates the trajectory of a representative of the scholarly classes, heir of a centuries-old tradition of learning in the Sudan, through the upheavals of the Mahdist revolt and the subsequent constitution of a new order under European colonial domination.[29]

Aḥmad *al-Ḥājj* ʻAlī was born around 1842/3 and thus probably in the "old" al-Ṣūfī/Ḥillat al-Fuqarā' on the upper Atbara. His mother was Bint Ḍiyāb from the old Jaʻalī ruling family, the Saʻdāb with whom the Majādhīb had intermarried previously.[30] As a teenager, he moved with his father and his uncle Muḥammad "al-Azraq" to the "new" al-Ṣūfī in al-Qaḍārif, where he studied Qur'ān and *fiqh*. There, he succeeded his father as teacher of the Qur'ān before his uncle's death (1289H: 1872/3) and continued in this position until the early days of the Mahdist state, together with his cousin Muḥammad w. al-Azraq, who inherited his father's task of teaching *ʻilm*.

In the absence of contemporary sources, we can only speculate about the Azāriqa's position toward the Mahdiyya. On the one hand, their material interests were closely bound up with the Abū Sinn

29. My sources for the life of Aḥmad *al-Ḥājj* ʻAlī are: ʻAbd al-ʻAzīz ʻĀbidīn ʻAbd al-Muʻīd, interview with ʻUmar b. Muḥammad al-Azraq al-Aṣghar, Kasalā 1941, in ʻAbd al-ʻAzīz Amīn ʻAbd al-Majīd 1949, 38–43; interviews, Wad al-Naqar, interviews with al-Amīn and al-Zākī al-Ṭayyib, Mar. 16, 1987, 1; interview, ʻUthmān ʻAbd al-Raḥmān al-Azraq, Mar. 19, 1987, 4–7.

30. Qamar al-Dīn b. *al-Fakī* Ḥamad w. "al-Majdhūb" (d. 1822) married Sitt al-Jīl, daughter of al-Makk Saʻd w. Idrīs w. Muḥammad al-Faḥl (d. c. 1800), who was allied to the Hamaj regents of Sinnār. Qamar al-Dīn also married Jāra, daughter of the Hamaj regent al-Makk Nāṣir w. Muḥammad Abū Likaylik (r. 1202–13H 1788/7–98/9), who had deposed the Fūnj sultan. Intermarriage between the Majādhīb and the Saʻdāb continued throughout the nineteenth century. In light of the rivalry between the Saʻdāb and the Nimrāb, it is interesting to see that no intermarriage is on record between the Majādhīb and the Nimrāb ("al-Shaykh" Muḥammad Majdhūb b. al-Ṭāhir b. al-Ṭayyib b. Qamar al-Dīn al-Majdhūb, "Tanāsul al-buṭūn wa'l-shuʻūb min āl al-faqīh Muḥammad al-Majdhūb," [1338H] 1920, MS, Bergen 506, Hofheinz Collection).

family, whose head, 'Awaḍ al-Karīm Pāşā Aḥmad Abū Sinn (d. 1886), was a Khatmī and loyal supporter of the Turkish government (Hill 1967, 63–64; Holt 1970, 167). On the other hand, the Mahdī's Islamic call may well have sounded reasonable to these teachers of Islamic law; this is at least what oral accounts suggest. In general, however, it seems that the Azāriqa joined the Mahdī only reluctantly, like many of the Majādhīb in al-Dāmar but contrary to their relatives in the Red Sea Hills under the leadership of Muḥammad al-Ṭāhir Majdhūb (1832/33–90), who had already given the oath of allegiance (*bay'a*) to 'Uthmān Diqna in July 1883, thus becoming instrumental in rallying the Hadendowa to the Mahdist cause.[31]

When Mahdist troops threatened al-Qaḍārif in 1884, the Majādhīb were allegedly involved in bringing about the peaceful surrender of the town on April 21.[32] Initially, the Mahdī permitted the

31. Only one member of the Azāriqa family is singled out in all reports as having joined the Anṣār: Muḥammad al-Azraq al-Aṣghar w. Muḥammad w. "al-Azraq" al-Kabīr (d. 1937/8). Being the eldest of his brothers (i.e., the only one old enough to serve in the army), he "was obliged" (*iḍṭarra*, according to his son) to join the Mahdist troops in 1304H: 1887/6 and was first stationed in al-Dāmar. Later—perhaps around 1890—he was apparently transferred to the East. A "Muḥammad al-Azraq" is listed as a soldier in the *muqaddamiyyat al-Makkī Muḥammad al-Makkī, rāyat Muḥammad b. al-Ṭāhir al-Majdhūb*, Mahdia 2/1, no. 2, National Records Office (NRO), Khartoum, Sudan. His service with the troops commanded by 'Uthmān Diqna earned him the *laqab* "al-Diqnāwī," under which he is commonly known today. After the Mahdiyya, he reestablished the main mosque in al-Qaḍārif (Jāmi' al-Sūq), where he gave introductory *fiqh* lessons (while Aḥmad *al-Ḥājj* 'Alī took care of the higher levels). He stopped teaching owing to eye failure in 1930 (see the interview with his son in 'Abd al-'Azīz Amīn 'Abd al-Majīd 1949, 38–43). Present-day Azāriqa informants emphasize their family's distance vis-à-vis the Mahdiyya. This distance is also noticeable in opinions expressed by informants from the Sawākin/Red Sea Hills area, where the Majādhīb were the most important supporters of 'Uthmān Diqna (interview, Sheyba Yāsīn 'Alī Karrār, Nov. 4, 1987, 1). On the social side, there is no intermarriage between the Azāriqa and these "eastern" Majādhīb. The Majādhīb of Wad al-Naqar to whom the Azāriqa are closely related are, in all but name, loyal followers of the Khatmiyya.

32. Interview, 'Uthmān 'Abd al-Raḥmān al-Azraq, Mar. 19, 1987, 5; cf. Shuqayr 1967, 896–97 (Shuqayr does not mention the Majādhīb).

continuation of Qur'ānic education in al-Qaḍārif; but in his letter to Aḥmad b. *al-Ḥājj* 'Alī,[33] he clearly stated that primary importance had to be given to the jihad: Qur'ān teaching was allowed only as long as the Mahdist *amīr* responsible for the area did not personally go on a campaign. Aḥmad served as imam and teacher in al-Qaḍārif for some time,[34] but continuing war, drought, and hunger led to a disruption of the school, and the Mahdists' hostility to traditional *fiqh* did not make the situation any better. Allegedly, they burned almost all books kept by the Azāriqa.[35] Eventually (before 1306H: 1889/8), the Khalīfa summoned Muḥammad w. al-Azraq (like many other notables) to Omdurman, where he died a week after his arrival; and Aḥmad *al-Ḥājj* 'Alī left al-Qaḍārif to join al-Ṭāhir al-Majdhūb and 'Uthmān Diqna in Tokar, where his nephew, Muḥammad al-Azraq w. Muḥammad w. al-Azraq, served as a *qāḍī*.[36]

When Tokar fell to the Anglo-Egyptian forces on February 19, 1891, Aḥmad *al-Ḥājj* 'Alī became a prisoner but was allowed to leave for Medina together with his wife.[37] He stayed there ("studying and

33. Mahdia 3/1/37, NRO (cf. Abū Salīm 1969, 509).

34. Letter, [Aḥmad *al-ḥājj* 'Alī] to Abū 'l-Qāsim [Aḥmad] Hāshim, [1912], manuscript 10 in the appendix.

35. Such reports on the fate of books during the Mahdiyya are quite common in the eastern Sudan. The books are said to have either been burned or else buried to hide them; when the attempt was made to recover them after the war, they had allegedly been eaten away by insects or could no longer be found. Book burning or the hiding of books to prevent them from being destroyed is of course a phenomenon also known from other parts of the Islamic and the wider world, most recently illustrated by the dramatic events surrounding the libraries of Timbuktu in 2012 (on which see the—rather sensationalist—account by Joshua Hammer [2017]; cf. also the story of the reconstitution of Timbuktu's oldest library in Hofheinz 2004).

36. On "Muḥammad al-Azraq," see also note 31.

37. The names of three of Aḥmad *al-Ḥājj* 'Alī's wives are preserved in "al-Shaykh" Muḥammad Majdhūb b. al-Ṭāhir b. al-Ṭayyib b. Qamar al-Dīn al-Majdhūb, "Tanāsul al-buṭūn wa'l-shu'ūb min āl al-faqīh Muḥammad al-Majdhūb," [1338H] 1920, MS, Bergen 506, Hofheinz Collection: (1) Bt. al-Nūr (of the Shā'addīnāb), whose maternal grandmother was Nūr bt. al-Aḥmar b. *al-Fakī* Ḥamad and who was the mother of *Fakī* Muḥammad al-Bashīr; (2) Fāṭima bt. al-khalīfa 'Umar (of the Nifey'āb, a section of

teaching," as a common topos has it) probably until the defeat of the Mahdiyya in 1898/9. One of his teachers was the traditionist 'Alī Ṭāhir; another was Yaḥyā al-Shinjīṭī, although he said he learned but little from him. Other men with whom he had contact in the Ḥijāz were the Shādhilī scholars 'Umar BāJunayd and 'Alawī b. 'Aqīl from Mecca.[38] In Medina, Aḥmad married another Sudanese woman and had children with her.

Eventually, he moved to Cairo, where he pursued his studies with Mālikī teachers, concentrating in particular on hadith, perhaps an indication that even "conservative" Muslims were influenced by the growing importance of hadith studies in the wake of the eighteenth- and nineteenth-century reform movements. He contacted the Mālikī scholar 'Abd al-Raḥmān b. Muḥammad 'Illaysh (son of the famous Shaykh al-Azhar), but more significant for him were two other scholars: Aḥmad al-Rifā'ī (a Mālikī teacher at al-Azhar), from whom he heard the first part of Mālik's *Muwaṭṭa'* as well more than half of al-Suyūṭī's *al-Jāmi' al-Ṣaghīr*, and Aḥmad al-Rifā'ī's recently graduated[39] student Muḥammad b. 'Abd al-Ghanī b. Muḥammad al-Mālikī al-Malawī, with whom he studied Muslim's *Ṣaḥīḥ* as well as getting permission to use the Shādhilī *Ḥizb al-Kabīr*.[40]

The *ijāza*s he obtained from these two teachers put him in a line of Mālikī teaching tradition "codified" by Muḥammad b. Muḥammad al-Amīr Sr. (1154–1232H: 1741/2–1817/6).[41] Al-Amīr, a student of the

---

the Ja'aliyyīn originally from al-Matamma), who gave birth to one daughter named Fāṭima, suggesting that the mother died in childbed; (3) Nafīsa bt. Muḥammad "al-Azraq al-Aṣghar" al-Diqnāwī b. Muḥammad w. *al-Fakī* Muḥammad "al-Azraq," who was still alive in 1920 and who became the mother of most of Aḥmad *al-Ḥājj* 'Alī's children (al-Ḥājj 'Alī, al-Azraq, 'Abdallāh, Muḥammad, and a daughter).

38. On the latter two, see manuscript 8 in the appendix.

39. The seal on his *ijāza* is dated 1315H: 1897/8; see manuscript 3 in the appendix.

40. An analysis and translation of this important litany is provided in McGregor 1993; the Arabic text and an English translation have also been published in Durkee [1411H] 1991.

41. Al-Ziriklī 1986, 7:71; Brockelmann 1943–49, S2:738; cf. also Vikør 1995, 84, with further sources.

influential 'Alī al-Ṣa'īdī al-'Adawī (1112–89H: 1700/1701–1775), was a grammarian and Mālikī scholar who left a "catalog" (*Thabat*) of his teachers, giving their biographies and scholarly affiliations. He wrote mainly commentaries and glosses on grammar books (Ibn Hishām's *Mughnī al-labīb*; Ibn Turkī's commentary on the *'Ashmāwiyya*; *shaykh* Khālid's commentary on the *Azhariyya*; a commentary on *al-Shudhūr*), on *fiqh* works (Khalīl's *Mukhtaṣar*; al-Zurqāwī's commentary on the *'Izziyya*), and on theology ('Abd al-Salām's commentary on the *Jawharat al-tawḥīd*), plus an exegesis of sūras 97, 113, and 114. The *ijāza*s Aḥmad *al-Ḥājj* 'Alī received emphasize that they comprise not only the books he directly "heard" (*sami'a*) from his teachers but also all the works listed in al-Amīr's *Thabat*.[42] Among the passages Aḥmad took care to

42. Muḥammad 'Abd al-Ghanī's *ijāza* is dated 17 Muḥarram 1319H: May 6, 1901; Aḥmad al-Rifā'ī's 19 Muḥarram 1319H: May 8, 1901. Additional information is provided by three documents detailing Aḥmad *al-Ḥājj* 'Alī's *sanads*; see manuscripts 2–6 in the appendix. Aḥmad al-Rifā'ī's teacher was Aḥmad Minnatallāh al-Shabāsī al-Mālikī, whose teacher was Muḥammad al-Amīr Jr., who in turn studied with his father, al-Amīr Sr. Muḥammad 'Abd al-Ghanī first studied with his father (who took from 'Abd al-Wahhāb al-Ḥusaynī, who in turn studied with al-Amīr Sr.) before becoming a student of Aḥmad al-Rifā'ī.

• The line of transmission for the *Muwaṭṭa'* is given as: Muḥammad al-Amīr Sr. ← 'Alī al-'Arabī al-Saqqāṭ ← Muḥammad [b. 'Abd al-Bāqī] al-Zurqānī [1055–1122H: 1645/6–1710/1; Egyptian Mālikī traditionist who wrote a famous commentary on the *Muwaṭṭa'*] ← 'Abd al-Bāqī [b. Yūsuf al-Zurqānī] [1020–99H: 1611/2–88/7; Egyptian Mālikī *faqīh* who wrote a well-known commentary on Khalīl's *Mukhtaṣar*] ← 'Alī [b. Muḥammad] al-Ujhūrī [967–1066H: 1560/59–1656/5; Egyptian Mālikī *faqīh* and traditionist] ← Muḥammad b. Aḥmad al-Ramlī [919–1004H: 1513/4–1596/5; Egyptian Shāfi'ī *muftī*] ← Zakariyyā [al-Anṣārī] [823–926H: 1420–1519/20; Egyptian Shāfi'ī jurisprudent and traditionist whose most famous work, *Manhaj al-ṭullāb fī 'l-fiqh*, became a standard Shāfi'ī law primer] ← [Aḥmad b. 'Alī] Ibn Ḥajar al-'Asqalānī [773–852H: 1371/2–1448/9; Egyptian Shāfi'ī traditionist and historian] ← Najm al-Dīn Muḥammad b. 'Alī [b. Muḥammad] b. 'Aqīl al-Bālisī [730–804H: 1330/29–1402/1; Shāfi'ī *faqīh*, originally from Syria, lived in Egypt] ← Muḥammad b. 'Alī al-Mukaffà ← Muḥammad b. Muḥammad al-Dalāṣī ← 'Abd al-'Azīz b. 'Abd al-Wahhāb b. Ismā'īl b. al-Ṭāhir ← Ismā'īl b. al-Ṭāhir ← Muḥammad b. al-Walīd al-Ṭurṭūs[h]ī [451–520H: 1059/60–126; Andalusian Mālikī *faqīh* who settled in Egypt] ← [Abū

copy from this catalog, we note al-Amīr's line of initiation into the Nāṣiriyya *ṭarīqa*, which he took from Muḥammad b. 'Abd al-Salām b. Nāṣir; the latter had come through Cairo on his way to the pilgrimage and had spent the night at al-Amīr's house.[43] The Nāṣiriyya had gained importance in the eighteenth century as a reformist Shādhilī order noted for its emphasis on learning, Prophetic piety, and complete adherence to the Prophet's Sunna. Along with his focus on hadith

---

'l-Walīd] Sulaymān b. Khalaf al-Bājī [403–474H: 1013–81; noted Andalusian poet and scholar whose short commentary on the *Muwaṭṭa'* gained wide circulation] ← Yūnus b. 'Abdallāh b. Mughīth ["Ibn al-Ṣaffār"] [338–429H: 949/50–1038/7; Andalusian *qāḍī*, Ṣūfī and traditionist who wrote a commentary on the *Muwaṭṭa'*] ← Abū 'Īsā Yaḥyā b. Yaḥyā ← (his ['Ubaydallāh's] father's uncle) 'Ubaydallāh b. Yaḥyā b. Yaḥyā ← Yaḥyā b. Yaḥyā al-Laythī al-Andalusī [152–234H: 769–848/9] ← Mālik [c. 90/7–179H: 708/16–95/6].

• For Muslim's *Ṣaḥīḥ*, al-Amīr Sr.'s *sanad* is given as: Muḥammad al-Amīr Sr. ← 'Alī al-Saqqāṭ ← Ibrāhīm [b. Mūsā] al-Fayyūmī [1062–137H: 1652/1–1725/4; Mālikī, *Shaykh al-Azhar*] ← Aḥmad [al-Fayyūmī] al-Furqāwī al-Mālikī [d. 1101H: 1690] ← 'Alī al-Ujhūrī [967–1066H: 1560/59–1656/5] ← Nūr al-Dīn 'Alī al-Qarāfī ← al-Suyūṭī [849–911H: 1445–1505] ← [Ṣāliḥ b. 'Umar] al-Bulqīnī [791–868H: 1389/8–1464/3; Shāfi'ī Grand Qāḍī of Cairo, *fiqh* teacher of al-Suyūṭī] ← al-Tanūkhī ← Sulaymān b. Ḥamza [al-Maqdisī] [628–715H: 1231/30–1315/6; Syrian Ḥanbalī scholar] ← Abū 'l-Ḥasan 'Alī b. Naṣr ← 'Abd al-Raḥmān b. [?] ← Abū Bakr Muḥammad b. 'Abdallāh ← Makkī al-Nīsābūrī ← Muslim b. al-Ḥajjāj [202/6–61H: 817/21–75/4].

• The line of transmission for Suyūṭī's *Jāmi'* is given as: Muḥammad al-Amīr Sr. ← 'Alī al-Ṣa'īdī al-'Adawī (1112–1189H: 1700/1–1775] ← [Muḥammad b. Aḥmad] 'Aqīla [d. 1150H: 1737/8; Meccan Ḥanafī historian and traditionist] ← Ḥasan ← [Muḥammad b. 'Alā' al-Dīn Shams al-Dīn] al-Bābilī [1000–1077H: 1592/1–1666/7; Egyptian Shāfi'ī *faqīh*] ← [Sālim b. Muḥammad] al-Sanhūrī [945–1015H: 1538/9–1603/4; Egyptian Mālikī *faqīh*] ← [Muḥammad b. 'Abd al-Raḥmān] al-Shams al-'Alqamī [897–969H: 1492/1–1562/1; Egyptian Shāfi'ī *faqīh* and traditionist who wrote a commentary on *al-Jāmi' al-Ṣaghīr*] ← al-Suyūṭī [849–911H: 1445–1505].

43. The *sanad* continues: Muḥammad b. 'Abd al-Salām b. Nāṣir ← (his uncle) Abū Ya'qūb Yūsuf b. Muḥammad ← Abū 'Abdallāh Muḥammad b. 'Abd al-Salām al-Bannānī [d. 1163H: 1750; traditionist from Fās] ← ("*al-quṭb*") Abū 'l-'Abbās Aḥmad [b. Maḥammad] b. Nāṣir [1057–1129H: 1647–1717] ← (his father, "*al-ghawth*") [Maḥammad b. "Nāṣir" Muḥammad b. Aḥmad b. Muḥammad b. al-Ḥusayn b. Nāṣir b. 'Amr al-Dar'ī al-Aghlāfī, 1015–85H: 1602/3–74], and so on back to Aḥmad Zarrūq.

studies, Aḥmad's affiliation with this order is another sign of the spread of a Prophet-centered, Sunna-minded understanding of Islam from consciously reformist circles to relatively conservative ulama.[44]

Provided with these new credentials, Aḥmad *al-Ḥājj* 'Alī left Egypt in or shortly after May 1901 and returned to the Sudan, where he became involved in efforts to reorganize religious education under the new political regime. It is unclear whether he spent much time in Omdurman, but he did have contacts with leading ulama, and, according to one report, he was appointed a member of the "Board of Ulema" created by Reginald Wingate in 1901.[45] Eventually, however, he returned to al-Qaḍārif,[46] where he again worked as an imam and resumed teaching *fiqh*.

There is some reason to believe that the school he reopened took a while to get off the ground and that his first students were mainly members of his own family.[47] The curriculum was perhaps also

44. See further Meier 2001, 2005.

45. Muḥammad al-Mubārak 'Abd Allāh [1392H] 1973, 11. I have no independent confirmation for this and rather doubt that it is true; it may be a misunderstanding on the part of Muḥammad al-Mubārak.

46. This may have happened quite early. In Dhū 'l-Qa'da 1319H: February/March 1902, Aḥmad *al-Ḥājj* 'Alī issued a Shādhilī *ijāza* to 'Uthmān w. Muḥammad w. al-Azraq of al-Qaḍārif (see manuscript 7 in the appendix). The *silsila*s mentioned in this *ijāza* run as follows: (1) for the Shādhilī *awrād*: Aḥmad ← his father ← his uncle *Fakī* al-Makkī ("*Rājil al-Ṣūfī*") ← his brother Aḥmad *Ab Jadarī* (1746–1804/8) ← his father *Fakī* Ḥamad w. al-Majdhūb (1105–90: 1694/3–1776/7); (2) for the *Dalā'il al-Khayrāt*: Aḥmad ← his father ← his uncle *Fakī* al-Makkī ← Muḥammad b. Hāshim al-Fallātī; (3) for both, Aḥmad also possesses *ijāza*s from his Medinese teacher 'Alī Ṭāhir (a *muḥaddith*) and from the Egyptian Mālikī scholar 'Abd al-Raḥmān b. Muḥammad 'Illaysh (probably a son of the famous *muḥaddith*, supreme Shādhilī leader and Mālikī mufti of Egypt, Muḥammad b. Aḥmad 'Illaysh [1802–82], on whom see de Jong 2004).

47. Other than his successor 'Uthmān Muḥammad al-Azraq, his students included al-Amīn and al-Ṭayyib (sons of Aḥmad Ḥamad al-Naqar), Muḥammad and *Ḥājj* Aḥmad (sons of Muḥammad Sa'īd w. Wideyda), and *Fakī* Masā'ad Ṭayyib al-Asmā'.

• Aḥmad Ḥamad al-Naqar (d. 1872/6) must have been an extraordinarily enterprising man. Born in al-Dāmar, he spent about two years in the Ḥijāz in the 1820s before

restricted to the bare essentials that had been at the core of instruction in the Sudan for centuries: Khalīl's *Mukhtaṣar*, Ibn Abī Zayd's *Risāla*, grammar, and hadith are mentioned as the subjects his most talented student and successor, 'Uthmān w. Muḥammad w. al-Azraq (b. before 1879, d. November 15, 1939), studied with him;[48] and according to a letter Aḥmad *al-Ḥājj* 'Alī wrote in 1912, it was as late as 1910 that he started teaching a regular one-year course in the *Risāla*.[49] Later

---

returning to the Sudan. The year 1831 saw him in al-Dāmar ("al-Shaykh" Muḥammad Majdhūb b. al-Ṭāhir b. al-Ṭayyib b. Qamar al-Dīn al-Majdhūb [1332H] 1914), but he was to spend the rest of his life in the East, where he moved to various places before finally establishing himself (c. 1839) as a farmer on land granted to him by the leader of the Ḍabāyna. He founded the village known after him as "Wad al-Naqar" on the upper Atbara, about an hour's walk south of al-Ṣūfī, where he died in 1872. His sons al-Amīn and al-Ṭayyib studied with the Azāriqa in al-Qaḍārif before joining the Mahdist armies. When Tokar fell, they temporarily moved to al-Dāmar, but after the defeat of the Mahdiyya they returned to the East. Both studied with Aḥmad *al-Ḥājj* 'Alī for a while; then al-Ṭayyib established himself as a farmer and Qur'ān teacher in al-Ṣūfī al-Bashīr, while al-Amīn remained in al-Ṣūfī al-Azraq. Al-Ṭayyib died in the early 1920s. Two of his sons, al-Amīn (c. 1910–Feb. 1988) and al-Zākī (b. 1912), returned to their ancestors' village, Wad al-Naqar, in January 1943, together with four other Ja'alīs, and revitalized agriculture there (interviews, Wad al-Naqar, Mar. 15–17, 1987).

• Muḥammad Sa'īd w. Wideyda belonged to a branch of the Ṣādiqāb family of *mashā'ikh* in Abbāyō/al-Qaḍārif. He was married to Fāṭima, a sister of Aḥmad *al-Ḥājj* 'Alī. His sons Muḥammad and Aḥmad were, however, from another wife (interview, 'Uthmān 'Abd al-Raḥmān al-Azraq, Mar. 20, 1987, 5).

• *Fakī* Masā'ad of al-Qaḍārif/Wad al-Kibayyir belonged to the eastern Zaydāb, who after 1820 had settled around al-Ṣūfī (interview, 'Uthmān 'Abd al-Raḥmān al-Azraq, Mar. 19, 1988).

48. 'Uthmān's "classical" interests are reflected in some books he acquired. In 1316H: 1898/9, he bought Abū 'l-Ḥasan 'Alī b. Muḥammad al-Shādhilī's *Kifāyat al-ṭālib al-rabbānī*, a commentary (completed in 1519) on Ibn Abī Zayd's *Risāla*; in 1320H: 1902, he copied the *Azhariyya* on grammar; and in 1326H: 1908/9, he copied Khalīl's *Mukhtaṣar* and Taqīy al-Dīn Abu 'l-Ḥasan 'Alī al-Subkī's (683–756H: 1284–1355) *Tā'iyya*, a famous poem in praise of the Prophet (these books are kept by 'Uthmān 'Abd al-Raḥmān al-Azraq).

49. Letter, [Aḥmad *al-Ḥājj* 'Alī] to Abū 'l-Qāsim [Aḥmad] Hāshim, [1912] (see also note 34 and manuscript 10 in the appendix).

reports list many more books in the curriculum—all of them manuals traditionally used in the Sudan's colleges[50]—but it is doubtful how intensively they were studied in al-Qaḍārif in the early years of the Condominium, when people presumably were preoccupied with reorganizing their lives and adjusting to the new administrative and economic circumstances.

When in 1912 Abū 'l-Qāsim Aḥmad Hāshim (1861–1934) succeeded Muḥammad al-Badawī as president of the "Board of Ulema," Aḥmad *al-Ḥājj* 'Alī approached him for government support for his school.[51] He was granted a monthly salary;[52] soon, however, Abū 'l-Qāsim brought him to Omdurman to teach at the newly established Religious Institute (Muḥammad al-Mubārak 'Abd Allāh [1392H] 1973, 11; Bāsharī [1411H] 1991, 33). The seventy-year-old man was

50. 'Uthmān Muḥammad al-Azraq (in 'Abd al-'Azīz Amīn 'Abd al-Majīd 1949, 3:42) lists the following: for Mālikī *fiqh*, Khalīl's *Mukhtaṣar*, Ibn Abī Zayd's *Risāla*, the *'Ashmāwiyya*, Abū 'l-Ḥasan 'Alī b. Muḥammad's *'Izziyya*, and al-Dardīr's *Aqrab al-Masālik*; for grammar, the *Ājurrūmiyya*, the *Azhariyya*, *al-Quṭr*, *al-Shudhūr*, and Ibn Mālik's *Alfiyya*; for hadith, the *Muwaṭṭa'*, al-Bukhārī, and al-Suyūṭī's *al-Jāmi' al-Ṣaghīr*; for *tafsīr*, al-Jalālayn (with al-Ṣāwī's gloss); and for *tawḥīd*, *al-Sanūsiyya* and the *Jawharat al-Tawḥīd*. One may ask, however, if this list adequately reflects the actual curriculum in al-Qaḍārif or whether it is "enriched" by works 'Uthmān studied in Omdurman (where he was trained in 1910–13 in the Madrasat al-'Urafā', the predecessor of the Ma'had al-'Ilmī).

51. Letter, [Aḥmad *al-Ḥājj* 'Alī] to Abū 'l-Qāsim [Aḥmad] Hāshim, [1912] (see also note 34 and manuscript 10 in the appendix).

52. See two letters (one by the Azāriqa, manuscript 12 in the appendix, and one by 'Abdallāh 'Awaḍ al-Karīm Abū Sinn) written to Abū 'l-Qāsim Hāshim upon Aḥmad *al-Ḥājj* 'Alī's death, asking to confirm 'Uthmān b. Muḥammad al-Azraq (b. before 1879, d. November 15, 1939) as Aḥmad's successor and to transfer the salary to him. The request was granted in a letter by Muḥammad 'Umar al-Bannā (1848–1919, at the time *mufattish shar'ī* of the Sudan) to Muḥammad ("al-Diqnāwī", d. 1937/8), Abū Bakr (Bābikr), 'Uthmān, and 'Alī (1879/80–1940), sons of Muḥammad al-Azraq, and to al-Amīn Aḥmad al-Naqar al-Majdhūb, dated May 24, 1914 (although these two letters are not included in the appendix, photocopies are in my possession and have been deposited at the NRO).

described not only as very learned but also as witty and sociable with his students. He died in Jumādà I 1332H: April 1914, never seeing the first batch of graduates.[53]

The Majādhīb of al-Qaḍārif, collectively known as the "Azāriqa," today constitute one of three distinct sections of the venerable "holy family" originating in al-Dāmar. Because of their history, local tradition has some reason to regard them as the most direct inheritors of the family's learned tradition. The brothers Muḥammad "al-Azraq" and *al-Ḥājj* 'Alī were the human link providing continuity in carrying this tradition of teaching Qur'ān and Mālikī *fiqh* from the Nile to the Abyssinian exile and on to the old and the new "Ṣūfī" settlements in the eastern planes. Although their line and their school continued to produce graduates of the religious sciences who were able to make their mark also on the "national" scale, the history of the Majādhīb who returned to al-Dāmar after 1825 is characterized more by efforts to rebuild the ruined town and to vie for economic influence on their home turf than by a focus on reviving al-Dāmar's former significance as a center of learning.[54] Meanwhile, a third section of the

53. The date of Aḥmad *al-Ḥājj* 'Alī's death and his age are mentioned in a document kept by 'Uthmān 'Abd al-Raḥmān 'Uthmān, which I was allowed to read but not able to photocopy.

54. There was consensus among my informants in both al-Qaḍārif and al-Dāmar that the *'ilm* tradition of the Majādhīb basically came to an end in al-Dāmar in the wake of the Turkish campaign against the Ja'aliyyīn. Al-Ṭayyib "Shaykh al-'Allāma" (b. Muḥammad b. al-Ṭayyib b. *al-Fakī* Ḥamad) (d. 1885) is sometimes quoted as an exception (e.g., 'Uthmān Muḥammad al-Azraq, in 'Abd al-'Azīz Amīn 'Abd al-Majīd 1949, 3:42). "Shaykh al-'Allāma," however, appears to have been knowledgeable mostly in magic and related areas (*ḥikma*, *ṭibb*, *'ilm al-ḥarf*) (interview, al-Fakī al-Ḥusayn 'Abd al-Mājid, Feb. 3, 1987; interview, al-Jaylānī al-Ḥusayn 'Abd al-Mājid, Feb. 2, 1987). This oral account is supported by the existence of a book on these subjects that al-Ṭayyib in 1866 had his student 'Umar al-Qāḍī (d. 1915) make a copy of: Muḥammad b. Muḥammad al-Kuntāwī's commentary on 'Abd al-Raḥmān al-Jurjānī's *al-Durar wa'l-tiryāq* (a poem on onomatomancy, *'ilm al-ḥurūf*); the manuscript was kept by al-Jaylānī).

Majādhīb emerged in Sawākin and the Red Sea Hills: the *awlād al-Shaykh*, the descendants of *al-Shaykh* Muḥammad Majdhūb b. Qamar al-Dīn ([1210–47] 1795/6–1831), the pietistic preacher who founded a distinct reformist *ṭarīqa* and whose successors became culturally and linguistically assimilated to Beja society.[55] The three sections of the Majādhīb maintained contact but operated largely independently of each other, each in its respective sphere. Perhaps one of the reasons why the Azāriqa and the *awlād al-Shaykh* rested their influence on affirming their position as religious leaders is that they had migrated to "foreign" territory, where they could not benefit from inherited land rights. In the twentieth century, once the political and economic situation had stabilized, al-Dāmar tried to reassert itself as the center of a newly imagined "Ṭarīqa Majdhūbiyya." The town that previously had been known as "Dāmar Ḥamad," the summer pasture protected by the Majādhīb's ancestor *Fakī* Ḥamad, was now restyled as "Dāmar al-Majdhūb," adopting the name and identifying with the heritage of Majdhūb b. Qamar al-Dīn.[56] These efforts, however, met only with partial success. The *awlād al-Shaykh*, though economically much less successful than their cousins on the Nile, were quite conscious of the fact that they were the original inheritors and successors of *al-Shaykh* Majdhūb. And the Azāriqa of al-Qaḍārif proudly affirmed that they had been the teachers of this shaykh and had kept going the *tuqāba*, the "fire of the Qur'ān," since young Majdhūb was sitting at the feet of *al-Ḥājj* 'Alī and "al-Azraq." To this day, the Azāriqa remain aloof from the *ṭarīqa* bearing Majdhūb's name, priding themselves instead on being heirs to an older and more erudite tradition of learning.[57]

55. On Majdhūb b. Qamar al-Dīn, see Hofheinz 1996.

56. On the twentieth-century re-construction of a Ṭarīqa Majdhūbiyya centered on Majdhūb's tomb in al-Dāmar, see Hofheinz 1991.

57. Characteristically, the Azāriqa differ from all other Majādhīb today in that they do not use Muḥammad Majdhūb's *mawlids* in their rituals; they stick to al-Ja'far b. Ḥasan al-Barzanjī's (1690–1765/6) *'Iqd al-Jawāhir*, the eighteenth-century *mawlid* that marked the beginning of this genre's popularity.

Appendix
Manuscript Documents from al-Ṣūfī al-Azraq

The originals of the manuscript documents reproduced and transcribed here are held at the mosque of al-Ṣūfī al-Azraq in al-Qaḍārif. I photocopied them and deposited the copy at the National Records Office in Khartoum. The documents are reproduced here with the kind permission of the collection's curator, *Shaykh* 'Uthmān 'Abd al-Raḥmān al-Azraq. In transcribing them, I have strived to preserve the characteristic spelling but have added some punctuation and paragraph breaks for better readability. Obvious amendments are added in square brackets []; words that remain unclear are marked by [?]; passages that are lost owing to damage to the manuscript are indicated by [. . .]. I thank Professor Aḥmad Abū Shōk, Qatar University, for his assistance in deciphering a number of problematic words.

Manuscript 1

A brief note on *al-Fakī* al-Azraq *al-Kabīr*.

نبذة من اخبار الفقه الازرق الكبير

فنقول هو العلامة الطيب النسيب الشيخ محمد الفقه الأزرق الكبير هو من ذرية الفقه حمد بن محمد المجذوب الكبير فهو جعلي عباسي ونسبه متصل بالعابس رضي الله عنه كما هو في مناقب المجذوب الصغير الي ان يتصل بالعابس ولد رضي الله عنه في سنة الف ومايتين وواحد [= ١٧٨٧م] بقرية ءاباية الكرام وتربي في حجرهم الي ان حفظ كتاب الله تعالي وتفقه علي الشيخ ابن عيسي تلميذ الدرديري بالجزيرة[58] وقرا القرءان علي ءاباية الكرام بالقرية المشهور [هك] بالدامر لفظا وبالثامر معني ومدة اقامته بها ستة وثلاثون سنة ثم هاجر منها الي الحبشة واقام بها سبع عشرة سنة ثم ارتحل منها الي الصوفي البشير وهي قرية باتبره واقام بها يدرس العلم عشرون سنة ومنها ارتحل الي القضارف واقام بقريته المشهورة بالصوفي الأزرق واجتمع عليه المسلمون من جميع الأقطار يلتقون منه العلوم الشرعية من منقول ومعقول وكان له الباع الطويل في العلوم الفقيه [هك، = الفقهية]

58. Aḥmad wad 'Īsā (c. 1737–1826), famous Mālikī scholar whose school in Kutrānj was extremely influential (see O'Fahey 1994, 15, and note 5 in this chapter). In the 1780s, Aḥmad traveled to Egypt, where he studied with, among others, the leading Mālikī jurist at al-Azhar, Aḥmad al-Dardīr (d. 1786) (Brockelmann 1943–49, 2:353, S2:479–80; McGregor 2011).

نبذه من اخبار الفقه الازرق الكبير

فنقول هو العلامة الحسيب النسيب الشيخ محمد الفقه الازرق الكبير هو من ذرية الفقه
حمد بن محمد المجذوب الكبير فهو جعلي عباسي ونسبه متصل بالعباس رضي الله عنه
كما هو في مناقب المجذوب الصغير الى ان يتصل بالعباس ولد رضي الله عنه في سنة
الف ومايتين وواحد بقرية ءابايه الكرام ونشا في حجرهم الى ان حفظ كتاب الله
تعالى وتفقه على الشيخ ابن عيسى تلميذ الدرديري بالجزيرة وقرا القرءان على
ءابايه الكرام بالقرية المشهورة بالدامر لفظا وبالثاعر معنى ومدة اقامته بها
ستة وثلاثون سنة ثم هاجر منها الى الحبشة واقام بها سبع عشرة سنة
ثم ارتحل منها الى الصوفي البشير وهي قرية باتبره واقام بها يدرس العلم
عشرون سنة ومنها ارتحل الى القضارف واقام بقريته المشهورة بالصوفي الازرق
واجتمع عليه المسلمون من جميع الافاق يتلقون منه العلوم الشرعية من منقول ومعقول
وكان له الباع الطويل في العلوم الفقهية وغيرها وكان ملازما لتدريس المختصر
والرسالة وغيرها وقرا عليه خلق كثير ورزقه الله القبول عند الحكام كان محترما
مجللا واقام بها خمس عشرة سنة الى ان توفاه الله ودفن بها بجوار
مسجده وقبره ظاهر يزار وصار مقبرة يدفنون الناس من موتاهم وحاشه
وله من العمر ثمان وثمانون سنة ومناقبه مشهورة نفعنا الله به وبعلومه
ءامين ١ه ثم تولى بعده الدرس ابنه محمد ولا زال المسجد معمورا بالتدريس
وافادة العلوم الى اليوم بابنائه الكرام

كتبه محمد احمد بن عبد الله
بامر مرع خليفة المحل
الشيخ عبد الرحيم الازرق

وغيرها وكان ملازما لتدريس المختصر والرسالة وغيرها وقرا عليه خلق كثير ورزقه الله القبول عند الحكام كان مكرما مجللا واقام بها خمس عشرة سنة الي ان توفاه الله ودفن بجوار مسجده وقبره ظاهر يزار وصار مقبرة يدفنون الناس معه موتاهم ومات وله من العمر ثمان وثمانون سنة ومناقبه شهيرة نفعنا الله به وبعلومه ءامين اهـ ثم تولي بعده الدرس ابنه محمد ولا زال المسجد معمور [هك] بالتدريس وافادة العلوم الي اليوم بابنآيهم الكرام »

كتبه محمد احمد بن عبد
الله
بامر من خليفة المحل
الشيخ عبد الرحمن الازرق[59]

Manuscript 2

Mālikī *ijāza*, Aḥmad al-Rifāʻī to Aḥmad [al-Ḥājj ʻAlī b. Muḥammad al-Azraq] Majdhūb, 19 Muḥarram 1319H: May 8, 1901.

٢ [. . .] صد [. . .] الاحد الا
٣ [. . .]ير في ربض الجنة ومظلاتها ولا بد [. . .]س باب المهامه [؟] وا [. . .]
من حميم التو[. . . ؟]
٤ [. . . ؟] والفضائل فان المسند ينسب وغيره من ظلمات [؟] الرد وكونه دعيًا قريب
[. . .] فالاشياخ علم الآبا في العلم دروبهم
٥ وكان ممن اقتفى اثر المتقدمين وارتحل لنيل سند ما يمكن من سند خير المرسلين وكذا
[. . .] من علوم الدين وآلاتها المحصلة [. . .] المتين
٦ احمد المجذوب العباسى السودانى فقدم بالديار المصرية وسمع مني اول الموطّأ وكثيرا
[من الجامع الصغير وطلب مني الاجازة بما اجازني به مـ[ـشائخي
٧ لظنه اني مثل الرجال الاوائل وهذا من حسن طويته فاني ضعيف البضاعة فكيف يليق
بي ان انيله بعض امنيته لكن جرّأني على [ذلك ما]

59. ʻAbd al-Raḥmān b. *Sheykhnā* ʻUthmān (b. before 1879, d. 1939) b. Muḥammad al-Shahīd (d. pre-1890) b. *al-Fakī* Muḥammad "al-Azraq" al-Kabīr, *al-khāṭib al-Rasūl* (1787/6–1872/3) b. *al-Fakī* Aḥmad *Ab Jadarī* (1746–1804/8) b. Ḥamad *Ab Diqn* (1694–1776) b. Muḥammad *al-Majdhūb* (fl. c. 1720). ʻAbd al-Raḥmān was imam of the mosque in al-Ṣūfī al-Azraq and still alive in 1956. It was his son and successor ʻUthmān who in 1987 let me photocopy the documents reproduced here. The present brief on *al-Fakī* "al-Azraq" al-Kabīr was penned sometime during the first half of the twentieth century; it is written on paper produced by the North Italian Binda paper mill.

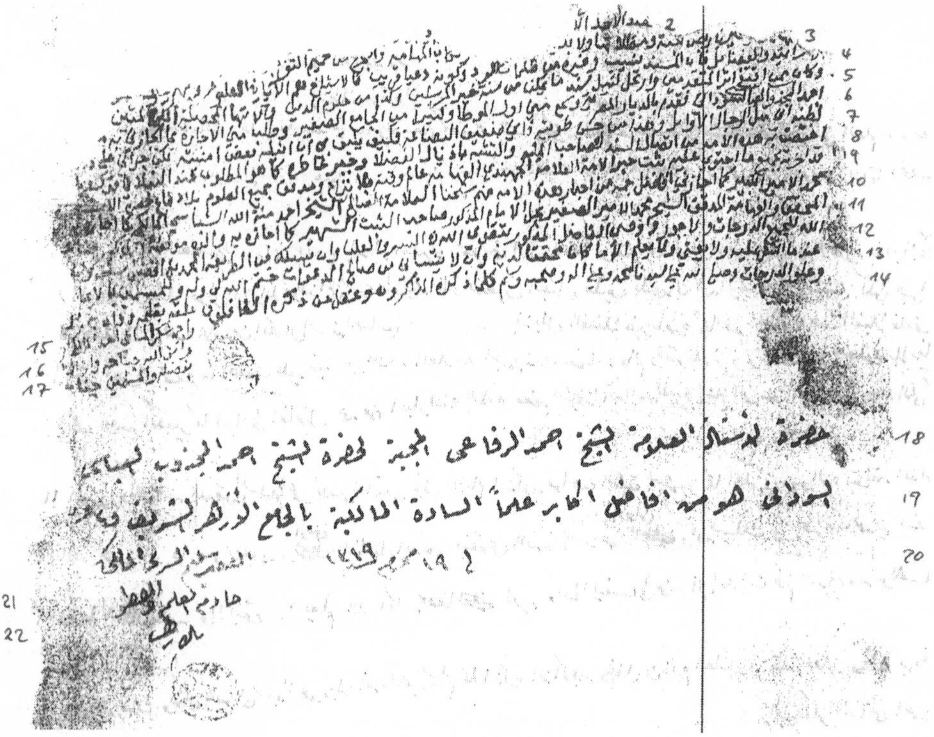

٨ اختصت به هذه الامة من اتصال السند لصاحب المنى والتشبه باذيال الفضلا وخير مخاطره [؟] كما هو المطلوب عند النبلا واقول و[بالله التوفيق]
٩ قد اجزته بجميع ما احتوى عليه ثبت حبر الامة العلامة الجهبذي الفهامة عالم وقته بلا نزاع ومدقق جميع العلوم بلا دفاع حضرة الاستاذ
١٠ محمد الامير الكبير كما اجازني افاضل جمة من احبار هذه الامة منهم شيخنا العلامة الصالح الشيخ احمد منة الله الشباسي المالكي كما اجازه به العلامة
١١ المحقق والفهامة المدقق الشيخ محمد الامير الصغير نجل الامام المذكور صاحب الثبت الشهير كما اجازه به والده مؤلفه المذكور ضاعف
١٢ الله للجميع الدرجات والاجور واوحى الفاضل المذكور بتقوى الله في السر والعلن وان يسلك في الطريقة المحمدية افضل سنن وان يقف
١٣ عندما اشكل عليه ولا يفتي ولا يعلّم الا ما كان محققا لديه وان لا ينساني من صالح الدعوات ختم الله لي وله وللمسلمين بالايمان
١٤ وعلو الدرجات وصلى الله على سيدنا محمد وعلى آله وصحبه وسلم كلما ذكره الذاكرون وغفل عنه الغافلون علقه بقلمه وفاه به بفمه
١٥ راجي شكر المساعي احمد المالكي الرفاعي
١٦ وامّن الله جناحه وازال عنه
١٧ بفضله والمسلمين جناحه [او: جناح ذنبه؟]

١٨ حضرة الاستاذ العلامة الشيخ احمد الرفاعي المجيز لحضرة الشيخ احمد المجذوب العباسي
١٩ السوداني هو من افاضل اكابر علما السادة المالكية بالجامع الأزهر الشريف فـ[. . . ؟]
٢٠ ١٩ محرم سنة ١٣١٩ الفقير سليم البشري المالكي
٢١ خادم العلم والمعرفه [؟]
٢٢ بالازهر
٢١ [الختم:] سليم البشري[60]

Manuscript 3

Ijāza in *Ṣaḥīḥ Muslim*, Muḥammad ʿAbd al-Ghanī Muḥammad al-Mālikī al-Malawī to Aḥmad *al-Ḥājj* ʿAlī, 17 Muḥarram 1319H: May 6, 1901.

بسم الله الرحمن الرحيم
الحمد لله حمدا يوافي نعمه ويكافي المزيد وينافي نقمه ويجافي العنيد والصلاة و[السلام على سيدنا] محمد اشرف المخلوقين المبعوث رحمة للعالمين وعلى اله الطيبين الطاهرين واصحابه [الغر الميامين؟] والتابعين وتابع التابعين لهم باحسان الى يوم الدين

60. Salīm al-Bishrī (1832–1916) was a Mālikī scholar and Shaykh al-Azhar from 1900 to 1916.

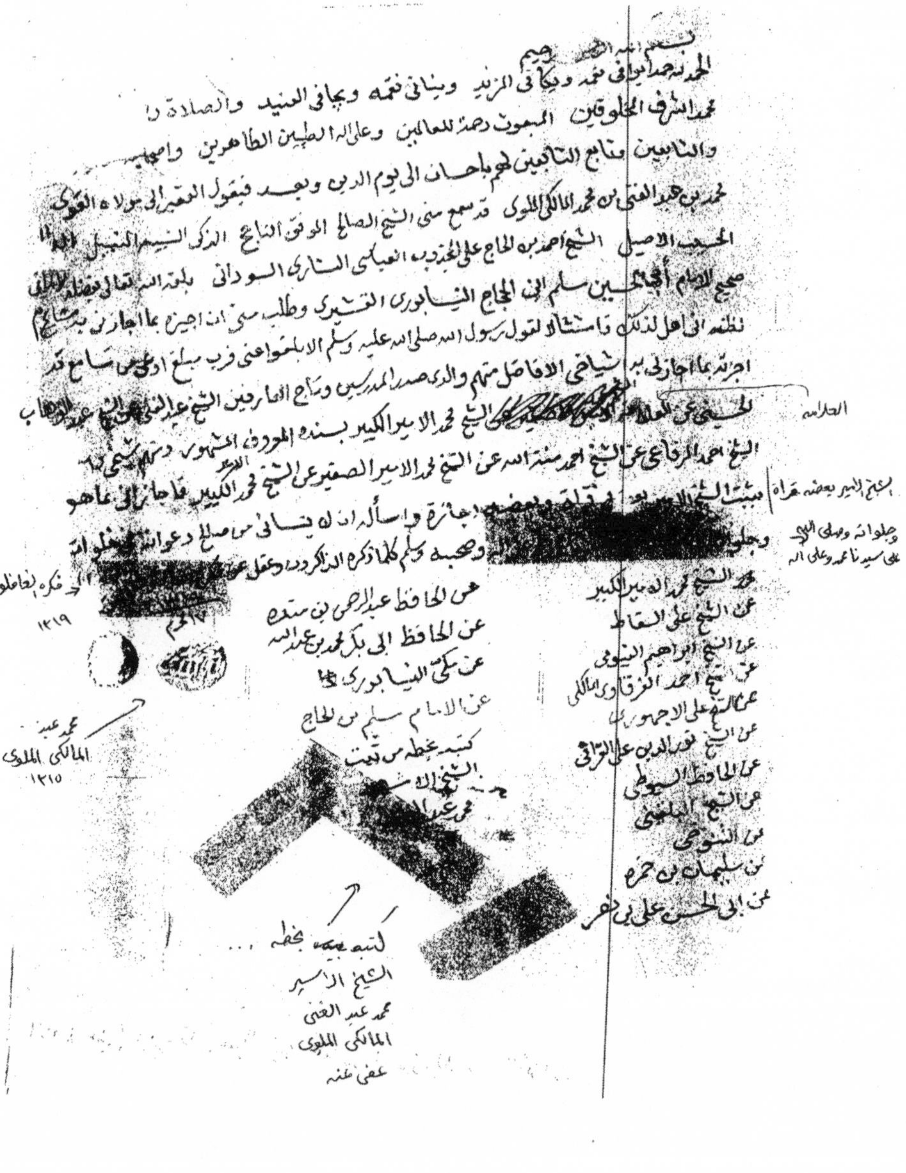

بسم الله الرحمن الرحيم

الحمد لله حمدا يوافي نعمه ويكافي المزيد ويداني نعمه ويجافي العبيد والصلاة وا
محمد اشرف المخلوقين المبعوث رحمة للعالمين وعلى اله الطيبين الطاهرين واصحابه
والتابعين ومتابع التابعين لهم باحسان الى يوم الدين وبعد فيقول الفقير الى مولاه القوي
محمد بن عبد الغني بن محمد المالكي الملوي قد سمع مني الشيخ الصالح الموفق النابغ الذكي النبيل الهمام
الحسيب الاصيل الشيخ احمد بن الحاج علي المجذوب العباسي الشاذلي السوداني بلغه الله تعالى بفضله الامال
صحيح الامام ابي الحسين مسلم ابن الحجاج النيسابوري القشيري وطلب مني ان اجيزه بما اجازني به مشايخي
نظنه انه اهل لذلك وامتثالا لقول رسول الله صلى الله عليه وسلم الا بلغوا عني فرب مبلغ اوعى من سامع قد
اجزته بما اجازني به مشايخي الافاضل منهم والذي صدر المدرسين وتاج العارفين الشيخ عبد الغني عن الشيخ عبد الوهاب
الحسيني عن العلامة ... على الشيخ محمد الامير الكبير بسنده المورود المشهور وعن شيخي
الشيخ احمد الرفاعي عن الشيخ احمد منة الله عن الشيخ محمد الامير الصغير عن الشيخ محمد الكبير فاجازني عامه
بثبت الشيخ الامير بعضه قراءة وبعضه اجازة واسأله ان لا ينساني من صالح دعواته في خلواته
وجلواته ... وصحبه وسلم كلما ذكره الذاكرون وغفل عن ذكره الغافلون

العلامة

الشيخ الامير بعضه قراءة

وجلواته وصلى الله على سيدنا محمد وعلى اله

فكره الغافلون

١٧ المحرم

١٣١٩

عن الحافظ عبد الرحمن بن ...
عن الحافظ ابي بكر محمد بن عبد الله
عن مكي النيسابوري
عن الامام مسلم بن الحجاج

كتبه بخطه من ثبت
الشيخ الاسير
محمد عبد ...

عن الشيخ محمد الامير الكبير
عن الشيخ علي العقاد
عن الشيخ ابراهيم الفيومي
عن الشيخ احمد الزرقاوي المالكي
عن الشيخ علي الاجهوري
عن الشيخ نور الدين علي القرافي
عن الحافظ السيوطي
عن الشيخ البلقيني
عن النووي
عن سليمان بن حمزة
عن ابي الحسن علي بن نصر

محمد عبد
المالكي الملوي
١٣١٥

كتبه بخطه ...
الشيخ الاسير
محمد عبد الغني
المالكي الملوي
عفي عنه

وبعد
فيقول الفقير الى مولاه القوي محمد بن عبد الغني بن محمد المالكي الملوي قد سمع مني الشيخ الصالح الموفق الناجح الزكى النبيه النبيل الـ[. . .] الحسيب الاصيل الشيخ احمد بن الحاج على المجذوب العباسي السناري السوداني بلغه الله تعالى بفضله الاماني صحيح الامام ابي الحسين مسلم ابن الحجاج النيسابوري القشيري وطلب مني ان اجيزه بما اجازني به مشائخ [. . .] لظنه اني اهل لذلك وامتثالا لقول رسول الله صلى الله عليه وسلّم "الا بلِّغوا عني فرُبَّ مُبلَّغ أوعى من سامعٍ"
قد اجزته بما اجازني به اشياخي الافاضل منهم والدى صدر المدرسين وتابع العارفين الشيخ عبد الغني عن الشيخ عبد الوهاب الحسيني عن العلامة الشيخ محمد الامير الكبير بسنده المعروف المشهور ومنهم شيخي و[. . .] الشيخ احمد الرفاعى عن الشيخ احمد منة الله عن الشيخ محمد الامير الصغير عن الشيخ محمد الامير الكبير فاجازاني بما هو بثبت الشيخ الامير بعضه قراة وبعضه اجازة واسأله ان لا ينساني من صالح دعواته في خلواته وجلواته وصلى الله على سيدنا محمد وعلى اله وصحبه وسلم كلما ذكره الذاكرون وغفل عن ذكره الغافلون

الشيخ محمد الامير الكبير
عن الشيخ على السقاط
عن الشيخ ابراهيم الفيومى
عن الشيخ احمد الفرقاوى المالكى
عن الشيخ على الاجهورى
عن الشيخ نور الدين على القرافى
عن الحافظ السيوطى
عن الشيخ البلقيني
عن التنوخى
عن سليمان بن حمزه
عن ابى الحسن على بن نصر
عن الحافظ عبد الرحمن بن منده
عن الحافظ ابى بكر محمد بن عبد الله
عن مكّى النيسابورى
[عن الامام مسلم بن الحاج [هك، = الحجاج
كتبه بخطه من ثبت الشيخ الامير
محمد عبد الغنى
المالكي الملوى
عفى عنه
١٧ محرم سنة ١٣١٩
ختم:] محمد عبد الغنى المالكى الملوى ١٣١٥]

Manuscript 4

Aḥmad *al-Ḥājj* ʿAlī gives his *silsila*s (copy, not original handwriting), 1319H: 1901.

قد سمعته بالمدينه الا قليلا عن يحيى [؟] محمد [؟] [. . .] يحيى [؟] الشنجيطى
الحاج على المجذوب مولا الامام مالك بن انس سماعا لاوايله واجازة في باقيه [. . .]
[. . .] احمد الرفاعى قال رضي الله عنه اجازني فيه افاضل جمه ورويته عن [. . .]
احمد منة الله [. . .]
عن الشيخ محمد الامير الصغير
عن والده الشيخ محمد الامير الكبير عن الشيخ على العربي السقاط [قال سماعا منه عليه من اوله الخ][61] عن شارحه سيدي محمد الزرقاني عن والده الشيخ عبد الباقي عن الشيخ على الاجهوري عن الشيخ محمد بن احمد الرملي عن شيخ الاسلام زكريا عن الحافظ بن حجر العسقلاني عن نجم الدين محمد بن علي بن عقيل البالِسي عن محمد بن علي المكفى عن محمد بن محمد الدلاصي[62] عن عبد العزيز بن عبد الوهاب بن اسماعيل عن جده اسماعيل عن الطاهر عن محمد ابن الوليد الطرطوشي عن سليمن بن خلف الباجي عن يوسف بن عبد الله بن مغيث عن ابي عيسى يحيى بن يحيى بن يحيى عن عم ابيه عبيد الله بن يحيى عن ابيه يحيي بن يحيي الليثي الاندلسي عن الامام مالك الا ما فاته سماعه علي مالك اوشك فيه ثلاثه ابواب في ورقه من ءاخر باب الاعتكاف فرواه عن زياد بن عبد الرحمن المعروف بشبطون عن مالك وكان يحيى سمع الموطأ قبل رحلته الي مالك ويحيى الاندلسي هذا لا رواية له في شيء من الكتب السته وروي الموطا ايضا عن مالك يحيى بن يحيى التميمى النيسابوري شيخ الشيخين وغيرهما وهو المروى عنه في الكتب السته ومن لا خبره له يلتبس عليه هذا
سنه ١٣١٩

واما الجامع الصغير للعلامة السيوطي فقد سمعت كثيرا منه ازيد من نصفه علي شيخنا العلامه المتقدم ذكره الشيخ احمد الرفاعي واجازني بباقيه قال كما اجازني له القاضى الشيخ احمد منة [الله] عن الامير الصغير عن والده الشيخ محمد الامير الكبير عن الشيخ علي الصعيدي العدوي عن الشيخ عقيله عن الشيخ حسن عن البابلي عن السنهوري عن الشمس العلقمي عن المولف السيوطي جلال الدين عبد الحمن السيوطي

61. The Azhar manuscript *Thabat [. . .] Muḥammad al-Amīr*, penned 1200: 1786/5 (at https://www.alukah.net/manu/files/manuscript_4811/makhtotat.pdf, f. 5), as well as al-Amīr al-Kabīr and ʿAlam al-Dīn Muḥammad b. ʿĪsà al-Fādānī al-Makki n.d., 19, have here: ارويه سماعا لجميعه عن شيخنا السقاط.

62. Both the Azhar manuscript and al-Amīr al-Kabīr and ʿAlam al-Dīn Muḥammad b. ʿĪsà al-Fādānī al-Makki n.d. vocalize المُكَفًّى. Dalāṣ is a village just north of Banī Suwayf in Upper Egypt.

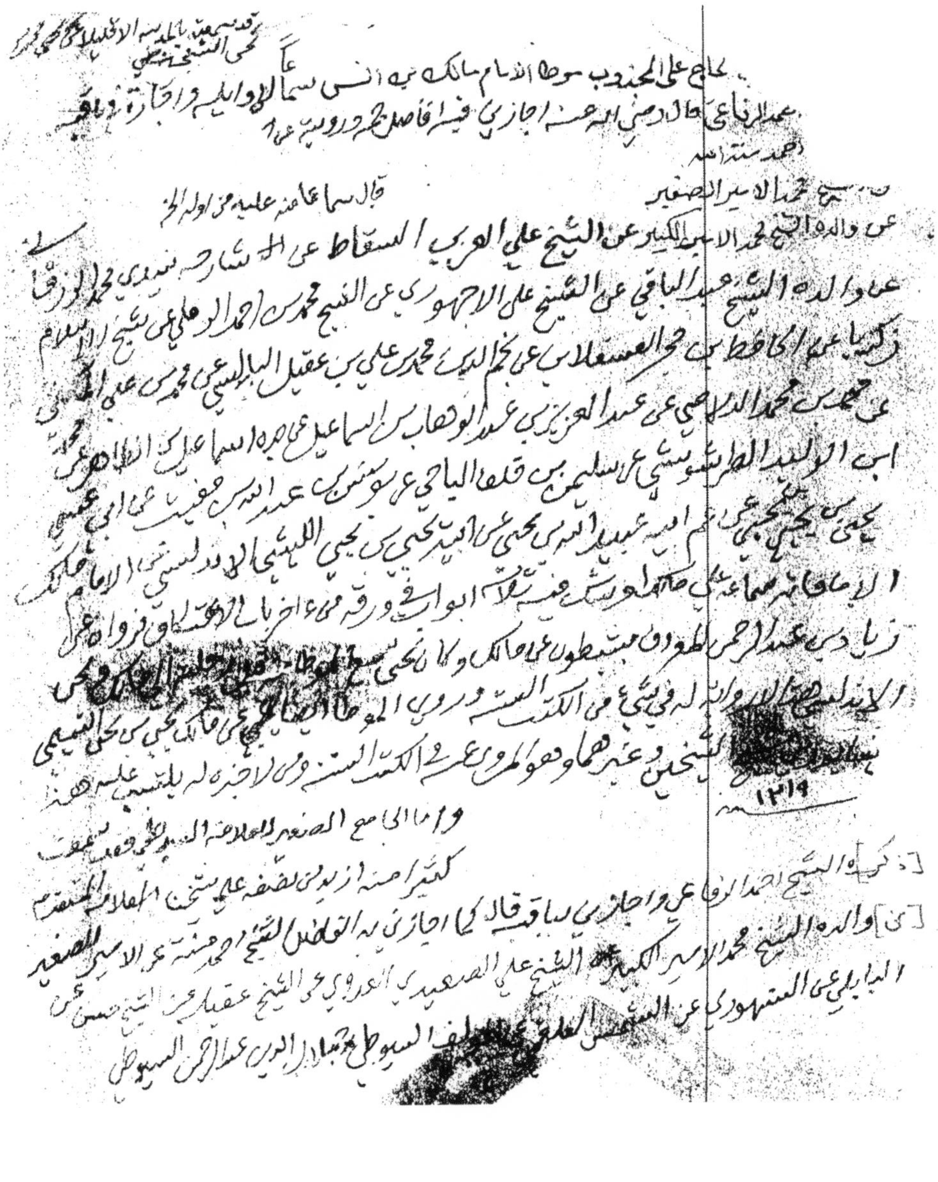
طالع علي المجذوب موطأ الامام مالك بن انس سماعاً للاوائل واجازة لباقيه

[illegible] رضي الله عنه اجازني فيه [illegible]

عن شيخه محمد الامير الصغير قال سماعا منه عليه من اوله الخ

عن والده الشيخ محمد الامير الكبير عن الشيخ علي العربي السقاط عن [illegible] سيدي محمد الزرقاني

عن والده الشيخ عبد الباقي عن الشيخ علي الاجهوري عن الشيخ محمد بن احمد الرملي عن شيخ الاسلام

زكريا [illegible] عن الحافظ ابن حجر العسقلاني عن نجم الدين محمد بن علي بن عقيل البالسي عن محمد بن علي [illegible]

عن محمد بن محمد [illegible] عن عبد العزيز بن عبد الوهاب بن اسماعيل [illegible]

ابي الوليد الطرطوشي عن [illegible] سليمان بن خلف الباجي عن يونس بن عبد الله بن مغيث عن ابي عيسى

يحيى بن يحيى عن عم ابيه عبيد الله بن يحيى عن ابيه يحيى بن يحيى الليثي الاندلسي عن الامام مالك

[illegible]

١٣١٩

[illegible]

Manuscript 5

Quotation from al-Amīr al-Kabīr's *Thabat*, deploring the latter-day focus on externalities, followed by Aḥmad *al-Ḥājj* 'Alī's *sanad* in grammar and in Mālikī *fiqh*.

ظاهرا و باطنا. وقد ورد تعميم النبي لبعض اصحابه في الجهاد وعقده اللوا له [. . .]
واغتفاره انشاد الشعر والتبختر بين الصفين وجعل الشعار في القوم ليجتمع بعضهم علي
بعض فكذلك القوم تبركوا بالباس [هك] الخرقه وانما الاعمال بنياتها ونشروا الاعلام واغتفروا
هز الجسم في الذكر والانشاد اعانة علي المجاهده وليجتمع بخرقتهم اصحاب طريقتهم
الذين هم يتعاونون بحال واحد من غير معصية [ولا] بغض لغير خرقتهم بل على حد ما قيل
فنادمني بمثل لسان حالي * تريحني واطرب من قريب
والمدعون اليوم افسدوا الاوضاع واقتصروا على الصور الظاهريه
واعلم ان طريق القوم اليوم دارسة * وحال مدعيها اليوم كيف ترى[63] اهـ
من ثبت الامير من اصله نقلت
واما علم النحو قد قراته علي عمي وابنه الشيخ محمد الازرق ببلادنا وعمنا يرويه عن ابن
عمي عن الدردير عن العدوي
وعلم الفقه فقد اجازني فيه شيخنا الشيخ احمد الرفاعى بسنده المتقدم الي الامير الكبير
قال الأمير في ثبته: واما علم الفقه فارويه[64] "عن شيخنا العدوي عن الشيخ عبدالله البناني
[والـ]ـسيد محمد السلموني عن الشيخ محمد الخرشي والشيخ عبد الباقي الزرقاني كلاهما
عن الشيخ [علي الا]جهوري والشيخ ابرهيم اللقاني كلاهما عن الشيخ محمد البنوفري عن
الشيخ [عبد الـ]ـرحمن الاجهوري عن شمس الدين اللقاني عن الشيخ على السنهوري عن
الشيخ البساطي عن الشيخ تاج الدين بهرام عن الشيخ خليل صاحب المختصر وهو [تفقـ]ـه
علي الشيخ عبدالله المنوفي وقد اخد الشيخ على السنهوري ايضا عن الشيخ طاهر بن علي
[بن محمد النويري وهو عن الشيخ حسين بن علي وهو][65] عن ابى العباس احمد بن عمر
بن هلال الربعي وهو عن قاضي القضات فخر الدين بن المخلطة [وهو عن ابـ]ـي حفص
عمر بن فراج الكندي وهو عن ابي محمد عبد الكريم بن عطاء الله السكندري وهو عن

63. This line is from a poem generally attributed to the famous Maghribī saint Abū Madyan Shu'ayb al-Andalusī al-Tilimsānī (Sidi Boumediène) (d. 589H: 1193 or 594H: 1198). The original differs slightly in that it reads:

واعلم بأن طريق القوم دارسة * وحال مدعيها اليوم كيف ترى

64. Cf. al-Amīr al-Kabīr and 'Alam al-Dīn Muḥammad b. 'Īsà al-Fādānī al-Makki n.d., 238–44.

65. The passage mentioning Ḥusayn b. 'Alī is omitted in the manuscript at hand; there is no space for it on the page. It has been added here from al-Amīr al-Kabīr and 'Alam al-Dīn Muḥammad b. 'Īsà al-Fādānī al-Makki n.d., 242.

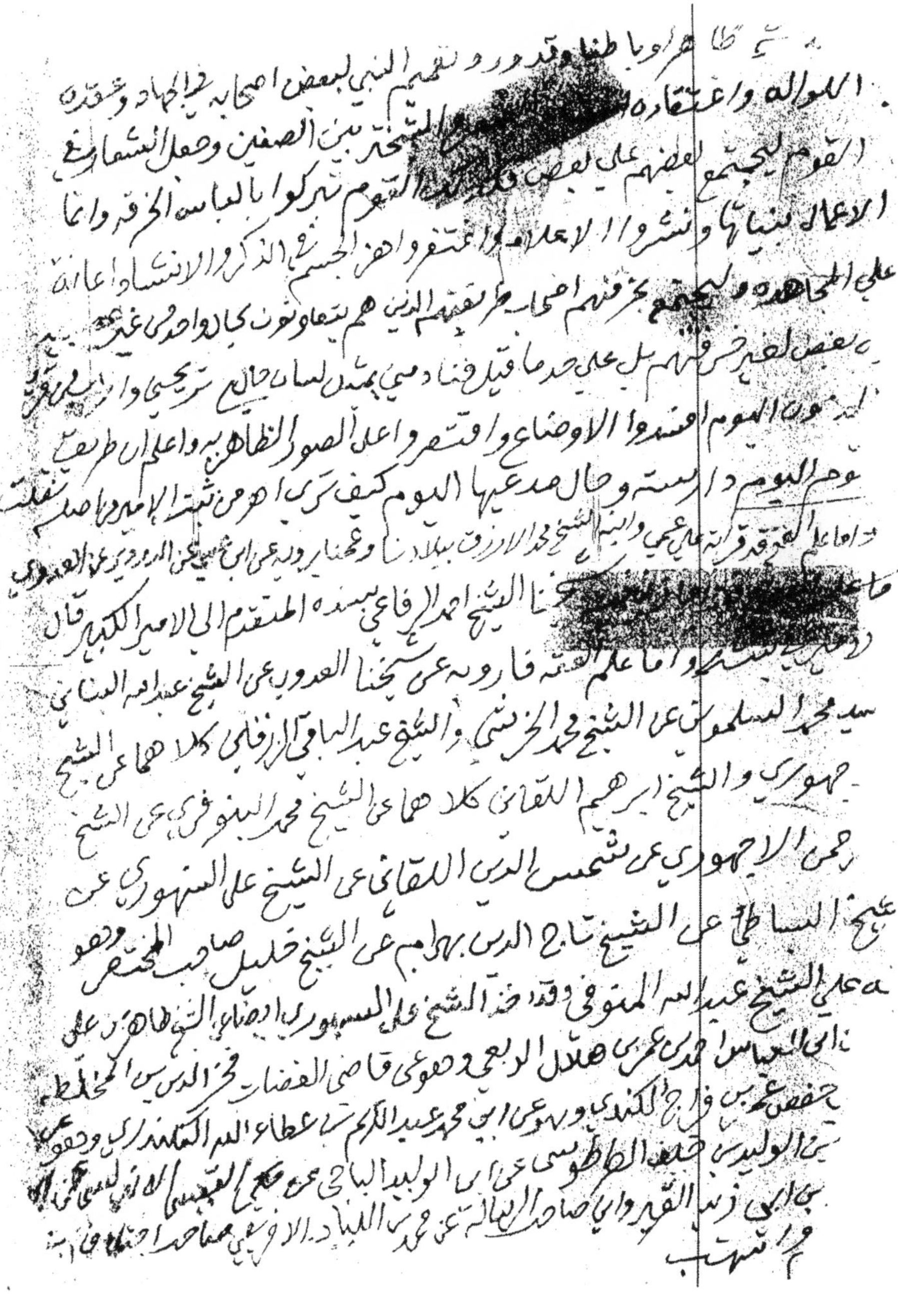

للموالاة واعتقاده [illegible] ظاهرا وباطنا وقد ورد تقديم النبي لبعض اصحابه في الجهاد وتقديم
القوم ليجتمع [illegible] الشيخ بين الصفين وجعل الشعار في
الاعمال بنياتها بعضهم على بعض فكذلك القوم تبركوا بالعباس الخرقة وانما
على المجاهدة وليجتمع ونشروا الاعلام واعتقدوا هز الجسم في الذكر والانشاد اعانة
بعضهم لبعض فمنهم اصحاب طريقتهم الذين هم يتعاونون كل واحد في غيره
[illegible] فهم على حد ما قيل فنادمني بمثل لسان حالي [illegible]
الذين اليوم اعتمدوا الاوضاع واقتصروا على الصور الظاهرية واعلم ان طريقة
القوم اليوم دارسة وحال من ادعاها اليوم كيف ترى [illegible] الامير [illegible] فقط
واما علم [illegible] قرأته على عمي والشيخ محمد الازرق ببلادنا وغيرهما وله عن ابن الشيخ [illegible] عن العدوي
[illegible] شيخنا الشيخ احمد الرفاعي بسنده المتقدم الى الامير الكبير قال
[illegible] الشيخ واما علم الفقه فارويه عن شيخنا العدوي عن الشيخ عبد الله [illegible]
سيد محمد السلموني عن الشيخ محمد الخرشي والشيخ عبد الباقي الزرقاني كلاهما عن الشيخ
[illegible]جهوري والشيخ ابرهيم اللقاني كلاهما عن الشيخ محمد البنوفري عن الشيخ
[illegible]حمن الاجهوري عن شمس الدين اللقاني عن الشيخ على السنهوري عن
شيخ البساطي عن الشيخ تاج الدين بهرام عن الشيخ خليل صاحب المختصر وهو
على الشيخ عبد الله المنوفي وقد اخذ الشيخ على السنهوري ايضا عن الشهاب [illegible] على
ابي العباس احمد بن عمر بن هلال الربعي وهو عن قاضي القضاة فخر الدين بن المخلطة
حفص عمر بن فارح الكندي وهو عن ابي محمد عبد الكريم بن عطاء الله الاسكندري وهو عن
ابي الوليد بن خلف الطرطوسي عن ابي الوليد الباجي عن [illegible] العبسي [illegible]
بن ابي زيد القيرواني صاحب الرسالة عن محمد بن اللباد [illegible]
[illegible]

[ابي بكر محمد] بن الوليد بن خلف الطرطوسي عن ابي الوليد الباجي عن مكي القيسي الاندلسى عن ابي [محمد عبد الله] بن ابي زيد القيرواني صاحب الرسالة عن محمد بن اللباد. الاخرُ بقي صاحب اختلاف [ابن القاسم] واشهب"

Manuscript 6

Supra: *isnād* for the Shādhilī *Ḥizb al-Kabīr*, from Muḥammad ʿAbd al-Ghanī. *Infra*: al-Amīr al-Kabīr's *silsila* for the Nāṣirī *ṭarīqa* (from his *Thabat*). No date (ca. 1901) (copies).

واجازة الحزب الكبير حزب شيخنا وولي نعمتنا الشيخ ابي الحسن الشاذلي فاني ارويه اجازة عن شيخنا الشيخ محمد عبد الغني عن والده الشيخ عبد الغني عن شيخه الشيخ عبد الوهاب الحسيني عن الشيخ محمد الامير

قال العلامة الامير الكبير في ثبته[66] : "واما طريقة ابن ناصر فارويها من طرق شتي منها روايتي عن العارف الفاضل سيدي محمد بن عبد السلام بن ناصر عام حجه[67] وقد بات بمنزلى وهو عن عمه شيخ الجماعة الامام ابي يعقوب يوسف بن محمد وهو [عن][68] العلامه ابي عبد الله محمد بن عبد السلام البناني عن ابي العباس القطب احمد بن ناصر عن الغوث والده عن عمود خباينا[69] الشيخ عبد الله بن حسين القباب حرفة الرفي نسبة لبلدة[70] عن الشيخ ابي العباس احمد بن علي الخزرجي عن امام الطريقة الغازي السجلماسي عن

66. Cf. al-Amīr al-Kabīr and ʿAlam al-Dīn Muḥammad b. ʿĪsà al-Fādānī al-Makki n.d., 365. The text here is somewhat shortened compared to the original.

67. Muḥammad b. ʿAbd al-Salām b. ʿAbd Allāh b. Muḥammad b. Muḥammad al-Nāṣirī (1142–1239H: 1729/30–1823), Moroccan *muḥaddith* and leader of the well-known Nāṣirī *ṭarīqa*, traveled to the East twice, in 1196H: 1782 and 1211H: 1796/7.

68. عن is missing in the manuscript and has been added here from the published text.

69. عمود خِبائنا, "our tentpole."

70. The text here suggests that it was copied from a North African manuscript that contained common errors. The form الرفي reveals the North African spelling ڡـ for قـ. All manuscripts used by the editor of *Sadd al-arab* (al-Amīr al-Kabīr and ʿAlam al-Dīn Muḥammad b. ʿĪsà al-Fādānī al-Makki n.d.) use the form <r-q-y>, which is itself an error; the correct form of the *nisba* is الدرعي (al-Darʿī). بلدة is spelled with a *tāʾ marbūṭa* in this manuscript as well as in the published *Sadd al-arab*; clearly, the correct reading of the text must be الدرعي نسبةً لبلده, "al-Darʿī, after his home in Wādī Darʿa."

وجاء الحزب الكبير حزب شيخنا وولي نعمتنا الشيخ ابو الحسن الشاذلي فاني ارويه
اجازة عن شيخنا الشيخ محمد عبد الغني عن والده الشيخ عبد الغني عن شيخه الشيخ عبد
الوهاب الحسيني عن الشيخ محمد الامير

قال العلامة الامير الكبير في ثبته واما طريقة ابن ناصر فما رويناها من طرق شتى منها روايتي
عن العارف الفاضل سيدي محمد بن عبد السلام بن ناصر عام حجه بقدومه لمنزلي وهو عن عمه
شيخ الجماعة الامام ابي يعقوب يوسف بن محمد وهو عن العلامة ابو عبد الله محمد بن عبد السلام البناني
عن ابي العباس القطب احمد بن ناصر عن الغوث والده عن عمود خبانينا الشيخ عبد الله
بن حسين القباب حرفة الدرعي نسبة لعله قرية عن الشيخ ابي العباس احمد بن علي الحارثي
عن امام الطريقة الغازي السجلماسي عن ابي الحسن علي بن عبد الله عن ابي العباس
احمد بن يوسف الملياني عن الشيخ الامام احمد زروق قال الامير وبهذا السند نروي
جميع ما ينسب لسيدي احمد زروق من الوظيفة والاوراد والتاليف ونروي الصلاة التي
فيها ذاتك التي الوفا الشاذلية بالسند عن زروق عن الشيخ ابي عبد الله القوري عن سيدي
عبد الله بن احمد عن سيدي علي وفا واما لبس الخرقة فقد اثبتنا ذكره واعلم ان لبس
الخرقة وعلم الرواية والاحكام ونحو ذلك ليست هي المقصود من الطريق بل
مجاهدة النفس والذهاب بالشريعة

ابي الحسن علي بن عبد الله عن ابي العباس احمد بن يوسف الملياني عن الشيخ الامام احمد زروق". قال الامير : "وبهذا السند نروى جميع ما ينسب لسيدى احمد زروق من الوظيفة والاوراد والتاليف ونروي ايضا طريق ساداتنا بني الوفا الشاذليه بالسند عن زروق عن الشيخ ابي عبد الله القوري عن سيدي عبد الله بن احمد عن سيدي على وفا." واما لبس الخرقه ففي اشياخ كثيره "واعلم ان [71] الخرقه وعلم الراية والحزام ونحو ذلك ليست هي المقصود من الطريق بل [مدار اصل الطريق[72]] مجاهده النفس والزامها بالشريعه

Manuscript 7

Shādhilī *ijāza*, Aḥmad *al-Ḥājj* ʻAlī to ʻUthmān w. Muḥammad w. al-Azraq, Dhū 'l-Qaʻda 1319H: February–March 1902.

بسم الله الرحمن الرحيم الحمد لله والصلاه والسلام على رسول الله
اما بعد
فقد اجزت الابن المبارك عثمان بن شيخنا وبركتنا الفقير محمد محمد الازرق باستعمال اوراد الطريقة الشاذليه واحزابها التى ناثرها ونرويها عن اسلافنا كما اجازنى بها والدي وهو قد اخذها وتلقاها عن عمه الولي الصالح الفقير المكي وهو اخذها عن اخيه وهو جدنا الفقير احمد أبو جدري وهو عن والده الفقير حمد بن المجذوب المتلقي عن شيخه الشيخ علي الدراوى عن الولي الكبير الشيخ محمد بن ناصر المغربي الشهير المتصل اسناده بسيدى احمد زروق ومنه الى الشاذلي كما يعلم من اسناد جدنا الفقير حمد الشهير المحفوظ في كتاب المناقب[73] وغيره
وكذلك اجزته بقراءة دلايل الخيرات باسنادها المتصل بمولفها الذي ارويه عن والدي وقد اخذه عن عمه الفقير المكي قرا[ء]ة واجازة وهو اي الفقير المكي يرويها عن العلامة محمد بن هاشم الفلاتي باسناده المتصل وكذا قد اجازنا بها وبقرا[ء]ة احزاب الشاذلي شيخنا السيد علي طاهر المحدث بالمدينة المنوره . واجازنا بذلك كله اعني اوراد الطريقه ودلايل الخيرات الفاضل سيدي عبد الرحمن بن سيدي محمد عليش عن والده مشاقة منه الينا وكتابة بيده وكذا الشيخ علي طاهر . واسال الله ان ينفعنا جميعا ببركتهم ويوفقنا لاتباع طريقتهم ويحسبنا في زمرتهم ويغنينا عن دنيتنا حتي نحشر مع المنعم عليهم من النبيين والصديقين امين

71. The page is cut off here; it is thus uncertain whether what looks like لي or لن here precedes some other word. The published version has only واعلم ان الخرقة.

72. The passage in brackets is supplied here from a text quoted from al-Amīr al-Kabīr, published at http://darelkhalil.blogspot.com/2009/03/blog-post_25.html as well as at http://almasheikh.com/AlshakMohamedAltaherFolder/Auth_2Almatia_F.html.

73. The reference is to "al-Shaykh" Muḥammad Majdhūb b. al-Ṭāhir b. al-Ṭayyib b. Qamar al-Dīn al-Majdhūb [1332H] 1914.

بسم الله الرحمن الرحيم الحمد لله والصلاة والسلام على رسول الله
اما بعد فقد اجزت الابن المبارك عثمان ابن شيخنا وبركتنا الفقيه محمد الازرق
باستعمال اوراد الطريقة الشاذلية واحزابها الى ... ورودها عن
اسلافنا كما اجازني بها والدي وهو قد اخذها وتلقاها عن عمه الولي
الصالح الفقيه المكي وهو اخذها عن اخيه وهو جدنا الفقيه حمد ابو جدري
وهو عن والده الفقيه محمد المجذوب المتلقي عن شيخه الشيخ علي الدراوي
عن الولي الكبير الشيخ محمد بن ناصر المغربي الشهير المتصل اسناده بسيدي
احمد زروق ومنه الى الشاذلي كما يعلم من اسناد جدنا الفقيه حمد الشهير المخطوط في [في اسناده]
كتاب المناقب وغيره وكذلك اجزته بقراءة دلائل الخيرات باسنادها المتصل
بمؤلفها الذي ارويه عن والدي وقد اخذه عن عمه الفقيه المكي قراءة واجازة وهو
اي الفقيه المكي يرويها عن العلامة محمد بن هاشم الفلالي باسناده المتصل وكذا
قد اجازنا بها وبقراءة احزاب الشاذلي شيخنا السيد علي طاهر المحدث المدني المتوفي
واجازنا بذلك كله اعني اوراد الطريقة ودلائل الخيرات الفاضل سيدي عبد الرحمن
سيدي محمد عليش عن والده مشافهة منه الينا وكتابة بيده وكذا الشيخ علي طاهر واسال
الله ان ينفعنا جميعا بكل ذلك وان يوفقنا لاتباع طريقتهم ويحشرنا في زمرتهم ويعيننا على
ديننا حتى نحشر مع المنعم عليهم من النبيين والصديقين امين

كتبه الفقير
احمد المجذوب
عفي عنه
١٣١٩
العمدة

كتبه بيده الفانيه احمد الحاج على عفى الله عنه
سنة ١٣١٩ ذي القعدة
ختمان:] [احمد] علي مجذوب]

Manuscript 8

Muḥammad al-Shaykh ʿAlī al-Naqar, Mecca, to Aḥmad *al-Ḥājj* ʿAlī (probably in al-Qaḍārif), 1 Shaʿbān 1320H: November 3, 1902.

حضرة العالم العلامه والحبر البحر الفهامه عمدت الفاضلين وسلاله الطاهرين عمدتنا واستاذنا والدنا الشيخ احمد الحاج علي مجذوب متعنا الله بلقائه [؟] وافاض علينا من بركاته ءامين
السلام عليكم ورحمة الله وبركاته وازكي تحياته ثم المبدي ترقيمه لحضرتكم سيدي شدت الشوق وانقطاع اخباركم عنا وما كنا نظن بعض ذالك [هك] منكم لعلمكم باحوالنا ووحدتنا وغربتنا ومثلكم لا يحتاج للتعريف في ذالك وان سالتم عنا فنحن بحمد الله الان مقيمين بمكه شرفها الله وثبتنا فيها ببركة دعايكم ولم [= ليس؟] بنا شاغل سوي فقد الاحبة والاهل والوطن ونرجوا الله ان يرينا وجوهكم بخير واشدّ ما كان عند فراقكم وانقطاع اخباركم عنا فنرجوا الله ان لا يكون في خاطركم شيئا من قبلنا حين تقصيرنا وبلغوا سلامنا الي الاهل كافه صغير وكبير ذكر وانثي وعرفونا عن الميت والحى وعرفونا عن حالكم واقامتكم وراحتكم نرجوا الله ان تكونوا في ارغد عيش واوفر نعم وان سالتم عن الاخ ابو بكر فهو بخير وعافيه ويهدي لحضرتكم جزيل السلام وهو مشغول الخاطر عن ما كان من قطع اخباركم
هذا ودمتم في حفظ الله ورعايته ءامين
غرة
شعبان
سنه ١٣٢٠
ابنكم محمد الشيخ
على
النقر
مجذوب
[ختم]
ويقريكم جزيل السلام مولا الشيخ عمر باجنيد ويسئل عنكم كثير وكذالك السيد علوي ابن عقيل[74] يسئل عنكم ويقريكم جزيل السلام

74. Both ʿUmar b. Abī Bakr BāJunayd (1263 or 1273–1354H: 1847 or 1857/6–1935) and ʿAlawī [b. Ṣāliḥ] b. ʿAqīl (b. 1263H: 1847) were Meccan Shāfiʿī scholars of Ḥaḍramī origin; ʿUmar BāJunayd later was appointed mufti and adviser to Sharīf

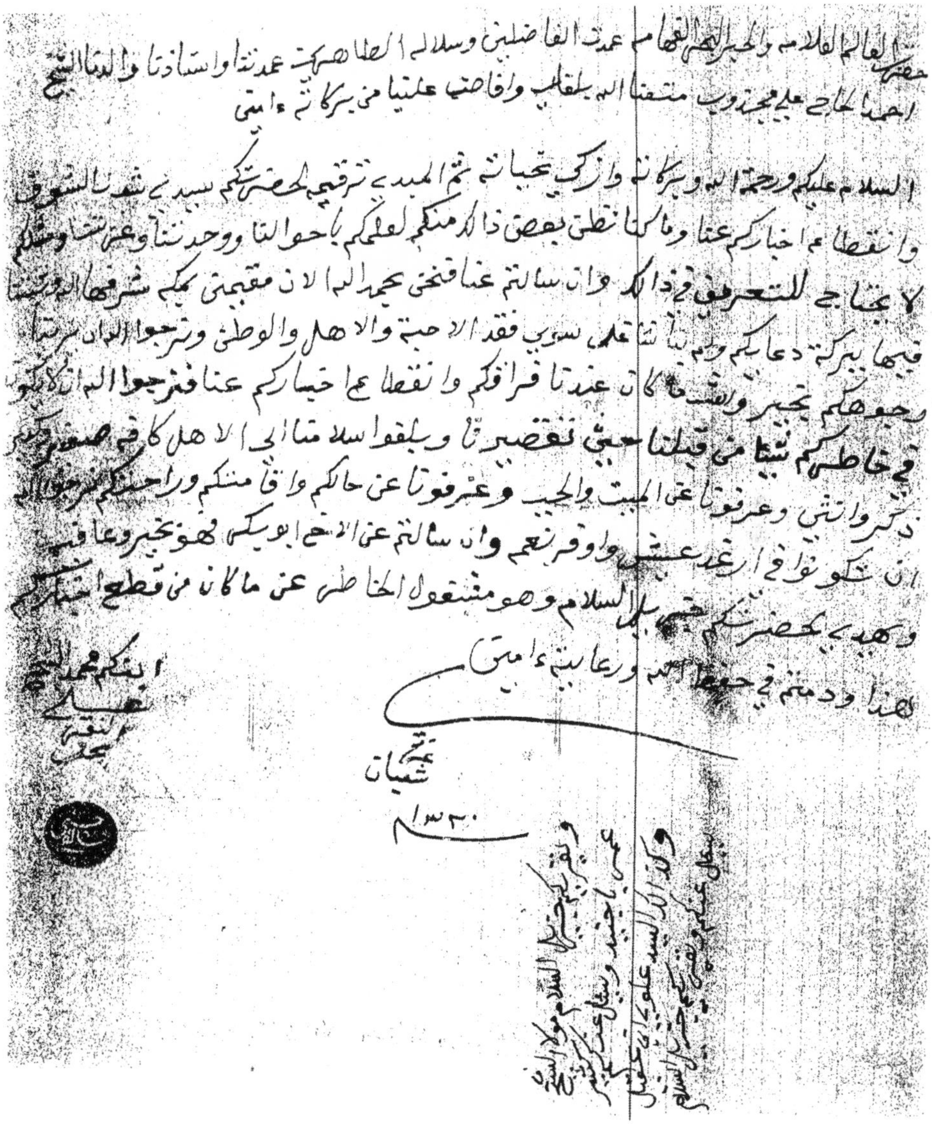
حضرة العالم العلامة والحبر البحر الفهامة عمدة الفاضلين وسلالة الطاهرين عمدتنا واستاذنا ووالدنا الشيخ
احمد الحاج علي مجذوب متعنا الله بطلعته وافاض علينا من بركاته امين

السلام عليكم ورحمة الله وبركاته وازكى تحياته ثم المبدي ترقيمه لحضرتكم بسبب شدة الشوق
وانقطاع اخباركم عنا وما كنا نطلع بعض ذلك منكم لعلمكم باحوالنا ووحدتنا وغربتنا وشغلكم
لا نحتاج للتعريف في ذلك وان سالتم عنا فنحن بحمد الله الان مقيمين بمكة شرفها الله وشرفنا
فيها ببركة دعائكم ... بسوى فقد الاحبة والاهل والوطن ونرجوا الله ان يردنا
وجوهكم بخير وبعد ما كان عندنا فراقكم وانقطاع اخباركم عنا فنرجوا الله ان لا يكون
في خاطركم شيئا من قبلنا حتى تقصيرنا وبلغوا سلامنا الى الاهل كافة صغير وكبير
ذكر وانثى وعرفونا عن الميت والحي وعرفونا عن حالكم واتفاقكم وراحتكم ونرجوا الله
ان يكون ... رغد عيش ... وان سالتم عن الاخ ابو بكر فهو بخير وعافية
ويهدي لحضرتكم جميل السلام وهو مشغول الخاطر عن ما كان من قطع اخباركم
هذا ودمتم في حفظ الله ورعايته امين

ابنكم محمد الحاج ...

محرم ... شعبان ١٣٠١

Manuscript 9

Shādhilī *ijāza*, [Aḥmad *al-Ḥājj* ʿAlī] to Muṣṭafà b. Muḥammad,[75] undated.

الحمد لله القوي الحنين الذي حفظ هذا الدين عن دسائس المفسدين وتحريف الملحدين
وجعل هذه الامة تروي امر دينها بالاسانيد الصحيحة المنقولة عن الثقات المتقنين حتي
تتصل بسيد المرسلين وامام المتقين المبلغ بالوحى المصون عن رب العلمين صلى الله عليه
وسلم
وجعل هذا الاسناد تسببا للوصال والاتصال لينخرط به المقصر في سلك اهل الكمال وساعته
[؟] تحصل له شفاعة اوليك الابرار وتعود عليه في الدارين بركة تلك السلسلة المنظمة من
جواهر الاخبار
ثم ان الابن الفاضل مصطفى بن محمد طلب مني ان اجيزه في اوراد الطريقة الشاذلية
باسانيدها المتصله المروية ظنا منه اني اهل لذلك فاجبته لذلك ~~[لحسن نيته]~~
~~. . . ؟[لحسن] . . . ؟[و] . . . ؟]~~[76] وان كنت لست اهلا لذلك تحقيقا لرجاءه وحسن
طويته فاجزته في اوراد الطريقة الشاذلية وجميع احزابها حسب ما وريته فاني اروي ذلك
عن والدي وهو اخذ عن عمه الولي الشهير الفكي المكي عن والده الفقيه حمد بن
المجذوب

Manuscript 10

Letter [probably from Aḥmad *al-Ḥājj* ʿAlī] to Abū ʾl-Qāsim Hāshim, congratulating him on his appointment as *Shaykh ʿUlamāʾ al-Sūdān* and asking him to include his school in al-Qaḍārif among the government-supported schools, 1912.

حضرة العالم الفاضل والماجد الكامل سماحة الاستاذ [. . .] شريعه ابي القاسم الشيخ
ابي القاسم هاشم

Ḥusayn (r. 1908–24) (al-Ghāmidī [1988], 88, 126–32; al-Marʿashlī [1427H] 2006, 278, 367, 1327, 1417).

75. Muṣṭafà b. Muḥammad was perhaps a son of Fāṭima bt. Ḥājj Aḥmad al-Naqar, a sister of al-Ṭayyib Aḥmad Ḥamad al-Naqar who was married to a rich Zaydābī named Muḥammad Muṣṭafà w. Mukhtār.

76. Struck out in the manuscript.

الحمد لله القوي المتين الذي حفظ هذا الدين عن أهو دسائس
المفسدين وتحريف الملحدين وجعل هذه الأمة تروي أمر دينها
بالأسانيد الصحيحة المنقولة عن الثقات المتقنين
حتى تتصل بسيد المرسلين وإمام المتقين المتلقي بالوحي
المصون عن رب العالمين صلى الله عليه وسلم وجعل هذا الإسناد سببا
للوصال والاتصال لينخرط به المعتصم في سلك أهل
الكمال ووسيلة تحصل له شفاعة أو لتكمل الأوراد ويعود
عليه من الدارين بركة سلك السلسلة المنتظمة من
جواهر الأخيار ثم إن الأخ الفاضل مصطفى بن محمد
طلب مني أن أجيزه في أوراد الطريقة الشاذلية بأسانيدها
المتصلة المروية ظنا منه أني أهل لذلك فأجبته لذلك تحقيقا لحسن ظنه
تحقيقا لحسن ظنه بي شيخه وإن كنت لست أهلا لذلك
تحقيقا لرجائه وحسن ظنه فأجزته في أوراد الطريقة
الشاذلية جميع أجزائها حسبما رويته فإني أروي ذلك
عن والدي وهو أخذ عن عمه الولي الشهيد الشيخ المكي عن والده
العمدة حمد بن المجذوب

حضرة العالم الفاضل والماجد الكامل سماحة الأستاذ ....
شريعة ابي القاسم الشيخ ابي القاسم هاشم
وقد صدق المادح المثني عليك ان يقول انك الرجل الذي تضرب
به الامثال والمهذب الذي لا يتساوى معه اي الرجال واذ اخلت
مشيخة علماء السودان فقد حظيت منك بشد ازرها
واصبحت وانت صدر القلب وتحلى لصدرها فهو مزدان بك بالفضل المتين
معانة بالقوي الامين ونسال الله ان يوفق فضيلتكم لهذا الامر الذي نثقل
حمله وعدم اهله فقد جيء بنا في زمان اصبح الناس فيه سدى وعاد الاسلام
غريبا كما بدئ وان يعينكم على تحمل عناه وان يصلح بكم الزمن وابناءه
ويعيد بهم بفضلكم الدين والعلم قايما على اصوله ويرفعه من خموله وحيث
يا سيدي ان المقصود نشر العلم واحياء السنة والفقر من خدمة

وفي وصية الامام مالك للشافعى "اتخذ لك ذا جاه ظهرا لئلا يستخف [هك] بك العامة"
وعن سحنون "وجدت كل شى يحتاج للجاه بمصر حتى العلم اى فلا بد ان يكون العالم ذا
جاه قال بعض الشيوخ هو كلام صدق وقول حق" اهـ عدوي على الخرشى[77]

بعد السلام عليكم ورحمت الله تعالى وبركاته سيدى كنت رايت مناما قبل ظهور تقليد
حضرتكم بالمشيخة فحواه ان حضرتك والشيخ رايتكما لابسين كساوى مزركشة في محل [؟]
مدخل [؟] الراس من [الجبة؟] فحين سمعت بتقليد حضرتكم المشيخه علمت ان ذلك مصداق
روياي وان لى نصيب من البشرى بذلك لان الرويا من المبشرات فمن قلدك هذا المنصب
السامى فعلى الخبير بها سقط وعند ابن بَجْدتها حطط وقد صدق الله لهجة المثنى عليك
وقد صدّق الله لهجةَ المُثْنِي عليك أنْ يقول انك الرجل الذي تضرب به الامثال، والمهذّب"
الذى لا يقال معه واى [هك، والصواب: اي] الرجال، واذا قُلدتَ مشيخة علماء السودان فقد
حُظيتْ منك بِشَدِّ ازرها، وسَدِّ ثَغْرِها، واصبحتَ وانت صدر لقلبها، وقلب لصدرها، فهى
مزدانة بك بالفضل المتين، معانة بالقوى الامين".[78] ونسال الله ان يوفق فضيلتكم لهذا الامر
الذي ثقل حمله وعدم اهله فقد جيء بنا في زمان اصبح الناس فيه سدى وعاد الاسلام غريبا
كما بدي وان يعينكم على تحمل عناه وان يصلح بكم الزمن واريناه ويعيد بفضلكم الدين
والعلم قايما على اصوله ويرفعه من خموله
وحيث يا سيدي ان المقصود نشر العلم واحياء السنه والفقه من خدمة العلم بحكم الوراثة
والتعليم من الوالد والجد وانى من زمن الحكومه السابقه معين بجامع القضارف امام
ومدرس والان بعد الفتوح تعينت لخدمة الجامع لاقامة الشعاير الدينيه وقد عقدت فيه درسا
علميا قراة على الاخوان رسالة ابن ابى زيد القيروانى منذ سنتين اختمها في كل سنة مرة مع
فتور اهل الزمن ورغبتهم عن تلقى العلم فارجوا من مكارمكم الشيخ شمول النظر وعدى في
سلك المنخرطين في خدمة العلم الشريف اذ ان خدمة العلم تحتاج لتعضيد ذى جاه يذب
عنك من يتعرض لك من المتصيدين لمعارضة العلم والاستهوان باهله خصوصا نحن في بلدة
بعيدة عن المعاهد العلميه وتعقد خدمه العلم ونشره وان كانت بضاعتنا مزجاة ولسنا من
اهل هذا المقام فقد يكرم الطفيلي في ساحة الكرام سعدى [؟؟] معكم [؟؟]

77. Both quotations are from al-ʿAdawī's gloss on al-Kharashī's gloss on Khalīl's abrégé of Mālikī law; cf. ʿUmayrāt 1997, 1:67–68. The published text has *tastakhiff* and *kalām ṣadūq*.

78. Taken literally (with the exception of the Sudan reference) from the section on the appointment of a minister in Ḍiyāʾ al-Dīn Naṣr Allāh b. Muḥammad b. ʿAbd al-Karīm Ibn al-Athīr al-Jazarī (558–637H: 1163–1239), *al-Mathal al-sāʾir fī adab al-kātib waʾl-shāʿir*, an influential work of literary theory (*ʿilm al-bayān*) and composition; see the edition edited by Aḥmad al-Ḥūfī and Badawī Ṭabāna (Ibn al-Athīr al-Jazarī 1959, 1:276). On *al-Mathal*, see Noy 2016, passim. Vocalization and phrasing as supplied here are not in the manuscript at hand; the published text has *muzdāna minka* instead of *muzdāna bika*.

Manuscript 11

Letter to Muḥammad al-Azraq from his son ʿUmar,[79] student in Omdurman, March 1912.

تحريرًا بأم درمان في ٢ [؟ ١][80] مارس سنة ١٩١٢
حضرة المحترم الفاضل والدي الشيخ محمد محمد الأزرق ادام الله سروره آمين
بعد السلام عليك وعلى من معك اعلمك أن جوابك المورخ يوم ٢١ فبراير سنة ٩١٢ وصل
وجميع ما تذكرونه فيه صار معلوما. اما من جهة محمد الحسن واخباره فلا هم لي من
جهتها حيث انى لم اكن مستلفًا من احد شيئا أخاف [؟؟؟] من الاطلاع [؟] عليه وبحمده
تعالى انت [؟] موجود لا احتاج الى أحد باذن الله تعالى كما انك تعلم ان اولاد الفكى
وغيرهم لا يهم امرهم [. . . ؟؟] الا من نقص عقله فان هؤلاء ليسوا بمن يخشى منهم
فيكفيهم ما هم فيه من دائرة [؟] السيرة [؟] وعدم التطبع وما علينا لو اشتغلنا بما يعود
علينا من النفع لو تكلموا او سكتوا فهكذا كانت الامم الذين قبلنا يذم كل وضيع [رفيعا ؟؟]
وكل عديم حسب يذم حسيبا فكيف بمن لهم [. . . ؟؟] اشتراك معك لا بد وان يروا ان لهم
[؟] الحق [؟] عليك وعلى من غيرك [؟] وهذه عادة كل ناقص [؟]

79. Muḥammad al-Azraq *al-Aṣghar* b. Muḥammad (d. 1937/8) was a grandson of *al-Fakī* Muḥammad *al-Azraq* (1787/6–1872/3). After the Mahdiyya, which he in part spent in al-Dāmar and in part with ʿUthmān Diqna, he built the Old Mosque (Jāmiʿ al-Sūq) in al-Qaḍārif and was responsible for primary *fiqh* teaching, including *tafsīr* and hadith, in al-Ṣūfī al-Azraq. Owing to failing eyesight, he stopped teaching in 1930. He used to excerpt important passages from the books he read on pieces of paper and in a booklet; some of what I photocopied may thus be in his hand. His son, ʿUmar (1888/9–1951), was born in al-Dāmar while Muḥammad al-Azraq was stationed there. After memorizing the Qur'ān in al-Dāmar and al-Qaḍārif and receiving elementary *fiqh* education at the hands of Aḥmad *al-Ḥājj* ʿAlī, from 1910 to 1913 ʿUmar studied at the teacher-training college in Omdurman (Madrasat al-ʿUrafāʾ, the predecessor to al-Maʿhad al-ʿIlmī). The letter at hand stems from this period; note the "modern"/Egyptian influence in his *ruqya* style of handwriting and that he uses the Gregorian, not the Hijri date. ʿUmar later worked as a teacher in Kasalā (until 1940/41) and eventually succeeded his father as imam of the Jāmiʿ al-Sūq in al-Qaḍārif. For more detail, see the interview with ʿUmar in ʿAbd al-ʿAzīz Amīn ʿAbd al-Majīd 1949, 38–43.

80. The date appears to have been amended, but it is unclear from the photocopy whether from 1 to 2 or vice versa.

ثم ان قطع الجوابات منكم ذلك لأمر تعلمونه وهو عدم الفضاء كما ان هذه الأيام ايام اشتغال خصوصا هذا الاسبوع فانه اسبوع امتحان نصف السنة وهو يكون بكرة يوم تاريخه نسأل الله النجاح وبعد الانتهاء نخبركم بالنتيجة. نقل قاضى ام درمان الى كسلا ونقل اليها الشيخ على حسيب ولكن لعدم الـفضاء لم اتمكن من مقابلته الى الآن. واما ابن الشيخ احمد البدوى فقد نقل درسه منا وابدل بالشيخ عبد الرحيم حامد وقد اطلعنى على جواب والده وفيه [؟] جملة [واحيانا ان شمل ؟؟؟] بها واعلم ان ما تسمعونه من المساعدات [؟] فذلك امر ليس بالمعمول به في ايام الدراسات بل المدار على العمل سابقا عرفتكم بان الكتب لم يرد لنا منها خبر وقد ظهر الخبر بان انكـ[. . . ؟ . . .] احتكر ارسالها لنفسه ولذلك لم يجب طعبنا وبناء عليه وردت له الكتب المذكوره وتكلمت معه بواسطة الشيخ على ابو قصيصه[81] فحجز عليها باسمى الى ان توجد الفلوس وهى كتاب شذا [. . .] العرف[82] وكتاب التطبيقات العربية[83] ولوعدنى ان دفعت ثمن هذه الكتب ودفعت نصف [؟] ثمن كتاب ادريس انه [؟؟] في الحساب يحضره [؟] بامن [؟] وزمن الوعد قريب جدا فارجوا ان لا تفوتني [؟] هذه الكتب واعلم ان ماهية هذا الشهر لم تفت [؟] ما كان من امرها وخصوصا ايام الامتحان فان العيش [؟] لا يكون الا بالشاى [؟] وكثرة النور [؟؟] وفي هذه الايام مشدد علينا في النظافة وذلك لان ايام الامتحان لا يقصر [؟؟] فيها من المفتشين [؟؟] وانى لا اقصد بالارسال مطلق فلوس بل ما يسهل لديكم من يد [؟] وغيره ولا يـ[. . . . ؟؟]ـكم ذلك على التبذير ولا تنظروا اليها بعين الكثرة بل انظروا لحال ام درمان وما [. . . . .؟؟] يظهر لكم الحال. يسلم عليكم المامون [؟] يوسف ووالدته واخواته واهل منزل [؟] ابرهيم يوسف يسلم عليكم وقد آن [؟] على ان اكتب لكم سلامه [؟]في كل بوستة فلز[. . . ؟؟؟] حصل مني سهو في بعض الأيام فالرجا [؟؟؟] في كل جواب يصدر منكم لا بد من كتب اسمه وخبر اولاده مهما ا[. . . ؟؟؟]ـكم [. . . ؟]

ولدكم

[عمر]

تقدم في البوسته السابقة جواب
وخبر [؟؟] جواب من بنت عكاشة لاخيها
على
هو وصلكم في لانسو [؟]

81. ʿAlī Abū Quṣayṣ, who at some point worked for the Sudan government as education inspector, later became the second director of al-Madrasa al-Ahliyya (Omdurman Ahlia School), founded in 1926/7 as the first of several such private initiatives to expand education opportunities beyond the limited circles admitted to the public school (al-Madrasa al-Amīriyya) that the British had established in 1904 (Abdin 1985, 128; Khiḍr 1986; al-Shaʿrānī 2006).

82. Al-Ḥamalāwī [1312H] 1894.

83. Ibrāhīm ʿAbd al-Khāliq 1910.

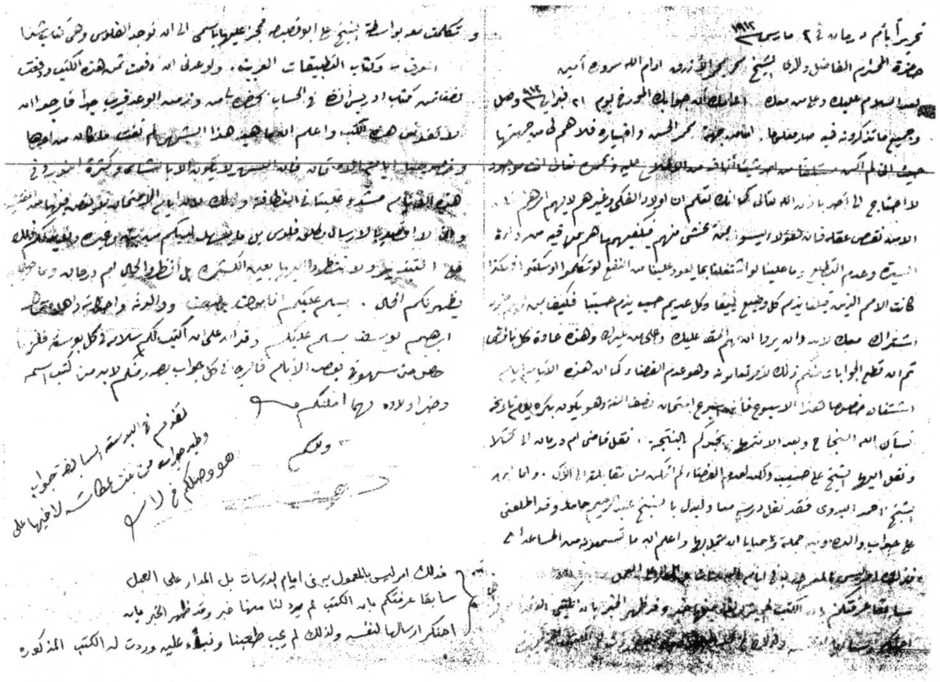

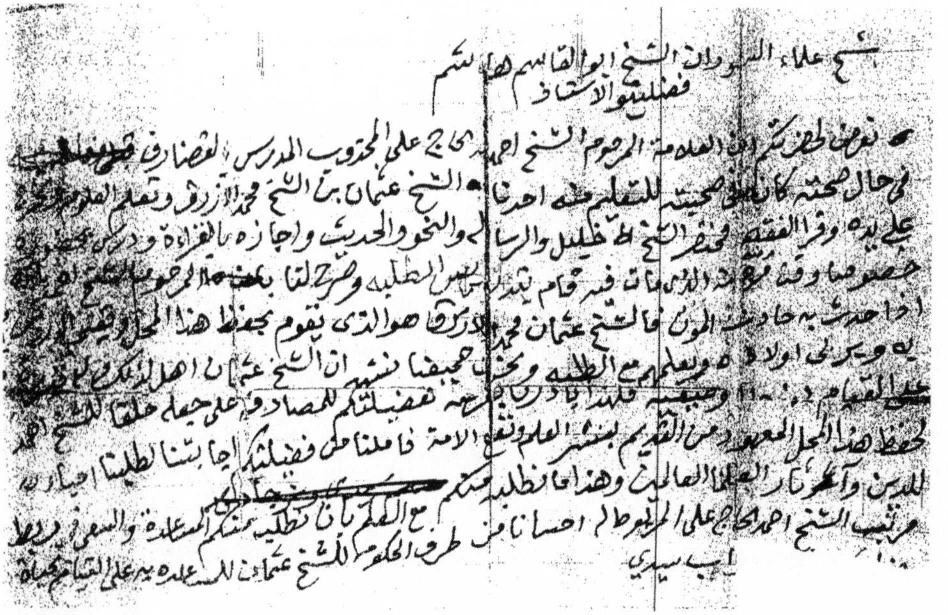

Manuscript 12

Letter [from the Azāriqa] to *Shaykh* Abū 'l-Qāsim Hāshim (*Shaykh 'Ulamā' al-Sūdān*), asking to confirm 'Uthmān al-Azraq as successor to Aḥmad *al-Ḥājj* 'Alī (d. Jumādà I 1332 [April 1914]).

شيخ علماء السودان الشيخ ابو القاسم هاشم
فضيلتو [؟] الاستاذ
نعرض لحضرتكم ان العلامة المرحوم الشيخ احمد بن الحاج على المجذوب المدرس بالقضارف قبل وفاته في حال صحته كان في صحبته للتعليم منه احدنا الشيخ عثمان بن الشيخ محمد الازرق وتعلم العلوم وتخرج على يده وقرا الفقه مختصر الشيخ خليل والرساله والنحو والحديث واجازه بالقراءة ودرس بحضوره خصوصا وقت مرضه الذي مات فيه قام بتدريس الطلبه وصرح لنا بان المرحوم الشيخ احمد بانه [؟] اذا حدث به حادث الموت فالشيخ عثمان محمد الازرق هو الذي يقوم بحفظ هذا المحل ويقيم الدروس به ويربى اولاده ويعلمهم مع الطلبه ونحن جميعنا نشهد ان الشيخ عثمان اهل لذلك وله قدرة على القيام بهذ[ا وخلفيته ؟] فلهذا بادرنا [؟] بعرض [؟] لفضيلتكم للمصادقه على جعله خلفا من القديم بنشر العلم ونفع الامة فاملنا من للشيخ احمد لحفظ هذا المحل المعهود فضيلتكم اجابتنا لطلبنا احياء به للدين وآثار العلما العالمين وهذا ما نطلبه منكم مع العلم بان نطلب منكم المساعدة والسعى في ربط مرتب الشيخ احمد الحاج على المربوط له احسانا من طرف الحكومه للشيخ عثمان للمساعده به على القيام بحياة [. . . .]اب سيدي

References

Interviews

'Abd Allāh al-Ṭayyib (1921–2003). 1988. The twentieth-century Sudan's foremost scholar of Arabic language and literature, from the Majādhīb of al-Dāmar. Interviewed by the author. Khartoum, Sudan, Feb. 18.

Al-Fakī al-Ḥusayn 'Abd al-Mājid. 1987. From the Majādhīb of al-Dāmar (younger brother of al-Jaylānī). Interviewed by the author, al-Dāmar, Sudan, Feb. 3.

Al-Jaylānī al-Ḥusayn 'Abd al-Mājid (c. 1900–c. 1990). 1987. From the Majādhīb of al-Dāmar. Interviewed by the author, al-Dāmar, Sudan, Feb. 2.

Majdhūb al-Naqar (1933–87). 1986. From the Majādhīb of al-Dāmar. Interviewed by the author, al-Dāmar, Sudan, Nov. 19.

Muḥammad Aḥmad b. 'Uthmān al-Hawwārī. 1988. Student of Majdhūb al-Naqar. Interviewed by the author, al-Dāmar, Sudan, Mar. 1.

Muḥammad al-Azraq Aḥmad *al-Ḥājj* 'Alī Aḥmad Ab Jadarī (b. c. 1937). 1987. Son of Aḥmad *al-Ḥājj* 'Alī, inspector of religious affairs in the Qaḍārif area. Interviewed by the author, al-Qaḍārif, Sudan, Mar. 21.

Sheyba Yāsīn 'Alī Karrār. 1987. A Khatmī from Sawākin. Interviewed by the author, Erkowit, Sudan, Nov. 4.

'Uthmān 'Abd al-Raḥmān ['Uthmān Muḥammad] al-Azraq. 1987. Imam of the Azāriqa mosque in al-Qaḍārif. Interviewed by the author, al-Qaḍārif, Sudan, Mar. 18–21.

Wad al-Naqar. 1987. Group interviews, including with the brothers al-Amīn (c. 1909–88) and al-Zākī (b. 1912) al-Ṭayyib, founders of the Naqarāb settlement at Wad al-Naqar. Interviewed by the author, Wad al-Naqar, Sudan, Mar. 15–17.

Published Sources

'Abd Allāh al-Ṭayyib. 1980. *Min nāfidhat al-qiṭār*. Khartoum, Sudan: Khartoum Univ. Press.

———. [1412H] 1992. *Aṣdā' al-Nīl*. Khartoum, Sudan: Khartoum Univ. Press.

'Abd al-Maḥmūd b. Nūr al-Dā'im b. Aḥmad al-Ṭayyib w. al-Bashīr. 1973. *Azāhīr al-riyāḍ: Fī manāqib [al-'ārif bi'llāh ta'ālā] {quṭb al-zamān, wa-shams al-'irfān, wa-tāj al-'ārifīn, wa-'umdat al-muqarrabīn,} al-ustādh al-shaykh Aḥmad al-Ṭayyib b. al-Bashīr*. Cairo: Mk. al-Qāhira.

'Abd al-'Azīz Amīn 'Abd al-Majīd. 1949. *Al-Tarbiya fī 'l-Sūdān wa'l-usus al-ijtimā'iyya wa'l-nafsiyya allatī qāmat 'alayhā*. Vol. 3: *Mulḥaqāt—Mujallad al-Wathā'iq: Min awwal al-qarn al-sādis 'ashar ilā nihāyat al-qarn al-tāsi' 'ashar*. Cairo: Mṭ. al-Amīriyya.

Abdin, Hasan. 1985. *Early Sudanese Nationalism, 1919–1925*. Khartoum, Sudan: Institute of African and Asian Studies, Univ. of Khartoum.

Abū Salīm, Muḥammad Ibrāhīm Aḥmad, ed. 1967. *Al-Fūnj wa'l-arḍ / Some Land Certificates from the Fung: Wathā'iq tamlīk*. Khartoum, Sudan: Univ. of Khartoum, Sudan Research Unit.

———. 1969. *Al-Murshid ilā wathā'iq al-Mahdī*. Khartoum, Sudan: Dār al-Wathā'iq al-Markaziyya.

Al-Amīr al-Kabīr, Abū 'Abd Allāh Muḥammad, and 'Alam al-Dīn Muḥammad b. 'Īsà al-Fādānī al-Makki. n.d. *Sadd al-arab min 'ulūm al-isnād wa'l-adab, wa-nihāyat al-maṭlab ta'līqāt 'alà Sadd al-arab, aw Itḥāf al-samīr bi-awhām mā fī Thabat al-Amīr*. N.p.: Mṭ. Ḥijāzī.

Baker, Samuel White. 1867. *The Nile Tributaries of Abyssinia and the Sword Hunters of the Hamran Arabs*. London: Macmillan.

Bāsharī, Maḥjūb 'Umar. [1411H] 1991. *Ruwwād al-fikr al-Sūdānī*. Beirut: D. al-Jīl.

Brockelmann, Carl. 1943–49. *Geschichte der arabischen Litteratur.* 2 vols. and 3 supplementary vols. Leiden: Brill.

Burckhardt, John Lewis. 1819. *Travels in Nubia*. London: John Murray.

De Jong, Frederick. 2004. "'Illaysh." In *The Encyclopaedia of Islam*, 2nd ed., vol. 12 Supplement, edited by Peri Bearman, Thierry Bianquis, Clifford Edmund Bosworth, Emeri Johannes van Donzel, and Wolfhart Peter Heinrichs, 411. Leiden: Brill.

Durkee, 'Abdullah [*sic*] Nur ad-Din, ed. [1411H] 1991. *Al-Madrasa al-Shādhuliyya li-ṭuma'nīnat al-nufūs wa-tanwīr al-qulūb / The School of the Shādhdhuliyyah* [*sic*] *for Being and Illumination of Hearts*. Vol. 1: *Aḥzāb al-Shādhuliyya / Orisons*. Alexandria, Egypt: D. al-Kutub.

Ewald, Janet Joran. 1989. "The Nile Valley System and Red Sea Slave Trade 1820–1880." In *The Economics of the Indian Ocean Slave Trade in the Nineteenth Century*, edited by William Gervase Clarence-Smith, 71–92. London: Cass.

Al-Ghāmidī, 'Abd Allāh b. Aḥmad Āl 'Allāf. [1988]. *A'immat al-Ḥaramayn, 1343–1436 h*. Al-Ṭā'if, Saudia Arabia: D. al-Ṭarafayn.

Al-Ḥamalāwī, Aḥmad b. Muḥammad b. Aḥmad. [1312H] 1894. *Shadhā al-'arf fī fann al-ṣarf.* Cairo: n.p.

Hammer, Joshua. 2017. *The Bad-ass Librarians of Timbuktu and Their Race to Save the World's Most Precious Manuscripts*. New York: Simon and Schuster.

Hassenstein, Bruno (unter A. Petermann's Anleitung). 1861. *Ost-Afrika zwischen Chartum und dem Rothen Meere bis Suakin und Massaua: Eine vornehmlich zum Verfolg der v. Heuglin'schen Expedition bestimmte Karte. Anhang: Theodor von Heuglin: "Ein Arabischer Schriftsteller über die Bedja-Länder.*" Gotha, Germany: Perthes.

Hill, Richard Leslie. 1967. *A Biographical Dictionary of the Sudan*. London: Frank Cass.

Hofheinz, Albrecht. 1991. "From Fakī to Duktōr: Changing Attitudes towards Tradition among Sudanese Rural Intellectuals." In *Conference Papers, Second International Sudan Studies on Sudan: Environment and People 3*, 96–106. Durham, UK: Sudan Archive.

———. 1996. "Internalising Islam: Shaykh Muḥammad Majdhūb, Scriptural Islam, and Local Context in the Early Nineteenth-Century Sudan." Dr.philos. diss., Univ. of Bergen.

———. 2004. "Goths in the Lands of the Blacks: A Preliminary Survey of the Ka'ti Library in Timbuktu." In *The Transmission of Learning in Islamic Africa*, edited by Scott Reese, 154–83. Leiden: Brill.

———. 2018. "The Islamic Eighteenth Century: A View from the Edge." In *Islam in der Moderne, Moderne im Islam: Eine Festschrift für Reinhard Schulze zum 65. Geburtstag*, edited by Florian Zemmin, Johannes Stephan, and Monica Corrado, 234–53. Leiden: Brill.

Holt, Peter Malcolm. 1967a. *A Modern History of the Sudan: From the Funj Sultanate to the Present Day*. London: Weidenfeld and Nicolson.

———. 1967b. "The Sons of Jābir and Their Kin: A Clan of Sudanese Religious Notables." *Bulletin of the School of Oriental and African Studies* 30, no. 1: 142–57.

———. 1970. *The Mahdist State in the Sudan, 1881–1898: A Study of Its Origins, Development, and Overthrow*. Oxford: Oxford Univ. Press.

———. 1988. "Mansfield Parkyns's Manuscript of the Funj Chronicle." *Die Welt des Islams* 28, nos. 1–4: 244–63.

Ibn al-Athīr al-Jazarī, Ḍiyā' al-Dīn Naṣr Allāh b. Muḥammad b. 'Abd al-Karīm. 1959. *Al-Mathal al-sā'ir fī adab al-kātib wa'l-shā'ir*. Edited by Aḥmad al-Ḥūfī and Badawī Ṭabāna. 2 vols. Cairo: D. Nahḍat Miṣr.

Ibrāhīm 'Abd al-Khāliq. 1910. *Al-Taṭbīqāt al-'arabiyya li-talāmīdh al-madāris al-thānawiyya*. Cairo: Mk. al-Tawfīq.

Khiḍr, Bakrī. 1986. Interview with 'Abd al-Raḥmān Mukhtār. *Jarīdat al-Siyāsa al-Sūdāniyya*, Oct. 18. At https://www.tawtheegonline.com/vb/showthread.php?t=18326.

Lejean, Guillaume. 1865. *Voyage aux deux Nils (Nubie, Kordofan, Soudan oriental), exécuté de 1860 à 1864 par ordre de l'Empereur*. Paris: Hachette.

Al-Mar'ashlī, Yūsuf 'Abd al-Raḥmān. [1427H] 2006. *Nathr al-jawāhir wa'l-durar fī 'ulamā' al-qarn al-rābi' 'ashar, wa-bi-dhaylihi 'Iqd al-jawāhir fī 'ulamā' al-rub' al-awwal min al-qarn al-khāmis 'ashar*. Beirut: D. al-Ma'rifa.

McGregor, Richard J. Addison. 1993. "The Shādhiliyya in Tunis: Prayer and Brotherhood." MA thesis, McGill Univ.

———. 2011. "Al-Dardīr, Aḥmad, and Dardīriyya." In *Encyclopaedia of Islam, THREE*, edited by Kate Fleet, Gudrun Krämer, Denis Matringe,

John Nawas, and Everett Rowson. Leiden: Brill. At https://referenceworks-brillonline-com/browse/encyclopaedia-of-islam-3.

Meier, Fritz. 2001. *Nachgelassene Schriften.* Vol. 1: *Bemerkungen zur Mohammedverehrung.* Part 1: *Die Segenssprechung über Mohammed.* Leiden: Brill.

———. 2005. *Nachgelassene Schriften.* Vol. 1: *Bemerkungen zur Mohammedverehrung.* Part 2: *Die taṣliya in sufischen Zusammenhängen.* Leiden: Brill.

Muḥammad ʻAbd al-Raḥīm. [1371H] 1953. *Al-Nidāʼ fī dafʻ al-iftirāʼ.* Cairo: Mṭ. al-Barlamān.

Muḥammad al-Mubārak ʻAbd Allāh. [1392H] 1973. *Maʻa al-taʻlīm al-dīnī fī ʼl-Sūdān.* Vol. 1: *Mudhakkirāt wa-dhikrayāt fī Maʻhad Umm Durmān al-ʻIlmī, ṭāliban wa-ustādhan wa-shaykhan liʼl-ʻulamāʼ.* Cairo: Mṭ. Muḥammad ʻAlī Ṣubayḥ.

Muḥammad al-Nūr b. Ḍayf Allāh. 1970. *Kitāb al-Ṭabaqāt fī khuṣūṣ al-awliyāʼ waʼl-ṣāliḥīn waʼl-ʻulamāʼ waʼl-shuʻarāʼ fī al-Sūdān.* Edited by Yūsuf Faḍl Ḥasan. Khartoum, Sudan: Khartoum Univ. Press.

Nöldeke, Theodor. 1909–38. *Geschichte des Qorāns.* 3 vols. Leipzig: Dieterich.

Noy, Avigail. 2016. "The Emergence of *ʻilm al-bayān*: Classical Arabic Literary Theory in the Arabic East in the 7th/13th Century." PhD diss., Harvard Univ.

O'Fahey, R. S., comp. 1994. *The Writings of Eastern Sudanic Africa to c. 1900.* Vol. 1 of *Arabic Literature of Africa.* Leiden: Brill.

Parkyns, Mansfield Harry Isham. 1966. *Life in Abyssinia: Being Notes Collected during Three Years' Residence and Travels in That Country.* 2 vols. London: Cass.

Al-Qaddāl, Muḥammad Saʻīd. 1973. *Al-Mahdiyya waʼl-Ḥabasha, 1881–1898.* Khartoum, Sudan: Khartoum Univ. Press.

Al-Qindīl, Ibrāhīm b. Muḥammad b. ʻAbd al-Dāfiʻ [urjūza]. 1982. *Ṭabaqāt Wad Ḍayf Allāh: Al-dhayl waʼl-takmila.* Commmentary by Aḥmad b Muḥammad b Nāṣir al-Salāwī [al-Sillāwī] al-Andalusī al-Maghribī al-Ṣāwī. Edited by Muḥammad Ibrāhīm Aḥmad Abū Salīm and Yūsuf Faḍl Ḥasan. Khartoum, Sudan: Univ. of Khartoum, Institute of African and Asian Studies.

Reichmuth, Stefan. 1990a. "Aufstieg unter Fremdherrschaft: Aḥmad Bêk Abû Sinn (1789–1869) und die Shukriyya." Paper presented at the colloquium "Laufende deutschsprachige Forschung in der Republik Sudan." Universität Bayreuth, Feb. 16–17.

———. 1990b. "Genealogie und Geschichte bei den Shukriyya." In *Tradition, Migration, Notstand: Themen heutiger Sudanethnographie*, edited by Bernhard Streck, 29–42. Göttingen, Germany: Edition Re.

Ri'āsat al-Jumhūriyya. 2019. "Ri'āsat al-Jumhūriyya taḥtasib al-Shaykh Muḥammad Majdhūb Ḥājj 'Alī al-Azraq." Feb. 8. At https://www.presidency.gov.sd/ara/news/The%20presidency%20of%20the%20Republic%20is%20calculated%20by%20Sheikh%20Mohammed%20Majzoub%20Haj%20Ali%20Azraq.

Al-Sha'rānī, Amīr. 2006. "Talāshà sūr al-Mahdiyya al-'aẓīm wa-ṣamadat al-Madrasa al-Ahliyya." Muntadà al-Ḥiwār, Muntadayāt Sūdāniyyāt, July 10. At http://sudanyat.net/vb/showthread.php?t=2762.

"Al-Shaykh" Muḥammad Majdhūb b. al-Ṭāhir b. al-Ṭayyib b. Qamar al-Dīn al-Majdhūb. [1332] 1914. *Al-Wasīla ilā 'l-maṭlūb fī ba'ḍ mā ishtahara min manāqib wa-karāmāt walī Allāh al-Shaykh al-Majdhūb*. Cairo: Mk. al-Taqaddum.

Shuqayr, Na'ūm Bey. 1967. *Jughrāfiya wa-tārīkh al-Sūdān*. Beirut: D. al-Thaqāfa.

The Sudan of the Three Niles: The Funj Chronicle, 910–1288/1504–1871. 1999. Translated and annotated by Peter Malcolm Holt. Leiden: Brill.

'Umayrāt, Zakariyyā, ed. 1997. *Ḥāshiyyat al-Kharashī 'alà Mukhtaṣar Sayyidī Khalīl, wa-waḍa'nā bi-asfal al-ṣafaḥāt Ḥāshiyat al-Shaykh 'Alī b. Aḥmad al-'Adawī 'alà al-Kharashī*. 8 vols. Beirut: D. al-Kutub al-'Ilmiyya.

'Uthmān [b.] Ḥamad Allāh. [1965] 1966. *Dalīl al-ma'ārif li'l-Ḍabāniya wa'l-Bawādira wa-Awlād al-Jābirī wa-sukkān al-Ṣūfī bi'l-Qaḍārif wa-ba'ḍ sukkān Ḥalfā wa-uṣūl usar sharq wa-gharb al-Sūdān: Wa-hādhā mulḥaq li-Kitāb al-Ta'āruf wa'l-'ashīra [fī Rufā'a wa'l-Ḥaṣāḥeyṣā wa-baḥrī 'l-Jazīra bi'l-Sūdān. Beirūt: D. al-Thaqāfa, 1965] wa-muqaddima li-Kitāb Rawābiṭ al-ikhwān*. Cairo: Sharikat al-Ṭibā'a al-fanniyya.

Vikør, Knut S. 1995. *Sufi and Scholar on the Desert Edge: Muḥammad b. 'Alī al-Sanūsī and His Brotherhood*. London: Hurst.

Voll, John Obert. 1975. "Muḥammad Ḥayyā al-Sindī and Muḥammad ibn 'Abd al-Wahhāb: An Analysis of an Intellectual Group in Eighteenth Century Madīna." *Bulletin of the School of Oriental and African Studies* 38:32–39.

———. 1980. "Hadith Scholars and Tariqahs: An Ulama Group in the 18th Century Haramayn and Their Impact in the Islamic World." *Journal of Asian and African Studies* 15, nos. 3–4: 264–73.

———. 1982. *Islam: Continuity and Change in the Modern World.* Boulder, CO: Westview.

———. 2002. "'Abdallah ibn Salim al-Basri and 18th Century Hadith Scholarship." *Die Welt des Islams* 42, no. 3: 356–72.

Wehr, Hans, and J. Milton Cowan, eds. 1976. *A Dictionary of Modern Written Arabic.* Ithaca, NY: Spoken Language Services.

Al-Ziriklī, Khayr al-Dīn. 1986. *Al-A'lām: Qamūs tarājim li-ashhar al-rijāl wa'l-nisā' min al-'arab wa'l-musta'ribīn wa'l-mustashriqīn.* 8 vols. Beirut: D. al-'Ilm li'l-malāyīn.

Part Three

Setting the Political Stage for the Modern Islamic World

5

Relational History, the Long Great War, and the Making of the Modern Middle East

Jonathan Wyrtzen

In the early 1920s, the British Institute of International Affairs, directed by Arnold Toynbee, published a series of volumes documenting the history of the Paris Peace Conference. They then continued publishing the annual *Survey of International Affairs* to track developments after the postwar peace settlement. For the 1925 edition, which was to cover the "Islamic World," Toynbee and the committee realized "that the amount of material to be dealt with was so great that it could not be treated adequately as a single section in a volume of five hundred pages." They had to dedicate the entire volume of six hundred pages to the Islamic world to cover the ongoing events that had transformed the region since the signing of the Treaty of Sèvres in 1920 (Toynbee 1927, v).

A significant amount of that material was generated during 1925 as large swaths of a region extending from Northwest Africa to Central Asia were in dramatic flux. In the western part, 'Abd al-Karim and his Rif Republic had achieved de facto sovereignty over close to 80 percent of the Spanish northern zone in Protectorate Morocco in the early 1920s. In April 1925, Rif forces pushed south into the French zone, overrunning French military posts in the fertile Ouergha Valley. By June, they had moved within forty kilometers of Fes, threatened the communication and transport corridor to French Algeria, and were poised to spatially link up to large autonomous areas of the Atlas Mountain ranges, possibly uniting an uprising that would imperil France's entire position in Morocco. In the former Ottoman provinces claimed as Italy's "fourth coast," Italy had expanded its control from an enclave around Tripoli to encompass most of Tripolitania and Fezzan by 1924, but Cyrenaica remained almost completely autonomous. There, a Sanusi proto-state exercised sovereignty from the Jabal Akhdar massif on the coast far southward across a network of Saharan oases.

In the eastern Mediterranean, France's Syrian Mandate began to come apart in the summer of 1925. In July, just as 'Abd al-Karim's Rif forces were advancing on the French protectorate zone in Morocco, a revolt initiated by Sultan Atrash broke out in Jabal Druze and encompassed much of Syria, including Damascus, by the end of the year. In Iraq, the British put down another uprising in 1924 led by Shaykh Mahmud Barzanji, who had created the Kingdom of Kurdistan based in Sulaymaniyah. In March 1925, the newly founded Turkish Republic faced a massive Kurdish revolt in northern Kurdistan. It was mostly put down that summer with the execution of Shaykh Said and other leaders in Diyarbakir, but resistance continued into the next year. Farther east, large areas of Iran and Afghanistan remained in revolt against state-building reforms imposed by Reza Shah and Amanullah Khan. The Arabian Peninsula also remained in flux in 1925, with Ibn Saud's Najdi forces having almost completely absorbed the Hashemite Kingdom of the Hijaz, while Ikhwan parties raided unchecked across ill-defined borders to the east and north into British Mandate Transjordan and Iraq.

This brief survey of the Islamic world five years after the signing of the Treaty of Sèvres in August 1920 highlights two important interrelated points. First, it demonstrates how little the post–World War I peace settlement actually settled. The Sèvres Treaty, the final of the five treaties negotiated in Paris between 1919 and 1920, marked the culmination of a series of bilateral and multilateral negotiations among the Allied Powers during and after the war (the Sykes-Picot, London, and Cairo Conferences; the San Remo Conference) through which these countries, in particular the British and French, negotiated the partition of the Ottoman Empire, supposedly "making" the modern Middle East. The 1925 overview of the actual state of play reveals the fundamental flaws of this traitial explanation for how the post-Ottoman Middle East was refashioned. European officials might have drawn (and redrawn) maps of the Middle East during and after the war, but these cartographic constructions and the treaty terms they informed did not create reality on the ground. Any semblance of a unilaterally dictated postwar settlement was proved specious, even while the agreements themselves were being negotiated, with the outbreaks of widespread revolts from Egypt to Iraq to Afghanistan in 1919–20. Over the next decade, the region extending from Morocco to Afghanistan was characterized by a near constant state of armed conflict over the shape and content of the postwar political map.[1]

The second point Toynbee's 1925 survey makes clear is that it was absolutely necessary, well into the interwar period, to keep the Islamic world—at least a greater Middle Eastern portion of it stretching from Morocco to the Iranian Plateau—in a single frame of reference. This interregional perspective had to be maintained owing to the fact that the political boundaries were so fluid, and anticolonial military activity across the region was interlinked within and across French, British, Italian, and Turkish colonial and national boundaries. Reducing the scope to proto-national units—protectorates, colonies, and mandates—supposedly "imposed" on the region after the Great War would have been incoherent.

This chapter, keeping this wider lens in place, reexamines how the political stage of much of the modern Islamic world was dramatically reshaped during the course of what I call the "Long Great War," a period of transregional conflict that extended from Italy's invasion of Ottoman Africa in 1911 through the mid-1930s. In rethinking the

1. Arguably, this period of violent contention over the post-Ottoman order continued right up to the eve of World War II if the Palestinian Great Revolt of 1936–39 and other cases such as Turkey's genocidal response to the Kurdish uprising in Dersim in 1937–38 are taken into account.

origin story of the modern Middle East, my deeper intervention is to highlight the importance of historiographical relationalism. The first section suggests how a family of historiographical "turns"—including world, global, international, and transnational histories—might productively be gathered together by a historiographical ontology and epistemology that *more explicitly* presumes and analyzes how the local, regional, and global are presumed to be connected and interacting. The second section gets practical, sketching out how methodological relationalism can be used to fundamentally reassess the seminal event in the history of the modern Islamic world: World War I. I argue that a relational account challenges widely held causal assumptions about the war's impact—namely, that the British and French imposed artificial boundaries on the post-Ottoman Middle East. In place of this dominant narrative, I trace a more complicated story in which the political topography of the greater Middle East was transformed as local and colonial political projects mobilized during the latter phases of the Long Great War came into violent conflict, with winners and losers on both sides.

Methodological Relationalism and Postnational Historiography

To set off the distinctions of a relational research agenda, it is helpful to use methodological nationalism as a foil to explain why history (in particular non-Western history, including that focused on the Islamic world) has largely been inoculated against it in contrast to neighboring social sciences. At first glance, history seems a disciplinary poster child for the methodological nationalism—the presuppositional naturalization of the "national" with respect to relevant actors, boundaries, units, and objects of social scientific analysis—that has been periodically critiqued since the 1970s.[2] Modern historiography was birthed in and alongside powerful movements toward nationalism

2. See Martins 1974, Beck 2000, Wimmer and Schiller 2003, and Chernilo 2006.

in nineteenth-century Europe. If anthropology served colonialism, European history was frequently the handmaiden of nationalism, positing the nation back in time, then tracing this actor's narrative along a more or less linear historical trajectory. Anticolonial nationalists in the Global South often mirrored this pairing, also using history to anchor the nation in time, to rebut colonial narratives denying peoplehood, and to legitimate political claims for self-determination.

Methodological nationalism's shortcomings are obvious—anachronistically imposing a national unit of reference onto historical periods prior to its relevance or assuming that political, economic, social, or cultural activity occurs primarily within the national unit rather than above (empire), below (village, city, region), or across the unit's boundaries—but it continues to provide a persistent analytical and categorical episteme through which many unreflexively think. In history, vestigial evidence of this episteme can be seen in labels used on faculty websites and associations denoting French, German, British, Russian, American, Japanese, or Chinese history. Tellingly, though, only imperial national cores are referenced, while peripheries are typically grouped in regional and area designations.

In reality, compared to neighboring disciplines in the humanities and social sciences, history has long resisted methodological nationalism. In contrast to sociology's and political science's preoccupation with the modern nation-state/society, the temporal breadth of historians' work, much of which includes premodern periods before the nation-state was relevant, inoculates the discipline, forcing the considerations of other units and processes. In the interwar period, in addition to Toynbee's work on international and civilizational global history, the Annales school began to take up local, rural, regional, and transregional history, flourishing through the 1960s and 1970s. Also in the post–World War II period, a Chicago school of historians including Marshall Hodgson and William McNeill laid the groundwork for the world history movement, explicitly provincializing Europe within a broader hemispheric frame that opened up cross-cultural, comparative, and global perspective beyond the national. For Hodgson, the Islamic world constituted the empirical grounding from which to recenter world history, and his work influenced a next generation of historians of the Islamic world—including John Voll, Edmund Burke III, and Ross Dunn—who directly contributed to the development of world history (which gained an institutional footing with the founding of the World History Association in 1982 and the *Journal of World History* in 1990).[3] Through this period, historians and sociologists working on the Islamic world also critically engaged with world systems analysis (by which Immanuel Wallerstein and others pointedly critiqued the methodological nationalism of modernization theory), including Janet Abu-Lughod's (1989) intervention against the Eurocentrism of the "modern" world system framework and John Voll's (1994a) exploration of how Islam functions as a "special world system."

Since the late 1990s, another major wave of historiographical approaches transcending national-scope limitations have trended under a variety of labels, including *global history*, *international history*, and *transnational history*. As is perhaps to be expected in a discipline where empirics are prioritized over explicit theorization or methodological boundary policing, these labels fuzzily encompass a family of overlapping orientations focused above, between, across, and sometimes below the "national" level. Global history seems to encompass two phenomena: globalization as itself a process and processes that are best understood as global (Mazlish 1998; Iriye 2013). International history and transnational history implicitly retain the nation as a reference, focusing between and across this unit, sometimes in a more traditional state-centric concentration on Great Power politics in a form of rebranded diplomatic history, or focusing on objects such as multinational corporations, transnational firms, nongovernmental organizations, and other nonstate actors that transcend national borders. Both of these labels can also be attached to variegated historical work on culture, licit

3. For examples of these historians' impact, see Voll 1994a, 1994b; Burke and Pomeranz 2009; Dunn and Mitchell 2014; Dunn, Mitchell, and Ward 2016; and Burke and Mankin 2018.

and illicit economic activity, migration, social mobilization, networking, and other objects that do not fit within a national horizon.[4]

The recent proliferation of various global-international-transnational-transoceanic-transregional labels represents a continuation of history's disciplinary resistance to methodological nationalism, but it is not quite clear what this "turn" means in concrete terms with respect to how we view and do history or what connects these approaches. Although I would agree that arguing over nomenclature is less important than just doing the work, clarifying our presuppositions and getting more precise about our historical ontology and methods can help us better train students, compare across cases, and facilitate transdisciplinary connections.

One way to gather these various postnational historiographical approaches together is to build on their shared relationalist orientation and reflexively think through how a more explicit "methodological relationalism" (Bourdieu and Wacquant 1992, 15–16) might provide a legible shared research agenda. What would this process entail in practice? First, it would challenge us to think hard about what we are studying and how we go about studying it. Instead of a substantivist ontological/epistemological dyad—that the objects of our analysis exist as things in and of themselves, moving through time and interacting in a Newtonian system of cause and effect—the starting point is relationalist—that things exist in a relation to other things and are situated in networks and that historical processes themselves are relationally conditioned pathways of interactions that produce historical outcomes.[5] This shift in perspective forces us to think through the type of cases we select, what conditions we uncritically presume, and what type of causation we assume. These questions are often implicit in our research design and in our writing but could productively be made more explicit.

4. See the discussion in Bayly et al. 2006.

5. Julian Go and George Lawson outline this application of relational sociology (Emirbrayer 1997) to historical social science (2017, 23).

In terms of practice, much of the work in world history, in world systems analysis, and transregional Islamic history already provides a wealth of examples for what relational history looks like. With respect to the latter, the work of Marshall Hodgson, Ira Lapidus, and John Voll emphasizes linkages across the Islamic world, shows how the local and global were connected, and demonstrates how Islamic revival and reform, religious, scholarly, and trade networks, as well as states, society, and culture spanned and moved far beyond the national from western Africa to southeastern Asia. Building on those legacies, the rest of this chapter sketches out how a methodological relationalism can help us rethink the seminal event in the making of the modern Middle East: the Great War.

A Relational Account of the Great War and the Making of the Modern Middle East

To put into relief what a transregional relational approach contributes to our understanding of the making of the modern Middle East, it helps first to briefly overview the existing standard narrative. How is World War I and its impact usually taught in a Middle East or Islamic world survey course? My own lecture outline for this topic has typically started off with the Ottoman Empire's entry into the war on the side of the Central Powers, overviewed the course of the war, and then zeroed in on a litany of contradictory wartime and postwar agreements that are the keys to understanding the making of the postwar Middle East order. These agreements include the Hussein–McMahon correspondence of 1915–16 promising an Arab Kingdom as a quid pro quo for the Hashemites' mobilization of an anti-Ottoman Arab revolt from the Hijaz; the Sykes-Picot Agreement of 1916 between Britain and France (as well as Russia and, later, Italy) dividing up zones of control and influence in the region; and the Balfour Declaration of 1917 promising British support for the creation of a Jewish national homeland in Palestine. We then conclude with the Treaty of Sèvres of 1920, the final treaty of the Paris Peace Conference in which the Ottoman Empire was subdivided into zones of direct and less-direct

European and local control in a series of mandates that maintained much of the Sykes-Picot Agreement, built in the Balfour promises, and contravened the Hussein–McMahon promises to Arabs for self-determination. As class is ending, rushing to beat the bell, I try to tack on a quick denouement explaining that Mustafa Kemal pushed back a bit, leading in 1923 to the Treaty of Lausanne revision of the postwar settlement that recognized the independence and boundaries of the Turkish Republic.

This telling—what we might call the "Sykes-Picot Standard Narrative"—offers a quick and compelling shorthand to explain how the Ottoman Middle East was transformed into the modern Middle East. In terms of periodization, the temporal focus is the expected 1914–18 bracket and the 1919–20 peace conference. The geographic unit of analysis is the eastern Mediterranean (northern Africa and the Iranian plateau are not in the picture), with attention to Gallipoli, perhaps the Battle of Kut al-Amara in Mesopotamia, and definitely the Arab Revolt as well as Faisal I and T. E. Lawrence's progress toward Damascus. This regional perspective is maintained through the postwar negotiations in Paris, San Remo, London, and Cairo as the outlay of post-Ottoman units is decided, but the analysis quickly switches to the (proto)national individual units in the region.

The interwar history of the Middle East is told in the next lecture through the mandate containers of Syria, Lebanon, Iraq, Palestine, and Transjordan and independent Turkey (note the quick shift to methodological nationalism). The causal story focuses on the agency of the Great Powers and is more or less linear: the British, with the French as a sidekick, were the architects of the post-Ottoman Middle East, imposing artificial boundaries and denying national self-determination, thereby committing the original sin that continues to curse the region from the Palestinian–Israeli conflict to the Syrian Civil War to the Kurdish Question.

Now let us turn to how a relational reanalysis and retelling of this genesis story fundamentally challenges the Sykes-Picot narrative, raising new questions and new insights about the (1) causes of the war, (2) the course of the war in the Middle East theater, and (3) the negotiation of postwar agreements versus the negotiation of the actual facts on the ground during the interwar period. Applying a methodological relationalism across these phases forces us to reconsider our periodization of the Great War and what geographic units make sense as well as to deeply rethink the Sykes-Picot Standard Narrative's causal explanation for how the war and the postwar settlement transformed the Middle East.

Why, where, and when did World War I start? The proximate cause of the war was the assassination of Archduke Ferdinand of Austria-Hungary in Sarajevo by a Serbian nationalist in June 1914, an event that activated a system of intra-European power alliances that brought the European continent to war the first week of August. If we zoom out with a non-Eurocentric lens, though, our view of the war's origins shifts to the greater Middle Eastern region stretching from northwestern Africa to the Hindu Kush, where overlapping European imperial rivalries escalated in the late nineteenth and early twentieth centuries in competition for direct and indirect influence in the Ottoman Empire, the Qajar Empire, and the Alawite Sultanate—all geostrategically situated astride key nodes of transhemispheric waterways linking the Atlantic, Mediterranean, and Indian Ocean.

From this vantage point, the year 1911 arguably stands out as much as 1914 as the starting point for a period of transregional warfare that would continue through and beyond the 1914–18 bracket in the Middle East. In the spring and summer of 1911, the Agadir Crisis brought France and Germany to the brink of war over competing claims to Morocco after France deployed troops to the interior to quell unrest in Fes (Mortimer 1967; Williamson 2011). Both countries mobilized troops on the Franco-German border, and it took until the fall for a diplomatic resolution to avert the clash. In late September, Italy did start a war, unilaterally attacking and attempting to occupy the Ottoman Empire's provinces of Tripolitania and Cyrenaica, a move that inaugurated more than a decade of continuous warfare in the region. The Italo-Ottoman war drew a host of Ottoman officers to North Africa who would play substantial roles through the Great War, including Enver Pasha, part of the Committee of Union and Progress (CUP) triumvirate who would command the Ottoman armies during the war; Mustafa Kemal, the celebrated hero of Gallipoli who would found modern Turkey; and Jaafar al-Askari, an Arab Ottoman officer who would serve in the Arab army with Faisal and later help found the Iraqi army. In 1912, the Italians spread the conflict to the Red Sea, where they attacked Ottoman vessels at the Kunfuda Bay on the Arabian Coast; to the eastern Mediterranean, where they shelled Beirut; and, finally, in September 1912 through the Aegean to the Dardanelles, where they threatened Istanbul. The Italo-Ottoman conflict flowed directly into the Balkan Wars after Montenegro, at Italy's urging, and then the rest of the Balkan League joined the attack on the Ottoman Empire. The Balkan–Ottoman conflict primed a relationally connected system of tensions—including competitive expansionism among the Balkan states, Ottoman defensive reactions, and Russian and Austro-Hungarian patronage relationships in the region—that created the context for the archduke's assassination and the July Crisis of 1914 that brought the rest of Europe into a transregional war.

A relational reading of the course of the war between 1914 and 1918 distinguishes among the multiple Ottoman fronts on which the empire fought, the ways these fronts were connected to each other, and how they were linked to other theaters of the war. They include the eastern Anatolia/Caucasus front versus the Russian army, the Mesopotamia front against British imperial forces, the southern Syria front (including Sinai and the Hijaz) against the British and the Arab army, the Dardanelles and Thrace against the British and French, and the North Africa front, where the Ottomans rallied Sanusi forces against British-controlled Egypt. The other important front was the "home front," where the Ottomans mobilized, conscripted, and (in some cases brutally) disciplined the civilian population (Akin 2018).

All of these fronts were connected in terms of strategic decision making, logistics, personnel movement, and wartime hardship. A methodologically relationalist approach shifts our understanding of multiple significant episodes of World War I often thought of in isolation by showing how they were connected.[6] Right at the start, days after an Ottoman–German naval attack on Russian Black Sea ports on October 29, 1914, Russian forces pushed into Ottoman eastern Anatolia the same week that the British landed troops in Basra province. Just after the Ottoman's worst defeat of the war, the Battle of Sarıkamış in January 1925 on the Caucasus front (where Enver Pasha had launched an offensive in December), Ottoman forces stormed across Sinai against the Suez Canal and were held off by the British. In March 1915, the Armenian Genocide was launched through directives emanating from the CUP leadership in Istanbul only weeks after the Allies had launched the assault on Istanbul through the Dardanelles that developed into the Gallipoli campaign. The Ottomans' greatest triumph, the Gallipoli victory achieved when Allied forces withdrew in January 1916 after eight months of fighting, was immediately offset by Russia's massive offensive in eastern Anatolia, which resulted in the Ottomans' loss of the key stronghold of Erzurum in February. Mustafa Kemal, the Gallipoli hero, had to rally Ottoman forces to defend against the Russian offensive that reached Erzincan that summer.

Elsewhere, British urgency in the Hussein–McMahon negotiations about the Arab Revolt increased after the humiliating surrender of thirteen thousand British and Indian soldiers at the Siege of Kut Amara. Ottoman dramatic advances through the Caucasus to Baku and the Caspian Sea in 1917–18 after the Russian Revolution forced the withdrawal of Russian troops from the area were offset by the steady advance of the British and Arab army forces into southern Syria. Throughout 1914–18, the Ottoman fronts were linked not only to each other but also to events taking place far away, from the Western Front (constantly factoring into French, British, and German calculations) to the Russian Revolution (which lifted pressure off respective eastern fronts for the Germans and Ottomans) and to the

6. Eugene Rogan's book *Fall of the Ottomans* (2015) provides an unparalleled synthetic history of the Ottomans' Great War and makes many of these connections.

British Raj (a vital source of manpower and materiel for multiple theaters of the war, including the Middle East).

Finally, a relational lens also transforms how we analyze and understand the postwar "settlement," which, as this chapter's opening described, did not actually settle much in 1920. This lens corrects against the historical error of reading wartime and postwar agreements as substantive, fixed objects that can be used to cleanly periodize starting and end points. Instead, many, if not all, of these agreements and treaties marked relationally negotiated statements signposting aspirations. These aspirations, even those enshrined in treaties, almost invariably had to be amended and redefined over time as processes on the ground reshaped what was thinkable and not thinkable. This is true for the bundle of British commitments made during the war—the Hussein–McMahon negotiations in 1915–16 about a post-Ottoman Arab Kingdom, the Sykes-Picot Agreement in 1916 about post-Ottoman French and British zones of direct and indirect influence, and the Balfour promise in 1917 to support a Jewish national home in Palestine—as well as for the San Remo and Sèvres agreements in 1920 and the Treaty of Lausanne in 1923. These agreements have to be seen in relation to other colonial and local political aspirations, none of which was unilaterally realized; rather, they all were negotiated, contested, amended, partially consummated, and in some cases denied through processes that worked out over the next decade. The postwar settlement has to be critically interpreted with attention to how little it actually settled.

A relational account more accurately reflects how a wide range of colonial and local actors reimagined what political futures might be possible in the post-Ottoman Middle East between 1918 and 1920, how these imaginings clashed, and how they had to be readjusted again and again through the 1920s. As the Allied powers convened in early 1919 for the Paris Peace Conference, a plethora of plans was being articulated and debated. On the colonial side, David Lloyd George and Georges Clemenceau were at odds over the Sykes-Picot provisions, in particular France's claim to Mosul province, the status of Palestine, and the future of Faisal's Damascus-based Arab Kingdom;

Italy wanted its Libyan claims acknowledged and vied with Greece for control of western Anatolia. On the local side, various visions for a unified Arab Kingdom, a Greater Syria under Faisal, a unified Iraq, a Kingdom of the Hijaz, a Greater Armenia, an independent Kurdistan, a separate Lebanon, and a Jewish polity in Palestine were also articulated. In 1920, the Treaty of Sèvres enshrined a particular Great Power construct—negotiated among the British, French, Italians, and Greeks—of the post-Ottoman Middle East, but it was an aspiration immediately abrogated by developments on the ground.

As Robert Gerwarth (2016) has shown with respect to how the Great War "failed to end" in eastern Europe and the Balkans, the war also continued in the Middle East long after the peace terms were dictated to the Ottoman Empire in 1920. In Mesopotamia, a massive uprising in the summer of 1920 against the British, which included Basra and Baghdad and eventually the Mosul province, took until the end of the year and massive aerial bombardment targeting civilian populations for the British to quell. In Anatolia, there was continuous warfare from the fall of 1919 through the fall of 1922 as reconstituted former Ottoman units under the command of Mustafa Kemal mobilized to defend and achieve the aims of the National Pact. These Turko-Kurdish forces first repelled attempts to consolidate the Greater Armenia outlined in the Sèvres Treaty, pushing out Armenian forces from the three easternmost provinces. By the fall of 1921, they had also ousted the French and Armenian forces from Cilicia and forced out Italian troops that had occupied parts of the southern coast. These struggles in the northern part of France's allotted mandate area were interlinked with major revolts in the Alawite highlands of Latakia and Ibrahim Hananu's mobilization in Aleppo province, both of which received logistical support and supplies from the Turkish military. In western Anatolia, Kemal's forces held off a Greek advance at the Battle of Sakarya near Ankara in October 1921. Having signed treaties that month with France and Russia that secured the eastern and southern borders, the Turko-Kurdish army redeployed to this front and steadily pushed the Greeks all the way back to the coast, ousting them from Izmir (Smyrna) in September 1922. That fall, the

Kemalists' continuing advance toward the Straits zone provoked the Chanak Crisis, in which the British Commonwealth countries refused London's call for military support, forcing the British to sit down with the Turks at Lausanne to begin renegotiating the Sèvres Treaty terms. Elsewhere in the region, Ibn Saud's military had expanded in the early 1920s from the Najd to include Hasa, Jabal Shammar, and 'Asir and took the Hijaz in 1924; in the Rif, 'Abd al-Karim devastated the Spanish army at the Battle of Anual in the summer of 1921 and set about consolidating an independent Rif Republic; and in Libya, the Italians began to subdue Tripolitania and Fezzan, but the Sanusis continued to function in Cyrenaica as a semi-independent state through the 1920s.

The Treaty of Lausanne signed in August 1923 recognized the facts that the newly founded Turkish Republic had created on the ground, but, again, this date does not mark the end of the Long Great War. The treaty left the Mosul Question, whether Turkey or Britain should get the province (or whether Kurdish autonomy should be recognized), unanswered, relegating the issue to bilateral negotiations and then to a League of Nations commission if negotiations failed (which they did). In addition to Turko-British diplomatic tensions over Mosul, a series of military conflicts started in the mid-1920s among competing political, colonial, and local actors over the shape and control of the post-Ottoman map. As Toynbee's post–Peace Conference survey of major conflicts across the Islamic world in 1925 indicated, both the local and the wider transregional perspectives have to be held in view because several of these conflicts were relationally linked.

The first wave of major military clashes in these last phases of the Long Great War occurred between 1925 and 1927. In March 1925, as the League of Nations Mosul Commission visited the province, the Turkish state faced a massive Kurdish revolt just to the north around Diyarbakir, led by Shaykh Said, that quickly spread throughout southeast Anatolia. In April 1925, the Rif War climaxed as 'Abd al-Karim's forces advanced against the French zone in Morocco, provoking a Franco-Spanish counteroffensive that involved more than two hundred thousand troops, massive aerial bombardment (the Spanish had been using chemical weapons since 1923), and coordinated pincer movements against the thirteen thousand Riffi troops (Pennell 1986). In Syria, a Druze revolt started in July 1925 and began to spread that fall. In early October, Fawzi al-Qawuqji, aware the French had deployed many of their forces from Syria to help with the Rif War, launched a revolt in Hama, while others moved against Damascus later that month (Provence 2009). The simultaneous Rif War and Great Syrian Revolt required the French to engage in their largest military operations of the interwar period and took until 1927 to finally quell. The Kurdish mobilization against the Turkish Republic was partially subdued with the capture and execution of Shaykh Said in late June 1925, but Kurdish lower-level resistance continued in the Southeast. From 1927 to 1934, a second wave of major conflicts climaxed, signaling the last phase of the Long Great War. They included the brutal Italo-Sanusi clash in Cyrenaica, which ended with the capture and execution of Omar al-Mokhtar in 1931; the internal Saudi civil war with the Ikhwan and war with the imamate in Yemen; and the Kurds' mobilizations within and across emerging borders to defend their autonomy against the Turkish and Iraqi states, which continued far into the 1930s and included the Ararat, Dersim, and the Barzani revolts.

Over the long decade after the Paris Peace Conference, the political order of the post-Ottoman greater Middle East remained highly fluid. As with the causes and course of World War I, the postwar settlement was relationally produced not in Paris but through intense, violent conflict on the ground in the region between rival political visions that had been catalyzed by the war's onset. It took until the 1930s for the modern Middle East's new political order to become more settled than not and for a series of new treaties to recognize the realities that had been forged on the ground.[7]

7. These treaties include the Hadda agreement between Transjordan and the Kingdom of the Najd and Hejaz in 1925 (settling part of the border from Aqaba to Wadi Sirhan); the Ankara Treaty among Turkey, Iraq, and Britain in 1926; the Iraq–Najd good-neighbor treaty in 1931 (settling disputes over the neutral-zone border exacerbated by the Ikhwan revolt); the Turko-Persian boundary accord in

Conclusion

Throughout the nineteenth century, European imperial expansion pressured the area stretching from northern Africa to the Iranian Plateau. The Long Great War was the final cataclysm that ended the Alawite, Ottoman, and Qajar political systems that had ordered the region for centuries. The modern Middle East was birthed during this pivotal period; the British and French did not just unilaterally impose artificial new political boundaries with the stroke of a pen. In contrast to the unidirectional causal arrow outlined by the Sykes-Picot Standard Narrative and to the latent methodological nationalism expressed in mandate-oriented interwar Middle East history, a methodologically relational account of a Long Great War that spanned from 1911 to the mid-1930s keeps a transregional scope in place and captures the complex interactions by which the modern Middle East's political stage was created.

A new narrative of the genesis moment of the modern Middle East that accounts for the contingencies, agencies, and complex interactions that occurred over time across the region—rather than using a simplifying shorthand of key dates and agreements—is important for understanding the early twentieth-century history of the region on its own terms. It is also highly relevant to the present as the region experiences a parallel moment of widespread upheaval and a range of political visions has again become thinkable as nation-state structures and boundaries become more unstable and fluid. Many of the early twenty-first-century friction points—in Kurdistan (Turkish, Iraqi, and Syrian), Iraq, Syria, Yemen, Libya, and the Rif region in Morocco—are places where contending political visions clashed so violently in the 1920s and 1930s and the collective memory of earlier polities—imagined, briefly realized, and denied—has been reactivated. It is possible

1932 (demarcated on the ground in 1934); the Franco-British Protocol on the Syria-Transjordan frontier in 1931 (demarcated in 1932); the League of Nations Syria–Iraq Boundary Commission of 1932; and the Franco-Turkish Mutual Aid Agreement of 1939 ceding the Sanjak of Alexandretta to Turkey.

that future historians will periodize a truly *long*, "hundred years" Great War over the political topography of the post-Ottoman Middle East that goes on into the twenty-first century. Analyzing continuities and changes over this century will require a relational, transregional historical approach, so well exemplified by mentors such as John Voll, that encompasses the breadth of much of the Islamic world.

References

Abu-Lughod, Janet. 1989. *Before European Hegemony: The World System A.D. 1250–1350*. Oxford: Oxford Univ. Press.

Akin, Yigit. 2018. *When the War Came Home: The Ottomans' Great War and the Devastation of an Empire*. Stanford, CA: Stanford Univ. Press.

Bayly, Chris, Sven Beckert, Matthew Connelly, Isabel Hofmeyr, Wendy Kozol, and Patricia Seed. 2006. "AHR Conversation: On Transnational History." *American Historical Review* 111, no. 5: 1441–64.

Beck, Ulrich. 2000. *What Is Globalization?* Cambridge: Polity Press.

Bourdieu, Pierre, and Loïc J. D. Wacquant. 1992. *An Invitation to Reflexive Sociology*. Chicago: Univ. of Chicago Press.

Burke, Edmund, III, and Robert Mankin, eds. 2018. *Islam and World History*. Chicago: Univ. of Chicago Press.

Burke, Edmund, III, and Kenneth Pomeranz, eds. 2009. *The Environment and World History*. Berkeley: Univ. of California Press.

Chernilo, Daniel. 2006. "Social Theory's Methodological Nationalism: Myth and Reality." *European Journal of Social Theory* 9, no. 1: 5–22.

Dunn, Ross, and Laura Mitchell. 2014. *Panorama: A World History*. New York: McGraw-Hill Education.

Dunn, Ross, Laura Mitchell, and Kerry Ward, eds. 2016. *The New World History: A Field Guide for Teachers and Researchers*. Berkeley: Univ. of California Press.

Emirbrayer, Mustafa. 1997. "Manifesto for a Relational Sociology." *American Journal of Sociology* 103, no. 2: 281–317.

Gerwarth, Robert. 2016. *The Vanquished: Why the First World War Failed to End*. New York: Farrar, Straus, Giroux.

Go, Julian, and George Lawson. 2017. "Introduction: For a Global Historical Sociology." In *Global Historical Sociology*, edited by Julian Go and George Lawson, 1–34. New York: Cambridge Univ. Press.

Iriye, Akira. 2013. *Global and Transnational History: The Past, Present, and Future*. Basingstoke, UK: Palgrave Macmillan.

Martins, Herminio. 1974. "Time and Theory in Sociology." In *Approaches to Sociology*, edited by John Rex, 246–93. London: Routledge & Kegan Paul.

Mazlish, Bruce. 1998. "Comparing Global History to World History." *Journal of Interdisciplinary History* 28, no. 3: 385–95.

Mortimer, Joanne Stafford. 1967. "Commercial Interests and German Diplomacy in the Agadir Crisis." *Historical Journal* 10, no. 3: 440–56.

Pennell, C. R. 1986. *A Country with a Government and a Flag: The Rif War in Morocco, 1921–1926*. Wisbech, UK: Middle East and North African Studies Press.

Provence, Michael. 2009. *The Great Syrian Revolt and the Rise of Arab Nationalism*. Austin: Univ. of Texas Press.

Rogan, Eugene. 2015. *The Fall of the Ottomans: The Great War in the Middle East*. New York: Basic Books.

Toynbee, Arnold J. 1927. *Survey of International Affairs 1925*. Vol. 1: *The Islamic World since the Peace Settlement*. London: Oxford Univ. Press, 1927.

Voll, John O. 1994a. "Islam as a Special World System." *Journal of World History* 5, no. 2: 213–26.

———. 1994b. *Islam: Continuity and Change in the Modern World*. 2nd ed. Syracuse, NY: Syracuse Univ. Press.

Williamson, Samuel. 2011. "German Perceptions of the Triple Entente after 1911: Their Mounting Apprehensions Reconsidered." *Foreign Policy Analysis* 7, no. 2: 205–14.

Wimmer, Andreas, and Nina Schiller. 2003. "Methodological Nationalism, the Social Sciences, and the Study of Migration: An Essay in Historical Epistemology." *International Migration Review* 37, no. 3: 576–610.

6

Turkish Liberal Conceptions of the Caliphate

1909–1924

York Norman

As a student of John Voll, I can safely say that the compatibility of Islam and democracy has been a major focus of his work. Voll and his writing partner John Esposito have succinctly argued that Islamic political identity has remained central to the development of more representational government not only in the Middle East but also in Africa as well as in South, Central, and Southeast Asia and beyond. Governments that have tried to suppress this identity and not seek strategies to include it in a democratic process have done so at their own peril (Esposito and Voll 1996, 192–202).

This chapter seeks to contribute to examining this broader issue in the history of the first years of the Republic of Turkey—my own current area of study—by examining a key moment of tension between the emerging secular state and its denial of the nation's roots in Islamic political culture: the abolition of the caliphate by the Turkish Grand National Assembly on March 1, 1924. Indeed, as Esposito and Voll have highlighted, this act effectively repudiated the Turkish claim to be the leading Islamic governing and judicial authority (1996, 26). The abolition of the caliphate also led to the abdication of Abdülmecid II, the last member of the Ottoman dynasty who served for that last year as the caliph, the symbolic head of state and the global Islamic community. The post of caliph had been formally instituted on November

1, 1922, to replace the sultan, the traditional title of the ruler of the Ottoman Empire. Mustafa Kemal (Atatürk) (1881–1938)—the heroic leader of the Turkish nationalist forces who, after having played a primary role in stopping the Allied invasion at Gallipoli during World War I, then led the Turkish nationalists to a successful victory over the Greeks from 1919 until 1922—was dedicated to a revolutionary program. He sought to use the enormous prestige and political capital he had built up as the savior of his nation to fundamentally remake it according to a progressive vision in which almost all of the former Ottoman Empire's political, cultural, and religious traditions would be jettisoned. Definitively ending the monarchy by terminating the caliphate paved the way for even more radical secular reforms, including the end of the Islamic legal courts, Islamic family law, and the pious foundations so central to customary urban life. Atatürk would also go so far as to ban Islamic schools and civic organizations, push for the abandonment of traditional Islamic head gear for both women and men,[1] and even attempt to secularize the Turkish language by shedding its traditional Arabic alphabet and eliminating as many Arabic and Persian loanwords as possible. The ultimate hope was that future generations of Turks, educated in a scientific manner free from the superstition and humiliation of their imperial past, could march in tandem to a new era of modern national greatness on par with even the most advanced Western nations (Hanioğlu 2011, 129–59).

Atatürk saw the French Revolution and the subsequent rise of Napoleon as a model for his own country to follow. He no doubt viewed the Ottoman sultan and caliph in much the same light as Louis XVI, a weak king who stood for a corrupt aristocratic order cynically supported by the neighboring European Great Powers. The toppling of that monarch after much complaint by the peasants and emerging middle classes came after a wave of nationalistic fervor, desire for social

1. Here I refer to the general Kemalist prohibition of women workers wearing head scarves in the public sector and the Hat Reform of 1925, which banned all men from wearing the fez or turban.

justice, and the attempt to establish a secular parliamentary republic. The fact that Napoleon, the country's most charismatic and capable general, established a military dictatorship over the new state likely also impressed Atatürk as a necessary precaution to prevent counter-revolution (Turan 2008, 178–82, and 2010, 9–17). The threat of religious and monarchist reaction loomed large not only to Napoleon and the French revolutionaries in the late eighteenth century but also to most of the Turkish political elite, who always saw the possibility that they might lose mass support to more traditional-minded Islamists intent on founding a state of their own. The solution, as far as Atatürk and his supporters were concerned, was to set up a regime founded on republican and ethnic Turkish nationalist principles.

Yet there were many in the new Turkish state who did not share Atatürk's revolutionary vision. Arguably the most significant of these opponents were those who believed in more gradual, evolutionary liberal reform. The bulk of these liberals were one-time supporters of the Young Turk Revolution, which in 1908 had led to the reestablishment of a constitutional monarchy in which the military played the role of guardian and the sultan the nominal head of state. Theirs was an elite movement that included a variety of military officers such as Rauf Orbay (1881–1964) and journalist/politicians such as Celal Nuri (İleri) (1888–1938), Lütfi Fikri (1872–1934), and Hüseyin Cahit (Yalçın) (1875–1957) (Demirel 2005). Many, such as Rauf Orbay, Celal Nuri, and Hüseyin Cahit, were official members of the Committee of Union and Progress (CUP), the dominant political organization within the Young Turk movement. Others, such as Lütfi Fikri, an opponent of the CUP's policies during World War I, were non-CUP-affiliated Young Turks (Birinci 2012, 40–42).

In general, these Turkish liberals believed that a parliamentary regime should be established with the caveat that there be a symbolic tie to the Ottoman dynasty and that Islam be recognized as the official state religion. Not to maintain these links to the past would, in their view, be an open invitation to reactionaries to reestablish an absolutist dynastic regime, such as that of Abdülhamid II (1875–1908/1909), the ruler whom the Young Turks had originally pressured to reconvene

Parliament in 1908 during the original takeover. Ironically, Abdülhamid II was the Ottoman ruler most responsible for conflating the traditional title of sultan with that of caliph, the successor of Prophet Muhammad and the head of Muslims globally. Abdülhamid II had done so to rally the Muslims of the empire in the wake of their country's defeat in the Russo-Turkish War (1877–78), which led to massive waves of Muslim refugees from significant lost territories in the Balkans. Ottoman sultans prior to Abdülhamid II had periodically claimed the title of caliph since 1517, when the Ottomans had originally established their authority over Mecca and the Hijaz. Arguments that the sultan was also the caliph and therefore responsible for the interests of the Islamic community had been stipulated in the Ottoman Constitution of 1876, as discussed later.

The Young Turks remembered with fear the events of April 1909, when the conservative partisans of Abdülhamid II briefly took over Istanbul and nearly succeeded in reinstating him as an absolutist ruler free of parliamentary oversight. Thereafter, the Young Turks would install Mehmet V (1909–18) and then his brother Vahdettin (1918–22) as sultan, but only on condition that they be subject to the laws of the Ottoman Constitution. The Constitution, originally promulgated in 1876, was revised under the Young Turks in 1909 to make sure that the sultan had no power to prorogue or disband the Parliament (Tanör 1985).

The wars that plagued the Ottoman Empire from 1911 until the foundation of the Turkish Republic in October 1923 largely discredited this political arrangement. The Ottoman Parliament continued to function only from 1909 until 1913, when Enver Pasha, a leading Young Turk military general, took over the state in a military junta. Parliament thereafter remained irrelevant up until the British occupation of Istanbul in October 1918 but was quickly prorogued when it denounced the British and declared its support of Atatürk and the Turkish nationalists. Those few deputies that could escape capture soon fled to Ankara, where they gathered under the auspices of Atatürk and his army (Mango 1999, 272–73). The Ottoman declaration of Islamic holy war against the British, French, and Russians in November 1914 tainted the caliphate in the wake of World War I because both the British and the French viewed it as a tool to incite rebellion among their numerous Muslim colonial subjects (Aksakal 2011). The sultanate likewise fell into disrepute during the British occupation of Istanbul because Vahdettin was always vulnerable to outside pressure. This was demonstrated most clearly in 1920, when he and his government were forced to agree to the humiliating Treaty of Sèvres, which ceded to foreign powers almost all Ottoman territories except for central Anatolia (Budak 2002, 202–17).

Nonetheless, the Turkish liberals believed that restoration of the previous constitutional monarchical system would be the most assured path to democratic development and that they could perhaps play the role of the loyal opposition to the ruling Turkish nationalists under Atatürk. They looked toward the model of Great Britain, where both the more conservative Tories and the more progressive Whigs worked under the rubric of a parliamentary system that recognized the monarchy and the historical legacy of the United Kingdom. The Turkish liberals saw the benefits Great Britain reaped from its living legal and literary traditions because these traditions meant that a country did not have to give up its past political and cultural identity in order effectively to modernize[2] (Celal Nuri [1339/1341H] 1923, 180–92; Fikri 2014).

The realities of Turkey in the immediate aftermath of the Independence War seriously limited liberal prospects, however. Allied recognition of Atatürk and the Parliament in Ankara as the true representatives of the Turkish nation in the Lausanne Treaty negotiations from July 1923 to August 1924 gave the revolutionaries the chance to gain international recognition of the new republic and the consequent abolition of the monarchy. Getting rid of the monarchy paved the way for abolishing the caliphate as well, given that the Ottoman

2. The Turkish liberals did not explicitly compare the Turkish caliph to the British king/queen in his/her role as the head of the Anglican Church, although this is a logical conclusion from their line of argument.

sultan traditionally held the title *caliph* as well. Atatürk and the Turkish nationalists also feared that if members of the dynasty remained, they could use the cause of Islamic unity to unite latent opposition, particularly in the conservative, Kurdish-majority region of eastern Anatolia (van Bruinessen 1992, 287–91). Indeed, Atatürk's main political testimony, the five-day speech he delivered in Parliament on October 15–20, 1927, highlighted a liberal plot among the former caliph, Muslim reactionaries, and liberal elements within the Grand National Assembly and army to instigate just such a rebellion. Yunus Nadi, one of Atatürk's chief publicists and the head of the Revolutionary Tribunal, characterized these liberals' desire to enshrine the caliphate through a constitutional act as a fallacy that would undermine the foundation of the future political structure of the country: "There are people who do not like the Republic; who conceal in their heads thoughts that they do not want to confess; such people are among us. The heads of these people will be smashed" (quoted in Atatürk 1981, 728).

It was nearly impossible under these conditions for the Turkish liberals to have any realistic chance of achieving their program of a constitutional monarchy with the caliph as a symbolic head of state. Their lonely voices could be heard primarily in newspaper articles and political speeches from 1923 to 1924, but they could not convince Atatürk or the Grand National Assembly to back away from a full abolition of the caliphate.

Even so, it is important to consider these Turkish liberal arguments in light of the consequences of abolishing that post. There was indeed a rebellion within a year in the Kurdish-majority regions of southeastern Anatolia led by the Nakshibandi Shaykh Said, who called for the restoration of that institution. Atatürk and the Revolutionary Tribunal soon also banned the liberal oppositional Progressive Republican Party (PRP, Terakkiperver Cumhuriyet Fırkası) on the charge that it, too, wished to restore that holy office. Full-fledged secularization of the laws, language, and popular customs soon alienated the large conservative elements of Turkish society, effectively dividing the country into two different spheres of political culture.

Having placed the debate over the caliphate in historical context, the chapter now turns to examine the Turkish liberal arguments for adopting a constitutional-bound version of the caliphate in order to prevent such political divisions. After examining Celal Nuri's initial liberal vision of this office in the first years of the Young Turk era, I then examine how this debate was eventually picked up by the liberal opposition to Atatürk in 1923 and 1924, resulting in the denunciation and defeat of that opposition by Atatürk and his revolutionary followers.

Celal Nuri first penned his thoughts on the caliphate and constitutional monarchy in the wake of the rebellion against the Young Turks in 1909. He wrote glowingly about Sahip Bey, the minister of religious affairs (*şeyhülislam*), who had written a religious opinion (*fetva*) arguing that Sultan Abdülhamid II needed to abdicate in favor of Mehmet V because he had failed to live up to his responsibilities as caliph. Thus, Sahip Bey's *fetva* conflated the office of sultan with the caliph in order to prevent tyrannical rule. Sahip Bey noted that the caliph could not be autocratic in nature because the caliphate was subject to the will of the Muslim community (Djelal Noury 1909, 3–4, 7). This principle of communal sovereignty went back to Abu Bakr, the beloved companion of Prophet Muhammad and the first caliph or "successor of the messenger of God." Abu Bakr announced after being chosen successor by consensus in 632 CE: "Oh mankind! I was appointed as your governor (*vali*) and commander (emir) yet I am hardly worthy of you. Support me if I do my task well and correct me when I am wrong. . . . The strongest among you is the weakest in my eyes because the strongest can abuse the rights of the weakest. . . . None of you has given up the principle to fight for justice. . . . All the time I have respected God, his Prophet, and his law. If I do not respect them, you are no longer required to listen to me" (quoted in Djelal Noury 1909, 10–11).[3]

3. I thank Dr. Birsen Bulmuş for graciously translating this article for me from French to English.

The Ottoman sultan Selim (1512–20) was the first to also assume the title of caliph after taking Mecca, Medina, and Hijaz from the Mamluks in 1517. In Celal Nuri's eyes, the sultan was thereafter subject to the principle of responsible popular governance. This principle was enshrined in the Constitution of 1876, which proclaims: "Ottoman sovereignty, which includes in the person of the Ottoman sovereign the supreme caliph, is subject to its rules from antiquity." This principle meant that a caliph who was no longer following the will of the Muslim community could be removed from office. Celal Nuri likened the "election" and possible "impeachment" of Mehmet V and other Ottoman caliphs to that of "the president of the United States of America" (Djelal Noury 1909, 20). This argument was thereby emblematic of the Young Turks' characterization of their successful struggle against Abdülhamid II and their restoration of parliamentary and constitutional rule as analogous to the American War of Independence and the formation of the United States.

Celal Nuri's views on the caliphate were also inspired in part by Wilfred Scawen Blunt's *The Future of Islam* (1882). After consulting a council (*şura*) made up of leading Islamic scholars from al-Azhar, the greatest Muslim Arab university based in Cairo, Blunt claimed that the caliph should be a member of the Hashemites, Prophet Muhammad's own lineage. Celal Nuri and other like-minded Turkish liberals were mindful in the run-up to World War I that the British planned to use the idea of a reformist caliphate to justify Arab separatism and to weaken Ottoman Turkish claims to be the leading Islamic power (Celal Nuri [1331H] 1913, 170; Dželal Nuri 1918). Therefore, it was necessary, according to Celal Nuri, to guarantee such a political reform in the Ottoman Empire in order to obviate this threat.

Celal Nuri's enthusiasm for the reform did not die in the wake of the Arab Revolt and the Ottoman surrender to the Allies at the end of World War I. In September 1919, he would propose a new Ottoman constitution that would endorse a "public sultanate" (*saltanat-i umumiye*) that would acknowledge Parliament's legislative authority but retain the caliph from the Ottoman dynasty as the symbolic head of state. This proposal would legitimize the Turkish nationalists who dominated the Parliament in the wake of the Greek occupation of Izmir in March 1919 and, in effect, demote Vahdettin, the reigning sultan, to an office where he could no longer appoint grand viziers and ministers amenable to the British, who were present in Istanbul until 1922.

Others made final efforts to retain the caliphate when the issue came up for debate following Atatürk's declaration of the Republic of Turkey on October 29, 1923. In an open letter published in the *Times* of London on November 23, 1923, Aga Khan and Ameer Ali, two prominent Indian Muslim spokesmen, urged Atatürk and the Turkish Grand National Assembly not to abolish the caliphate so that "the religious and moral solidarity of Islam" could be maintained. Eradicating the office, in their judgment, "would cause discord in the world of Islam" (Toynbee 1927, 571–72). Lütfi Fikri, the head of the Istanbul Bar Association and longtime member of the former Freedom and Accord Party (Hürriyet ve İtilaf Fırkası), who had fallen into disgrace because of his failure to support the Turkish nationalist movement during the Independence War, broached the topic after Aga Khan and Ameer Ali's letter was reprinted in a number of Istanbul newspapers on December 5 (Zürcher 1991, 36). In Fikri's opinion, there was no way to distinguish between the Grand National Assembly and the caliphate, which was to be chosen by the Assembly. Because of this, he concluded that the Assembly was duty bound to choose the caliph as the head of state (as given in Atatürk 2011, 283–84). Hüseyin Cahit, a prominent journalist and critic of Atatürk, openly wondered what other purpose there was for retaining the caliph and not the sultan besides recognizing the holy office as the head of state (Cahit 2014, 593–94).

Rauf Orbay, deputy head of the Assembly, saw the Assembly, not the commander of the armed forces, as having the sole right to decide the fate of the caliphate (Atatürk 1981, 679).

Yet the Grand National Assembly was hardly able to dictate terms to the military hero who had delivered independence to the country. None of these liberals was willing to go so far as to defend the right of Abdülmecid II to retain the caliphate per se, only to state that the Grand National Assembly was the only legitimate body to make the choice. To them, the symbolic value of the office as a way to unite the vast majority of the new state as sharing a common Sunni Muslim identity was more important than retaining the tie to the Ottoman dynasty, a house that had fallen into disrepute as a result of Vahdettin's alleged collaboration with the British during the Turkish Independence War. Thus, they feared a purely secular state might endanger those bonds of loyalty, particularly in the more conservative areas of central and southeastern Anatolia.

Rasih Efendi, a member of Parliament and a trained Muslim cleric, personally suggested that Atatürk become caliph. Moreover, if Atatürk were to accept this post on behalf of the Assembly, it would resolve the political dilemma. Atatürk had, after all, taken on the title of "Islamic holy warrior" (*gazi*)[4] when he had led the Turkish nationalist forces to victory. During that struggle, he had successfully appealed to the Muslims of Anatolia, regardless of ethnicity, in their struggle against foreign Christian occupation (Atatürk 1981, 702).

Atatürk declined this offer on the spot for a number of reasons (Atatürk 1981, 702). One of the problems, he declared, was the fact that the caliph was duty bound to lead all of the Muslim peoples, not just the Turks. By accepting this post, he would be diluting Turkey's independence. Moreover, he would lay the groundwork for the republic's enemies to plot for the return of the Ottoman dynasty. Had not the caliph's declaration of jihad in 1914 been responsible for World War I, which sealed the fate of the empire, and had not the sultan totally disgraced his throne by collaborating with the British in the conflict that followed? Most members of Parliament and Turkish nationalists in general strongly agreed with such arguments.

What Atatürk left unstated, however, was his desire to retain the political initiative as de facto head of state by making decisions on his own and then passing them on to the Grand National Assembly for

4. It should be noted that the term *gazi*, although often synonymous in Ottoman Turkish with the term *mucahid*, "one who wages jihad," also had specific tribal connotations that date back to the Seljuk era. Atatürk's choice of this term therefore emphasized his people as "Anatolian Muslims" (Özcan 1996, 443–45).

further approval. This initiative was indeed revolutionary because it broke from the Constitution of 1921, which stated that the executive as well as legislative authority was vested only in the Grand National Assembly. The new Constitution of 1924, approved on April 20, only some six weeks after the abolition of the caliphate, granted the president executive authority (Kocatürk 2000, 413).

Ironically, Celal Nuri played an important collaborative role with Atatürk in drafting the new constitution. Named as the secretary of the Constitutional Committee in the Grand National Assembly, Celal Nuri endorsed the position of president. The one concession that Celal Nuri presumably won from Atatürk and Yunus Nadi, the head of the Constitutional Committee, was the declaration that "the religion of the Turkish state is Islam" (Earle 1925, 89). Thus, Celal Nuri hoped the new regime would avoid "hostile secularism" (*lâ-dinilik*) and recognize the consultative, parliamentary nature of the government (*meşveret*) as an Islamic tradition that dated as far back as Prophet Muhammad and the first four caliphs (Celal Nuri [1339/1341H] 1923, 204–7).

Celal Nuri would be profoundly disappointed. Atatürk and the ruling Republican People's Party (RPP, Cumhuriyet Halk Partisi) removed the reference to Islam in the Constitution on April 10, 1928. Some ten years later, a new sentence was inserted describing Turkey's government as "republican, nationalist, populist, statist, secular, and revolutionary," an enumeration of the RPP's "six arrows" (Parla 2002, 25).[5] Popular response to this change was muted because Atatürk had established near unquestioned control of the state structure by the early 1930s, when the government tried to eliminate all civic society organizations that were not linked to the RPP (Bengi 2000, 229–30; Zürcher 2010b, 253).

Other liberal advocates of the reformist caliphate would also suffer defeat. Atatürk's Revolutionary Tribunal would find both Lütfi Fikri

5. These principles were adopted earlier into the RPP party program of 1931 (Zürcher 2010a, 181).

and Hüseyin Cahit guilty for their journalistic support of the caliphate, although the Grand National Assembly would ultimately pardon both men for this "crime" (Birinci 2012, 234). Rauf Orbay, one of the leaders of the liberal opposition PRP, would go to Europe in exile after his party was closed in 1925 (Sitembölükbaşı 2007).

Atatürk's shutting down of the Turkish liberals was final proof that there was no room for a consensus-based parliamentary order analogous to what had happened in England in the wake of the Glorious Revolution in 1688. The English system of peaceful reconciliation of "progressive" Whigs and "royalist" Tories had developed only after some fifty years of civil war in which their own monarch was beheaded. The strongest supporter of such consensus in England was an affluent commercial middle class that was about to lead its country into the Industrial Revolution (Coward and Gaunt 1985, 217).

Such a model of evolutionary political development lay in stark contrast with Turkish political realities. The Republic of Turkey had adopted a constitution and parliament shortly after its establishment in 1923, but they were initiated immediately on the heels of the Independence War. The Turkish middle class was decimated because it had been made up of significant numbers of Greek and Armenian merchants, who fled or died after supporting the losing side. Refugees flooded what was left of Turkey's urban centers, and much of the countryside was also suffering economic and social disarray (Göçek 1996, 1–7).

Atatürk, a Napoleon-like figure, was bent on reassembling the country under the protection of the army, the one institution that had survived the war intact. Compromising that command structure by lending power to the Assembly and the caliphate was, in Atatürk's view, a dangerous mistake because it would build a bridge between the Turkish liberals and what he saw as the reactionary masses. He would repress such voices if they would not heed his warning and accept the new republican regime he was putting in place (Atatürk 1981, 698–700).

Turkish liberals increasingly accepted that their country most resembled the France of the French Revolution. Indeed, figures such as Celal Nuri, Lütfi Fikri, and Hüseyin Cahit resembled the "Girondists."[6] Unable to secure a liberal world order with a symbolic constitutional monarchy, they were doomed to become the scapegoats for Atatürk and revolutionaries such as Yunus Nadi. They stood by speechless as Atatürk's radical secularization and authoritarianism would create an enduring political gulf between the progressive elite and an embittered conservative majority. Indeed, Shaykh Said, a Kurdish tribal leader, would raise the standard of revolt in February 1925, claiming that the Muslims of Anatolia should regain the caliphate. Atatürk felt so threatened by the revolt that he declared the Law of the Maintenance of Order and built an authoritarian regime that would punish not only the rebels but ban the opposition PRP and effectively end any dissent in the press (Zürcher 2010a, 171–72, 176–77). The rebellion exposed the fact that much of the population continued to identify with their religion rather than with their ethnic community—an issue that helps explain the challenge that political Islamic movements have posed toward the republic since that time until today.

References

Aksakal, Mustafa. 2011. "'Holy War Made in Germany'? Ottoman Origins of the 1914 Jihad." *War in History* 18, no. 2: 184–99.

Atatürk, Mustafa Kemal. 1981. *A Speech Delivered by Mustafa Kemal Atatürk*. Ankara: Başbakanlık Basımevi.

———. 2011. *Atatürk'ün Bütün Eserleri*. 3rd ed. Vol. 14. Edited by Şule Perinçek and others. Istanbul: Kaynak Yayınları.

Bengi, Hilmi. 2000. *Gazeteci, Siyasetçi, ve Fikir Adamı Olarak: Hüseyin Cahit Yalçın*. Ankara: Atatürk Araştırma Merkezi.

Birinci, Ali. *Hürriyet ve İtilaf Fırkası*. Vol. 2: *Meşrutiyet devrinde İttihat ve Terrakki'ye Karşı Çıkanlar*. Istanbul: Dergâh Yayınları, 2012.

6. Celal Nuri went so far as to laud the liberal French Constitution of 1791, promulgated shortly before the Jacobins took power (Celal Nuri [1339/1341H] 1923, 111–12).

Blunt, Wilfrid Scawen. 1882. *The Future of Islam*. London: Kegan, Paul, Trench.

Budak, Mustafa. 2002. *Misak-ı Milli'den Lozana: İdealden Gerçeğe Türk Dış Politikası*. Istanbul: Küre Yayınları.

Cahit, Hüseyin. 2014. "Şimdi de Hilafet Meselesi." In *Hilafet Risaleleri, Altıncı Cilt: Cumhuriyet Devri*, edited by Ismail Kara, 591–94. Istanbul: Klasik Yayınları.

Celal Nuri. [1331H] 1913. *Tarih-i İstikbal: Mesail-i Siyasi*. Istanbul: Yeni Osmanlı Matbaası.

———. [1339/1341H] 1923. *Taç Giyen Millet*. Istanbul: Cihan Biraderler Matbaası.

Coward, Barry, and Peter Gaunt. 1985. *The Stuart Age: England, 1603–1714*. New York: Routledge.

Demirel, Ahmet. 2005. "Milli Mücadele Döneminde Birinci Meclis'teki Liberal Fikirler ve Tartışmalar." In *Modern Türkiye'de Siyasi Düşünce: Cilt 7: Liberalizm*, edited by Murat Belge, Tanıl Bora, Ahmet Çiğdem, Bağış Erten, Murat Gültekingil, Ahmet İnsel, and Ömer Laçiner, 164–84. Istanbul: İletişim Yayınları.

Djelal Noury. 1909. *La Droit publique et l'Islam*. Constantinople: Imprimerie du "Courier d'Orient."

Dželal Nuri. 1918. "Panislamizam: Islam u prošlosti, sadašnjosti i budućnosti." Translated by Salih Bakamović. *Biser: List za Širenje islamske prosvjete* (Mostar, Bosnia-Herzegovina) 3, nos. 13–14 (July 1 and 15): 196–99.

Earle, Edward Mead. 1925. "The New Constitution of Turkey." *Political Science Quarterly* 40, no. 1: 73–100.

Esposito, John L., and John O. Voll. 1996. *Islam and Democracy*. New York: Oxford Univ. Press.

Fikri, Lütfi. 2014. "Meşrutiyet ve Cumhuriyet." In *Hilafet Risaleleri, Altıncı Cilt: Cumhuriyet Devri*, edited by Ismail Kara, 213–42. Istanbul: Klasik Yayınları.

Göçek, Fatma Müge. 1996. *Rise of the Bourgeoisie, Demise of Empire: Ottoman Westernization and Social Change*. New York: Oxford Univ. Press.

Hanioğlu, Şükrü. 2011. *Atatürk: An Intellectual Biography*. Princeton, NJ: Princeton Univ. Press.

Kocatürk, Utkan. 2000. *Atatürk ve Türkiye Cumhuriyeti Tarihi Kronolojisi: 1918–1938*. Ankara: Türk Tarih Kurumu Basımevi.

Mango, Andrew. 1999. *Atatürk: The Biography of the Founder of Modern Turkey*. New York: Overlook Press.

Özcan, Abdülkadir. 1996. "Gazi." In *İslam Ansiklopedisi*, 13:443–45. Ankara: Diyanet İşler Bakanlığı.

Parla, Tarla. 2002. *Türkiye'de anayasalar.* Exp. 3rd ed. Istanbul: İletişim.

Sitembölükbaşı, Şaban. 2007. "Hüseyin Rauf Orbay." In *İslam Ansiklopedisi*, 33:356–57. Ankara: Diyanet İşler Yayınları.

Tanör, Bülent. 1985. "Anayasal Gelişmelere Toplu Bir Bakış." In *Tanzimat'tan Cumhuriyet's Türkiye Ansiklopedisi*, edited by Murat Belge and others, 1:22–26. Istanbul: İletişim Yayınları.

Toynbee, Arnold J. 1927. *Survey of International Affairs 1925.* Vol. 1: *The Islamic World since the Peace Settlement.* London: Oxford Univ. Press.

Turan, Şerefettin. 2008. *Mustafa Kemal Atatürk: Kendine Özgü Bir Yaşam ve Kişilik.* Istanbul: Bilgi Yayınları.

———. 2010. *Atatürk'ün Düşünce Yapısını Etkileyen Olaylar, Düşünürler, Kitaplar.* Ankara: Türk Tarih Kurumu Basımevi.

Van Bruinessen, Martin. 1992. *Agha, Shaikh, and State: The Social and Political Structures of Kurdistan.* London: Zed Books.

Zürcher, Erik J. 1991. *Political Opposition in the Early Turkish Republic.* Leiden: Brill Academic.

———. 2010a. *Turkey: A Modern History.* 3rd ed. London: I. B. Tauris.

———. 2010b. *The Young Turk Legacy and Nation Building.* London: I. B. Tauris.

Part Four

Religion, Revival, Reform, and Globalization

A Contemporary Assessment

7

Taking Religion Seriously in the Study of Islamist Movements

Shadi Hamid

Why do people join groups such as the Muslim Brotherhood? Considering the potential costs—repression, surveillance, or denial of employment, for example—doing so is not necessarily "rational" in the strictest sense of the word. Any number of factors can contribute to an individual's decision to join, including a desire for community and belonging, economic grievances, underemployment and unemployment, rural–urban migration, and even opposition toward US foreign policy.[1]

But doesn't religion presumably play a role in a movement that claims to be fundamentally religious in orientation? As one Muslim Brotherhood official reminded me just before the Arab Spring began, many join the movement so they can "get into heaven." Discussing his own reasons for joining, he told me: "I was far from religion, and this was unsettling. Islamists resolved it for me" (interview, August 2010). These are deeply personal decisions that can involve something as weighty as one's relationship to God.

How do we model or measure a desire for paradise—for eternal salvation—from the standpoint of political science? It might be tempting to dismiss pronouncements like that of the Brotherhood official

1. For incentive structures of Islamist activists, see Wickham 2002.

as irrational bouts of fancy. However, if one looks at it another way, what could be more rational than wanting eternal salvation and doing whatever possible in this life to make such an outcome more likely in the next?

Political scientists, myself included, have often viewed religion and ideology more generally as "epiphenomenal"—products of a given set of material factors. They are things to be explained rather than things that have real explanatory power of their own. In political science and in the humanities more generally, the reluctance to attribute too much (or any) causal power to religion also derives from understandable fears about essentializing an entire faith and its practitioners.[2] Here, the criticisms of Edward Said and a new generation of scholars helped to temper the sometimes singular focus on "Islam" emanating from academics such as Bernard Lewis in the 1960s and 1970s. Lewis in particular found himself in tense exchanges with Said that defined some of the contours of a still ongoing debate over how to talk about Islam and, perhaps just as importantly, *who* should talk about it. It didn't help that after the attacks on September 11, 2001, Lewis achieved considerable influence among top US officials, including Vice President Dick Cheney. Lewis—and his ideas around Islam's centrality and causal power—became associated with (and tainted by) a US invasion of Iraq that was nearly unanimously opposed by Middle East scholars (Buruma 2004).

The rise of the Islamic State in Iraq and Syria, or ISIS, brought new attention to this set of questions, with endless discussions about how "Islamic" the group actually was. Here, the understandable instinct was to establish as much distance between a group that seemed to have no limit to its savagery and the faith that its members claimed was theirs alone. But to insist that ISIS was not Islamic was to run the risk of dismissing the relevance of religious motivations and religious appeals to the group's rise. Once one decided that ISIS had "nothing to do with Islam," as United Nations secretary-general Ban Ki-moon

2. On the dangers of essentializing, see Mneimneh 2016.

once put it (Ban 2014), it became that much harder to assess how the group's interpretations of Islamic law, however perverted or unrepresentative, might shape its approach to governance.

Bringing Religion Back in—But Carefully

John Voll was a key interpreter in the emerging debate over the Islamic revival and its causes that began in earnest in the 1970s. At the time, it was not clear how long the phenomenon would last. Some academics dismissed its staying power or simply did not feel it required changing traditional approaches to studying the region. Others, such as Lewis, seemed to overstate the singular influence of religion and, perhaps more problematically in the eyes of some, did so without the requisite sympathy for the people and cultures being studied. There isn't one right way to write about Islam's role in politics, but there are certainly better ways. To read John Voll's book *Islam: Continuity and Change in the Modern World* is to be struck by how a book published in 1982 could preview, anticipate, and address so many of the debates and arguments over Islamist movements that would grow in importance in the 1990s—particularly in light of the Algerian military coup against the country's largest Islamist party—and intensify in the 2000s and 2010s.

Voll quoted Tareq Ismael, who could write in 1974 that "in recent years Islam has so declined in authority and vitality that it has become a mere instrument for state policy, although it is still active as a folk religion" (1982, 2). Voll, however, had a different set of starting premises. "This book," he wrote, "is based on the assumption that the currently visible resurgence of Islam is not simply the last gasp of a dying religious tradition" (2).

But even if this Islamic resurgence was real, wasn't it still possible that religion was a cover for more prosaic concerns or that Islam was "providing familiar forms for basically non-Islamic ideas and institutions" (Voll 1982, 2)? In this reading, Islam is a mode and a means but rarely an end unto itself. Even when faith is expressed with seeming sincerity, the individuals who express it may be suffering from false consciousness, thinking that they are doing things for the noble cause of religion or for God when what's really driving them is something altogether simpler and considerably less romantic. "Another alternative," cautioned Voll, "is that the Islamic community is entering a new phase, not the end, of its history" (1982, 2).

The argument that Islam still mattered and would continue to matter may seem more obvious today, but it wasn't at the time. In 1974, the Muslim Brotherhood in Egypt was only just emerging from prison, so it wasn't self-evident that the Brotherhood and Islamism more generally would rise so rapidly in subsequent years. However, to assume as a default position that modernization, through its own inherent power, could so definitively render Islam politically irrelevant suggested a blind spot. It was possible to look at Egypt during the so-called liberal era and see nothing but secular parties such as the Wafd and the Liberal Constitutional Party dominating parliamentary life (Gordon 1989, 193). According to this thinking, history is unidirectional, necessarily leading to Westernization and modernization. But even where Western or secular ideas were being adopted, they were being retranslated by actors—Islamist and secular alike—who themselves had agency.

It was precisely during this liberal era that an illiberal or post-liberal movement such as the Muslim Brotherhood was reaching its peak, not measured in electoral power (it had none) but in sheer numbers. By the 1940s, as many as six hundred thousand Egyptians—in a population of only around twenty million—were Brotherhood members, a proportion it would never come close to during or after Egypt's Islamic revival decades later (Mitchell 1969, 328). To focus only on parliamentary or elite politics was to miss a strong and resilient undercurrent of explicitly Islamic and Islamist sentiment.

There was also another bias—namely, that coercion and repression could kill an idea that enjoyed broad popular support. It is certainly true that Gamal Abdel Nasser had achieved a level of popularity that made everything else seem irrelevant, but Nasser could reach such unrivaled dominance only by employing extreme levels of repression against the Brotherhood and its organizational structures. In this sense, the dominance of Arab nationalism and Arab secularism was *not* the natural outcome of political and electoral competition.

Voll problematized the simplistic narrative of "secularism winning over Islam." Arab nationalism, rather than being exclusively one thing or another, was a fusion of Arab, nationalist, and Islamic concepts. More importantly, ostensibly secular governments, however socialist or progressive they claimed to be, made ready use of Islam in both domestic and foreign policy. They nationalized their religious establishments (as in the case of al-Azhar in Egypt and Zaytouna in Tunisia), making the state *more* intimately involved in matters of religious production. There never stopped being a "correct" Islam that regimes wanted their subjects to embrace—or at least to acquiesce to. However authoritarian these regimes were, they were not—and could not be—insulated from the reality that faith, to varying degrees, continued to play a significant role in the everyday lives of citizens.

In the 1950s and 1960s, Arab nationalism was capable of attracting and inspiring a large number of Arabs (without necessarily requiring them to do away with their Islamic commitments). Yet its weakness, as would soon become clear, was that its legitimacy was inextricably linked to performance, whether with respect to military prowess or economic development. As an ideology, Arab nationalism had little intrinsic value beyond its ability to provide something temporal and tangible. After the trials of colonialism, it could and did offer pride, dignity, and self-esteem, but those sentiments eroded under the weight of accumulated failure.

Although Islamist ideologies are not immune from some of these same concerns, they tend to be more resilient in the face of material and military disappointments. Islamists might fail, but Islamism, broadly understood, is an argument about the centrality of religion in public life, an argument that is difficult to discredit. As Francis Fukuyama writes in *The Origins of Political Order* (2011), "Religious beliefs are never held by their adherents to be simple theories that can be discarded if proved wrong; they are held to be unconditionally true, and there are usually heavy social and psychological penalties attached to asserting their falsehood" (38).

But although it is difficult to "disprove" Islamism on performance grounds, the link between commitment to the faith and temporal success—whether in terms of military, technological, or scientific progress—is in some ways still a profound one for Islam, and this is a theme that Voll returns to. The predicament Muslims found themselves in from the seventeenth century onward—which came to a head under the indignities of colonialism—was one of making sense of a growing dissonance. If Islam was the one true faith, then why were Muslims failing and losing ground to other faiths and empires? Unlike Christianity, which was in a relatively weak position in its early centuries, Islam had achieved fairly consistent, impressive earthly success from its founding. Until the modern era, there was never a period without a great Islamic empire or caliphate or even several empires that coexisted in various parts of the Muslim world. The various religious reform movements emerging in the eighteenth and nineteenth centuries that Voll documents in painstaking detail were attempts to respond to the increasingly inescapable reality that "the link between faith and worldly success appeared to have been broken" (1982, 351).

The Role of Doctrine

Ideas matter, but they don't matter in isolation, and the ideas themselves do not appear unmediated out of some unchanging essence, as if they always were and always will be. Ideas—and in this case religious ideas—emerge out of the complex interaction between doctrine and theology, on one hand, and the political context in which those ideas are first introduced or revealed, on the other.[3]

When it comes to how Muslims interpret their faith, however, the role of doctrine can easily be overstated, as if Muslims passively

3. Muslim Brotherhood branches in the Persian Gulf have received relatively little scholarly attention, in particular those in the United Arab Emirates, Qatar, and Kuwait. These oil-rich countries with small populations present vastly different contexts from the rest of the region. Not surprisingly, then, we see Brotherhood movements evolving there in distinctive ways. See Freer 2018, 18–21, 25–27.

absorb Qur'anic verses and then proceed to act as mere automatons, instructed, absent free will, by divine command. Even if this description were somewhat close to the truth, it would not tell us *which* interpretation of the Qur'anic verses in question Muslims would act according to. At the same time, it is not quite right to minimize the power of doctrine altogether. In 1982, Fouad Ajami wrote, "The turning toward religious symbols is in very small measure explained by the doctrine itself, by Islam's classical teachings" (15). Doctrine doesn't necessarily shape political behavior, but it does make the resort to religion more or less likely in a given context, all other things being equal. As Voll remarks, "It is often noted that Islam has not experienced a huge change similar to the Protestant Reformation in Europe, and some feel that such a change is needed if Islam is to adapt successfully to the challenge of modernity. Such a viewpoint is thought provoking, but it often ignores the fundamental differences between the structures of Western and Islamic societies" (1982, 3–4).

Voll also writes that "the success or failure of actual communities of Muslims becomes a major concern, with political structures, economic practices, and social customs all being relevant to the historic vocation of faithful Muslims" (1982, 7). Presumably, this relevance has at least *something* to do with a theology that draws heavily from the fact that Muhammad was both a prophet and the head of a proto-state in Medina, where his religious and political functions were intertwined (and, from a Muslim perspective, not by accident but by design). If in an alternative history Muslims after the Prophet's death were not in a position to govern territory, then early Islam would have needed to focus on a different set of questions, including the challenge of how to live as a minority community under the constraining and even repressive rule of others.

Not all religions are the same, and not all religions are the same when it comes to their relationship to law, politics, and governance. As Michael Cook notes, religions are not "putty in the hands of exegetes" (2014, xv). If they were, that condition would undermine the very fact of religious difference and diversity, with each faith tradition characterized by its own theological contentions and methodological approaches.

But to simply state that Islam plays an outsize role in politics (at least compared to Christianity, in particular Western Christianity) tells us relatively little about the nature of that role. To understand that role requires looking beyond powerbrokers and urban elites, which can be difficult to do in authoritarian societies where access is often restricted. Although those who advocate for and organize politically around Islam's centrality in public life are today generally "conservative" in the sense of subscribing to a stricter interpretation of Islamic law, they wouldn't have been considered as such in the premodern era.

Before the relatively recent introduction of secularism—in the sense of reducing Islam's relevance to political authority and privatizing the role of religion—Islam's status and place in public life was inescapable and, more importantly, unquestioned. It imbued nearly everything. The scholar of Islamic law Wael Hallaq refers to Islam's "overarching moral apparatus" and "hegemonic moral system" (2013, 11). Hallaq and other chroniclers of medieval Islam—as well as no doubt many modern Muslims—sometimes idealize the shari'a for what it claimed to be rather than what it actually was. But they are right to point to its enveloping power. In being everywhere and imbuing nearly everything, the shari'a had no need to announce itself. No one was an Islamist because everyone was.

Within this uncontested Islamic sphere, there was considerable diversity not only in terms of narrower questions of ritual and practice but also in competing and sometimes conflicting philosophical and metaphysical approaches to Islam (captured, for example, in the ideological contests between the Mutazalites and Asharis). Although Islam's public role was constant, this diversity meant that some interpretations of this role were, in modern parlance, more "conservative," whereas others were more "progressive," with a pronounced emphasis on rationality and reason as a means of divining God's will. In other words, just because Islam plays a central or even dominant role in politics doesn't mean that this role is invariably a rigid one.[4]

4. In various caliphates, perhaps most notably in the Abbasid Caliphate and in Andalusia, Islam, by definition, played a central, dominant role but produced what

This diversity within conservatism also applies to the world of mainstream Islamism today. Islamists in Tunisia and Morocco have increasingly been developing a different approach to questions of pluralism, freedom of expression, and gender equality than their counterparts in, say, Egypt, Malaysia, and Pakistan.[5] Each of the Muslim Brotherhood or Muslim Brotherhood–inspired organizations in these countries began with a similar set of starting ideological premises based on what might be called the Brotherhood "school of thought." Yet one can track how over time this basic ideological orientation evolved in sometimes quite different ways in these different countries through the complex interaction between religious ideas and otherwise mundane political realities. The importance of local and regional context—as well as of the diverse relationships between each movement and the regimes it lives under—shapes Islamism, providing incentives and constraints for diverging approaches to religious and political behavior.

Islamism as a Vehicle of Democratization

In 1996, John Esposito and John Voll argued that Islamist parties not only had a right to participate in the democratic process but also could be, and often were, vehicles for democratization. At the time, this was a controversial argument; in some ways, it still is. In this respect, Voll's influence can be felt among a younger generation of scholars who were willing to suspend their personal ideological preferences to understand who Islamists were rather than merely condemning what they believed.

Looking back, Esposito and Voll's linking of Islamism and democratization was more prescient than they may have expected, particularly in light of developments during and after the Arab Spring. In a

---

would today be considered relatively progressive theological positions. On this topic, see, for example, Ahmed 2016.

5. For more on the distinctive approaches taken by Ennahda in Tunisia and the Justice and Development Party in Morocco, see Marks 2014 and Spiegel 2015.

sort of sequel work, they, with coauthor Tamara Sonn, write: "Thus, while in Europe, secular discourse was the vehicle of political opposition to authoritarian governments, in Muslim-majority countries, religious discourse has often expressed populist opposition to authoritarianism" (Esposito, Sonn, and Voll 2016, 25).

To understand how Islamist movements were challenging autocrats and why they were increasingly adopting the language of (at least procedural) democracy required understanding not only the region's changing political context but also the doctrinal justifications that Islamists were growing more comfortable using. As Esposito and Voll wrote earlier, "It is important to examine the conceptual resources within Islam for democratization" (1996, 7).

There have long been arguments within the classical Islamic tradition not necessarily for dictatorship itself but for obeying or resigning oneself to a despot (as long as the despot is nominally Muslim and does not prevent believers from practicing their religion). But this view was largely one of and by elites, including the religious scholars and clerics who saw themselves as protectors of the faith. Rebellion threatened to upturn and undermine the security and order that allowed Muslims to observe Islam. And most rebellions, despite any initial idealism they may have had, led merely to other forms of dynastic rule. With the spread of Islam and the development of a corpus of law, so much had been gained that a conservative bent inevitably seeped into legal judgments around obedience and rebellion, in the process creating, if not in intent then in effect, an intellectual and theological framework for the justification of authoritarianism.

But what were Islamists if not modernists, inherently suspicious of the preserved wisdom of the past? Almost by definition, the Islamic reformers of the eighteenth and nineteenth centuries—rising to prominence before *Islamism* became a recognizable term—respected the Islamic tradition while at the same time feeling unbound by it. They had to adapt to a radically new political context. The state, either administered or backed by colonial powers, was changing: it was becoming centralized and domineering, finding new ways to intrude into both public and private life. By the second half of the twentieth century, the modern state was a far cry from the caliphates of the premodern era, reaching levels of repression that the old sultans could only begin to imagine (and perhaps envy).

Conceivably, those who wished to challenge autocrats, monarchs, or colonial powers could have relied on secular ideologies. They didn't. Islam proved a powerful resource, offering a natural language of defiance and opposition that these reformers and would-be revolutionaries could readily draw upon. Because Muslim-majority societies retained relatively high levels of religious belief and awareness, even after secularization, Islam was one of the few things that could speak to a large cross-section of citizens.

Islamists didn't particularly have to stretch themselves to find Islamic concepts that could sustain opposition to newly independent regimes that also happened to be quite repressive. The Islamist project was, at least in one sense, an attempt to reconcile premodern Islamic law with the modern nation-state, however unideal the latter was. Ideas around the equality of citizens and representative democracy, particularly in the 1980s and intensifying after the triumphalism of the post–Cold War period, were shaping Islamists' behavior and their desire to enter parliamentary politics. But even well before this, Islamist ideologues such as Abul A'la Mawdudi were repurposing foundational Islamic concepts for expanding political participation. One such concept was *tawhid*, or oneness. In theory as well in practice, *tawhid* "might be used as a basis for a nondemocratic state" (Esposito and Voll 1996, 25)—as it has been by Salafi movements—but, here, it also offered a rallying cry for egalitarian politics. *Tawhid* itself might not be obviously antiauthoritarian, but taking theological ideas seriously enables scholars to understand the intuitive, if not necessarily the intellectually coherent, power of an idea such as *tawhid* that can inspire and animate political action. As Esposito and Voll write, "Tawhid provides the conceptual and theological foundation for an active emphasis on equality within the political system" (1996, 25). They quote the Iranian revolutionary and sociologist 'Ali Shari'ati, who argued that in "the world-view of tawhid, man fears only one power" (quoted on 25). *Tawhid*, in theological terms, speaks to the uncompromising indivisibility of God, intended to draw a strong contrast with Christian doctrine. But it could be (and was) broadened to an antiauthoritarian message: repressive leaders who had no interest in the consent of the governed—raising themselves as absolute arbiters of mercy and punishment—were undermining and challenging God's absolute dominion.

Polarization Not Because of Religion but over Religion

A common question that Middle East scholars have had to contend with, perhaps now more than before, is the question of authoritarian durability (Bellin 2004). One answer—that Islam and democracy are incompatible—has (fortunately) fallen out of favor, yet this doesn't mean that debates over religion and politics are unimportant when assessing the causes of authoritarian persistence. To understand why requires reflecting on why the words *Islamism* and *Islamist* even exist.

The very idea of Islamism would have been met with confused looks and blank stares at any point prior to the nineteenth century. As Voll, Hallaq, and others have outlined in considerable detail, modernity and Islamism were and are inseparable. It is difficult to imagine one without the other. Voll writes, for example, that "it may be possible that part of the Islamic resurgence is putting modern sentiments into Islamic garb, but it may also be possible to discern new and modern forms of the continuing Islamic vitality" (1982, 2; see also Hallaq 2013). This Islamic impulse, then, is a long-standing one, but it has adapted and evolved in response to and in the context of modern concepts of democratic participation and the nation-state.

Islamism, in other words, is a relatively new introduction in the Middle East. Its insertion into politics is a product of foundational divides over the appropriate role for Islam in public life. Islamism—an attempt to make Islam into a self-conscious and "applied" political program—cannot exist without its (perceived) opposite, secularism.

The struggle to establish a legitimate political order in Middle Eastern nations—with disagreements about Islam informing perceptions of legitimacy—has remained unresolved. In this sense, Islam itself is not the problem. The problem is and has been the continued inability to resolve the questions of whether, how, and to what extent to accommodate Islam's public role and specifically its relationship to the state and its legal status vis-à-vis "secular" law and legal sources. Accordingly, the turmoil of the Arab Spring and its aftermath is only the latest iteration of the failure to come to anything resembling a consensus around basic questions of what it means to be a citizen and what it is to be a state. Islamism, in its various iterations, offers a particular set of answers to the question of legitimacy and the nature of the state. But in offering its own answers, it provokes strong and sometimes violent responses from those who see even mild forms of Islamist politics as an existential threat, as became all too clear during the Arab Spring. In short, no account of authoritarian durability is complete without reference to the contested role of religion.[6]

Faith as an Advantage

Ideological polarization over these foundational questions has consistently undermined democratization in countries as diverse as Algeria and Egypt. Even in countries that appear less ideologically polarized and where the Muslim Brotherhood has never been banned, such as Jordan, fear of Islamist dominance at the polls remains a major factor contributing to authoritarian durability (Hamid 2014, 101–6). The striking success of the Muslim Brotherhood and independent Islamists in Jordan's landmark elections in 1989, the freest the country has ever seen, provoked a backlash, leading to the passing of new electoral legislation to limit Islamist gains.

Ideological divides are fueled by a lopsided power imbalance between Islamists and their opponents. In religiously conservative societies where large constituencies favor (or at least say they favor)

6. The contested role of religion is no longer just a Middle East preoccupation, if it ever was. The role of Islam and Muslim minorities in public life has become a central political and ideological divide even in the most advanced Western democracies.

implementation of Sharia, liberals and secularists fear that democratization will reflect this religious conservatism in the form of electoral support for Islamist parties and Islamist policies. It is not enough, however, to condemn liberals and other non-Islamists for what are effectively antidemocratic attitudes. Their fears, after all, are understandable—liberals, by definition, are likely to prioritize liberalism over democracy if the two come into conflict. More importantly, these fears reflect a political reality, one that is difficult to alter.

For example, in Egypt liberal parties underperformed in successive elections and referenda in the 2011–13 period, contributing to a perception that liberals were fundamentally disadvantaged by democratic competition. If liberals were underperforming, was it simply a matter of building a party organization—and of the time required to do so—or did it also reflect something deeper? As the liberal activist and parliamentary candidate Shadi Taha put it, referring to his Islamist counterparts, "To them, it's faith. You tell me how you can add faith to liberalism, and I'll build you an organization like [the Brotherhood's]. That's why religion always beats politics in any match" (interview by the author, November 20, 2011).

In the early days of democratic transition, the field tends to be quite crowded with dozens of parties and hundreds of candidates. It can be confusing to those casting votes for the first time, with many of those who run repeating the same old platitudes. Who, after all, *isn't* for fighting unemployment and combating poverty? Islamist parties are able to distinguish themselves because they're immediately identifiable as having a particular ideological orientation. Liberal parties in the Arab world, for their part, are not free of ideology. Liberalism is also an ideological orientation. However, because liberalism and more secular approaches to politics more generally do not have a strong natural constituency outside of major urban centers, liberal parties do not tend to emphasize their liberalism. They may even refuse to identify as such. As Mustafa al-Naggar, founder of the Justice Party, explained it to me during the campaign for Egypt's first free parliamentary elections in 2011, "We help people understand liberalism through behavior and example, through an understanding of citizenship." At the same time, he said, "none of us is using the word *liberalism* because for the Egyptian street 'liberalism' equals disbelief" (interview, October 15, 2011).

It is somewhat ironic that in countries plagued by economic crisis, the one thing that dominated public discourse during the Arab Spring was the role of religion in politics, something that has relatively little day-to-day impact on the lives of ordinary people. Looked at another way, though, it is little surprise that foundational questions over religion's role in public life and the relationship between Islam and the state were—and certainly *felt* as if they were—existential for many citizens. And this is not necessarily unique to the Arab world or Muslim-majority contexts. As we are seeing throughout Europe, the United States, Israel, India, the Philippines, and numerous other countries, cultural and identity-based cleavages have increasingly predominated over more traditional class and economic divides. In such contexts, to be without a discernible (or popular) ideology is to join an electoral battle with a hand tied behind one's back.

This holds even in more secularized contexts such as Tunisia, where the Islamist party Ennahda has remained the largest single party in Parliament despite the fact that a secular party, Nidaa Tounes (Call of Tunisia), won the parliamentary and presidential elections in 2014. In 2016, Nidaa split into two, once again illustrating a different kind of secular–Islamist imbalance, this time regarding internal cohesion and organizational discipline. Nidaa Tounes always lacked real coherence because it was mostly an otherwise unwieldy coalition of interests, individuals, and smaller parties that couldn't quite agree on much beyond their staunch opposition to Ennahda. In one study of Tunisian secularists, Anne Wolf writes that the "focus on anti-Islamism is one of [Nidaa's] greatest weaknesses" (2014). But what other option did Nidaa Tounes have? Without a clear ideological or programmatic raison d'être of its own—it included both leftists and old-regime businessmen, after all—it needed, at the very least, an enemy against which to define itself.

How Religion Affects Party Structures

In Tunisia, anti-Islamism may have been effective in an election, but it was unlikely to be enough while trying to govern, especially when not everyone agreed on exactly *how* anti-Islamist to be. Without an obvious ideological impulse, it was also challenging to get Nidaa Tounes members to attend parliamentary sessions because, for many, getting into Parliament was its own end rather than a means to a particular policy or ideological objective. The attendance gap between Ennahda and Nidaa Tounes was significant (Marsad Majles n.d.), and similar gaps have been evident in Egypt (Shehata and Stacher 2006).

Such attendance gaps hint at another important difference between Islamist and non-Islamist parties. Islamist parties are not traditional political parties. They act politically with a mind to nonpolitical considerations. Most are political wings of religious movements or at least remain tied to such movements through informal links and overlapping memberships. To the extent it is permitted to do so, the Muslim Brotherhood, as a religious and social *movement*, operates as a kind of state-within-a-state with its own set of parallel institutions, including hospitals, schools, banks, cooperatives, daycare centers, thrift shops, social clubs, facilities for the disabled, and even Boy Scout troops. There is also the preaching (*da'wa*) wing of the organization, which is in some ways the foundation upon which everything else is built. On this more basic level, the Brotherhood is concerned with strengthening the religious and moral character of its members through an extensive educational process that has its own structured curriculum.

When leaders of the parent movement establish an affiliated political party in a given country, they always are at pains to say that the party will be independent. Even where these intentions are real, it is exceedingly difficult to disentangle the parent and the child. The new party inevitably depends on the broader movement for everything from financial backing to grassroots support, name recognition, and, perhaps most importantly, legitimacy. However, although this dependence can be a problem from the standpoint of defining party–movement relations and stoking the liberal and secular groups' fears, it is a boon to the party in electoral terms, giving it tremendous mobilizational capacity and organizational discipline.

The party benefits from the movement's member base, which offers up a ready population of committed supporters, volunteers, and voters who need no convincing. In Egypt, for example, Brotherhood "election marches" were deceptively simple but difficult for non-Islamist parties to replicate. This meant that in many neighborhoods, particularly in less-central areas, prospective voters would generally hear of (and from) Brotherhood volunteers but not necessarily from volunteers for other parties. For the Brotherhood, the gathering point was almost always outside a mosque just after the evening prayer, which Brotherhood members were likely to be attending anyway, thus guaranteeing the group a critical mass with relatively minimal effort.

In one march I attended in the Ard al-Liwa' neighborhood in November 2011, the participants, numbering in the low hundreds, organized themselves in rows of three or four, often filling the width of the street. Two of the Brotherhood's parliamentary candidates led the way, introducing themselves to residents and shaking hands. Behind them, the marchers were trailed by a pickup truck with a loudspeaker. If you happened to be in the area, the march was impossible to ignore. There were around thirty designated "coordinators"—all volunteers—each of whom had a laminated Freedom and Justice Party card hanging around his or her neck, engaged residents in conversation, and signed them up if they appeared interested. Volunteers were at pains to repeat at regular intervals that the Freedom and Justice Party was founded by the Brotherhood (*hizb essasuha al Ikhwan*). There was no effort to paint the party as a distinct entity. As a young volunteer explained to me, "Some people still don't know it's the Brotherhood's party, so this is something we always try to make clear" (interview, November 2011).

Theoretically, other political parties could have tried to do something similar, but even parties that had, at least on paper, tens of thousands of members did not necessarily have the ability to turn out enough volunteers in enough areas. Here, again, the advantages of having a movement over a party were critical. For a member of the Brotherhood, participating in an election march wasn't merely about expressing a political preference; it was effectively a religious obligation. All members were expected, by virtue of being members, to do their part and commit to supporting the movement's party during the campaign.

In traditional parties, becoming a member is usually fairly easy and comes with relatively few requirements or obligations (and in many democracies often no obligations at all). Contrast this with Brotherhood branches and affiliates, where each member is part of an *usra*, "family," that meets on a weekly basis to discuss religious topics and other matters relevant to the organization. Until fairly recently, even the most "progressive" of Islamist movements, Tunisia's Ennahda, was both a movement and a party simultaneously—reflected in its formal designation "Hizb Harakat al-Nahda," the Ennahda Movement Party. Because Ennahda was still, in part, a movement, there were conditions for becoming a "party" member. Someone had to vouch for your moral character, a process known as *tazkiya*. Those who were interested in joining were a self-selecting group. At some level, this is true of all parties, but in the case of Brotherhood and Brotherhood-inspired movements, the private behavior of party applicants is relevant, which can include activities such as alcohol consumption and mixed-gender interaction.

"Party-movements," as opposed to parties, are well suited for Middle Eastern contexts in light of persistently high levels of repression. Collective-action dilemmas are always a feature of any political and social activity, but these dilemmas are even more pronounced in countries that have suffered for long periods under authoritarian rule, where citizens resign themselves to thinking that nothing will change because nothing has changed. Religious commitments and motivations help inspire action under these circumstances, even when political or electoral gratification might be delayed for decades.

Conclusion

Ideologies can sometimes appear as revelations, existing outside and beyond time and space. But the religious and ideological gulfs that today sometimes seem insurmountable were not necessarily inevitable. They became what they are. They were, in a sense, manufactured. And once the "Islamist–secular" divide—to use an oversimplified description—solidified, it was difficult to undo.

The divide gained its own momentum. Individuals played an important role, choosing what to believe in and what to oppose at particular historical junctures. Whereas the main ideological divide during early (and often failed) democratic transitions in western Europe often fell along class and economic lines, the cleavage in Middle Eastern countries became a "religious" one—even if it wasn't about Islam per se but rather about disagreement over what Islam meant in relation to the nation-state and political legitimacy. Over time, these dimensions of political competition and conflict have become institutionalized—or, in the terminology of Seymour Lipset and Stein Rokkan (1967), "frozen" in the form of groups and parties and "sides" that self-define as being more or less secular or more or less religious in orientation.

The examples of two of the most influential "secular" and "Islamist" political figures of the twentieth century—Gamal Abdel Nasser and Muslim Brotherhood ideologue Sayyid Qutb—capture how what begins as ideological fluidity can give way to something deeper and rigidly demarcated. Nasser was always a nationalist, but he was also, in effect, an Islamist. It isn't a secret that Nasser was a Muslim Brotherhood member in the 1940s. But some recent studies, including Fawaz Gerges's *Making the Arab World* (2018), show that Nasser's relationship to the Brotherhood was closer than is generally acknowledged. In an interview by Gerges, Farid Abdel Khaleq, a close aide to Brotherhood founder Hasan al-Banna and to al-Banna's successor Hassan al-Hudaybi, recounted how Nasser "trained [Brotherhood] youth on how to use firearms. I saw him with my own eyes" (166). Khaled Mohieddin, one of Nasser's closest associates, recalled that Nasser was "ecstatic" about joining the Brotherhood's secret paramilitary wing, the so-called Special Apparatus (166).

Yet the story of Nasser and Qutb—friends turned enemies—ultimately points to the stickiness of ideologies once they have taken root and been sometimes cynically deployed by charismatic authoritarians. More than fifty years after Nasser ordered the execution of Qutb in 1966, the Middle East remains divided, perhaps even more so, along Islamist–secular and Islamist–nationalist lines.

Nasser himself was a socialist who wanted to redistribute wealth, ratchet up industrial production and growth in gross domestic product, and create a modern bureaucratic state capable of driving and sustaining economic modernization. This was, in other words, an economic vision, one in which religious concerns were secondary. But foundational divides around the role of Islam in public and political life were left to fester, and so they returned. In the future, when it will seem again that religious divides have taken a backseat, we can safely assume that they will return, and so on—until there is a more consensual approach to Islam and politics as well as to Islam *in* politics.

In the early 1980s, when Voll was writing *Islam: Continuity and Change in the Modern World* and building on its arguments, he sensed something that would become more obvious only with time—that much of politics is inherently "religious" in the broader sense of the word. Toward the end of the book, he notes that "even the most clearly antireligious ideologies are increasingly recognized as assuming a religious form. They are not so much antireligious as attempting to replace one religion with another" (1982, 275). He also writes: "The giant structures of modern and modernizing societies, the great international corporations, the large bureaucracies, and the large political organizations [are] too large to provide a satisfying identity for individuals" (279).

Where does this leave us? It is possible to recognize Islam's power without making it into a problem to be solved (or reformed). At the same time, to take seriously the primacy of politics is to take seriously the primacy of religion and religious ideas. Religious reform cannot be separated from political reform, and religious pluralism is impossible without political pluralism. It is now as it was then: Muslim-majority societies will have to find a way to live with Islamism as well as secularism. There cannot—and likely will not—be one without the other, for both better and worse.

References

Ahmed, Shahab. 2016. *What Is Islam? The Importance of Being Islamic.* Princeton, NJ: Princeton Univ. Press.

Ajami, Fouad. 1982. *The Arab Predicament.* New York: Cambridge Univ. Press.

Ban Ki-moon. 2014. "Secretary-General's Remarks to Security Council High-Level Summit on Foreign Terrorist Fighters." United Nations, Sept. 24. At https://www.un.org/sg/en/content/sg/statement/2014-09-24/secretary-generals-remarks-security-council-high-level-summit.

Bellin, Eva. 2004. "The Robustness of Authoritarianism in the Middle East: Exceptionalism in Comparative Perspective." *Comparative Politics* 36, no. 2: 139–57.

Buruma, Ian. 2004. "Lost in Translation." *New Yorker,* June 14. At https://www.newyorker.com/magazine/2004/06/14/lost-in-translation-3.

Cook, Michael. 2014. *Ancient Religions, Modern Politics: The Islamic Case in Historical Perspective.* Princeton, NJ: Princeton Univ. Press.

Esposito, John L., Tamara Sonn, and John O. Voll. 2016. *Islam and Democracy after the Arab Spring.* Oxford: Oxford Univ. Press.

Esposito, John L., and John O. Voll. 1996. *Islam and Democracy.* Oxford: Oxford Univ. Press.

Freer, Courtney. 2018. *Rentier Islamism: The Influence of the Muslim Brotherhood.* New York: Oxford Univ. Press.

Fukuyama, Francis. 2011. *The Origins of Political Order: From Prehuman Times to the French Revolution.* New York: Farrar, Straus and Giroux.

Gerges, Fawaz A. 2018. *Making the Arab World: Nasser, Qutb, and the Clash That Shaped the Middle East.* Princeton, NJ: Princeton Univ. Press.

Gordon, Joel. 1989. "The False Hopes of 1950: The Wafd's Last Hurrah and the Demise of the Old Order." *International Journal of Middle East Studies* 21:193–214.

Hallaq, Wael. 2013. *The Impossible State: Islam, Politics, and Modernity's Moral Predicament.* New York: Columbia Univ. Press.

Hamid, Shadi. 2014. *Temptations of Power.* New York: Oxford Univ. Press.

Lipset, Seymour Martin, and Stein Rokkan. 1967. *Party Systems and Voter Alignments: Cross-National Perspectives.* London: Free Press.

Marks, Monica. 2014. "Convince, Coerce, or Compromise: Ennahda's Approach to Tunisia's Constitution." Brookings Doha Center, Feb. 2014.

At https://www.brookings.edu/wp-content/uploads/2016/06/Ennahda-Approach-Tunisia-Constitution-English.pdf.

Marsad Majles (website). n.d. "Al Bawsala." At https://majles.marsad.tn/2014/.

Mitchell, Richard P. 1969. *The Society of the Muslim Brothers*. London: Oxford Univ. Press.

Mneimneh, Hassan. 2016. "The Dangerous Stipulation of Islamic Exceptionalism." Middle East Institute, July 28. At https://www.mei.edu/publications/dangerous-stipulation-islamic-exceptionalism.

Shehata, Samer, and Joshua Stacher. 2006. "The Brotherhood Goes to Parliament." *Middle East Report* 240:32–39.

Spiegel, Avi Max. 2015. *Young Islam: The New Politics of Religion in Morocco and the Arab World*. Princeton, NJ: Princeton Univ. Press.

Voll, John Obert. 1982. *Islam: Continuity and Change in the Modern World*. Boulder, CO: Westview.

Wickham, Carrie Rosefsky. 2002. *Mobilizing Islam: Religion, Activism, and Political Change in Egypt*. New York: Columbia Univ. Press.

Wolf, Anne. 2014. "Can Secular Parties Lead the New Tunisia?" Carnegie Endowment for International Peace, Apr. 30. At http://carnegieendowment.org/2014/04/30/can-secular-parties-lead-new-tunisia.

8

Islamists and the State

The Egyptian Muslim Brotherhood's Evolving Mission

Abdullah al-Arian

During the fall of 2011, the Muslim Brotherhood's newly established Freedom and Justice Party (FJP) launched an ambitious electoral program by declaring the foundation of Egypt's "second republic" (FJP 2011, 2). As millions of Egyptians prepared to go to the polls for the first free parliamentary elections since the Free Officers Revolution in 1952, which brought a military regime into power, the FJP was poised to win the largest share of seats in the revamped legislature. Buried within the lengthy document detailing the FJP's legislative agenda, party leaders affirmed their commitment to upholding the integrity of the Egyptian state, rooted in equal citizenship, constitutionalism, democracy, and checks and balances between governing institutions (FJP 2011, 10–11). Given the frequent charge to which Islamist movements are often subjected—namely, their alleged rejection of the nation-state as a basis for modern political organization—it was not particularly surprising to see the Muslim Brotherhood go out of its way to affirm its allegiance to the Egyptian state. Indeed, before the movement ever harbored ambitions of taking the reins of Egypt's chief legislative body, the rise of Islamism as a distinct movement occurred in parallel with the emergence of the modern state as the definitive force in the lives of Egyptians to such an extent that it has defined the evolution of this form of political expression throughout the past century.

Lasting a little more than two years, the period roughly from February 2011 until August 2013 encapsulated both the highest and lowest points in the Muslim Brotherhood's nine-decade history. During that time, the movement founded in 1928 by Hasan al-Banna, an idealistic schoolteacher in Ismailiyya, found itself in the unprecedented position of controlling the Parliament as well as the highest elected position in the land, the presidency. Coming on the heels of a revolutionary movement that unseated an authoritarian ruler who had maintained his grip on power for thirty years, the Muslim Brotherhood's fortunes quickly turned. Always lurking in the background, the Egyptian armed forces seized on the frustrations expressed by many Egyptians in the midst of a turbulent transition from a deeply entrenched dictatorship to a free and democratic political order.

The military coup led by Field Marshal Abdel Fattah al-Sisi overthrew the FJP's Mohamad Morsi from the presidency, dissolved the country's first freely elected parliament, and sent most of the Muslim Brotherhood's leading members to prison, where Morsi would later succumb to conditions that a prominent human rights organization described as possibly amounting to torture (Human Rights Watch 2019). Those who protested the military's actions were met with an unprecedented use of force, as occurred during the massacres at Rab'aa al-'Adawiyya and al-Nahda Squares in Cairo on August 14, 2013, in which nearly one thousand Egyptians were killed, the largest single death toll by security forces in the country's modern history. When the dust settled, the military coup had completely displaced the country's democratic transition, and the ensuing security operation threatened to eradicate the nation's oldest social movement organization. While campaigning for the presidency the following spring, al-Sisi proclaimed, "There will be nothing called the Muslim Brotherhood during my tenure" (quoted in Loveluck 2014).

Understandably, in the immediate aftermath of these developments, much of the assessment, whether by outside observers or by Muslim Brotherhood members, tended to focus on the lessons from the movement's brush with power. These lessons revolved largely around issues of tactics employed by the Muslim Brotherhood's leadership during its brief time as the dominant political actor within Egypt's revolution. Critics lamented that these leaders should have been more forceful in purging the authoritarian state's institutions; that they should have been more confrontational with the military at an earlier stage when the movement enjoyed popular support; that they also should have been more politically inclusive, siding with the revolutionary factions and forming a united bloc against the counter-revolutionary forces that ultimately succeeded in undoing all the gains of a fleeting revolutionary moment.

There is much validity in these critiques, and they warrant continued engagement as Egyptians reflect on what might ultimately prove to have been a series of missed opportunities. However, of equal importance is the need to reexamine the roots of the Islamic activist mission that began in the early twentieth century and gave rise to a political vision that came to define the movement's posture during the critical revolutionary opening of the past decade. In the wake of the Muslim Brotherhood's downfall and the sheer scale of the subsequent repression by the al-Sisi regime and its allies across the Arab region, the current period presents an opportune moment to reevaluate this movement's ideological core, goals, and modes of operation.

The first step in this process demands that we historicize the development of Islamic movements: that is, we must recognize that their emergence corresponded with the period of transition to modern nation-states and that this was no mere coincidence. The proximity of the nation-building process to the emergence of Islamic social movements has largely been overlooked or mischaracterized as a purely antagonistic relationship. The classical literature on the emergence of Islamic activism as a significant political force in the twentieth century characterized the phenomenon as one of opposition to the modernization process at work in Middle Eastern societies, contending that it represented either a Mahdist-style movement with messianic aspirations or a militant reactionary force unwavering in its commitment to outmoded religious dogma.[1] In one of the earliest studies of the Egyptian Muslim Brotherhood, one scholar posited the following assessment of the movement's supposed political aims: "The whole of Hasan al-Banna's teachings, exhortations, activities were directed to the removal of the present constitutional government in Egypt, and to replace it by imposing upon the country a government the principles of which would be entirely Islamic according to the doctrines and laws established over a thousand years ago. The only interpreter of this body of doctrine would be Hasan al-Banna" (Heyworth-Dunne 1950, 54).

Richard Mitchell's seminal study of 1969 (Mitchell [1969] 1993) offered an important corrective to the prevailing narrative, situating the Muslim Brotherhood within the legacy of Islamic modernism and contemporary reform movements, though it fell short of incorporating the organization into the broader Egyptian national movement. Subsequent studies shifted their focus to exploring the roots of antistate violence by Muslim Brotherhood offshoots in the aftermath of the repressive Nasser era or were concerned by the movement's fixation on establishing the shari'a as the basis of law and political legitimacy.[2] More recently, scholars have integrated their studies of the Muslim Brotherhood within the literature on Egypt's social and economic development by examining the organization's establishment of a robust social services provision sector or in observing the upwardly mobile social class of the movement's expanding base of support.[3] Nevertheless, these works are more concerned with exploring the contemporary place of the Muslim Brotherhood within Egyptian society than with tracing the process by which the movement developed in full view of the challenges presented by the modern state. They also confront renewed challenges from literature that largely recycles some well-worn tropes: the classical messianic

1. For example, see Heyworth-Dunne 1950 and Harris 1964.
2. See, for example, Ibrahim 1980, Sivan 1985, Kepel 1993, and Shepard 1987.
3. See, for example, Clark 2004, Wickham 2015, and Brooke 2019.

portrayal was recently repackaged as "religious determinism," and the depictions of violent militarism have been retrofitted for the age of the war on terror.[4]

In the face of such lingering questions regarding the viability of the Islamist project and its compatibility with modern forms of governance, this chapter excavates the Muslim Brotherhood's historical relationship with the modern state, an entity with which it has maintained an allegedly hostile relationship. Even among critics who accept the organization's commitments to democratic participation within existing state structures, the frequent refrain has been that it has done so only recently and out of a pragmatic need to secure its survival, while nevertheless seeking to impose a radically different order. By situating the movement's development within the broader political and socioeconomic transformations under way in Egypt during the first half of the twentieth century, a more accurate trajectory can be formed.

From the colonial experience through the struggle for independence, the logic of the modern state became a deeply internalized force that guided the formation and articulation of the Islamically inspired mission of the Muslim Brotherhood. So pervasive was the modern state as a framework for political and social organization that al-Banna built his ideological project entirely within its confines, while the movement's modes of contention in the decades that followed developed in accordance with the state's established limits. In other words, although the Muslim Brotherhood aimed to counteract the perceived secularization of society and the compartmentalization of the place of religion within society, it nevertheless acceded to the structural demands of social and political advocacy within a public space free of an overarching Islamic value system. A number of studies have shown this to be a relatively recent phenomenon, tracing it through the development of the Muslim Brotherhood's political

4. For an example of the former, see Kandil 2015, 175. For an example of the latter, see Aly 2018.

platforms, which it has publicized since the mid-1980s. As one scholar maintains, the Muslim Brotherhood's "Islamist vision is shaped by secularization as institutional and functional differentiation" (Dalacoura 2018, 330). Others have explored the recent development of the Muslim Brotherhood's notion of a "civil state" that explicitly adopts conceptions of popular sovereignty and civil liberties in the movement's bid to reform the political system in a far more limited fashion than previously thought.[5]

As this chapter contends, long before the Islamist movement could articulate a notion of a civil state, it had to signal its acceptance of the state writ large—that is, its acceptance that the traditional levers of political power and regulation of social life had transformed to such an extent that they demanded a reconceptualization of the means by which Islamic values could be deemed capable of informing their application. A similar process could be observed in Sudan's modern history. Writing on the Mahdiyya movement that came to power in the late nineteenth century, John Voll argued that it represented a high degree of "stateness" in its desire to establish far stronger and more centralized structures and practices with expanded control over the lives of Sudanese than those of premodern empires (1983, 8–9). In the case of Egypt's Muslim Brotherhood, the internalization of key features of the modern state left a strong imprint on the rise and evolution of Islamic activism, the articulation of movement goals, and the development of modes of contention since the interwar period. Indeed, the Muslim Brotherhood's and the modern state's fates have been irrevocably intertwined ever since.

The Legacy of Islamic Modernism

The emergence of popular mobilization rooted in a call for the return to Islamic values was pursuant to the decline of traditional centers of

5. See Harnisch and Mecham 2009 as well as Pahwa 2013.

religious and political authority that accompanied the era of Islamic empires.[6] So whereas today the question we hear asked quite often is "Who speaks for Islam?," a century ago it was "Who doesn't speak for Islam?" (Esposito and Mogahed 2007) or, perhaps more accurately, "Who can no longer speak for Islam?" Along with the fall of the caliphate, the symbol of religious and political authority in Islam for thirteen centuries, came the loss of status of traditional religious institutions. And with the rise of the modern state, the very nature of the relationship between society and those who ruled over it became radically transformed in both content as well as character. Islamic activists and intellectuals who encountered modernity became fixated on the emergence of these unprecedented entities in one way or another.

In attempting to guide, influence, and at times coerce the shah of Qajar Iran, the Ottoman sultan, and the khedive of Egypt, the nineteenth-century intellectual and activist Sayyid Jamal al-Din al-Afghani pursued a last-ditch effort to salvage traditional modes of political authority within a broadly Islamic—albeit modernizing—framework. In his writings, al-Afghani cautioned against the uncritical adoption of new forms of political legitimation that strayed from Islamic legal ordinances, declaring in the 1890s that "the amount of power given to Muslim rulers is a product of their observance of divine regulations, of the way in which they follow the good directions which these prescribe, and of the absence of all personal ambition in them" (al-Afghani 2007, 18). In expressing these concerns, al-Afghani predicted the changing norms of political legitimacy that would accompany European encroachment and seek to displace a traditional system of political authority rooted in the application of Islamic law. To be sure, colonial pressures often compelled Muslim reformers to construct an idealized Islamic legal order that had limited basis in

6. For a fuller discussion of the responses to the challenges posed by the decline of traditional political and religious authority across Muslim societies, see Voll 1994.

historical reality, and in turn, as Iza Hussin has shown, colonial authorities occasionally ceded ground to such demands as a means of legitimizing their control (2016, 212).

One of al-Afghani's leading disciples would attempt to navigate this difficult terrain. By codifying religious legal instruments and institutions under the auspices of British colonial rule, Muhammad Abduh, Egypt's mufti at the turn of the twentieth century, signaled the gradual acceptance of changing modes of authority and state organization. The reformed national court system brought the application of Islamic law under direct state control in unprecedented fashion. Several decades later, the scholar and writer Muhammad Rashid Rida witnessed the worst excesses of colonialism and the persistence of Western encroachment in the postcolonial era across the Muslim world. His critiques represented, on the one hand, the increased alienation from the emerging political, social, and economic orders among populations in the newly independent states and, on the other hand, an increased determination to bend these arrangements to accommodate a developing understanding of what constitutes an authentically Islamic order. In the absence of the recently abolished caliphate, he proposed a vision of Islamic renewal built not only upon the leadership of regional monarchs, such as King Fuad of Egypt, but also upon the broader Muslim community, or *umma*, as a whole. "Everyone is equally [responsible] for this renewal: individuals, groups, and governments," he stated in 1930 (Rida 2002, 84). In the same speech, Rida illustrated the holistic nature of this mission: "Legitimate renewal includes all that the *umma* and the state hold dear, such as the sciences, arts, and industries; financial, administrative, and military systems; land, naval, and air installations. All these are considered a collective duty in Islam, and the entire *umma* sins when it neglects them. The *shari'a* does not restrict the *umma* in pursuing them" (2002, 85). Indeed, a key feature of the modernist vision of renewal was the shift toward greater popular agency that resulted from the concomitant crisis of traditional religious authority and the development of modern notions of citizenship.

Hasan al-Banna and the Modern State

By the time Hasan al-Banna established the Muslim Brotherhood in 1928, he had internalized these different phases of the Islamic modernist movement and devised an actionable program encouraged by the latest of those approaches. In fact, as a contemporary of Rida, al-Banna not only found inspiration in Rida's critiques but also eventually inherited Rida's *al-Manar* magazine and utilized it as a vehicle to disseminate his movement's ideas. Echoing the modernist claims to renewal as a public obligation, al-Banna wrote in his widely distributed letters to followers that the material strength of a nation was the product of the moral rectitude of its people: "The Muslim Brotherhood believes this fervently, and are therefore diligently purifying their souls, strengthening themselves, and rectifying their moral character. And it is for this reason that they are striving to fulfill their mission, convincing people to accept their principles, and demanding that the umma reform itself and rectify its moral character" (al-Banna 2006, 105). As the Muslim Brotherhood's mission evolved to promote a program aimed at modern-style political and socioeconomic reforms, it implicitly and at times explicitly affirmed its commitment to operating within the bounds of the modern state. The modern state's only crime, as far as al-Banna was concerned, was that it was not sufficiently Islamic, beginning with its foundational document: "Each one of the Islamic nations has a constitution, and it is necessary that it derive the sources of its constitution from the prescriptions of the Noble Qur'an; that the nation which declares in the first paragraph of its constitution that its official religion is Islam must set down the rest of its paragraphs in conformity with this principle. Every paragraph which Islam cannot tolerate and which its prescriptions do not sanction must be expunged so that no contradiction will appear in the fundamental law of the state" (al-Banna 2006, 107).

Interestingly, debates about the place of Islam (and of the shari'a in particular) in the Egyptian Constitution have continued to play out ever since, with echoes of al-Banna's sentiments expressed by Muslim

Brotherhood leaders during their tussles with Anwar al-Sadat in the late 1970s and in their mission to devise a new constitution after the uprising of 2011.[7] Elsewhere, however, in articulating the movement's goals, al-Banna expressed tacit acceptance of the state's role in applying law, regulating social conduct, and standardizing systems of education. Once again, his call centered on bending those new processes to reflect an Islamic value system rather than on questioning the state's right to implement policy in areas that were historically removed from the role of political authority. Putting it another way, when the assertion was later made that "al-Islam din wa dawla" (Islam is both religion and state), there was rarely a discussion of what this *dawla* signified.

By not going as far as offering a critique of the structures and boundaries of the modern state, let alone putting forward an alternative model, the Muslim Brotherhood's founder implicitly ceded that ground to the modernizing efforts of colonial authorities and nationalist elites alike. Indeed, from his perspective, there was no need for an alternative. Al-Banna represents the first generation of Egyptians who had for all intents and purposes internalized the modern state and its vision of society to such an extent that its existence was beyond question. As Timothy Mitchell has posited, Egypt's colonial experience produced a conception of society as individuals "to be formed into an organized and disciplined whole. It was this obedient and regulated whole that was to be imagined under the name of the 'nation,' that was to be constructed as Egyptian 'society.' And the word for this political process of discipline and formation was education" (1991, 119). Exploring the impact of Émile Durkheim's ideas on an emerging Egyptian political elite, Mitchell continues that "the purpose of universal secular state education was to make the child 'understand his country and times, to make him aware of its needs, to initiate him into its life, and in this way to prepare him for the collective tasks which await him'" (121).

7. See, for example, Lombardi and Brown 2013, 33–37, and al-Arian 2014, 199–204.

Al-Banna bore witness to these crucial developments during the course of his life as a pious advocate for the application of Islamic values who nevertheless internalized the newly established tenets of modern life. Born in the rural town of Mahmudiyya in 1906, he was brought up in the wave of nationalist fervor that swept Egypt after World War I. He was educated in government schools and received his postsecondary degree at an institute of modern education, Dar al-'Ulum, in Cairo before going on to become a government functionary as a schoolteacher assigned to a district away from the village in which he grew up and the city in which he was educated. In other words, the modern state was a lived, breathed reality that shaped the formation of the opposition to it, even the religiously inspired opposition.

Nasserism and Its Discontents

By the end of his life, al-Banna had successfully articulated and disseminated a holistic vision of Islamic reform that hewed closely to the realities of state power vis-à-vis Egyptian society. The conception of Islam as "a way of life" that has since been advanced by Islamic activists represents a set of core values, historical experiences, common practices, institutions, and legal principles—all things that modern states claim as the basis upon which they were formed. In that light, the fixation on the state by early iterations of the modern Islamic activist mission becomes more comprehensible.

This is especially true when considering the state's responsibility for stripping public life of its religiously based value system and replacing it with a set of institutions conceived on an alternate basis and performing a far more pervasive function in society than the traditional political and social orders deemed permissible (or even possible). Writing on his vision regarding Egypt's future, the literary figure Taha Husayn proclaimed in 1938, "The dominant and undeniable fact of our times is that day by day we are drawing closer to Europe and becoming an integral part of her, literally and figuratively" (Husayn 1975, 12). Husayn, who also served as education minister in the early

1950s, contributed to a developing narrative that secularization played a crucial role in the modernization process.

Of course, that notion has been vigorously challenged in recent years by Western scholars of religion as well as by those engaged in religiously inspired movements. In his seminal study of the historical roots of the contemporary Islamic revival, Voll proposed that "the contemporary experience in Muslim societies shows clearly that the old assumption of a direct correlation between modernization and secularization must at least be reexamined, if not rejected" (1994, 3). Referring to a "new paradigm" of the sociology of religion, two scholars later posited that if religion traditionally represented the institution of social improvement, or "doing better," as they termed it, "what has come to be called 'secularization' is the process by which societies in the experience of 'modernization' have created competing institutions for doing better" (Swatos and Christiano 1999, 224–25). In other words, rather than signaling the triumph of secularism, the modernization process was marked by a pluralistic competition "between historical religious approaches to doing better and other systems of doing better" (225).

Although Husayn and other political and cultural figures embraced the traditional view of secularism during a crucial era in Egypt's development, the reality of it proved to be far from the conception. As the modern state developed in the postcolonial Middle East, it was not the secular enterprise it was often imagined to be. The process of consigning religious affairs to the private sphere and removing them entirely from politics was by no means a value-free project but rather witnessed attempts by supposedly secular regimes to assert their control over religious thought and practice in ways that were historically unprecedented.

In writing on Gamal Abdel Nasser's "rejection of religion as a basis for national identity and state policy," James Jankowski points out that this policy was hardly revolutionary. "The disavowal of religion as a political referent had been a prominent feature of Egyptian territorial nationalism under the parliamentary monarchy" (2003, 37). Nevertheless, in a crucial development Nasser's revolutionary socialist regime oversaw a massive expansion of the state. John Waterbury employs the term *bureaucratic authoritarianism* to describe a state "run by an alliance of the military and state technocrats . . . who were very much concerned with discipline, order, and production" (1983, 9). As the state took on a more pervasive role in the lives of Egyptians, it not only assumed control over levers of political, economic, and social life but also took unprecedented measures to incorporate religious institutions into its domain. The Nasser regime nationalized al-Azhar, an institution that had maintained its independence for a millennium. The state also took charge of appointing religious officials and placed the independent religious endowments, or *awqaf* institutions, in its control as well.

Both Jankowski and Waterbury acknowledge that the Nasser regime's actions were motivated, at least in part, by the presence of the Muslim Brotherhood as a leading opposition movement (Waterbury 1983, 9; Jankowski 2003, 37). Rather than a religious versus secular binary, the competition that has marked the contentious relationship between the authoritarian state and the Islamist movement during the course of the past six decades represents a desire to legitimize claims to religious authority on the part of all parties concerned. As Voll has written, "The real battles regarding religion and politics—both in the debates framing the wording in the various constitutions that have been recently written, and on the streets—are over the control of religious institutions and loyalties" (2014). Indeed, as Rached al-Ghannouchi, the leader of Tunisia's Ennahda Party, characterized the situation, contrary to the historical Western fixation on liberating the state from religion, "in our context the problem is one of liberating religion from the state and preventing [the state] from dominating religion, and keeping the latter in the societal realm" (2012).

It was only upon recognizing the pervasive role of the modern state in regulating the lives of citizens, including the freedom to live according to their interpretation of Islam, that the Islamist movement saw political action as necessary to the achievement of its broader objectives. One critic recently noted that when the state restrained the ability of traditional institutions to maintain society's Islamic credentials, "the gatekeepers of knowledge shifted from the ulama class to a body of professional religious entrepreneurs," represented in part by al-Banna and his successors (Kazmi 2014). Indeed, as Carrie Wickham has shown, by the 1980s the Muslim Brotherhood's base of supporters had become composed primarily of upwardly mobile urban middle-class professionals with a vested interest in challenging state hegemony over social and economic policies (2002, 36–62).

Sayyid Qutb's ideological intervention has traditionally been understood in the context of the Nasser regime's attempts to regulate religious interpretation and observance. However, some elements of Qutb's critique extend beyond his rebuke of the regime's tyranny and its role in returning society to a state of ignorance, or *jahiliyya*. When those critiques are juxtaposed with his consideration of the notion of divine sovereignty, or *hakimiyya*, it becomes apparent that Qutb was concerned with the emergence of the modern state writ large. As Sayed Khatab has shown, Qutb, long before producing *Milestones* in 1964, his prison-authored denunciation of the Nasser regime, expressed a similar conception of *hakimiyya* in earlier works such as *Social Justice in Islam* (1949) and *In the Shade of the Qur'an* (1951–65), his modernist exegesis of the Qur'an (2002, 151). Citing Qutb's construction of an Islamic past centered around divine sovereignty, Khatab argues that Qutb "means that Islam is a religion and a state 'din wa dawlah.' To him, Islam in its very nature is a political religion; the unity between religion and politics is a great principle in Islam, and the system of government is an important element in the Islamic creed" (154).

In offering an interpretation of a classical Islamic concept within a modern context, Qutb was therefore responding to the challenge presented by contemporary notions of political authority as represented by the state. Khatab continues regarding Qutb's conception of *hakimiyya* as it relates to a governing political order:

> From a practical prospective, *hakimiyyah* means that, in the Islamic state, God is the supreme legislator and the ultimate source of legal and political authority. This in turn reveals to us that the government in Islam is a limited form designed to implement the *shari'ah*

> and administer justice in accordance with the ordinance of *shari'ah*. There is no place in Islam for arbitrary rule by a single individual or a group. The basis of all decisions and actions in an Islamic polity should not be individual whim and caprice, but *shurah* (consultation) within the boundary of *shari'ah*. Imposing the *shari'ah* and facilitating its application requires a state; it must follow, then, that Islam is both religion and state. (2002, 155)

Although Qutb's critiques have been considered radical departures from the Islamic tradition (and, indeed, his remedies signified a call to action that was rare in Islamic history), Khatab points out that, in fact, Qutb's conception of *hakimiyya* was very much in line with the traditional interpretations of it as they have been articulated by establishment scholars within al-Azhar and across the Islamic world (2002, 155–58). Echoing some of these sentiments, Wael Hallaq posits in *The Impossible State* (2013) that the essential contours of the modern state remain immutable to the kinds of structural changes necessary to fulfill a truly Islamic state. As a scholar of Islamic law, Hallaq appears particularly concerned with the inherent contradictions in the traditional conceptions of the shari'a and modern notions of constitutionalism, sovereignty, and legislative and executive power. He argues that

> the state possesses a metaphysic that resides within its own boundaries as sovereign will. The metaphysic generates its own meanings, which is to say that its particular views of the world are of its own creation and bound by its own standards, however changeable these standards may be. . . . Second, and flowing from the former consideration, Islamic governance cannot permit any sovereignty or sovereign will other than that of God. If morality is to guide human actions, if it be autonomous, then it must rest on universal and eternal principles of truth and justice, principles that transcend the manipulation and whims of a positivist entity. . . . In Islamic governance, where—as we have seen—the rule of law takes on one of its most supreme expressions, no earthly sovereignty is allowed to compromise the dictates of moral autonomy. (2013, 157)

Therefore, in at least one respect, Qutb's intervention marks an important but ultimately exceptional footnote in the broader march of Islamic activism. By invoking the notion of *jahiliyya* as a state of renewed ignorance, Qutb looked forward to Hallaq's later critique that the modern state is a god in itself, one with which you cannot associate any other gods. In fact, much of the classical secularization literature argued that the end of religion's place in modern societies was inevitable precisely because of its supposed incompatibility with contemporary notions of social, economic, and political organization (Stark 1999).

As a Muslim Brotherhood veteran who gave voice to the movement's ideals at a time when it suffered the most repressive political climate in its history, Qutb offered general commentary on the inherent conflict between a state ruled by human will and one governed by divine sovereignty, but that commentary was reframed largely as a vociferous condemnation of the Nasser regime's excesses. The fact that Qutb was executed by the regime only gave further weight to the more limited critique of the contemporary political order that inspired a series of militant insurgencies in Egypt over the course of the next two decades. Meanwhile, successive Muslim Brotherhood leaders avoided confronting the deeper critiques against the modern state put forward by Qutb and instead offered a response that posited their movement as one of "preachers, not judges," as expressed in the title of Hasan al-Hudaybi's book in 1969 imploring followers to limit their mission to spreading Islamic values within society rather than calling for a complete overhaul of the existing political order, implied in Qutb's teachings. In fact, by the early 1980s the Muslim Brotherhood had fully consolidated its ideological position regarding the state and refashioned its activist mission in line with these parameters.

"Islam Is the Solution"

As I have explored elsewhere, the 1970s signaled the reconstitution of the Muslim Brotherhood's organization following its dismantlement and suppression under Nasser (al-Arian 2014, 146–74). While Hudaybi secured the ideological conformity of the veteran activists who continued to advocate on behalf of the movement following their release from prison, it was his successor as the organization's general guide, 'Umar al-Tilmisani, who ensured that a new generation of youth activists would carry the mantle of the Muslim Brotherhood going forward.

The student movement of the 1970s signaled a pivotal era in the evolution of Islamic activism in Egypt for several reasons. First, for a generation that came of age following the nation's defeat in the June War of 1967 and the total collapse of the Nasserist project, Islam offered an alternative ideological footing from which to challenge the residual effects of Arab nationalism. In fact, throughout the decade and in stark contrast to the secularization thesis, religious observance witnessed a notable rise across all segments of Egyptian society following the widespread disillusionment with leftist ideologies.

Second, Anwar Sadat's reorientation away from Nasserism and his economic and social liberalization policies created an atmosphere of greater openness for the public exchange of ideas, leading to the propagation of an Islamic political alternative by a wide array of forces within society. For its part, the Sadat regime also adopted a more outwardly religious character. Led chiefly by its "Believer President," the state thus became a more active participant in the impassioned discussions about the place of Islam in contemporary Egyptian society. Finally, the student movement itself operated within the bounds of a state institution, the university, and its various organs, including the student unions, and thus found the success of its mission to be inextricably linked to its ability to navigate the terrain of state bureaucracy and university administration. By the late 1970s, the student union presidents of nearly every major university had joined the Muslim Brotherhood and were responsible for the recruitment of thousands of new activists into the organization.

As many of those students graduated, they joined labor unions and professional syndicates as sites of political contestation and institutions with the potential to affect the functioning of state services such as medical care and infrastructure. The rejuvenation of the parallel

Muslim Sisterhood ushered in the participation of tens of thousands of Egyptian women, who evoked the legacy of pioneering Islamist activist Zaynab al-Ghazali by challenging the boundaries of women's involvement in public life (Cooke 1994). Nearly a decade later, the Muslim Brotherhood had become a permanent fixture within the narrow political space made available by the regime for independent movements and parties. Because the Muslim Brotherhood was legally banned from forming its own political party, it offered some of its members as independent candidates for Parliament, usually in alliance with established parties. Following the regime's crackdown on the Muslim Brotherhood's expanded political participation, the organization boycotted the election in 1990. But as some observers pointed out, its message remained unchanged irrespective of the shifting political winds: "Significantly, therefore, newspaper articles, speeches at conferences, announcements issued, and sermons at mosques all suggest that accommodation of the political system continues to be a major Brotherhood strategy, despite the 1990 election boycott. Because the Brotherhood's influence has become too pervasive for it to withdraw from the electoral process, it will continue to seek ways to more firmly entrench its presence" (Sullivan and Abed-Kotob 1999, 56).

Indeed, the movement's posture since the early 1990s would appear to challenge the notion that the Muslim Brotherhood embraced participation in the political system only on a conditional basis while continuing to challenge the state's legitimacy. By committing itself more heavily to the provision of social services and engagement in electoral politics alongside its traditional *da'wa* activity, the Muslim Brotherhood settled any lingering questions as to its ideological commitments. Its candidates ran under the banner of "Islam is the solution," a seemingly all-encompassing slogan that to its critics presaged an ominous call for the return of a traditional Islamic state led by a caliphate. Ironically, although "Islam is the solution" implied a comprehensive and universalistic message, in fact it was envisioned strictly within the parameters of the existing political structures, for which the Muslim Brotherhood's leaders championed a reformist approach. The proposed implementation of the shari'a similarly conceived of it as "a modern understanding of law as code, quite alien to how shari'a had been conceived of and functioned in Islamic settings in the premodern period" (Dalacoura 2018, 327). When asked how the Muslim Brotherhood expected to fulfill this broad vision, General Guide Ma'mun al-Hudaybi explained that the movement's goals sought only to address the flaws within the state's prevailing structures "by changing institutions with institutions" (quoted in Sullivan and Abed-Kotob 1999, 57).

During the mid-1990s, a number of intellectuals and activists associated with the Muslim Brotherhood's school of thought decided to commit more fully to the ideal of becoming more firmly entrenched within the political order. In launching the Wasat Party, they took yet another step away from a dogmatic reading of the Islamic legal tradition and instead advocated for an interpretation of Islamic law that broadened the scope of the general principles underlying important legal concepts rather than emphasizing specific rulings. The *wasatiyya* tradition, as they interpreted it, demanded that the Islamic tradition "be evaluated in the light of not only the texts but also an informed and pragmatic grasp of the realities of the actual world in which the faith must be lived" (Baker 2003, 274).

A State within a State

As a result of these key developments, the Islamist project of the late twentieth century was one in which success and failure were measured in relation to the movement's proximity to the centers of political power and authority. In other words, as the Muslim Brotherhood's ideological program presented no opposition to the modern state as such, its mission was geared almost exclusively toward fulfilling the state's functions and inhabiting its institutions. Establishing successful social services institutions, making electoral gains, and mobilizing in favor of reforms to state institutions were viewed as the measures of progress.

As described in a number of recent works, the Muslim Brotherhood's welfare sector emerged not in opposition to the regime but rather as an extension of the state's reoriented social and economic commitments. In what one scholar has termed the "imaginary of state developmentalism," the neoliberal reorientation that began under Sadat and continued vigorously throughout the Mubarak era allowed the regime to continue to play an active role in pursuing economic growth while steadily dismantling the state industries and welfare institutions established under Nasser (Vannetzel 2017, 222). To fill the ensuing void, groups within society were incentivized to take advantage of the economic opening and then channel the resulting revenues toward enhancing their public profile. Khairat al-Shater, the Muslim Brotherhood's deputy general guide who emerged as a leading presidential contender during the 2012 election, had gained prominence for his successful businesses, which in turn supported Muslim Brotherhood social welfare initiatives. For most scholars observing the growth of this phenomenon, the blossoming of a social welfare network would be examined almost exclusively through its ability to mobilize political support on behalf of the Muslim Brotherhood.[8]

As described by Wickham, the "lumpen intelligentsia" that became the target demographic for Muslim Brotherhood mobilization represented an educated middle class of Egyptians whose socioeconomic fate was determined by the state's inability to meet that class's demands for employment and social benefits (2002, 37). In contrast to the Muslim Brotherhood's early history, then, by the twenty-first century its organizational focus had shifted considerably to providing a complementary role to the state's failure to meet its obligations. By having already accepted the features and functions of the state as such, the movement's focus expanded in search of acceptance and inclusion from the regime in particular. As Hesham al-Awadi has argued, "The build-up of an organized informal legitimacy, and its politicization, should therefore be seen as a functional development aimed at persuading, or even pressuring the state finally to recognize the presence of the Brothers. This would not happen, or so the movement

8. See, for example, Masoud 2014 and Brooke 2019.

assumed, until the Brothers had succeeded in establishing a firm and broad presence in the society and in its civil institutions, and until they had cultivated a wide network of relations with different political and social forces" (2005, 78).

Within a closed, semiauthoritarian political climate, then, the organization's durability became measured not only by its visibility across society but also through its engagement with the political process. Indeed, inasmuch as the Muslim Brotherhood sought legitimation in the eyes of the regime, given its continued outlawed status (at least formally) since 1954, so, too, did the regime rely on the Muslim Brotherhood's continued participation in politics to enhance its own claims to legitimacy. By 2005, the Muslim Brotherhood vastly exceeded its previous electoral successes, winning one-fifth of all parliamentary seats, eighty-eight seats in total, through its independent candidates. Five years later, however, the organization found itself reaching a new low when it could not muster a single elected representative in the 2010 elections as a result of the regime's security crackdown and its procedural changes to the electoral process. Nevertheless, the group's commitment to operating within the bounds of the established political order remained. Far from "a state within a state," the Muslim Brotherhood viewed its mission as inextricably linked to the viability of the one and only state. If that was not clear in the era prior to Mubarak's overthrow in 2011, it would certainly become so after.

Revolutionary Brothers

The Muslim Brotherhood's posture in the aftermath of the uprising that overthrew Egypt's authoritarian ruler in February 2011 reflected a long-standing internalization of the state and its institutions. The group's leadership had long ago dispensed with the notion that the implementation of Islamic rule was a religiously inscribed mandate that demanded top-down enforcement, through the dismantling of existing structures if need be. Having already declared its approval of Sadat's largely symbolic incorporation of the shari'a as a basis for legislation in the Egyptian Constitution, by the late 1980s the Muslim

Brotherhood's leadership proclaimed that the question of implementing Islamic legal statutes would be subject to democratic approval, not divine will (Wickham 2015, 56).

Since this position set the organization on an accommodationist path, the Muslim Brotherhood was ill equipped to confront the revolutionary moment that erupted with the popular protests of 2011. As Egypt's revolutionary youth demanded a new social contract rooted in freedom, democracy, and social justice, the Muslim Brotherhood faced the challenge of radically reorienting a nearly century-old mission in a matter of days. This process would have entailed devising a fundamentally different outlook toward the functions of state institutions and their role in the fulfillment of Islamic principles, all while balancing the pressing demands of the nation's budding revolutionaries.

But rather than present an alternative to the state that had developed over the previous six decades, the Muslim Brotherhood remained content to operate within its existing institutions. As it won one election after another under the supervision of the nation's ruling military council, the organization's political arm, the Freedom and Justice Party, simply attempted to replace authoritarian rule with democratic legitimacy. Any discussion of reforming the state entailed little more than purging certain institutions of their corrupt figures and replacing them with uncompromised or more accountable ones. The implementation of democratic institutions amid the passage of a new constitution that placed additional guarantees for personal freedoms, accountability of public officials, and social justice never attempted to alter the basic arrangements of the state's role vis-à-vis some kind of idealized Islamic system. The controversy over the place of the shari'a in Morsi's proposed constitution in 2012 notwithstanding, the new language introduced by the Muslim Brotherhood's leadership was to have been little more than a frame of reference within an otherwise unchanged set of procedures and institutions for legislation, interpretation, and enforcement of the law. Debates surrounding the future of al-Azhar also lend credence to the argument that at no point did the Muslim Brotherhood depart from its commitment to a civil state. As several scholars at the time noted, the proposals ranged from restoring al-Azhar to its pre-Nasser-era position as an independent institution outside direct oversight by the state to granting it an extremely limited, nonbinding advisory role regarding state legislation (Brown 2011; see also Scott 2012).

A fundamental reimagining of the Islamist mission in revolutionary times would have entailed reopening what were largely moot intellectual debates about the nature of Islamic rule as it had developed in the premodern Islamic tradition, a project that none of Egypt's Islamist factions was interested in embarking upon at a time when political power over the existing state structures was seemingly within reach. Even the Salafis, who had historically shunned political engagement in the interest of maintaining ideological purity, rushed to form their own political parties in the aftermath of Mubarak's fall and proceeded to win one-quarter of parliamentary seats in the 2011–12 elections, where the Muslim Brotherhood took half the seats. In total, Islamist parties maintained a three-quarters majority in Egypt's legislature but did not offer a fundamentally different view of the legislature's role and functions.

Ultimately, by placing all of its eggs into the basket of state power, the Muslim Brotherhood would forego the opportunity to seize upon a revolutionary opening to reconceptualize the role of the state in governing the lives of Egyptians. Needless to say, such a process would have been fraught owing to the deep divisions among the revolutionary factions and the violent resistance unleashed by elements of the state's security apparatus in crushing the revolution. Nevertheless, even in the best of scenarios, the Muslim Brotherhood hoped for little more than that the existing state would absorb its leaders and its party organization into its structures, which would represent the fruition of its historic mission as it had evolved since the early twentieth century.

Islamism beyond the State

That the organization has since 2013 faced the most severe existential crisis in its history does not appear to have sparked a process of deep reflection on the movement's ideology, goals, and tactics. Rather, the Muslim Brotherhood's leadership remains committed to operating within the framework of existing instruments of governance, irrespective of their condition in the postcoup reality. The movement's highest-ranking figures who survived repression by going into exile have since maintained that Egypt's conflict is political in nature, a competition among rival factions and not an indication that the state has rejected the Islamist project outright (al-Arian 2015, 6). Despite the extreme measures to which the movement has been subjected, these surviving leaders have placed the movement's current predicament within the broader historical context of cyclical regime repression. One of the Muslim Brotherhood's chief strengths, they have argued, has been its ability to endure these trials until such time that it can resume its mission.

Challenging this outlook, a second group of exiled activists within the Muslim Brotherhood's ranks has expressed its desire for greater critical engagement with the organization's performance during Egypt's revolutionary moment. Communicated in a series of unpublished memorandums, their assertion that the movement failed to unite the nation's revolutionary factions as part of a broad coalition to take on the remnants of the authoritarian system was largely dismissed by the leadership. So, too, was this group's suggestion that the Muslim Brotherhood adopt a decidedly revolutionary path and seek to replace the existing state in its entirety with one rooted in democratic institutions and the rule of law (al-Arian 2015, 7–8). Although that sentiment has not gained traction beyond the middle and lower ranks of the organization, it signals a departure for the Muslim Brotherhood's traditionally accommodationist and reformist mission. Within a deeply divided organization, it stands as a measure of the possibilities for substantive transformation in the future, particularly amid the group's ongoing organizational crisis.

Asef Bayat has traced the evolution of traditional Islamist discourses from the quest "to establish some kind of an 'Islamic order'—a religious state, shari'a law, and moral codes in Muslim societies and communities"—to what he has termed "post-Islamism" (2013, 4). To Bayat, post-Islamism "represents an endeavor to fuse religiosity and rights, faith and freedom, Islam and liberty. . . . Whereas Islamism is defined by the fusion of religion and responsibility, post-Islamism emphasizes religiosity and rights" (8). Although this analysis offers a useful intellectual demarcation regarding the development of Islamist thought, when it is examined from the perspective of the Muslim Brotherhood's outlook toward the modern state, the differences between an Islamist and post-Islamist approach are barely perceptible. Even at the height of its call to establish an Islamic order, the Muslim Brotherhood did not put forward a vision of state power or institutions that veered from those that had developed under non-Islamic governance. Any indications that the movement may reassess its ideological roots are still in their infancy. In an unpublished memorandum circulated in 2019, the Muslim Brotherhood's internal opposition may have finally offered a critique that would indicate a shift in thinking. The document's authors declared the modern nation-state a foreign imposition that has dismantled Muslim unity and served to control the destinies of populations through its establishment of centralized education, taxation, and military conscription. The acts of counting and documenting its population are identified as more assertions of state power at the expense of freedom, including the freedom to live according to the Muslim Brotherhood's interpretation of the Islamic tradition. If the post-Islamist turn that Bayat describes is destined to have a fundamental impact on the Muslim Brotherhood's outlook, it must be in its call for "a civil and nonreligious state," which will ultimately shift the burden of an Islamic order onto society and require that Islamists begin thinking beyond the state.

References

Al-Afghani, Sayyid Jamal al-Din. 2007. "Islamic Solidarity" (c. 1890s). In *Islam in Transition: Muslim Perspectives*, edited by John J. Donohue and John L. Esposito, 16–19. New York: Oxford Univ. Press.

Aly, Abdel Monem Said. 2018. "The Truth about the Muslim Brotherhood." *Cairo Review*, Spring. At https://www.thecairoreview.com/essays/the-truth-about-the-muslim-brotherhood/.

Al-Arian, Abdullah. 2014. *Answering the Call: Popular Islamic Activism in Sadat's Egypt*. New York: Oxford Univ. Press.

———. 2015. "From the Ashes of Rabaa: History and the Future of the Muslim Brotherhood." Occasional Paper Series no. 4. Univ. of Denver, Center for Middle East Studies.

Al-Awadi, Hesham. 2005. "Mubarak and the Islamists: Why Did the 'Honeymoon' End?" *Middle East Journal* 59, no. 1: 62–80.

Baker, Raymond William. 2003. *Islam without Fear: Egypt and the New Islamists*. Cambridge, MA: Harvard Univ. Press.

Al-Banna, Hasan. 2006. *Six Tracts of Hasan al-Banna: A Selection from the* Majmu'at Rasa'il al-Imam al-Shahid Hasan al-Banna. Aachen, Germany: International Islamic Federation of Student Organizations.

Bayat, Asef. 2013. "Post-Islamism at Large." In *Post-Islamism: The Changing Faces of Political Islam*, edited by Asef Bayat, 3–32. New York: Oxford Univ. Press.

Brooke, Steven. 2019. *Winning Hearts and Votes: Social Services and the Islamist Political Advantage*. Ithaca, NY: Cornell Univ. Press.

Brown, Nathan. 2011. "Post-revolutionary al-Azhar." Carnegie Papers, Oct. 3. Carnegie Endowment for International Peace, Washington, DC.

Clark, Janine A. 2004. *Islam, Charity, and Activism: Middle-Class Networks and Social Welfare in Egypt, Jordan, and Yemen*. Bloomington: Indiana Univ. Press.

Cooke, Miriam. 1994. "Zaynab al-Ghazali: Saint or Subversive?" *Die Welt des Islam* 34, no. 1: 1–20.

Dalacoura, Katerina. 2018. "Islamism, Secularization, Secularity: The Muslim Brotherhood in Egypt as a Phenomenon of a Secular Age." *Economy and Society* 47, no. 2: 313–34.

Esposito, John L., and Dalia Mogahed. 2007. *Who Speaks for Islam? What a Billion Muslims Really Think*. New York: Gallup Press.

Freedom and Justice Party (FJP). 2011. *Election Program*. Cairo: FJP.

Al-Ghannouchi, Rachid. 2012. "Secularism and the Relation between Religion and the State from the Perspective of al-Nahdha Party." Speech given at the Center for the Study of Islam and Democracy, Washington, DC, Mar. 2. Transcript at http://archive.constantcontact.com/fs093/1102084408196/archive/1109480512119.html.

Hallaq, Wael. 2013. *The Impossible State: Islam, Politics, and Modernity's Moral Predicament*. New York: Columbia Univ. Press.

Harnisch, Chris, and Quinn Mecham. 2009. "Democratic Ideology in Islamist Opposition? The Muslim Brotherhood's 'Civil State.'" *Middle Eastern Studies* 45, no. 2: 189–205.

Harris, Christina Phelps. 1964. *Nationalism and Revolution in Egypt: The Role of the Muslim Brotherhood*. The Hague: Mouton.

Heyworth-Dunne, J. 1950. *Religious and Political Trends in Modern Egypt*. Washington, DC: McGregor & Werner.

Human Rights Watch. 2019. "Egypt: Independently Investigate Morsy's Death." At https://www.hrw.org/news/2019/06/17/egypt-independently-investigate-morsys-death.

Husayn, Taha. 1975. *The Future of Culture in Egypt*. New York: Octagon Books.

Hussin, Iza R. 2016. *The Politics of Islamic Law: Local Elites, Colonial Authority, and the Making of the Muslim State*. Chicago: Univ. of Chicago Press.

Ibrahim, Saad Eddin. 1980. "Anatomy of Egypt's Militant Islamic Groups: Methodological Note and Preliminary Findings." *International Journal of Middle East Studies* 12, no. 4: 423–53.

Jankowski, James P. 2002. *Nasser's Egypt, Arab Nationalism, and the United Arab Republic*. Boulder, CO: Lynne Reiner.

Kandil, Hazem. 2015. *Inside the Brotherhood*. London: Polity Press.

Kazmi, Zaheer. 2014. "The Limits of Muslim Liberalism." *Los Angeles Review of Books*, Apr. 4.

Kepel, Gilles. 1993. *The Prophet and Pharaoh: Muslim Extremism in Egypt*. Berkeley: Univ. of California Press.

Khatab, Sayed. 2002. "'Hakimiyyah' and 'Jahiliyyah' in the Thought of Sayyid Qutb." *Middle Eastern Studies* 38, no. 3: 145–70.

Lombardi, Clark, and Nathan Brown. 2013. "Islam in Egypt's New Constitution." In *The Battle for Egypt's Constitution*, Project on Middle East Political Science (POMEPS) Briefings no. 17, 33–37. Washington, DC: Elliot School of International Affairs.

Loveluck, Louisa. 2014. "Sisi Says Muslim Brotherhood Will Not Exist under His Reign." *Guardian*, May 5.

Masoud, Tarek. 2014. *Counting Islam: Religion, Class, and Elections in Egypt*. New York: Cambridge Univ. Press.

Mitchell, Richard. [1969] 1993. *The Society of the Muslim Brothers*. With a foreword by John O. Voll. New York: Oxford Univ. Press.

Mitchell, Timothy. 1991. *Colonizing Egypt*. Berkeley: Univ. of California Press.

Pahwa, Sumita. 2013. "Secularizing Islamism and Islamizing Democracy: The Political and Ideational Evolution of the Egyptian Muslim Brothers 1984–2012." *Mediterranean Politics* 18, no. 2: 189–206.

Rida, Muhammad Rashid. 2002. "Renewal, Renewing, and Renewers" (speech, 1930). In *Modernist Islam: 1840–1940*, edited by Charles Kurzman, 77–85. New York: Oxford Univ. Press.

Scott, Rachel M. 2012. "What Might the Muslim Brotherhood Do with al-Azhar? Religious Authority in Egypt." *Die Welt des Islams* 52, no. 2: 131–65.

Shepard, William E. 1987. "Islam and Ideology: Toward a Typology." *International Journal of Middle East Studies* 19:307–35.

Sivan, Emmanuel. 1985. *Radical Islam: Medieval Theology and Modern Politics.* New Haven, CT: Yale Univ. Press.

Stark, Rodney. 1999. "Secularization, R.I.P." *Sociology of Religion* 60, no. 3: 249–73.

Sullivan, Denis J., and Sana Abed-Kotob. 1999. *Islam in Contemporary Egypt: Civil Society vs. the State.* Boulder, CO: Lynne Rienner.

Swatos, William H., Jr., and Kevin J. Christiano. 1999. "Secularization Theory: The Course of a Concept." *Sociology of Religion* 60, no. 3: 209–28.

Vannetzel, Marie. 2017. "The Muslim Brotherhood's 'Virtuous Society' and State Developmentalism in Egypt: The Politics of 'Goodness.'" In *Development as a Battlefield*, edited by Irene Bono and Beatrice Hibou, 220–45. Leiden: Brill.

Voll, John O. 1983. *Islam and Stateness in the Modern Sudan.* Discussion Paper Series no. 4. Montreal: McGill Univ. Centre for Developing-Area Studies.

———. 1994. *Islam: Continuity and Change in the Modern World.* 2nd ed. Syracuse, NY: Syracuse Univ. Press.

———. 2014. "Not Secularism vs. Islamism." https://tif.ssrc.org/2014/03/25/not-secularism-vs-islamism/.

Waterbury, John. 1983. *The Egypt of Nasser and Sadat: The Political Economy of Two Regimes.* Princeton, NJ: Princeton Univ. Press.

Wickham, Carrie Rosefsky. 2002. *Mobilizing Islam: Religion, Activism, and Political Change in Egypt.* New York: Columbia Univ. Press.

———. 2015. *The Muslim Brotherhood: Evolution of an Islamist Movement.* Princeton, NJ: Princeton Univ. Press.

Part Five

Producing, Presenting, and Consuming Islamic Knowledge Today

9

A Short History of Modern Arab Knowledge Production on China

Shuang Wen

Despite the long history of Arab–Chinese interactions since the seventh century, *modern* Arab knowledge production on China has only a short story owing to the relative marginality of China/Chinese studies in Arabic academies. The global historical context that led to such a situation is Western dominance. Consequently, most Arab scholars research issues of their own countries with reference to and/or in interaction with the West. Only a handful cast their eyes on the "other East." Another major reason behind the paucity of scholarship on China is the inherent linguistic difficulty involved: in order to conduct research on China, an Arab scholar needs to know Chinese. Although some have mastered the language, most publish only in Arabic, so their research findings are not widely known. This article, therefore, attempts to summarize in English the Arabic scholarship on China in order to introduce it to a larger international audience that is keenly observing the increasing Arab–Chinese engagements in the twenty-first century.[1] In addition to providing synoptic overviews of major institutions, scholars, and their representative works, this article

1. As it is impossible to survey all of the academic developments and literature on Arab–Chinese relations, this article highlights only the major institutions, scholars, and their representative works.

also critically analyzes the historical contexts for the formation, development, and challenges of the field.

The development of China/Chinese studies in Arabic academies reflects the long-term aspiration of non-Western scholars to overcome Western academic hegemony since the first half of the twentieth century. This desire originated from the Chinese Hui modernists' attempt to improve religious education for Chinese Muslims and, at the same time, to earn respect for Muslims from the non-Muslim Chinese public by educating the latter about the Islamic and Arab culture.[2] To achieve these goals, these scholars sought knowledge from the Islamic educational center, Egypt, rather than going to the West, as many Chinese did at the time. While in Egypt, they made concerted efforts to spread knowledge about Chinese Muslims as well as about Chinese history and culture to the Arabs. Frustrated by Western colonialism and imperialism, Arab modernists took great interest in the Hui modernists' work, so the transfer of knowledge was bidirectional.

These two-way intellectual exchanges continue today, despite the ups and downs of Cold War politics. There are multiple reasons for the sustained knowledge transfer and production, ranging from diplomatic needs for personnel to the deepening of trade between China and the Arab world at present. The contents of the knowledge transfer have also been expanded to include language instruction, translation, literary critique, and political analyses.

China/Chinese Studies in Arabic Academies

The Republic of China (ROC, declared in 1912) recognized Egypt immediately after it declared independence from Great Britain in 1922. Later, the ROC signed a tariff agreement with Egypt and established a

2. The Huis are primarily or exclusively Chinese-speaking Muslims, or "Sino-Muslims," as defined by the historian Jonathan Lipman (1998). They are different from other Muslim groups in China, such as the Uyghur-speaking Muslims in Xinjiang.

consulate in Alexandria in 1930.[3] By the introduction of two Afghan scholars, Faḍl al-Rahman and Muhammad Dazan, who were traveling and teaching in Yunnan, al-Azhar University agreed to accept five Hui students to study there and covered their full expenses, including tuition, accommodations, and stipend (Na 1992, 3). In November, the first group arrived in Egypt: one English teacher, Sha Guozhen, who was appointed as the group leader; three students from the Mingde Middle School in Yunnan; and one student from the Shanghai Islamic Teachers College. The next year, when meeting with Sha, King Fu'ad promised to increase the enrollment of Hui students in the ensuing years and do his best to improve the educational level of Chinese Muslims in general. From 1931 to 1947, a total of thirty-five Chinese Muslims, including two Uyghurs from Xinjiang, studied at al-Azhar University.[4]

It was these Hui students who planted the seeds of China studies in Arabic academies. While in Egypt, they made conscientious efforts to publish in Arabic to spread general knowledge on China and Chinese Muslims to Arab readers. Among these graduates, Muhammad Makin, Muhammad Tawāḍu', and Badruddin aṣ-Ṣinī made the most impact. Since those early years, however, the development of China/Chinese studies in Arabic academies has been *uneven*. Although Egypt has a longer history in this area of Arab–Chinese educational exchange, because of its current political and economic conditions, some scholars have migrated to the Persian Gulf countries instead, which have little experience in China/Chinese studies but are eager to catch up, especially with China's generous financial investment. As for

3. Wizārat al-Khārijiyyah (Ministry of Foreign Affairs), folder no. 0078-023266, 1930, Dār al-Wathā'iq al-Qawmiyyah (Egyptian National Archives), Cairo.

4. Major studies in Chinese on this group of scholars include Ma, Na, and Li 2011 as well as Gao and Yao 2012. In addition to the main group of thirty-five visiting Chinese scholars, there were eleven "Xinjiang schoolmates" (*Xinjiang tongxue*) at al-Azhar as well. These individuals were sent by the Mengmai Xinjiang Tongxue Hui (Xinjiang Students Association in Mumbai) and arrived in Egypt between February 1940 and December 1945.

the major institutions focused on China/Chinese studies, they can be divided into two types: Chinese-language teaching departments and research centers.

The Early Years of Development

In 1934, Muhammad Makin (Ma Jian, 1906–78) published *Naẓrah āmi'ah ila tārīkh al-Islām fī aṣ-Ṣin wa aḥwāl al-Muslimīn fīhā* (A Comprehensive View on the History of Islam in China and on the Conditions of Muslims There). Because Makin had studied Arabic prior to arriving in Egypt, he could quickly start communicating with the locals. The book was based on a series of lectures that Makin gave on Chinese Islam at al-Azhar, which drew a large audience. After the lectures, the Jamā'ayyat at-Ta'āruf al-Islāmī (Association for Mutual Islamic Acquaintance) was also established to deepen mutual understandings between Egypt and China, with administrative members from both countries. Al-Muṭba'a as-Salafīyya wa-Maktabatuhā (Salafi Press and Its Library) in Cairo published the book. Although the word *salafīyya* may have a negative connotation today, at the time the publishing house aimed at giving voice to the modernist movement to revive the Arab-Islamic heritage.[5] Given the publisher's objectives, there was a keen interest in Chinese Muslims, about whom little was known. The book included chapters on the arrival of Islam to China; comparison of Islam with other religions in China; the political, economic, and social conditions of Chinese Muslims; mosques in China; madrasas; Islamic newspapers; Chinese Muslims' lack of development; matters related to *fiqh* that caused this backwardness; ways to improve the situation; and so on. The book filled in many knowledge gaps in the Arab academy. In 1935, the same press also published Makin's Arabic translation of *The Analects* as *Kitāb al-ḥiwār li Kūnfūshuys fīlsūf aṣ-Ṣin al-akbar* (The Book of Dialogue: China's Great Philosopher Confucius) to introduce

5. For more on the evolution of the term *salafīyya*, see Lauzière 2010.

Chinese philosophy to Arab readers.[6] The book quickly received the attention of the Egyptian philosophy scholar Mohammad Ghalāb at Cairo University. In his book *al-Filsafah as-Sharqiyyah* (The Eastern Philosophy) in 1938, Ghalāb used *Kitāb al-ḥiwār* as one of his major sources to introduce Chinese philosophy. Years later, the Egyptian Nobel laureate Naguib Mahfouz reflected that *Kitāb al-ḥiwār* left the deepest imprint on his understanding of the Chinese culture (Zhong 1983, 12–13).

In 1945, the Muslim Brotherhood's Qism al-Iṣāl bi al-'Ālam al-Islām (Outreach to the Islamic World Section) published *Aṣ-Ṣin wa-l-Islām* (China and Islam) by Muhammad Tawāḍu' (Pang Shiqian, 1902–58). Tawāḍu' was born in Henan and studied at Chengda Teacher's College before going to al-Azhar, where he studied from 1938 to 1946. During his studies in Egypt, he was even appointed as a consultant of King Faruq on eastern affairs and as a lecturer on Chinese culture at al-Azhar (Pang [1951] 1988, 20). Hasan al-Banna, founder of the Muslim Brotherhood, wrote a preface and introduction for the book and praised the kindness of its author. The major difference between Tawāḍu''s *Aṣ-Ṣin wa-l-Islām* and Makin's *Naẓrah* was that Tawāḍu' included some basic information about China because his intended readers were not just Muslims but also all who could read Arabic. Tawāḍu' arrived in Egypt during the time of the second Sino-Japanese War (1937–45), so one of his major tasks was to educate Arab readers on basic information about China, including Chinese ancient and modern history, philosophy, education, society, culture, economy, women, and even Sun Yat-sen's "Three Principals of the People." On the topic of Islam in China, in addition to the topics covered in Makin's book, Tawāḍu''s book also included information about Chinese translations of Islamic literature, Chinese Islamic associations, and Chinese Turkistan. Even the chapters on the conditions of Chinese Muslims in different parts of China included basic geographical and demographic

6. For more on Makin's translation of *The Analects*, see Benite 2014.

information about the specific provinces in order to provide a context for Arabic readers to understand the whereabouts and percentages of Chinese Muslims living among the non-Muslim Chinese. In addition, the book offered more than thirty pages of indexes, references, and addendums so that future scholars could conduct further research, all of which added to its academic value.

Another Hui student, Badruddin aṣ-Ṣinī (Hai Weiliang, 1912–2006) transferred from Nadwat al-'Ulama in Lucknow, India, to al-Azhar, where he studied from 1934 to 1942. Aṣ-Ṣinī was born in Hunan in central China but never returned to the mainland after studying in the Islamic world. While abroad, he was recruited by the Guomindang (Chinese Nationalist Party) to work as a diplomat for Taiwan. Throughout his career, he was appointed to the embassies in Tehran, New Delhi, and Jeddah and was fluent in Persian, Urdu, and Arabic. In 1937, he completed his manuscript "al-'Alaqāt bayna al-'Arab wa-l-Ṣin" (Relations between the Arabs and China) in Cairo, but the book with the same title was not published until 1950 by the Maktabat an-Nahḍah al-Miṣriyyah (Egyptian Nahḍah Library) in Cairo. The long delay was probably owing to his career change from scholar to diplomat.[7] *Al-'Alaqāt* is based on sources in all the languages that Badruddin aṣ-Ṣinī knew. It covers contacts between East and West Asia from Han/Roman times to Zheng He's voyages during the early Ming. The chapters are divided thematically into the political, intellectual, commercial, religious, diplomatic, and artistic relations between the Chinese and Arabs.[8] In 1974, aṣ-Ṣinī also published *Tārīkh al-Muslimīn fi aṣ-Ṣin fi al-māḍī wa-l-ḥāḍr* (History of Muslims in China in the Past and Present) in Beirut. On the cover of the book, the author's name is

7. For more on Hai Weiliang, see Chen 2018.

8. The manuscript was first translated into Chinese by Chen Keli in 1956, but the book *Zhongguo he Alabo de guanxi* (Relations between China and the Arabs) was not published until 2006 by the Tianma Publishing House in Hong Kong. Chen was educated at the Beiping Huijiao Jingxueyuan (Islamic Scripture Institute of Peking) and studied with Imam Wang Jingzhai, who had studied in Turkey and Egypt. Although Chen had great command of the Arabic language, he never studied abroad.

given as "Badruddin W. L. Hai," with his political title, "Counsellor of Chinese Embassy–Jeddah." This book was a reprinted combination of two books previously published by Badruddin. Whereas one was written in Arabic on Islam and Chinese Turkistan, the other was written in Urdu on Chinese Muslims (Tawāḍu' 1945, 98).

In addition to writing in Arabic, the Hui scholars also translated some Chinese literature into Arabic, such as Makin's translation of *The Analects* as *Kitāb al-ḥiwār* mentioned earlier. Another major translator was Nur Muhammad (Na Xun, 1911–89), who studied at al-Azhar from 1934 to 1947, probably the longest stay among this group of Hui scholars. While in Egypt, Nur Muhammad translated into Arabic the short stories of Lu Xun, Zhu Ziqing, and Cao Yu, which were well received (Suo 2012, 197), and inspired some Egyptian Sinologists to continue such endeavors many years later. These publications were produced before the Chinese Civil War in the late 1940s, so the content and political stance among the books were similar because the Hui scholars had a common objective: to introduce to Arabic readers the conditions of Chinese Muslims and China. They also had a common enemy: the Japanese during World War II. For example, in 1939 the three authors went on Hajj together with twenty-five other Chinese Azharites to dispel the misinformation spread by Japanese wartime propaganda.[9] They also collectively published "Risālah ba'athatu al-Islāmiyah aṣ-Ṣiniyyah ila al-'ālam al-Islāmi" (Letter from the Chinese Islamic Association Delegation to the Islamic World) in the newspaper *al-Ahram* so that Arabic readers could realize the aggressive behaviors of the Japanese government during the war. As a result of their efforts, King Faruq expressed support to the ROC government (Wang 2012, 57).[10] Moreover, at the time the term *China* used in their writings referred to the same political entity: the ROC. After 1949, however, the term *China* started to be politically contentious because it could refer to

9. For more details on Japanese efforts in the Islamic world during World War II, see Hammond 2017.

10. For more details on this Hajj, see Mao 2011.

either the ROC in Taiwan or the People's Republic of China (PRC) on the mainland. Because Taiwan's efforts to promote knowledge in the Arab world were and have been little known, the account in the following section comes from the available sources on Arab academic exchanges with the PRC, and "China" mainly means the PRC.

Chinese-Language Teaching

Two years after Egypt established diplomatic relations with the PRC, the first Chinese-language teaching department was established in 1958 at al-Madrasa al-Alsun (Egyptian School of Languages), which later was incorporated into Ain Shams University. The first two Chinese staff sent by the PRC were Jin Jiazhen, another Hui scholar but one who specialized in English language and literature at Xibei (Northwestern) University, and Bao Zhenggu, a professor in English at Fudan University. The initial purpose of the program was to train Egyptian personnel with Chinese-language skills for diplomacy. The Chinese professors taught the Chinese language in English at the beginning. The first group of ten Egyptian students graduated in 1962, including the Egyptian artists Hebay and Tamatir Anayat, who later studied Chinese painting in Beijing (Li 2010, 161).[11] From 1963 to 1977, however, owing to political tensions between Egypt and the PRC over the Sino-Soviet split and later to the Chinese Cultural Revolution (1966–76), the Chinese-language department at the Egyptian School of Languages stopped recruiting students for more than a decade. By the end of the 1980s, the first generation of Egyptian Sinologists had finally been well trained enough to start their own careers. With more than thirty Egyptian faculty members who have spent some time living in China, the program now grants degrees from the BA to the PhD. One of the excellent graduates of this program is Dr. Hassanein Fahmy Hussein, who has devoted his Chinese-language skills to translating Chinese literature and even to publishing literary critiques

11. The spelling of these names is approximate.

in Chinese academic journals. Hussein received his initial Chinese-language training at Ain Shams University and eventually earned a PhD in comparative literature from Beijing Language and Culture University in 2008. Hussein's most renowned translation, perhaps, is *Adh-dhurah al-rafī'ah al-ḥamrā'* (The Sublime Red Sorghum, 2012), an Arabic rendition of the Chinese Nobel laureate Mo Yan's most widely known novel, *Hong gaoliang jiazu* (The Red Sorghum Clan, 1986).[12]

Al-Azhar University established the Department of Chinese Language and Literature in its Faculty of Foreign Languages in the academic year 2001–2. One unique feature of al-Azhar's Chinese program is that it includes, in addition to Chinese language and literature, the subtrack "Islamic Studies in the Chinese Language," a five-year program that was later also incorporated into the Department of Islamic Studies in 2007. The objective of this special area of study, according to its website, is to increase communications and connections with Muslims living in China. It also seeks to spread *da'wa* among people living in the Islamic societies of Asia.[13] In addition to Chinese-language classes, other courses are "History of Islam in China," "Chinese Civilization," and "Life of Muslims in Chinese in Modern and Contemporary Times."

Outside Egypt,[14] in 1977 Institut Bourguiba des langues vivantes in Tunis established a Chinese-language program, offering selective courses. By 1998, the program had developed into a four-year BA-granting institution. In 1993, the University of Khartoum in Sudan established a Chinese-language department. Other Arab universities that have established a Chinese-language department include the University of Jordan (2009), the Royal Jordanian National Defense

12. The novel was adapted into the movie *Hong gaoliang* (Red Sorghum) in 1988. The novel was translated into English as *Red Sorghum* in 1993 by Howard Goldblatt.

13. See al-Azhar's website at http://www.azhar.edu.eg/languages/قسم-اللغة-الصينية-وآدابها, last accessed Aug. 10, 2019.

14. Other Egyptian universities that have a Chinese-language department include: Suez Canal University, University of Alexandria, Cairo University, Minia University, and Zaqāzīq University.

College (2009), the University of Nouakchott in Mauritania (2010), Mohammed V University in Rabat (2011), the Red Sea University in Port Sudan (2016), and University Hassan II in Casablanca (2017).

The Persian Gulf region came late to developing its Chinese-language teaching capabilities. Although Effat University in Saudi Arabia and Sultan Qaboos University in Oman have been offering some courses, no degree-granting program has been established so far. In the United Arab Emirates, al-Mushrif Chinese School officially opened in Abu Dhabi in 2010 at the elementary level. With strong backing from Crown Prince Shaykh Mohammed bin Zayed, it is the first school in the Gulf seeking to introduce Chinese culture and language to a younger generation. It was estimated that by 2020 there were sixty schools in the Emirates that teach Chinese to twelve thousand young students.[15]

In addition to the degree-granting Chinese-language university departments funded by Arab countries, the PRC has also established about fifteen Confucius Institutes in these countries, which are non-degree granting Chinese-language teaching schools in the Arab world. The first one opened in Lebanon in 2007. These schools offer different levels of long-term language courses to students of all age groups and from all walks of life, including businesspersons, government officials, and even police officers, who are dealing with an increasing number of Chinese tourists in the region. These Confucius Institutes also offer courses on Chinese culture, such as Gongfu (Chinese martial arts), painting, and calligraphy. They organize annual Chinese-speaking contests and summer trips to the PRC as well.

With the increased number of Chinese-language training departments and schools, many Arab students choose China (instead of a Western country) as the place to pursue their graduate studies in a variety of disciplines, such as Chinese language and culture,

15. See the website of the Dubai government-owned newspaper *al-Bayān* at https://www.albayan.ae/across-the-uae/news-and-reports/2019-07-20-1.3609538, last accessed Aug. 26, 2019.

Chinese–Arabic comparative linguistics, and even engineering and medical science. For example, by 2016 an estimated fourteen thousand Arab students were studying in China (Bouchaib 2017, 18). This figure comes from an MA thesis written in Chinese by a Moroccan student majoring in Chinese international education and teaching Chinese as a foreign language. According to these Arab students, they are following the hadith of Prophet Muhammad, "Seek knowledge, even unto China." One of the reasons why they choose China to study abroad is the tightening visa controls on Muslim students by some Western governments. China, in contrast, is warmly welcoming these students, often offering full scholarships and stipends.

China as an Area of Study in Arabic Academies

China as an area of study in the Arabic academies, however, is a relatively new development. Zaqāzīq University in al-Sharqiyyah *muḥāfaẓah* (governorate) in northern Egypt established Ma'ahad ad-Dirāsāt wa-l-Baḥūth al-Āsiyawīyah (Institute of Asian Studies and Research) in 1993. It is the first research organization in the Arabic academies that specializes in the study of Asia. Since its inception, the institute has established its reputation as one of the best programs for training Arab Asianists. Undergraduates from any disciplinary background, even the natural sciences, can enter the program to pursue MA and PhD degrees as long as their regional research focus is Asia. For example, Dr. Ibrahim al-Akhras, a graduate of this institute, wrote some well-received books that attracted the attention and stimulated the interest of Arab readers. His major publications include *At-Tajrabah aṣ-Ṣiniyyah al-ḥadīthah fi an-numū: Hal yumkin al-iqtidā' bihā?* (China's Modern Experience of Growth: Can It Be Emulated?, 2005), *Asrār taqadum aṣ-Ṣin: Dirāsah fi malāmiḥ al-quwah wa asbāb aṣ-ṣu'ūd* (Secrets of China's Progress: Study on Power Features and Reasons for Its Rise, 2008), and *Dawur ash-sharakāt 'ābirah al-qārāt fi aṣ-Ṣin: Tanmiyyah iqtiṣādīyah am isti'mārīyah wa taba'īyah?* (The Role of Transcontinental Companies in China: Economic Development or Colonialism and Dependency?, 2012).

Markaz ad-Dirāsāt al-Āsiyawīyyah (Center for Asian Studies) at Cairo University was established in 1994 as a policy-oriented research organization. Although it initially focused on Japan, more research has been done on China with the rise of China in recent years. The center houses the Faculty of Political Science and Economics because the disciplinary background of researchers at the center is mainly in political science. For example, the center's first director, Dr. Muhammad as-Said Salīm, is a political scientist who received his PhD in Canada in 1979. His major publications on China include *Mustaqbal Hong Kong* (The Future of Hong Kong, 1998) and *al-'Alaqāt al-Maṣriyyah Ṣinīyyah* (Egyptian–Chinese Relations, 1999). Unfortunately, Salīm does not know Chinese. His analyses are based mainly on Arabic and English sources. This shortcoming is also reflected in other publications coming from the center, such as the edited volume *Aṣ-Ṣu'ūd aṣ-Ṣinī* (The Rise of China) by Huda Mītkīs and Ghadījah 'Arafah Muhammad published in 2006.

Markaz al-Ahrām lil Dirāsāt as-Siyāsīyyah wal Istirātījīyyah (al-Ahrām Center for Political and Strategic Studies) is another major institute for research on the contemporary politics of China. The Ahrām Center has been publishing the periodical *as-Siyāsah ad-Dawuliyyah* (International Politics) since 1965. Since its very first issue, China has been a frequently discussed topic in it. For example, from 1965 to 2007 a total of 115 articles were published on China (Salīm 2008). The al-Ahrām Center has a unit on international relations where most of its China experts are based. One of its major publications is *Aṣ-Ṣin: Ma'ajizah nihāyyah al-qarana al-'ashrīn* (China: Miracle at the End of the Twentieth Century) by Ibrāhīm Nāfi'a, published in 1999.

Two research centers especially designed for the study of China were established in 2009. Markaz al-Baḥūth wa-l-Dirāsāt aṣ-Ṣinīyyah al-Maṣrīyyah (Chinese–Egyptian Research Center) at Helwan University in Cairo focuses on China–Egypt relations. It has held three conferences and has published its own journal since 2012, with contributions from scholars in China and Egypt as well as from other researchers who are interested in the relations between China and Egypt. The publications are in Arabic, Chinese, and English. Markaz

Dirāsāt aṣ-Ṣin wa Āsiyā (Center for China and Asia Studies) was established in Damascus. The center's director, Muhammad Khira al-Wādi, received his MA in journalism and advertising from the University of Moscow in 1974. He served as the director and editor in chief at radio stations, television stations, and newspapers in Syria for many years before becoming the ambassador to the PRC from 2000 to 2008. After completing his tenure in China, he established this research center. Al-Wādi is a member of both the Chinese Academy of Social Sciences and the Russian Academy of Sciences and Arts. His major publications on China include *Tajārub aṣ-Ṣin min at-taṭarruf ila al-i'tidāl* (The Experiences of China from Radicalism to Moderation) in 2008 and *al-'Alāqāt aṣ-Ṣinīyyah al-Isrā'ilīyyah: Al-ḥisābāt al-bāridah* (Chinese–Israeli Relations: The Cold Reflections) in 2012. Markaz al-Malak Faiṣal lil Baḥuth wal Dirāsāt al-Islāmīyyah (King Faisal Center for Research and Islamic Studies) in Saudi Arabia established a unit on Asian studies in 2015, seeking to promote understanding of East Asia within the Gulf and the wider Arab world. The unit's research agenda is bifurcated between a focus on contemporary East Asian international relations, politics, economics, and security topics, on the one hand, and a concentration on historical, anthropological, and cultural-social issues, on the other. This broad research agenda enables the unit to engage with multiple disciplines, generate a diverse set of studies, and, more importantly, maintain its fidelity to the spirit of the King Faisal Center as a think tank and academic institution. Although the unit was created only recently, it has hosted a variety of activities, such as seminars, workshops, and lectures, and has hosted visiting scholars as well as nonresident fellows and associates (including professors and PhD students) from Chinese universities. This activity demonstrates the intention of a major Gulf research institute to catch up in the field of Chinese studies. It even has a website in the Chinese language.[16]

16. See the King Faisal Center website at https://www.kfcris.com/ch/view/22, last accessed Aug. 31, 2019.

On the topic of Chinese–Arab relations, MA and PhD dissertations at various universities in Egypt have focused largely on Arab–China diplomatic relations since 1956. They rarely use primary sources, however. Dr. Zeinab Essa Abdul Rahman is an exemplary exception who wrote a PhD dissertation for the History Department of the University of Alexandria. She later turned the dissertation into a monograph titled *'Ālāqāt al-Maṣriyyah aṣ-Ṣiniyyah 1956–1970* (Egyptian–Chinese Relations, 1956–1970), which was published in 2011. In her research, Abdul Rahman used Egyptian Ministry of Foreign Affairs archival documents extensively, and the book was published by al-Hay'ah al-Miṣrīyah al-'Āmmah lil-Kitāb (General Egyptian Writers Association), an important publisher affiliated with the Egyptian National Archives. This is the best work on the history of Chinese–Egyptian relations written by an Egyptian scholar that I have ever come across.

In 2006, Muhammad Nu'aman Jalāl, former Egyptian ambassador to China, published an edited volume titled *Aṣ-Ṣin bi 'uyūn Maṣriyyah* (China in the Eyes of the Egyptians), which includes contributing articles from other Egyptian diplomats and public intellectuals who had lived in or visited China. The book, including firsthand accounts of the diplomats and intellectuals' observations on the development of China, was translated into Chinese in the same year of its Arabic publication, which shows the importance that Chinese scholars attach to Egyptian scholars' views.

The Challenges of China/Chinese Studies in Arabic Academies

The developments discussed in the preceding sections reveal some major challenges to China/Chinese studies in Arabic academies. First, whereas a growing number of Arabs have studied the Chinese language, most of them choose to work in the business sector rather than becoming academic researchers. For example, in Egypt, because academic researchers and university professors are paid poorly, students graduating from Chinese-language training programs often choose to work as tour guides for the increasing numbers of Chinese tourists or as translators/interpreters for trading companies that are benefiting from the tightening economic cooperation between China and Egypt, especially after the launch of the Second Suez Canal Project in Egypt by China in 2014. This is an unfortunate misplacement of the invaluable human talents produced by Arabic academies.

Second, while Chinese-speaking Egyptians seek financial rewards in the private sector, the Arab scholars who do research on China do not usually have the necessary Chinese-language skills. Most of the books mentioned earlier are based on Arabic sources or on Arabic translations of Western scholarship. As a result, their analyses tend to be one-sided and sometimes internalize the biases of their Western sources. Furthermore, the academic works produced by Arab scholars who do have the Chinese-language skills tend to narrowly focus on Chinese linguistics and the methodologies of teaching Chinese as a foreign language to native Arabic speakers. As a result, their works thus unfortunately circulate only among a few interested specialists in the field and are shelved mainly in university libraries and are not easily available to the general public, thus limiting their impact. Moreover, those books on China that *are* readily available in the bookstores, on the internet, or in the used/secondhand book market, such as the *sur al-azbakiyyah* in Cairo, are mostly translated works of Western scholarship or popular accounts. Arab commercial publishers employ translators with European-language skills to translate Western scholarship on China to elevate the general public's thirst for information and knowledge. Consequently, the general reading public also unconsciously internalizes the biases of Western perspectives. This is another unfortunate mismatch of academic production and public consumption on knowledge about China in the Arab countries.

Third, although Arab universities have been teaching Chinese language since 1956, so far no systematic textbook has been produced to suit the special needs of native Arabic speakers. Most Chinese-language teaching departments in the Arab world use *Xin shiyong hanyu keben* (New Practical Chinese Reader), a textbook for teaching Chinese to native English speakers. Even if the book has been translated into Arabic, its methodologies are not tailored to native Arabic speakers. To remedy this situation, some Chinese Arabists are cooperating with Egyptian Sinologists to publish a textbook especially designed for native Arabic speakers to study Chinese as a foreign language. In addition to textbooks, there is also a very limited supply of reference tools, such as grammar books, dictionaries, and thesauruses, as well as of other reading materials for native Arabic speakers to enhance their language-acquisition experience.

Fourth, no professional association in the Arabic academies is devoted to research on China, which is a major benchmark for the coming of age of an academic field. As a result, the exchanges between the Arab scholars on their common research interest in China are often ad hoc and limited. Most of them work on their own and oftentimes reinvent the wheel. Whereas Arab–Chinese contemporary relations have been overresearched, other topics on Chinese history and culture have rarely been explored.

Therefore, at present China/Chinese studies as an area of study in Arabic academies is still underdeveloped. Many Arab people are eager to know more about China, but few have in-depth knowledge and the necessary language skills. These problems are not unique to China/Chinese studies in Arabic academies. They tend to exist wherever a new academic field is developing. My purpose here is not to unjustly criticize but to point out the existing challenges so that the field can be further developed in the future. In his article "Wāqiʿa wa mustaqbal ad-dirāsāt aṣ-Ṣīniyyah fi Maṣr" (The Reality and Future of China Studies in Egypt, 2008), Dr. Salīm calls for support from the Chinese government to strengthen the development of China/Chinese studies in the Arab world and to improve the exchanges between Chinese and Arab scholars.

Conclusion

Since the 1930s, Chinese and Arab scholars have been striving to overcome the Western academic hegemon. Language training is an important first step. The next step is to encourage language specialists to utilize their hard-earned skills in rigorous academic research with firsthand field research and primary sources. Moreover, well-trained scholars should take up the crucial task of informing the general public about Chinese–Arab interactions rather than leaving it in the hands of those who do not have the necessary language skills or research experience, including the untrained or undertrained "talking heads" on TV, who might simply misinform the public with hidden biases inherited from Western sources. Only by rigorous academic work and the dissemination of its knowledge will the image of China in the Arab world no longer be a romanticized curiosity or biased stereotype but include practical and concrete realities that can deepen mutual understanding.

References

Abdul Rahman, Zeinab Essa. 2011. *'Ālāqāt al-Maṣriyyah aṣ-Ṣiniyyah 1956–1970* (Egyptian–Chinese relations, 1956–1970). Cairo: Al-Hay'ah al-Miṣrīyah al-'Āmmah lil-Kitāb.

Benite, Zvi Ben-Dor. 2014. "Taking Abduh to China: Chinese–Egyptian Intellectual Contact in the Early Twentieth Century." In *Global Muslims in the Age of Steam and Print*, edited by James Gelvin and Nile Green, 249–67. Berkeley: Univ. of California Press.

Bouchaib Chkaif. 2017. "Alabo guojia hanyu jiaoxue jianlun: Yi Moluoge wei li" (Brief study about teaching Chinese in the Arab Countries: Morocco as an example). MA thesis in Chinese International Education, Zhejiang Univ.

Chen, John. 2018. "Islam's Loneliest Cosmopolitan: Badr Aal-Din Hai Weiliang, the Lucknow–Cairo Connection, and the Circumscription of Islamic Transnationalism." *ReOrient* 3, no. 2: 120–39.

Gao Yuanfa and Yao Jide, eds. 2012. *Zhongguo xuesheng liuxue Aiji bashi zhounian jinian wenji 1913–2011* (Proceedings for celebrating the eightieth anniversary of Chinese Muslim students going to study in Egypt). Kunming, China: Yunnan Univ. Press.

Hammond, Kelly. 2017. "Managing Muslims: Imperial Japan, Islamic Policy, and Axis Connections during the Second World War." *Journal of Global History* 12:251–73.

Jalāl, Muhammad Nu'aman. 2006. *Aṣ-Ṣin bi 'uyūn Maṣriyyah* (China in the eyes of the Egyptians). [Cairo]: Mu'sasat al-Ma'āruf lil Ṭabā'ah wal Nasha.

Lauzière, Henri. 2010. "The Construction of Salafiyya: Reconsidering Salafism from the Perspective of Conceptual History." *International Journal of Middle East Studies* 42, no. 3: 369–89.

Li Zhenzhong. 2010. *Niluohe pan de huiyi: Xin Zhongguo di yi pi liu Ai xuesheng jishi* (Our sweet Days on the Nile: Memories of the first Chinese students in Egypt after 1949). Beijing: Shijie zhishi chubanshe.

Lipman, Jonathan. 1998. *Familiar Strangers: A History of Muslims in Northwest China.* Seattle: Univ. of Washington Press.

Ma Bozhong, Na Jiarui, and Li Jiangong, eds. 2011. *Li Cheng: Minguo liu Ai Huizu xuesheng paiqian shi yanjiu* (Experience: A historical study on the ROC Hui expatriate students in Egypt). Yichuan, China: Ningxia renmin chubanshe.

Mao, Yufeng. 2011. "A Muslim Vision for the Chinese Nation: Chinese Pilgrimage Missions to Mecca during World War II." *Journal of Asian Studies* 70, no. 2: 373–95.

Na Zhong. 1992. "*Aiji jiu nian*" (Nine years in Egypt). *Alabo shijie yanjiu* (Arab world studies) 10, no. 3: 3–8.

Pang Shiqian. [1951] 1988. *Aiji jiu nian* (Nine years in Egypt). Beijing: Zhongguo Yisilanjiao xiehui.

Salīm, Muhammad as-Said. 2008. "Wāqi'a wa mustaqbal ad-dirāsāt aṣ-Ṣīniyyah fi Maṣr" (The Reality and future of China studies in Egypt). *As-Siyāsah ad-dawuliyyah* (International politics) 43, no. 173: 71–73.

Suo Xinxiang. 2012. "Goujian Zhong: A wenxue qiaoliang de fanyijia Na Xun" (Na Xun: A bridge of translation for Chinese–Arabic literature). In *Zhongguo xuesheng liuxue Aiji bashi zhounian jinian wenji 1913–2011* (Proceedings for celebrating the eightieth anniversary of Chinese Muslim students going to study in Egypt), edited by Gao Yuanfa and Yao Jide, 196–200. Kunming, China: Yunnan Univ. Press.

Tawāḍu', Muhammad. 1945. *Aṣ-Ṣin wa-l-Islām* (China and Islam). Cairo: Qism al-Itṣāl bi al-'Ālam al-Islām.

Wang Zihua. 2012. "Sha Rucheng zai Aiji suo zuo de gongxian" (Sha Rucheng's achievements in Egypt). *Huizu Yanjiu* (Journal of Hui Muslim minority studies) 21, no 1: 52–60.

Zhong Jikun. 1983. "Yi Ma Jian xiansheng" (Memories about Professor Ma Jian). *Alabo shijie yanjiu* (Arab world studies) 2, no. 4: 8–15.

10

Muslim Media Preachers as Agenda Setters

Teaching Religion and Promoting Social Change

Tuve Buchmann Floden

Starting in the late 1990s and early 2000s, a new brand of Muslim preachers began to emerge, preachers who catered to the younger generation using modern media and a relaxed, informal style. Some people refer to these new preachers as "Muslim televangelists" or "Islamic televangelists"; I prefer to call them "media *du'ā*," which more precisely captures their roots and the tools they employ. "Media *du'ā*" is more appropriate than "televangelists" for several reasons. First, *televangelist* is a Christian word, composed of the prefix *tele-* for "television" and the word *evangelist*, referring to someone who preaches the Gospel. Using the Arabic word *du'ā*—literally meaning "callers to Islam"—captures the work of these popular preachers without the Christian context. Second, by definition, the term *televangelist* refers only to television and thus leaves out the full range of these Muslim preachers' output, which also includes books, websites, and social media (Floden 2017).

In addition, the media *du'ā* are a subset of Muslim preachers, with three characteristics setting them apart from the others. First, they do not hold formal religious degrees from al-Azhar or other such institutions. They instead have degrees in fields such as accounting, business, and engineering. Second, they use an informal style, addressing their audiences in a colloquial manner and mixing classical sources with modern examples. Third, they employ a wealth of modern media—not just television but also books, audio media (CDs and cassette tapes), websites, social media, and in-person lectures and workshops.

The recent focus on jihadists as a security threat, especially by people in the West, has tended to allow militants to speak for Islam. This study highlights, in contrast, that to understand the state of Islam today, we should pay attention to whom Muslims are listening and what those individuals are saying. The media *duʿā*'s broad global audiences suggest that they fit the bill for this exchange far better than the jihadists.

Modern scholars have studied the media *duʿā* to some degree but focus on distinctly different aspects of these preachers' work. Lindsay Wise (2003) and Yasmin Moll (2012), for instance, show how the media *duʿā* attract an audience disenchanted with the stricter, more rigid methods of the religious establishment, while Samuel Lee Harris (2008) and Mona Atia (2013) argue that these preachers focus on self-help and community development. Using audience theory, my study illustrates how the media *duʿā* tailor their message to pursue both of these goals and reveals the effect this modification has had on their success and influence. We can see how in using their messages about education and community development, these preachers are reformulating the relationship between television preachers and their audience by encouraging audience members to be active consumers and participants in the message.

Sources—Three Preachers from the Arab World

To explore the work of the media *duʿā*, my study examines three preachers from the twentieth and twenty-first centuries with roots in different parts of the Arab world, whom I selected based on their popularity, prominence, and prolific output: Amr Khaled from Egypt, Tariq al-Suwaidan from Kuwait, and Ahmad al-Shugairi from Saudi Arabia.[1]

1. The transliterated names of these preachers are ʿAmr Khālid, Ṭāriq al-Suwaydān, and Aḥmad al-Shuqayrī. I use simplified spellings for ease of reading and because the preachers themselves write their names like this in English. Regarding

They are not part of the religious establishment; they are popular preachers with a colloquial and informal style, and they extend their preaching into the public arena using books, audio media, television, websites, and social media.

Egyptian preacher Amr Khaled, born in Alexandria in 1967, is the individual most often mentioned in discussions of Muslim media preachers. An accountant by training, Khaled has amassed a vast array of religious programming that has made him one of the most popular Muslim television preachers in the Arab world. His books and shows fall into several broad categories: stories of the Qur'an, the Prophet Muhammad, and his Companions; calls for religious and cultural coexistence; and discussions of social and spiritual development—of the individual, the family, and the community as a whole. Since the broadcast of Khaled's first television show, *Kalām min al-qalb* (Words from the Heart), in 1999, he has hosted twenty-six different television programs (some encompassing several seasons), published twenty-seven books, and broadcast on the radio and YouTube, where his channel has more than 143 million total views.[2] Since 2009, he has regularly ranked in the top forty of the world's most-influential Muslims according to the annual publication *The 500 Most Influential Muslims*.[3] On social media platforms, Khaled has almost 11 million followers on Twitter, 30 million likes on Facebook, and 3.7 million followers on Instagram. By comparison, the Egyptian media-savvy *ālim* (Islamic scholar) Yusuf al-Qaradawi has 2.9 million Twitter followers

Ahmad al-Shugairi in particular, this simplified version also distinguishes him from a different Aḥmad al-Shuqayrī, the first chairman of the Palestinian Liberation Organization, who was born in 1908 in Tebnine, southern Lebanon, then part of the Ottoman Empire.

2. See the appendixes and references for links to these *du'ā*'s websites and social media accounts (Facebook, Instagram, Twitter, YouTube) as well as for full lists of their television programs and written works.

3. The annual publication *The 500 Most Influential Muslims*, published in English by the Royal Islamic Strategic Studies Centre in Amman, Jordan, is available for download at https://www.themuslim500.com/download/.

and about 2.2 million Facebook likes, and the *ālim* and former Grand Mufti of Egypt Ali Gomaa has 2.9 million Twitter followers, 1.6 million Facebook likes, and about 91,000 followers on Instagram. Social media for the current Grand Mufti, Shawky Allam, have barely any followers or likes, with less than thirty Twitter followers and about 8,000 Facebook likes.

Tariq al-Suwaidan was born in Kuwait in 1953 and is an engineer by training, with a PhD in petroleum engineering from the University of Tulsa in Oklahoma. He is famous as an expert on leadership and management, as a popular preacher on religious issues, and for his role in establishing and developing the popular religious satellite channel al-Risāla, where he served as general manager until 2013. Since starting with popular cassettes and videotapes and producing his first television show in 1999, al-Suwaidan has now hosted thirty television programs, published forty-nine books, and uploaded his works to YouTube, where his channel has more than 39 million total views. His television shows treat several main subjects: stories of the Prophets and Companions; the renewal of Islam and Islamic civilization; the attributes of a successful leader; and individual and spiritual development. His books (many of them multivolume works) cover history, general studies of Islam, as well as management, leadership, and education. Since 2009, al-Suwaidan has consistently ranked among the world's five hundred most-influential Muslims, and the preacher has 8.4 million likes on Facebook, almost 10 million followers on Twitter, and 435,000 followers on Instagram.

Saudi preacher Ahmad al-Shugairi was born in Jeddah, Saudi Arabia, in 1973 but obtained his bachelor's and master's degrees in business administration in California. He became famous on his return home to Saudi Arabia when he was a host for the television show *Yalla shabab* (Let's Go, Young People), a religious program geared toward the younger generation. In 2005, he launched his own program, *Khawāṭir* (Thoughts), which ran for eleven seasons. Since 2009, al-Shugairi has ranked among the world's five hundred most-influential Muslims. He is also one of the most popular Saudi personalities on social media, with a combined total of almost 45 million followers on Facebook,

Twitter, and Instagram (14.4 million, 18.2 million, and 12.2 million, respectively).

In terms of his literary and media production, al-Shugairi has produced fewer books and television programs than the other two preachers, but he surpasses Amr Khaled and Tariq al-Suwaidan in his online work. Al-Shugairi has published six books, produced three television movies, and hosted six television series (a combined total of twenty-one seasons of television). In total, his diverse works can be divided into the themes of social activism, individual and community development, and Islam in today's world. Al-Shugairi's YouTube channel has 424 million total views, almost three times more than Khaled and eleven times more than al-Suwaidan. Although al-Shugairi has no personal website, unlike Khaled and al-Suwaidan, he actively utilizes webpages to pursue his professional and social goals. Al-Shugairi's café and television programs have Facebook accounts, and his television series *Qumra* (Cockpit) was built around an online competition, where participants submitted short videos for cash prizes and possible inclusion in the television show.

These three men are representative of the media *du'ā* as a group and reveal the diverse forms that their message can take. Their success and popularity are based on more than just numbers, however. To be sure, these preachers have a big audience and a large number of television programs, books, and media accounts. However, by using a theoretical framework, we can see how the *du'ā* intentionally target different types of people and encourage their audiences to be active participants in their message.

Theoretical Model: The Diverse Roles of the Modern Audience

In 2004, the Norwegian media theorist Trine Syvertsen broke from the standard dichotomy of the public as either citizens or consumers by positing more nuanced roles. Her model divides the citizen–consumer division into four parts, maintaining the concept of citizens but splitting consumers into three types: audiences, customers, and players. As she explains, when the media think of the public as an audience, they aim simply to provide that audience with entertaining programming and do what it takes to keep passive viewers watching (2004, 368–69). Active consumers, however, are either customers or players. Customers want to purchase products and services, not only in stores but also through television and the internet. Players wish to join in media activities and do so by commenting and interacting online or by joining in-person audiences in the studio (370–74). These three consumer-based roles are complemented by Syvertsen's expansion of the traditional idea of citizens. In her model, the media see the public not only as political citizens but also as civil, social, and cultural citizens. In each case, these media producers want an active and engaged population and aim "not to keep people watching, but to help them turn off the set and involve themselves actively in society" (367).

This theoretical model offers unique insight into the aims and actions of Muslim media *du'ā*. To deliver their message, these preachers clearly need an audience, whether they are listeners, viewers, or readers. The preachers thus make a series of conscious choices before delivering their message, not only regarding the topics for discussion but also regarding how and where to discuss them. The way that their style, format, delivery, and subject matter address all four audiences in Syvertsen's theory helps explain why the media *du'ā* have been so successful.

A New Approach to Religious Television: Targeting All Types of Consumers

If you consider the basic principles of communication and marketing, the media *du'ā*'s approach makes sense. They are seeking an audience and, for this reason, are actively trying to set themselves apart from the work of other Muslim preachers. More traditional preachers such as Muhammad al-Sha'rawi and Yusuf al-Qaradawi have television shows that are either (1) in a style reminiscent of a madrasa, where a robed shaykh speaks in formal Arabic (*fuṣḥā*) to a male audience, or (2) in a one-on-one interview environment featuring only the preacher and a host (Wise 2003, 13–14; Gräf and Skovgaard-Petersen 2009, 154–57). The media *du'ā*, in contrast, have a more relaxed style and try to capture the attention of a passive audience with an informal approach and an engaging atmosphere.

This relaxed style takes many forms. The Egyptian preacher Amr Khaled frames himself as an everyday person sharing his wisdom with the audience. In his television shows, he does not use formal Arabic, and his colloquial language and demeanor mirror those of people on the street. He often wears a blazer with no tie, and his face is clean-shaven or sports a moustache but no beard, unlike al-Sha'rawi and al-Qaradawi, who wear traditional robes (*thawbs*) like the religious establishment and have long beards, following the hadith that Muslim men can trim their mustaches but must let their beards grow.[4] Khaled also speaks before mixed-gender groups and takes his show into public spaces, visiting venues or people that complement the subject of the day.

Ahmad al-Shugairi focuses more carefully on his role and demeanor and less on his physical appearance. He is comfortable on screen in either a traditional *thawb* or blue jeans and a jacket. Like Khaled, he speaks with both men and women in his shows, but his attitude is not one of teacher and student. He jokes and laughs with his participants, aiming for a closer, more collegial relationship. Furthermore, he does not hesitate to acknowledge his own faults. In *Law kāna baynanā* (If He Were among Us), a series about the Prophet Muhammad, al-Shugairi openly states that his position as host does not mean he is perfect: "We don't make a program on the Prophet because we are special in any way or even because we deserve it. It is an honor for us, even though we are wrongdoers" (*Law kāna baynanā* 2009b, season 2, episode 10).

Tariq al-Suwaidan's informal style incorporates his experience in leading management workshops and trainings. Although he speaks

4. This hadith is featured in *Ṣaḥīḥ al-Bukhārī* (the clothing chapter under the section "Kitāb al-libās, bāb i'fā' al-liḥān 'afū kathurū wa-kathurat amwāluhum": "Leave the Beard (as It Is). They Left Them to Grow, and Their Wealth Increased").

primarily in formal Arabic and wears a sharply pressed Gulfi *thawb*, he is equally at home lecturing on stage with a slideshow presentation, interviewing guests one on one, and working as a facilitator with small groups. When his programs show the audience, they reveal a mixed group of men and women.

These stylistic changes are supplemented by an emphasis on modern production techniques. Not only do these preachers employ multiple television cameras, but they also incorporate computer graphics into their work. In the series *Al-Rasūl al-insān* (The Messenger, the Person), al-Suwaidan walks between a set of columns to lecture in a computer-generated room of brown marble, suggesting that the preacher is really standing before a green screen and that the background is added in postproduction. This idea is reinforced in another series, *Asrār al-qiyāda al-nabawiyya* (The Secrets of Prophetic Leadership), where al-Suwaidan stands on a computer-generated stage, referencing charts and tables that float beside him as he talks. Ahmad al-Shugairi's work regularly features computer graphics, too, including vibrant maps and charts as well as three-dimensional reconstructions of Medina during the Prophet's time (*Law kāna baynanā* 2009a, season 1, episode 6). Contrast these graphics and colors with the approach adopted by a more traditional preacher such as Yusuf al-Qaradawi, whose popular show *al-Sharīʿa wa-l-ḥayāh* (Shariʿa and Life) employs no computer graphics or three-dimensional modeling, aside from the opening credits. The media *duʿā*'s emphasis on modern technology and new production techniques illustrates how religion can be up-to-date, not just reliant on printed books or traditional authority. In addition, the way these preachers bridge the old and the new caters to the younger generation, who may find more legitimacy in their smartphones and social media.

Such visual and stylistic changes set the media *duʿā* apart, yet these elements attract only passive audiences, not consumers, players, or citizens. The *duʿā* are well aware of this and so carefully consider other elements of their work to increase their audience and better engage with them.

First, these popular preachers have diversified their portfolio with a collection of books, cassettes and CDs, DVDs, social media, and websites, thereby targeting their audience as customers. The success of these ventures mirrors that of their television programs. Their taped sermons have become best sellers (Bayet 2002); their books have gone through numerous printings;[5] and, as demonstrated earlier, their viewers and followers on social media have grown into the millions. Using a diverse array of media serves multiple purposes, which include extending the reach of the preachers' religious message to larger audiences, allowing audiences to discuss and share issues on social media, and monetizing the preachers' work beyond the compensation they receive from television.

Using taped sermons, books, and social media is not unique to the media *du'ā*, of course. Recordings of Muhammad al-Sha'rawi's sermons are still popular, while al-Qaradawi, Salman al-Awda, and others are prolific authors and frequent users of social media. From a consumer's perspective, the *du'ā*'s most innovative aspect is their focus on the audience as players whom they entice to engage in religious discussions or to work on transforming themselves as a precursor to a broader social transformation. It is worth noting that jihadist preachers also try to engage their audience as players but in a different and more negative fashion, instead enticing them to be angry, protest, or fight back.

In 1999, Khaled's program *Kalām min al-qalb* (Words from the Heart) was one of the first religious shows to target the audience as players. Under the lights of a modern television studio, the Egyptian preacher led the series like a talk show, including famous actresses and athletes as his guests and soliciting stories and opinions from the studio audience (Wise 2004). Khaled would speak at length, then let

5. For example, Ahmad al-Shugairi's book *Khawāṭir shābb* (A young man's thoughts) (2011) is currently in its seventh edition, while Amr Khaled's *Ḥattā yughayyirū mā bi-anfusihim* (2012) is in its sixth edition.

others have a chance, passing the microphone to the young men and women in the studio. After their input, the preacher responded, creating a live dialogue. The Kuwaiti preacher al-Suwaidan picked up on this technique, too, with television shows such as *Al-Wasaṭiyya* (The Middle Path), which offered his audience the opportunity to voice their opinions live. Bringing the audience into the conversation in this fashion leads to a collective, collaborative way of teaching religion in place of using a one-way stream of preaching common in other religious programming. The impact of this collective approach leaves the audience feeling more vested in the conversation because they can participate as opposed to being preached at and acting as passive listeners.

The media *du'ā* have refined this approach even further, however, developing other ways to attract large groups of players both inside and outside the studio. In 2010, Khaled debuted the reality show *Mujaddidūn* (Renewers), extending his social development themes into a show based loosely on the American program *The Apprentice.* Contestants did not work on business projects but rather on charitable ones—helping orphans, coaching people on how to find jobs, and returning dropouts back to school. There was considerable interest in joining the show; 250,000 young men and women applied to be contestants, with 16 youth from nine Arab countries making the final cut (Ṭaha 2009).

Another series, launched in 2016, took the participatory role of its audience to the extreme. *Qumra* was marketed as part television show, part competition. Ahmad al-Shugairi recruited the public to film their own short videos for the series and post them online and then offered prizes worth a total of two million Saudi riyals (approx. US$530,000) (Khalaf 2015). Each episode drew directly from these submissions, focusing on a particular topic—marriage, the plight of refugees, coexistence, and so on—and providing commentary by al-Shugairi between segments from submitted videos. The show's success resulted in three seasons stretching from 2016 to 2018.

Targeting Syvertsen's three types of consumers (passive audiences, customers, and players) has paid off in big ways for the media *du'ā.* This diverse approach has given all of them a large following. Each has a combined total of more than 18 million followers on Facebook and Twitter as well as millions of views on his YouTube channel. In addition, each of these three preachers has produced twenty to thirty seasons of television programming and has earned millions of dollars in the process. One study from 2007 calculated that Khaled and al-Suwaidan's respective annual incomes were $2.5 million and $1 million in that year alone (*BBC Arabic* 2008).

Reframing Modern Issues in a Religious Light: Revitalizing Interest in Religion

Although the media *du'ā*'s focus on consumers has led to fame and a large following, that is not the ultimate purpose of their work. These preachers advocate for action and so push their followers to convert religious and social commentary into real change that focuses on (1) the revitalization of interest in religion and (2) community development. Khaled expressed the practicality of this approach in an interview in 2007: "Why are we talking about prayer and hijabs when the youth cannot find jobs? If you give them nothing but Islamic speeches, you will turn them into fanatics, or turn them off and towards drugs. You have to start with their practical needs" (White 2007).

Khaled's point is valid: unemployment rates among young people are high across much of the Arab world, with one report stating that one in every four Arab youth is unemployed (Arab Thought Foundation 2013). Underemployment is common as well, with college graduates settling for work as taxi drivers or opting for volunteer positions when other jobs elude them (AlJunaid 2014). Recent polling confirms the importance of this issue. The Arab Youth Survey of 2014 found that across the sixteen countries polled, almost three-quarters of the young men and women surveyed were very concerned or somewhat concerned about unemployment (ASDA'A Burson-Marsteller 2014).

Some Arab governments have tried to address these issues through employment programs that promote the hiring of their citizens, with initiatives thus known as "Saudization," "Kuwaitization," and so on. Under these programs, governments require companies to employ a certain number or percentage of local citizens. This hiring requirement reduces unemployment to some degree, at least in skilled fields such as engineering, medicine, and business, yet the programs also exhibit several flaws. First, nationality can take precedence over a candidate's skills and job experience. At times, these programs force companies to hire a local citizen over a more experienced foreigner, thus costing the company a more skilled employee and potentially damaging the company's growth and long-term success. Second, these initiatives struggle in many sectors of the job market, particularly with small businesses or labor-intensive jobs such as electrical work, plumbing, and construction, where the salaries are traditionally quite low (Hertog 2010, 191–92).

The media *du'ā* target both of these flaws. To help their audience members compete for job openings, the preachers stress the need for better education in schools and universities as well as additional skill building outside of school. They note that the Arab world has fallen behind other nations in the field of education. Both Khaled and al-Shugairi say that Arab teachers should not force students to memorize and regurgitate material, but should actively engage them in the learning process and allow them to discuss and apply what they learn in the classroom (al-Shugairi 2011b, 99–100; Khaled 2013, 20). In addition, although Arab governments have built many new universities and expanded their programs for citizens to study abroad, al-Suwaidan notes that opportunities for higher education in the Arab world are still woefully lacking, especially when compared to other nations (al-Suwaidan 2011c, 21).

Regarding overlooked sectors in the job market, these preachers note that labor-intensive positions are not bad and can serve as valuable stepping-stones in a long-term career. They tell young people to take advantage of all opportunities, even if it means working at a gas station or selling newspapers. Any job is better than lying idle around the house, they say, and the simplest of jobs can open doors to new opportunities through promotions or networking (al-Shugairi 2011c, 85–86; Khaled 2013, 77). Moreover, they add, skilled laborers are highly valued in many places. Plumbers in the United Kingdom can make an average of £150,000 per year, more than a doctor, exclaims al-Shugairi in the series *Khawāṭir 9* (2013, episode 11), while another episode shows that driving a London taxi is a coveted job requiring three to five years of specialized training (*Khawāṭir 9* 2013, episode 8). In this fashion, the preachers target social stigmas around these careers as well as the poor wages paid for such work in the region.

At first glance, these preachers' focus on educational reform and employment might appear out of place in religious programming and not relevant to discussions about Islam or the life of a devout Muslim. Yet the media *du'ā* infuse these discussions with religious examples, creatively framing the issues in a religious manner by blending in quotations from the Qur'an and Sunna. This framing not only strengthens their argument for devout listeners but also promotes religion for others, showing how Islam is relevant for contemporary issues and combatting what the *du'ā* see as a flaw in modern society: lack of religiosity.

Two common themes illustrate how the media *du'ā* mix religion into their discussion of education and employment. In the first theme, the preachers stress that society needs to improve education, both in and out of the classroom. Using the example of the Prophet Muhammad, they say that even in day-to-day activities Muslims have a responsibility to teach the younger generation. The Prophet knew how to handle youth, steering them to the correct path when they went astray and remaining calm in situations that would have provoked anger in others. Al-Shugairi cites the example of al-Fadl Ibn al-'Abbas sneaking furtive glances at a young woman during the farewell pilgrimage to Mecca (al-Shugairi 2011a, 21–22),[6] and Khaled references a young man who asked the Prophet for permission to fornicate (Khaled 2013,

6. This tale appears in many of the canonical hadith collections. See, for example, *Ṣaḥīḥ al-Bukhārī* (the chapter on asking permission under the section "Kitāb al-isti'dhān, bāb yā ayuhā alladhīna āmanū lā tadkhulū" ["Oh You Who Believe, Do Not Enter"]) and *Ṣaḥīḥ Muslim* (the Hajj chapter under the section "Kitāb al-Ḥajj, bāb al-Ḥajj 'an al-'ājiz li-zamāna wa-hiram wa-naḥwihimā aw li-l-mawt" ["The Hajj on Behalf of One Who Is Incapable due to Old Age, Senility, and the Like, or on Behalf of One Who Has Died."]).

95),[7] a practice explicitly condemned in the Qur'an. In both cases, the Prophet remained a patient teacher, acknowledging the young person's mistake and responding in a way that guided him to be a better person. In the first case, the Prophet simply turned al-Fadl's head away, while in the second he asked the young man if he would wish such a situation (sex out of wedlock) upon his mother, his sister, or his aunts. When the youngster responded with a categorical no, the Prophet replied: "Therefore do not wish upon others what you do not wish upon your family" (Khaled 2013, 95).

These stories illustrate the Prophet's mercy and remind audiences to be forgiving of mistakes and not to banish people for small infractions. There are no long lectures, finger wagging, or notes of anger—a relatively common practice for more traditional preachers. Instead, the *du'ā* present a softer approach to mistakes, acknowledging the difficulties and temptations of modern life. They thus make a shift from the rule-based approach to religion found in older generations to more of a guidance-based approach combined with mercy and forgiveness. In this fashion, the *du'ā* make religion more inviting and encourage young people to embrace Islam, not to fear it.

Education inside the classroom is also a concern for the media *du'ā*, who believe that the current practices of memorization and blind imitation are not the best means of education or development. They reinforce this view with religious evidence drawn from the Prophet's *sīra*. Al-Shugairi notes that the Prophet always said: "Oh God, provide me with useful knowledge (*'ilman nāfi'an*)." As the preacher explains, useful knowledge is information that can be applied, not just recited and remembered. Knowledge that is not turned into action has no benefit (al-Shugairi 2011b, 100). Indeed, such emphasis on action and

7. Other hadith collections also include this story, such as *al-Musnad* by Aḥmad Ibn Ḥanbal (under the section "Bāqī Musnad al-Anṣār, ḥadīth Abī Umāma al-Bāhilī" [The Remainder of Musnad al-Anṣar, the Hadith of Abī Umāma al-Bāhilī]) and *Al-Mu'jam al-kabir* by Sulaymān Ibn Aḥmad al-Ṭabarāni (under the section titled for hadith transmitters: "Ṣuday bin 'Ajlān Abū Umāma al-Bāhilī, Salīm bin 'Āmir Abū Yaḥyā al-Khabā'irī 'an Abī Umāma").

applicability closely matches the interests of the media *du'ā*'s target audience. A survey of Arab youth in six different countries found that 86 percent "want school curricula to be more relevant to the needs of the workplace" (ASDA'A Burson-Marsteller 2008, 17).

The second theme that these preachers stress is the fact that education is a life-long mission that individuals should take upon themselves. As evidence for this argument, the preachers turn to the Prophet Muhammad's discussion of *iḥsān*, a term that means "charity or the performance of good deeds" but also relates to the pursuit of perfection. Al-Shugairi cites a hadith where the Prophet said: "[*Iḥsān* is] that you worship Allah as if you are seeing Him, for though you don't see Him, He, verily, sees you."[8] The intention behind worship, al-Shugairi argues, is not merely prayer and fasting but all types of actions. Thus, he continues, the Prophet wanted people to act in the best way in all things, making *iḥsān*, the pursuit of perfection, relevant in both issues of faith *and* everyday life (al-Shugairi 2011b, 53–54). Al-Suwaidan's discussion of perfection reinforces this interpretation of *iḥsān*, citing a hadith that reads: "Verily, Allah loves that when anyone of you does a job, he should perfect it" (quoted in al-Suwaidan 2011c, 102).[9]

Adopting this goal of perfection across all aspects of life, the media *du'ā* apply *iḥsān* to a wide variety of contemporary ideas and issues. Al-Shugairi begins by discussing driving safely, being on time, parking your car correctly, and even placing your shoes in the appropriate cubbies before praying in a mosque (al-Shugairi 2011b, 54). In general, however, the *du'ā* devote their longest treatments of *iḥsān* to modern business applications, including organizing one's wallet and

8. Although al-Shugairi does not give a source, this hadith is featured in the canonical collection *Ṣaḥīḥ Muslim* (in the Faith chapter under the section "Kitāb al-Īmān, bāb bayān al-īmān wa-l-islām wa-l-iḥsān, wa-wujūb al-īmān" [Explaining Faith, Islam, and the Performance of Good Deeds, and the Obligations of Faith]).

9. Al-Suwaidan cites the work *Shu'ab al-iman* by Abu Bakr al-Bayhaqi, although this hadith is also found in earlier hadith collections: Sulaymān al-Ṭabarānī, *al-Mu'jam al-awsaṭ* (1995, 1:275), and Abū Ya'lā al-Mawṣilī, *Musnad Abī Ya'lā al-Mawṣilī* (1998, 4:20).

office, keeping one's finances, managing one's time, and building and maintaining relationships (al-Shugairi 2011b, 60–75; al-Suwaidan 2011c, 62–77, 106). Such skills are not only useful for self-improvement but also valuable in the workplace. Organizational skills, financial know-how, good time management, and strong networks are advantages in the business world. In the job search, they can make one's application more attractive as well. The fact that these skills are tied to Islam through the concept of *iḥsān* makes them even more enticing for young Muslims to learn and for society to accept.

These examples highlight the creative power of the media *du'ā*. Employment is a popular issue. By reframing this topic in a religious light, these preachers accomplish multiple goals—sharing tools to make their audience members more employable and reviving interest in Islam by introducing contemporary topics into religious discourse. The preachers' aims extend beyond religious education and skill building, however, which concentrate primarily on personal development and self-growth. They also target change at the community level, thereby addressing the final part of Syvertsen's model—the role of the public as citizens.

Community Development: Moving from Active Listeners to an Activist Audience

The media *du'ā* are particularly adamant that their audience can be active agents for change. Khaled deems this approach "faith-based development" (Atia 2013, 137–39), as explained in his television series *Ṣunnā' al-ḥayāh* (Life Makers). However, this concept of development through faith is not unique to Khaled's work.

All of the media *du'ā* agree that change requires work on a number of fronts—thought, faith, and ethical conduct (*akhlāq*)—each tied to a different aspect of daily life. In his book *Khawāṭir shābb* (A Young Man's Thoughts), al-Shugairi calls these ideas "thought" (*fikr*), "heart" (*qalb*), and "behavior" (*salūk*). Change is like driving a car, he says. Your thoughts are the driver, who knows where to go, while your heart is the fuel, which allows you to move. If you do not have good behavior (driving skills), then everything falls apart (al-Shugairi 2011c, 11). Tariq al-Suwaidan focuses on the same general principles, describing thought (*fikr*) and Islamic identity (*huwīya*), stemming from shari'a, as requirements for changing society. "Civilization is created on thought," he explains, "and torn down by corrupt ethical conduct" (al-Suwaidan 2011b, 64).

Khaled is the clearest in his approach to development, presenting the three elements mentioned earlier—thought, faith, and ethical conduct—as well as two additional ones, skills (*mahārat*) and movement or action (*ḥaraka*). These five components form the building blocks of Khaled's "*insān* al-Nahḍa" (Renaissance man), the type of person who will contribute to changing society and building a new civilization. It is important to note that Khaled does not describe exactly what this Renaissance will be. That is a task for the ulama and the great thinkers, he explains, and his role is only to define who will be qualified to carry out such changes (Khaled 2013, 45–46).

The fact that al-Shugairi and al-Suwaidan do not list skills and action in their theory of change does not mean that they ignore them. Quite the contrary. Although their theoretical framework is not as explicit as Khaled's, their emphasis on education and volunteerism reveals the importance they place on skills and action. In other parts of their work, too, they cry out for action. For example, al-Suwaidan criticizes young people who focus on shopping and fashion, both trivial issues in his mind. He says they should instead concentrate on doing what they can to develop their community (al-Suwaidan 2011c, 82). He proposes that, to do so, people should divide their lives in two. Before the age of thirty, they should focus on education and training, perfecting their skills. Then after the age of thirty, they can dedicate themselves to action, giving back to the community and the world and using their skills to achieve real results (al-Suwaidan 2011c, 108).

All three preachers also offer an array of religious examples to encourage their audience to take action, emphasizing in particular the central role of Muslim youth in development. Perhaps they see young people as the easiest implementers for change because of their numbers or their youthful energy or the fact that they are less indoctrinated in the current system than their older counterparts. Whatever the case may be, the media *du'ā* offer numerous examples to motivate youth, and they also work to change public opinion about the younger generation, arguing that young people can be successful leaders.

Both Khaled and al-Suwaidan cite the story of the Prophet's selection of the young Usama Ibn Zayd to lead an army into the Levant region as proof that a teenager can lead his elders, despite the availability of experienced leaders such as 'Umar and Abu Bakr (al-Suwaidan 2011a, 104; Khaled 2013, 218–19). In another case, the preachers note that the Prophet saw the intellectual promise in young 'Abd Allah Ibn 'Abbas, specifically his love of learning and his interest in fiqh. The Prophet pushed him to study the subject further, despite the protests made by some scholars, who thought Ibn 'Abbas was too young. The young man persevered and became a famous scholar, validating the Prophet's trust in him and showing how an individual's drive and effort can propel him or her to great heights (al-Suwaidan 2011a, 105, and 2011c, 13).

For a young audience today, these tangible examples and achievable models can be emulated. Although the Prophet is an excellent role model, his excellence and experience may seem daunting to young Muslims. Usama and Ibn 'Abbas provide younger role models and concrete examples of success in specific fields—as the commander of an army and as a popular and influential scholar. They also demonstrate the trust that early Muslims placed in the younger generation, something that the media *du'ā* want to emphasize to society today.

The media *du'ā* pair these classical examples with motivational messages from the modern era. Real results are attainable, they say, even within a short time. Al-Shugairi and Khaled cite the examples of Turkey and Malaysia, which rejuvenated their economies in ten to fifteen years (al-Shugairi 2011b, 118; Khaled 2013, 99–100), and al-Shugairi also uses Japan as a model of a country that changed and developed without sacrificing its culture, language, and traditions (al-Shugairi 2011b, 37–38). They call on the Arab world to follow this lead, reiterating that the answer lies with the region's youth.

This call to action is working: Khaled's programs resulted in independent Life Makers (Ṣunnāʿ al-Ḥayāh) organizations springing up across the Arab world and beyond and pursuing a range of projects, such as antidrug campaigns, educational programs, and the collection of food and clothing for the poor (Harris 2008, 25–29). Al-Shugairi's interactive website (at www.i7san.net) connected more than 60,000 individuals interested in volunteer work and, at its height, featured more than 4,000 different volunteering clubs and more than 3,000 different projects.[10] Al-Shugairi's show *Qumra* attracted video submissions from across the Arab and Muslim worlds—and in the process avoided problems with the Saudi government despite crackdowns on other media personalities. Al-Suwaidan runs an annual leadership camp, the Leadership Preparation Academy (Akādīmīya Iʿdād al-Qāda), drawing young people from across the Arab world, as well as two leadership centers in Kuwait, one for boys and one for girls (al-Suwaidan 2011d, 20). These organizations and activities motivate youth to take action in their communities and show the public the positive influence that young people and young leaders can have.

Conclusion

Examining the media *duʿā* through the lens of Trine Syvertsen's audience theory reveals not only the lengths to which these preachers have gone to secure their audience but also some of the reasons for their success and influence. They target all four roles described in Syversten's audience theory—the passive audience, the customer, the player, and the citizen. By actively pursuing this diverse approach—using new visuals, a relaxed style, interactive programming, and multiple media—they set themselves apart from their more conservative

10. This website is under reconstruction, but a snapshot from the Internet Archive reveals the volunteering data cited here. See "Shabkat Iḥsān," Internet Archive Wayback Machine, Apr. 24, 2014, at https://web.archive.org/web/20140424124537/http://www.i7san.net/.

competitors and have secured the attention of large audiences. Their vibrant and engaging style attracts viewers who were bored with the more formal style of al-Qaradawi and other preachers. Their use of social media, books, and interactive websites captures audiences that otherwise might not have participated in religious discussions. These charismatic and prolific preachers have thus expanded the reach of religion, educating their audience about Islam on multiple platforms while also encouraging them to develop themselves and their community.

To say that this emphasis on religion makes the *du'ā* religious leaders or authority figures in *all* religious matters is a step too far, however, and is a claim the preachers themselves deny. The *du'ā* repeatedly insist that they are ordinary Muslims, not muftis or religious scholars (Naggar 2005; al-Shugairi 2011c, 8). They do not issue fatwas or discuss Islamic law, and they state that those activities are reserved for religious scholars, not preachers like themselves (*al-Ahram Weekly* 2002).

What is clear, however, is that these popular preachers are motivating others to take action and helping set the agenda by introducing new topics into religious discussions and so pushing the boundaries of religious discourse. They do not explicitly tell people what to think, for they stress that they are not qualified to do so. Yet they are convincing people "what to think *about*," to cite Bernard Cohen, one of the early inspirations for the theory of agenda setting (1963, 13). This theory, found in studies of the press and mass communication, is easily transferable to our context. The popularity of these preachers gives them considerable influence on national and religious debates. They do not give legal rulings or fatwas, but they steer the public eye to issues such as educational reform and social change. Their large audiences and broad reach across the region force politicians, other preachers, and the general public to respond to their work on these issues. And by incorporating religion into their discussions, these agenda setters demonstrate how Islam is a key component of an activist lifestyle and an important tool for education and community development.

Appendix I

Amr Khaled's Television Productions and Publications

Note: All works are listed in chronological order of production or publication. Television shows include the year of their first broadcast, and written works include the date they were first published.

Television Shows

1. *Kalām min al-qalb*. Broadcast in 2001 but first produced on videotape in 1999.
2. *Islāmunā*. 2000.
3. *Wa-Nalqā al-aḥibba*. Three seasons, 2001–3.
4. *Kunūz*. Two seasons, 2003–4.
5. *Ḥatā yughayyirū mā bi-anfusihim*. 2003.
6. *Khawāṭir Qur'āniyya*. 2003.
7. *Ṣunnā' al-ḥayāh*. Three seasons, 2003–4; season 4 released online in 2009.
8. *'Alā khuṭā al-ḥabīb*. 2005.
9. *Bi-Ismik naḥyā*. 2006.
10. *Lamaḥāt insāniyya*. 2006.
11. *Ṣadaqa Rasūl Allāh*. 2006.
12. *Da'wa li-l-ta'āyush*. 2007.
13. *Al-Janna fī buyūtinā*. 2008.
14. *Qiṣaṣ al-Qur'ān*. 2008–9.
15. *Mujaddidūn*. 2010.
16. *Riḥla li-l-sa'āda*. 2010.
17. *Bukra aḥlā*. 2011.
18. *Ma'a al-tābi'īn*. 2011.
19. *'Umar: Ṣāni' ḥaḍāra*. 2012.
20. *Qiṣṣat al-Andalus*. 2013.
21. *Al-Īmān wa-l-'asr*. 2015.
22. *Al-Īmān wa-l-'asr: Ṭarīq li-l-ḥayāh*. 2016.
23. *Nabīy al-raḥma al-tasāmuḥ*. 2017.
24. *Al-Sīra ḥayā*. 2018.
25. *Fa-Udhkarūnī*. 2019.
26. *Ka-annak tarāha*. 2020.

Written Works

1. *Akhlāq al-mu'min*. 2002.
2. *'Ibādāt al-mu'min*. 2002.
3. *Yūsuf 'alayhi al-salām*. 2002.
4. *Ḥattā yughayyirū mā bi-anfusihim*. 2003.
5. *'Ibādāt al-tafakkur*. 2003.
6. *Iṣlāḥ al-qulūb*. 2003.
7. *Al-Ṣabr wa-l-dhawq*. 2004.
8. *Kalām min al-qalb*. 2004.
9. *Khawāṭir Qur'āniyya: Naẓarāt fī ahdāf suwar al-Qur'ān*. 2004.
10. *Inī jā'il fī al-arḍ khalīfa*. 2005.
11. *Khulafā' al-Rasūl ṣallā Allāhu 'alayhi wa-sallam*. 2005.
12. *Qirā'a jadīda wa-ru'ya fī qiṣaṣ al-anbiyā'*. 2005.
13. *'Alā khuṭā al-ḥabīb Muḥammad Rasūl Allāh*. 2006.
14. *Qiṣaṣ al-hidāya*. 2006.
15. *Bi-Ismik naḥyā*. 2007.
16. *Al-Janna fī buyūtinā*. 2009.
17. *Da'wa li-l-ta'āyush*. 2009.
18. *Qiṣaṣ al-Qur'ān*. 2009.
19. *Riḥla li-l-sa'āda*. 2011.
20. *Ma'a al-tābi'īn*. 2012.
21. *Binā' insān al-Nahḍa*. 2013.
22. *'Umar: Ṣāni' ḥaḍāra*. 2014.
23. *Qirā'a jadīda wa-ru'ya fī qiṣaṣ al-anbiyā'*. 2014.
24. *Rāfī barakāt wa-sirr al-rimāl al-ghāmiḍa*. 2014.
25. *Al-Īmān wa-l-'asr*. 2015.
26. *Ḥikam tatakhaṭṭā al-zaman: 200 ḥikma Qur'ānīya*. 2016.
27. *Al-Ahdāf al-insānīya li-l-Qur'ān min Sūra al-Baqara ilā Sūra al-Kahf*. 2016.

Appendix II

Tariq al-Suwaidan's Television Productions and Publications

Note: In general, all works are listed in chronological order of production or publication. Titles not followed by a date mean the date was difficult to determine with certainty. For all other cases, television shows include the year of their first broadcast, and written works include the date they were first published.

Television Shows

1. *Allāh 'azz wa-jall.*
2. *Asrār al-Ḥajj.*
3. *Fann al-iḥsān.*
4. *Al-Mubdi'ūn.*
5. *Nisā' khālidāt.*
6. *Qiṣaṣ al-anbiyā'.*
7. *Qiṣaṣ al-anbiyā' bi-l-lugha al-injlīziyya.*
8. *Qiṣaṣ wa-'ibar.*
9. *Qiṣṣat al-nihāya.*
10. *Al-Rasūl al-insān.*
11. *Rawā'i' al-qiṣaṣ.*
12. *Rawā'i' al-tābi'īn.*
13. *Siḥr al-Qur'ān.*
14. *Sajāyā.*
15. *Ṣinā'at al-najāḥ.*
16. *Sīrat Khālid bin al-Walīd.*
17. *Al-Sīra Al-khālida.* 1993–94.
18. *Ṣinā'at al-qā'id.* 2006.
19. *Al-Wasaṭiyya.* 2008.
20. *Akādīmīya i'dād al-qāda.* Two seasons, 2009–10.
21. *'Allamatnī al-ḥayāh.* Two seasons, 2009–10.
22. *Riyāḥ al-taghyīr.* Two seasons, 2011–12.
23. *Asrār al-qiyāda al-nabawiyya.* 2012.
24. *Tārīkhunā fī al-mīzān.* 2013.
25. *Qiṣṣa wa-fikra.* 2014.
26. *Kun najman.* 2016.
27. *Nūruka fīnā.* 2017.
28. *Ḥaṣād al-'umr.* 2018.
29. *Ḥaṣād al-fikr.* 2019.
30. *Al-Islām bil-basāṭa.* 2020.

Written Works: Management, Leadership, and Education

1. *Rattib ḥayātak*. 1999.
2. *Al-Qiyāda fī al-qarn al-ḥādī wa-l-ʿishrīn*. 2000.
3. *Idārat al-waqt*. 2001.
4. *Manhajiyyat al-taghyīr fī al-munaẓẓamāt*. 2001.
5. *Marrin ʿaḍalāt mukhkhik*. 2001.
6. *Al-Munaẓẓama al-mutaʿallima*. 2001.
7. *Qiyādat al-sūq*. 2001.
8. *Ṣināʿat al-najāḥ*. 2001.
9. *Khumāsiyyat al-walāʾ: Kayfa taḥfiz wa-tabnī walāʾ al-ʿāmilīn*. 2002.
10. *Mabādiʾ al-ibdāʿ*. 2002.
11. *Ṣināʿat al-qāʾid*. 2002.
12. *Fann al-ilqāʾ al-rāʾiʿ*. 2003.
13. *Ikhtabir maʿlūmātik ḥawla al-istrātījiyyāt*. 2004.
14. *Kayfa taktub khiṭṭa istrātījiyya: 100 Suʾāl wa-jawāb*. 2005.
15. *Al-Tadrīb wa-l-tadrīs al-ibdāʿī*. 2005.
16. *Al-Najūmiyya: Ikhtibār khāṣṣ li-qiyās mustawā istiʿdādik li-takūn najman*. 2007.
17. *Ṣināʿat al-dhakāʾ*. 2008.
18. *Ṣināʿat al-thaqāfa*. 4 vols. 2009.
    a. *Ṣināʿat al-thaqāfa*.
    b. *Kayfa aqrā*.
    c. *Al-Ṭifl al-qāriʾ*.
    d. *Mādhā aqrā*.
19. *Kayfa tatakhith qarārātik*. 2010.
20. *Miqyās al-qāʾid al-namūdhajī: Taḥdīd daqīq li-mustawāk bi-l-muqārana bi-ṣifāt al-qāʾid al-namūdhajī al-muḥaddada ʿālamiyyan*. 2011.
21. *Al-Muʾassasiyya: Ikhtibār khāṣṣ li-qiyās mustawā al-muʾassasiyya fī munaẓẓamatik*. 2011.
22. *Al-Qiyāda al-mawqifiyya*. 2011.
23. *Ikhtabir darajat ibdāʿik*. 2012.
24. *Al-Ittijāhāt al-ḥadītha fī al-idāra*. 2012.
25. *Al-Mawhiba al-qiyādiyya*. 2012.
26. *Al-Quwwa wa-l-nufūdh*. 2013–14(?).

27. *Fann al-ta'līf wa-l-nashr.* 2015.
28. *Al-Ibdā' khaṭwa khaṭwa bi-isti'māl ālla al-ibdā'.*[11]
29. *Ta'sīs wa-idāra al-mashārī'.* 2016. 8 vols.
    a. *Naḥwa al-'amal al-ḥurr.*
    b. *Asāsāt al-mashārī'.*
    c. *Al-Takhṭīṭ wa-l-taḥlīl li-l-mashārī'.*
    d. *Fann taswīq al-mashārī'.*
    e. *Idāra al-mawārid al-bashariyya.*
    f. *Ra's māl al-mashārī'.*
    g. *Idāra amwāl al-mashārī'.*
    h. *Inṭilāq wa-iftitāḥ al-mashrū'.*
30. *Qawānīn al-tadrīb al-iḥtirāfī.* 2017.
31. *Al-Minhāj al-mutakāmil li-i'dād al-qāda.* 2018. 3 vols.
    a. *Mafāhīm wa-asāsiyāt al-qiyāda.*
    b. *Al-Namūdhaj al-'āmm li-i'dād al-qāda.*
    c. *Khaṭawāt wa-manāhij i'dād al-qāda.*
32. *Al-Takhṭīṭ al-istrātījī al-ḥadīth.* 2018.
33. *Al-Intājīya.* 2019. 4 vols.
    a. *Waqt al-Muslim: 'Umruhu fīmā afnāhu.*
    b. *Ziyāda al-intājīya al-shakhsiyya.*
    c. *Ziyāda al-intājīya al-jamā'iyya wa-l-mu'assasiyya.*
    d. *Kayfa tudīr ijtimā'an fi'lan.*

Written Works: Religion

1. *Mukhtaṣar al-'aqīda al-Islāmiyya.* 1987.
2. *Al-Ṣawm: al-I'tikāf, zakāt al-fiṭr, ṣalāt al-'īdayn.* 1994.
3. *Al-Imām Aḥmad bin Ḥanbal: Al-Sīra al-muṣawwara.* 2006.
4. *Asrār al-Ḥajj wa-l-'Umra.* 2007.
5. *Al-Imām al-Shāfi'ī: Al-Sīra al-muṣawwara.* 2007.

11. This work is not a book but rather is printed on a set of cards that are bound in one corner by a metal pivot. No date of publication is given, but I found it in 2015, and its publisher is the same as the publisher of many of al-Suwaidan's other works, Sharikat al-Ibdā' al-Fikrī in Kuwait.

6. *Asrār al-ṣiyām*. 2009.
7. *Al-Imām Mālik: Al-Sīra al-muṣawwara*. 2009.
8. *Al-Imām Abū Hanīfa al-Nu'mān: Al-Sīra al-muṣawwara*. 2011.
9. *Stories of the Prophets in al-Quran*. 2013.
10. *Great Women in Islam*. 2013.
11. *Al-Rasūl al-insān*. 2016.
12. *Mustaqbal al-Islām*. 2018. 6 vols.
    a. *Al-Ḥaḍāra al-Islāmiyya al-qādima*.
    b. *Al-Khuṭṭa al-istrātījiyya li-Nahḍa al-umma*.
    c. *Al-Hurrīya fī dawla al-Islāmiyya al-qādima*.
    d. *Man anā? wa-mā hiya huwīyatī?*
    e. *Ikhtabir akhlāqik*.
    f. *Al-Dawla allatī aḥlam bi-hā*.
13. *As'ila li-l-tafkīr*. 2019. 5 vols.
    a. *Ikhtabir fahmik hawla usus al-dīn*.
    b. *Ikhtabir fahmik hawla al-dhāt wa-l-'alāqat*.
    c. *Ikhtabir fahmik hawla al-Mustaqbal wa-mushakil al-umma*.
    d. *Ikhtabir fahmik hawla al-ḥaqq wa-l-bāṭil*.
    e. *Ikhtabir fahmik ḥawla al-awwalīyāt wa-fahm-ḥayāh*.

Written Works: History

1. *Filasṭīn: Al-Tārīkh al-muṣawwar*. 2004.
2. *Al-Andalus: al-tārīkh al-muṣawwar*. 2006.
3. *Al-Yahūd: al-mawsū'a al-muṣawwara*. 2009.
4. *'Allamatnī al-ḥayāh*. 2011. Al-Suwaidan's autobiography. 5 vols.
    a. *Madrasat al-ḥayāh*.
    b. *Fahm al-dīn*.
    c. *Usus al-'aṭā'*.
    d. *Mahārāt al-ta'thīr*.
    e. *Taṣḥīḥ al-mafāhīm*.
5. *Tārīkh al-Islām al-muṣawwar*. 2015.
6. *'Allamatnī al-ḥayāh: Al-Juz' al-thānī*. 2015. The continuation of al-Suwaidan's autobiography. 5 vols.
    a. *Fahm al-mashā'ir*.
    b. *Azamāt al-umma*.
    c. *Nashr al-fikr*.

d. *Muthabbiṭāt wa-muḥarrikāt.*
e. *Mādhā nurīd.*

Appendix III

Ahmad al-Shugairi's Publications and Television Productions

Note: All works are listed in chronological order of production or publication. Television shows include the year of their first broadcast, and written works include the date they were first published.

Television Shows and Movies

1. *Yallā shabāb.* Three seasons, 2002–4.
2. *Khawāṭir.* Eleven seasons, 2005–15.[12]
3. *Law kāna baynanā.* Two seasons, both in 2009.
4. *Qumra.* Three seasons, 2016–18.
5. *Ṣunnā' al-amal.* 2017.
6. *Baṣma amal* 2. 2017.[13]
7. *Iḥsān min al-Ḥaram.* Movie made for TV, 2018.
8. *Iḥsān min al-Madīna al-Munawwara.* Movie made for TV, 2019.
9. *Iḥsān min al-mustaqbal.* Two-part movie made for TV, 2020.

Written Works

1. *Khawāṭir shābb.* 2006.
2. *Khawāṭir 2: Al-Juz' al-thānī.* 2008.
3. *Khawāṭir 3: Min al-Yābān.* 2009.
4. *Law kāna baynanā.* 2009.
5. *Riḥlatī ma'a Ghāndī.* 2011.
6. *40: Arba'ūn.* 2019.

12. The first season of this show was titled *Khawāṭir shābb,* but the title of all subsequent seasons was shortened to *Khawāṭir.*

13. Al-Shugairi did not host the first season of *Baṣma amal,* which ran on TV in 2016, hosted by the Arab actor Bassel Alzaro.

References

Personal Websites and Social Media Accounts

Allam, Shawky (Grand Mufti)
Facebook: https://www.facebook.com/DrShawkyAllamENG
Twitter: https://twitter.com/DrShawkyAllam
Gomaa, Ali
Facebook: https://www.facebook.com/DrAliGomaa/
Instagram: https://www.instagram.com/draligomaa
Twitter: https://twitter.com/draligomaa
Khaled, Amr
Website: http://amrkhaled.net
Facebook: https://www.facebook.com/AmrKhaled
Instagram: https://www.instagram.com/amrkhaled
Twitter: https://twitter.com/amrkhaled
YouTube: https://www.youtube.com/user/AmrKhaled
Al-Qaradawi, Yusuf
Facebook: https://www.facebook.com/alqaradawy
Twitter: https://twitter.com/alqaradawy
Al-Shugairi, Ahmad
Websites: http://www.i7san.net (networking site for volunteering) and http://qomrah.tv (website for the TV series *Qumra*)
Facebook: https://www.facebook.com/AhmadAlShugairi; https://www.facebook.com/AndalusiahCafe; https://www.facebook.com/khawatirTV; https://www.facebook.com/QomrahTV
Instagram: https://www.instagram.com/ahmadalshugairi/
Twitter: https://twitter.com/shugairi
YouTube: https://www.youtube.com/user/AhmadAlShugairi
Al-Suwaidan, Tariq
Websites: http://www.suwaidan.com; https://suwaidan.tv; http://www.leadersta.com (Leadership Preparation Academy)
Facebook: https://www.facebook.com/Dr.TareqAlSuwaidan
Instagram: https://www.instagram.com/dr.tareqalsuwaidan
Twitter: https://twitter.com/tareqalsuwaidan
YouTube: https://www.youtube.com/user/DrAlSuwaidan

Television Programs

Asrār al-qiyāda al-nabawiyya. Episode 1. Produced by Karim 'Umar and presented by Tāriq al-Suwaydān. First broadcast in 2012. At https://www.youtube.com/watch?v=tbSrkZXo-AI.

Khawāṭir 9. Episode 8. Directed by Jāsim al-Sa'adī and presented by Aḥmad al-Shuqayrī. First broadcast in 2013. At https://www.youtube.com/watch?v=lGXNpFvZpbk.

———. Episode 11. Directed by Jāsim al-Sa'adī and presented by Aḥmad al-Shuqayrī. First broadcast in 2013. At https://www.youtube.com/watch?v=MhEgON0Yd00.

Law kāna baynanā. Season 1, episode 6. Directed by Muḥammad Shawqī and presented by Aḥmad al-Shuqayrī. First broadcast in 2009. At https://www.youtube.com/watch?v=FgCYhLFTwDw.

———. Season 2, episode 10. Directed by Muḥammad Shawqī and presented by Aḥmad al-Shuqayrī. First broadcast in 2009. At https://www.youtube.com/watch?v=NLCE7Ih0eo4.

Al-Rasūl al-insān. Episode 1. Directed by Hishām 'Abd al-'Azīz al-Sa'adī and presented by Ṭāriq al-Suwaydān. First broadcast in 2012. At https://www.youtube.com/watch?v=UzvfHBgzeRc.

Other Published Sources

Al-Ahram Weekly. 2002. "Preaching with a Passion." Nov. 28–Dec. 4. Originally at http://weekly.ahram.org.eg/2002/614/fe2.htm and now available through the Internet Archive Wayback Machine at https://web.archive.org/web/20121111152159/http://weekly.ahram.org.eg/2002/614/fe2.htm.

Arab Thought Foundation. 2013. "Enabling Job Creation in the Arab World: A Role for Regional Integration." Dec. At https://www.pwc.com/m1/en/publications/enabling-job-creation-in-arab-world.pdf.

ASDA'A Burson-Marsteller. 2008. "The Arab Millennials: Understanding the Aspirations and Attitudes of Middle East Youth. A White Paper on the Findings of the First Annual ASDA'A Burson-Marsteller Arab Youth Survey 2008." At http://arabyouthsurvey.com/pdf/whitepaper/en/2008-AYS-White-Paper.pdf.

———. 2014. "'We Want to Embrace Modern Values': A White Paper on the Findings of the ASDA'A Burson-Marsteller Arab Youth Survey 2014." At http://arabyouthsurvey.com/pdf/whitepaper/en/2014-AYS-WhitePaper.pdf.

Atia, Mona. 2013. *Building a House in Heaven: Pious Neoliberalism and Islamic Charity in Egypt*. Minneapolis: Univ. of Minnesota Press.

Bayet, Asef. 2002. "Piety, Privelege, and Egyptian Youth." *ISIM Newsletter* 10 (July 2002): 23.

BBC Arabic. 2008. "Majallat *Forbes* al-'arabiyya: 'Amr Khālid aghnā nujūm al-du'ā 'arabiyyan." Feb. 28. At http://news.bbc.co.uk/hi/arabic/business/newsid_7261000/7261877.stm.

Cohen, Bernard C. 1963. *The Press and Foreign Policy*. Princeton, NJ: Princeton Univ. Press.

Floden, Tuve. 2017. "Defining the Media *Du'ā* and Their Call to Action." In "New Islamic Media," special issue of *POMEPS Studies* 23:9–13.

Gräf, Bettina, and Jakob Skovgaard-Petersen. 2009. *Global Mufti: The Phenomenon of Yusuf al-Qaradawi*. New York: Columbia Univ. Press.

Harris, Samuel Lee. 2008. "Development through Faith: The Ma'adi Life Makers and the Islamic Entrepreneurial Subject." MA thesis, Georgetown Univ.

Hertog, Steffen. 2010. *Princes, Brokers, and Bureaucrats: Oil and the State in Saudi Arabia*. Ithaca, NY: Cornell Univ. Press.

AlJunaid, Madiha. 2014. "The Challenge of Youth Unemployment." *Yemen Times*, Apr. 17. Originally at http://www.yementimes.com/en/1773/report/3744/The-challenge-of-youth-unemployment.htm and now available through the Internet Archive Wayback Machine at https://web.archive.org/web/20140417160228/http://www.yementimes.

Khalaf, May. 2015. "'Qumrah' . . . Furṣatak li-mushārakat al-Shuqayrī intāj barnāmajihi al-jadīd." *Al-Khaleej Online*, Dec. 24. At http://alkhaleejonline.net/ثقافة-وفن/قمرة-فرصتك-لمشاركة-الشقيري-إنتاج-برنامجه-الجديد.

Khaled, Amr. 2012. *Ḥattā yughayyirū mā bi-anfusihim*. 6th ed. Beirut: Dār al-Ma'rifa.

———. 2013. *Binā' insān al-Nahḍa*. Beirut: Arab Scientific Publishers.

Al-Mawṣilī, Abū Ya'lā. 1998. *Musnad Abī Ya'lā al-Mawṣilī*. 7 vols. Beirut: Dār al-Kutub al-'Ilmīya.

Moll, Yasmin. 2012. "Storytelling, Sincerity, and Islamic Televangelism in Egypt." In *Global and Local Televangelism*, edited by Pradip Thomas and Philip Lee, 21–44. New York: Palgrave Macmillan.

Naggar, Mona. 2005. "Amr Khaled: 'I Want to Move Arabic Youth!'" Qantara.de. At http://en.qantara.de/content/amr-khaled-i-want-to-move-arabic-youth.

Al-Shugairi, Ahmad. 2011a. *Khawāṭir 2: Al-Juz' al-thānī*. 4th ed. Riyadh: Al-'Ubaykān li-l-Nashr.

———. 2011b. *Khawāṭir 3: Min al-Yābān*. 3rd ed. Riyadh: Al-'Ubaykān li-l-Nashr.

———. 2011c. *Khawāṭir shābb*. 7th ed. Riyadh: Al-'Ubaykān li-l-Nashr.

Al-Suwaidan, Tariq. 2011a. *'Allamatnī al-ḥayāh*. Vol. 1: *Madrasat al-hayāh*. Kuwait City: Sharikat al-Ibdā' al-Fikrī.

———. 2011b. *'Allamatnī al-hayāh*. Vol. 2: *Fahm al-dīn*. Kuwait City: Sharikat al-Ibdā' al-Fikrī.

———. 2011c. *'Allamatnī al-hayāh*. Vol. 3: *Usus al-'aṭā'*. Kuwait City: Sharikat al-Ibdā' al-Fikrī.

———. 2011d. *'Allamatnī al-hayāh*. Vol. 4: *Mahārāt al-ta'thīr*. Kuwait City: Sharikat al-Ibdā' al-Fikrī.

Syvertsen, Trine. 2004. "Citizens, Audiences, Customers, and Players: A Conceptual Discussion of the Relationship between Broadcasters and Their Publics." *European Journal of Cultural Studies* 7, no. 3: 363–80.

Al-Ṭabarānī, Sulaymān. 1995. *Al-Mu'jam al-awsaṭ*. 10 vols. Cairo: Dār al-Ḥaramayn.

Ṭaha, Muḥammad. 2009. "'Amr Khālid min al-wa'ẓ al-mubāshir ilā tilīfizyūn al-wāqi'." *BBC Arabic*, Dec. 28. At http://www.bbc.com/arabic/artandculture/2009/12/091228_am_amr_tc2.shtml.

White, Lesley. 2007. "The Antidote to Terror." *Sunday Times* (London), May 13. At http://www.thesundaytimes.co.uk/sto/news/uk_news/article63246.ece.

Wise, Lindsay. 2003. "'Words from the Heart': New Forms of Islamic Preaching in Egypt." M.Phil. thesis, St. Antony's College, Oxford Univ.

———. 2004. "Broadcasting the Nahda." *TBS Journal* 13. At https://www.arabmediasociety.com/amr-khaled-broadcasting-the-nahda/.

11

Music with a Message

Maher Zain and the Rise of Awakening's New Global Sound

Sean Foley

In early June 2018, *Hasat vakti* (Harvest Time), a music video praising Recep Tayyip Erdoğan and Turkey emerged in Turkey's official media and in campaign rallies for the president (Sani 2018). Released weeks before one of Turkey's most contested elections in years, the Turkish-language music video soon went viral in the country and around the Muslim world. Newspapers from Germany to Southeast Asia reported on the video (*Malaysiakini* 2018; *Nex24.News* 2018), while versions of the song with subtitles in Arabic and other languages were posted on YouTube (TRT Arabi 2018). Even after Erdoğan won reelection on June 24, 2018, the song remained popular. By January 2019, the version of the *Hasat vakti* video that the state-run Anadolu News Agency in Ankara posted online on June 1, 2018, had been viewed nearly 13 million times (Anadolu Agency 2018).

The song "Hasat vakti," like modern Turkey, blends traditions from East and West. The song is a *našīd* (pl. *anāšīd*)—a type of vocal music that is sung either a cappella or accompanied by percussion instruments but that has been made catchy by speeding up the rhythm and westernizing the melody. The lyrics similarly mix secular and religious themes. While the song hails the leadership of Erdoğan and the people's commitment to unity and nationalist values, it also invokes the memory of the Prophet Muhammad and of legendary Ottoman and Turkish leaders, such as Mehmet the Conqueror. Indeed, Erdoğan is openly portrayed as the contemporary version of Ertuğrul, the thirteenth-century Ghazi warrior and the father of Osman I, the founder of the Ottoman Empire.[1]

Throughout "Hasat Vakti," one message is repeated over and over: Turks should unify around Erdoğan, the father of the nation. The message is positive and upbeat, with no attacks on the president's political opponents. Reinforcing that basic theme in the video are countless pictures of Erdoğan interacting with Turkish men and women of all ages and backgrounds in small groups and in massive rallies. Many are shown expressing their enthusiastic support for Erdoğan, often holding handmade signs and scarves bearing the president's name. Others are shown taking pictures of him with their cell phones, either selfies with him or photos of him speaking on stage, all presumably to be posted on social media. In a country seemingly plagued by deep divisions surrounding Islam and the place of women, there are many pictures of both veiled Turkish women and those in stylish Western clothing strongly supporting Erdoğan. Many are in fact shown in the same crowds next to one another.

No less striking, the singer of "Hasat Vakti" is not one of Turkey's leading pop singers, but Maher Zain—a Lebanese-born Swedish R&B superstar singer with a vast following on social media. His videos were viewed more than 2 billion times on YouTube between 2015 and 2017 (*OneFamily* 2017). Nor was the song's writer Turkish: Mesut Kurtis is a Macedonian poet who has worked with Zain[2] and been featured on his social media (Awakening Music [@Awakeningrecords] 2016).

1. Although little is known for certain about his life, Ertuğrul holds a central place in contemporary Turkish popular culture and has been portrayed since 2014 in *Diriliş: Ertuğrul* (Resurrection: Ertuğrul)—a popular historical adventure television series shown on Turkish television station TRT 1 and comparable to *Game of Thrones* (*Daily Sabah* 2018).

2. Kurtis wrote the Turkish version of Zain's song "Ramadan." See the credits in the video *Ramadan* (Awakening Music [@AwakeningMusic] 2013b).

The success of the video and Erdoğan's decision to enlist Zain and Kurtis point to the singer's talent and the importance of Awakening Music,[3] Zain's record label and one of the world's foremost Muslim media companies. The company aims to address the demand among Turks and other Muslims for popular music inspired by faith and driven by values. Over the past decade, Zain and Awakening Music's most successful works have been *našīd*-based videos and songs that show how Islam offers Muslims a framework for individual and collective action in the contemporary world. The songs and videos in particular show Muslims how to blur the seemingly hard lines between secular and religious forces, helping them to realize a more just future in which they don't have to choose between their faith and Western modernity.

Awakening Music and Zain's videos point to the importance of new communication technologies along with what John Voll has identified as the "religionization of what is called 'secular,' and a secularization of what is called 'religious" (quoted in al-Arian 2018). That social transformation—what Voll calls the rise of "seculigious" forces—touches everyone, from what many analysts identify as "secular" governments to the "pious" Muslim Brotherhood and everyone in between (al-Arian 2018).

Ultimately, the link between vast sociopolitical changes and Zain's songs reminds us that if scholars limit their focus to "traditional" political sources and to the men and women at the front of Muslim societies, then they may miss the individuals who shape culture and mass public opinion—critical elements in any country's politics. Carin Berg (2017), Jonathan Pieslak (2017), and others have demonstrated the importance of *našīd* and music to jihadis and other major Muslim social movements, but this chapter seeks to show that Zain and Muslim popular musicians can play a critical social and political role through art and social media. As Mark LeVine has observed, to understand the people and politics of the Muslim world, we have to follow

3. Awakening Music was known as Awakening Records before 2018.

the artists and "the musicians and their fans as much as the mullahs and their followers" (2008, 3).

Awakening Music, Globalization, and Maher Zain

When Awakening began at the start of the twenty-first century, there was no precedent for a singer like Zain, for a record label marketing to the entire Muslim World, or for a Lebanese Swedish singer serving a pivotal role in a Turkish presidential election. But the men who founded the company—Sharif Banna, a British Muslim of Bangladeshi origin; Bara Kherigi, a Tunisian Muslim; and Wassim Malak, an American Muslim who was born in Lebanon—believed that there was a viable market for Western-style pop that spoke to Muslims' religion and its values. The executives also aimed to provide a social space for the emergence of a musical alternative to the options available in most Muslim nations: secular popular music in a local language but modeled on Western songs or classic religious sermons in Arabic that had little appeal to younger audiences (Foley 2012).

Significantly, these musical choices mirrored the binary political choices that Muslims believed they faced following the terrorist attacks on September 11, 2001, and the US-led war on terrorism. In the West and in much of the Muslim world, Muslims could either side with Western modernity and the authoritarian Muslim regimes allied with Washington or back anti-Western extremism and terrorism. There was no space for any alternative perspectives, whether intellectually or musically.

To make this alternative path a reality, Awakening executives devised an innovative and labor-intensive business model. They supervised every detail of an artist's career through production and marketing; worked in multiple countries simultaneously via Skype and email; and spent generously on high-quality music videos that could compete with the finest Western ones. Their songs and videos synthesized Eastern percussive instrumentation and Western melodies and featured lyrics that were equally multicultural. They touched on recognizable Islamic themes and images along with the themes of personal freedom, women's rights, and a host of others that resonated among non-Muslims in the West and beyond. A new genre of music and implicitly a new seculigious way of thinking—the "religionization of what is called 'secular,' and a secularization of what is called 'religious'"—had emerged.

Among the artists whom Awakening has shepherded to stardom with this model, none has proven more successful than Maher Zain. Although Zain was born in Lebanon, he grew up in Sweden. After earning a degree in aeronautical engineering, he moved to the United States in 2006, where he worked in the music industry. While still in his midtwenties, Zain partnered with Nadir Khayat (widely known as RedOne), the American Moroccan record producer, who has worked with Lady Gaga and other leading international performing artists. But a personal spiritual crisis prompted Zain to return to Sweden and embrace Islam, an aspect of his heritage that he had largely ignored up to that point in his life.

In January 2009, Zain began to work with Awakening on songs that would allow him to merge his identity in the music industry with his new spiritual life. In particular, he focused on songs that, like "Hasat vakti," were *našīd*—an Islamic vocal genre whose roots extend back to pre-Islamic Arabs. Although many leading Muslims have for centuries debated whether *našīd* should be a legitimate part of their faith, this music genre had, by the time Zain joined Awakening in the early twenty-first century, become a central part of daily life for Muslim societies around the world. In addition, many Muslim reformers had sought to use it to renew their societies in periods of crisis. No less a figure than Anwar al-Awlaki, whose YouTube lectures remain some of al-Qaeda's most potent recruitment tools, observed that a "good *našīd*" spreads far faster and is far better at winning the attention of young Muslim audiences than either a sermon or a book are (Stjernholm 2013, 209).

One can see the wisdom in al-Awlaki's insight in the success of Raihan, a Malaysian *našīd* group that turned to music as the way to convince young Muslims about the virtues of Islam. Echoing language that Awakening executives would later use to describe Zain and his style of Muslim music, Raihan member Abu Bakar noted in 1998: "Entertainment and music are the closest thing to today's youngsters. If we are going to influence them, it will have to be through music" (quoted in Seneviratne 2012, 211). The group, whose name derives from the Arabic word for a fragrance from heaven, became a popular sensation after the release of their debut album *Puji-Pujian* (Praise God, 1996) a decade before Zain joined Awakening (Seneviratne 2012, 209). It sold a record 750,000 units in Malaysia alone, where the most successful music albums usually sell only 20,000, and more than 3.5 million worldwide (Seneviratne 2012, 209, 212–13). Not only did Raihan's success foreshadow Zain's success in Malaysia, but its lyrics and official motto, "Pray Hard, Work Smart," also foreshadowed the key themes of Zain's songs that resonated with Malays and other Muslims around the world (Seneviratne 2012, 209).

At the same time, although Raihan has performed around the world with leading non-Malay Muslim artists,[4] it remains a Malaysian Muslim group. Raihan often sings in Arabic and Bahasa Malaysian and appears on stage in traditional male Malay ceremonial outfits—the black Songkok hat and the Baju Melayu tunic.[5]

By contrast, Zain sought to use *našīd* to appeal to a much larger global audience not associated with a specific nation or region. Most of the songs in his debut album, *Thank You Allah*, released in November 2009, are in English, the most commonly spoken language around the world. Zain framed himself visually as a westernized Muslim comfortable in Voll's seculigious world. The album's cover shows him in jeans, a black jacket, and a dapper cap appropriate for an R&B concert in Stockholm or New York but seated in Islamic prayer. That combination is emblematic of the album's central message: faith in Islam, God, and personal dignity are the answer to the many systematic challenges

4. The group has sung with Yusuf Islam (formerly known as Cat Stevens) (Seneviratne 2012, 209).

5. For an excellent picture of the group in costume, see the photograph "Raihan" in *Voices of Islam in Southeast Asia* ("Raihan" 2006, 272).

facing Muslims throughout the world in the twenty-first century (Foley 2011).

Within months of *Thank You Allah*'s release, there was clear evidence that its message had touched a nerve in the Muslim world, starting with Egypt. There, listeners to Cairo-based Nogoum FM, the biggest Arab mainstream radio station, voted one of the album's songs, "Ya Nabi salam alayka" (Oh Prophet, Peace Be upon You), the Best New Song award for 2009 (Foley 2011). In March 2010, many of the station's listeners and others from as far away as Great Britain attended Zain's concert with Awakening singers at the American University in Cairo, an education institution that has portrayed itself as a critical bridge between the West and the Arab and Muslim worlds. Dahlia Radwan, a forty-five-year-old Egyptian human-relations consultant, spoke for many in the audience when she said to the *Daily News Egypt* that she loved "the revolutionary feel of music with a message." "This is not the usual empty lyrics," Radwan continued, that "we hear on TV, or the classic religious sermons that are not in touch with the new generation" (quoted in *Daily News Egypt* 2010).

Reinforcing the power of Zain's songs was his decision to avoid the standard formula for popular videos or songs, which glamorize and revolve around the singer. Instead, he focuses on a heroic person—such as President Erdoğan in "Hasat vakti"—or on being seen as an ordinary person who is no big deal except for his talent, which is given to him by Allah, whom he often thanks (Foley 2011).

But Zain's faith is not founded on a renunciation of either the West or of traditional liberal secular values. This is nothing like al-Awlaki's jihad. In "Awaken," Zain even calls on Muslims to reform themselves and not to fault others for their shortcomings, including the colonial powers that once controlled the Muslim world. Collective social action is also an important aspect of his message. In his videos—whose visual and sound quality far surpass Raihan's—we see him singing in many situations where there are problems, but people other than Zain address them.

Equally importantly, Zain encourages individuals to take ownership of their problems and to confront injustice, but not with violence.

For instance, in the music video for *Thank You Allah*'s third song, "Insha Allah," one sees pictures of dark and menacing riot police chasing innocents and even of violent torture as Zain sings that one should never lose hope because Allah is always on one's side. That video, which was released in May 2010 and foreshadowed the demonstrations that took place in Tahrir Square in 2011, has been seen more than 80 million times on YouTube (Awakening Music [@AwakeningMusic] 2010). Even more astonishingly, in the video for "Palestine Will Be Free" viewers see a schoolgirl holding a stone and standing in front of an Israeli tank—an image meant to invoke a very famous picture of a Palestinian child from the al-Aqsa Intifada holding a rock high to throw at a nearby Israeli tank. But the girl in the video drops the rock, stands defenseless in front of the tank, and implicitly puts her faith in God that her personal will is stronger than the Israeli tank. Her faith is rewarded as the tank withdraws. The video, released on August 2009, has been seen nearly 15 million times (Awakening Music [@AwakeningMusic] 2009).

At the same time, Awakening executives consciously married Zain's musical vision to an aggressive marketing campaign based almost entirely on Facebook, Twitter, YouTube, and other social media accessible on smartphones. Their decision to pursue this strategy reflected the fact that online media, as the cassette tape once was, are significantly cheaper to use for advertising than traditional media (Schewe 2017).[6] It also reflected the fact that there remains a reluctance among many mainstream advertisers and executives of global music labels to promote Muslim popular music (Foley 2011).

But there was also a clear profit motive in Awakening's decisions. Awakening executives realized that there was potentially a very lucrative market for Zain's music among the millions of people using social media and accessing the internet via smart phones in Muslim nations, especially in Southeast Asia. By December 2011, there were 12 million

6. The cassette tape played an especially important role in social change in Iran, especially during the Iranian Revolution (Siamdoust 2017).

Facebook users in Malaysia alone, a number equal to 42 percent of the nation's population and 70 percent of the country's internet users (Yung-Hui 2011). At the time, Malaysians maintained close ties to the West and the Middle East, where Zain's songs had already done well, and spoke English. And Raihan had shown that Malaysians were highly receptive to Islamic popular music based on *anāšīd* that utilized Western themes.

Thanks to this strategy, Zain's music spread rapidly online and took on a life of its own. The album *Thank You Allah* set new sales records throughout much of Southeast Asia—mirroring Raihan's success in the 1990s. Not only did Zain's likes on Facebook grow quickly, but he also was the most Googled personality in Malaysia in 2010 (Kamin 2012). In 2011, *Thank You Allah* went platinum[7] eleven times in Malaysia and was the best-selling album in the country (Kamin 2012). A year later, the television serial *Insha Allah*, based on Zain's songs, was filmed in Indonesia (Kamin 2012).

Zain's social media presence continued to grow quickly, fueled by the debuting of new songs and videos online to his followers. In 2019, he had more than 25 million followers on Facebook, while his top four videos had been viewed more than 400 million times on YouTube. One video from *Thank You Allah*, *Ya Nabi salam alayka*, has been viewed more than 200 million times (Zain 2018). He has further expanded his fanbase by releasing a cappella versions of *Thank You Allah* and his other albums—a recognition of the fact that some Muslims view music as *ḥarām* (forbidden) under Islamic law (Saeed 2015).[8] Although Zain clearly views music as *ḥalāl* (permitted) under Islamic law, he has consciously adopted a position in public that provides space for those who do not agree with him (Saeed 2015). In 2015, he told the *National*, an Emirati daily newspaper, "I'd rather not delve into the discussion of what is *ḥalāl* and *ḥarām*, as there are people and

7. Since July 1, 2009, an album is considered to "have gone platinum" in Malaysia if it has sold more than 15,000 copies (*Wikipedia* n.d.).

8. Sami Yusuf, who has worked with Awakening, has also released multiple versions of select songs to respect these types of differences (Saeed 2015).

scholars immensely more qualified than myself to comment on such things" (Saeed 2015).

As Zain has expanded his fanbase among Muslims, he has also won fans among non-Muslim populations in Southeast Asia. In Singapore, a city-state where Muslims account for just 15 percent of the country's 5 million population, Zain's concert in 2011 drew 5,000 people (Habi 2016). In Sarawak, a Malaysian province with large Chinese and Muslim populations, his concert in November 2011 drew a large crowd in Kuching, the state capital (author's fieldnotes, 2011). In a clear sign of the singer's importance, two mammoth posters—one of Sarawak's then chief minister (governor) Abdul Taib Mahmud and the other of then prime minister of Malaysia Najib Tun Razak—adorned the entrance to the concert venue (author's fieldnotes, 2011). Yet Zain did not make any public comments during the concert in support of either man, as he later did for Erdoğan.

Global Reach with Local Resonance: The Glocalization of Maher Zain

A year after Zain gave that concert in Kuching, he released his second album, *Forgive Me.* This album pointed to his vast online presence—the first video linked to the album was seen 500,000 times within five days of its release (Kamin 2012)—and to Awakening's desire to expand his fan base to include more non-Muslims and people whose native language was neither Arabic nor English.

On the album's cover, Zain sits in a contemplative position but wears black pants, a warm-weather jacket, a scarf, and a winter cap while sitting in picturesque European mountains. Although there are songs in English with Western chords that discuss the Prophet Muhammad, a visit to Mecca, and the Arab Spring, there are also songs in Arabic and in the popular styles of Arabic music. There are also songs about the untimely death of a friend, substance abuse, marriage, the joy of being a father to a daughter, personal regret, as well as Zain's and by extension any young man's appreciation and love for his mother.

The latter most universal of themes is at the heart of the first video released with *Forgive Me, You Are My Number One.* The video, which has been seen more than 96 million times on YouTube, is in English and features Western popular chords but has subtitles in seventeen languages, including Chinese and Russian. It is set in a Western bourgeois home and flips between the present and the singer's antics as a young boy. Zain asks for his mother's forgiveness and communicates with large white cards his desire to make her happy, a method analogous to Bob Dylan's classic video for the song "Subterranean Homesick Blues" (1965). The language and symbols on the large cards, such as a smiley face, are similar to those used in text messages in English around the world. Zain's ode to his mother endears him to women of all faiths. The video is the same quality as Zain's previous videos, but it is worthy of note that there are few outwardly Islamic themes or symbols in it (Foley 2014).

The absence of Islamic themes in this video is indicative of Awakening's growing confidence. Zain and his label are no longer focusing just on the global Muslim market; they are aiming to "mainstream" Muslim popular music. Zain's Facebook page has highlighted the comments of Muslims and non-Muslims to "You Are My Number One" (Foley 2014). Equally importantly, he retains a hopeful, optimistic, and generally upbeat message on even the most contentious issues. The album is neither a call to arms nor a rejection of the West or of existing governments in the Islamic world.

Yet Zain has not abandoned his original audience, either; there are still plenty of songs on Islamic themes. For instance, in the music video *Ramadan*, which was released in June 2013 and filmed in California, Zain sings an ode to the holy month in Arabic, English, and other languages. He wears Western clothing and appears in modern contexts, including in a large balloon and an outdoor dinner with a wide group of friends representing nationalities from around the world (Awakening Music [@AwakeningMusic] 2013b).

There are also both veiled and unveiled women as well as people of many ages and ethnicities: Arabs easily mix with African Americans, Africans, Asians, Southeast Asians, South Asians, and individuals of

European ancestry. We also see Zain reading a Qur'an in the blimp and people of different backgrounds preparing for the holy month and eating food associated with it, such as *sambusa*s and Vimto, a sweet beverage Arabs drink with festive meals during Ramadan. Strikingly, we see Zain pray next to a blond and blue-eyed young man during the dinner. The same young man proposes a toast that leads into a firework display at the end of the video (Awakening Music [@AwakeningMusic] 2013b).

Ramadan, which had the same high production values as Zain's earlier videos, was part of a series of increasingly successful videos that Awakening produced in the 2010s. Many of those videos starred a new generation of Western and Middle Eastern Muslim singers—such as Harris J, Humood AlKhudher, and Mesut Kurtis—and explored the same themes that had resonated with Zain's fans in 2009. Equally importantly, the new videos proved to be as popular as Zain's, while opening up new opportunities for the company. Two examples are significant.

Harris J, a British Muslim teenager who won an Awakening talent contest in which Zain served as a judge (*ZilzarLife* 2015), was an immediate success in August 2015 with his debut song "Salam alaikum" (Peace Be upon You). Later that same year, Harris J and Zain together sang Zain's song "Number One for Me" at the annual conference of the Muslim American Society/Islamic Society of North America (MAS/ISNA), the premier event of its kind for Muslims in the United States (Awakening Music [@AwakeningMusic] 2015). Thanks in part to his appearances with Zain in both videos and in social media, Harris has increased his profile and that of the *Salam alaikum* video, which has been viewed 86 million times on YouTube (Awakening Music [@ AwakeningMusic] 2015).

The Kuwaiti singer Humood AlKhudher has been even more successful than Harris J in building on Zain's business model and ability to employ new social media to great effect. In 2015, Malaysia and the other Southeast Asian musical markets that had propelled Zain to success in 2010 reacted strongly to AlKhudher when Awakening released *Aseer ahsan* (I Feel Better), the Kuwaiti singer's first album with the media company. Just as Zain harnessed Facebook and smartphones in 2010 to rapidly spread his music, AlKhudher publicized his album in Malaysia with a recording of himself parodying one of the songs on it, "Kun anta" (Be Yourself), using Dubsmash, a social media app. The parody was so successful that Malaysian actress Noor Neelofa binti Mohd Noor (Neelofa) and other celebrities produced versions of themselves singing it on Dubsmash (*Rakyat Post* 2015).[9]

Equally importantly, Maher Zain appeared alongside AlKhudher in YouTube videos, including one where the Kuwaiti launched *Aseer ahsan* at the Hala Festival, a major annual shopping festival in Kuwait City.[10] This type of publicity has produced great dividends. Not only was AlKhudher invited to perform at the MAS/ISNA conference, as Zain and Harris J had been, but the video *Kun anta* was also viewed more than 123 million times on YouTube, a number that rivals any video made by Zain. It has subtitles available in nineteen languages, is aimed at a global audience similar to Zain's, and has won global financial backing. Al-Jaber, a major Saudi conglomerate, and one of its business partners, Haier, China's biggest producer of consumer electronics, sponsored the video.[11] Notably, Haier plays a more prominent role in *Kun anta* than any company has in Zain's musical videos: there are multiple shots of Haier televisions in the video, and the message "Powered by Haier Al-Jaber Electronics" appears after the credits.[12]

9. Neelofa may have paved the way for Awakening to sign Eman, the company's first female singer. Although Awakening produced a brief music video featuring Eman in 2019, the video of the Moroccan female singer was subsequently removed from the company's website. As of August 2020, the six artists featured in the company's promotional materials are men.

10. In the video, Zain is shown standing alongside AlKhudher, smiling and holding the album (Anisfitt22 2015).

11. The two companies have been partners since at least 2012 (*Saudi Gazette* 2013).

12. Tasyorah Cheesecake, the Kuwaiti media company Bustop, and Kuwait's Love Restaurants have sponsored AlKhudher's videos with Awakening (Awakening Music [@AwakeningMusic] 2017, 2018).

Partnering with al-Jaber and Haier also points to Awakening executives' drive to open new markets in Asia and the Middle East, especially in Turkey. Zain helped pioneer the company's efforts with Turkish singers,[13] a process that coincided with his deepening emotional and personal commitment to Syrians, the Rohingya in Myanmar (Burma), and other Muslims whom he saw as suffering from persecution. Not only did he frequently comment on Syria on Twitter and other social media, but he also produced a song that reflected the darker mood, especially in Syria. Entitled "Love Will Prevail," the song was dedicated to Syrian refuges and released with a music video on May 11, 2013—just a few weeks before the start of Ramadan, when it was watched more than 7 million times on YouTube (Zain 2013b). In subsequent weeks, Zain dedicated the song to victims of violence in Myanmar and other places (Zain 2013a).

The song shares important characteristics with "Palestine Will Be Free." Much like the girl/tank video in 2010, this video portrays a strong girl forced to survive on her own in a terrifying warzone and features uplifting lyrics that promise a better future, including "love will prevail" and "I will never give up." She—not Zain—is the center of the video. But whereas in the video *Palestine Will Be Free* we see the young girl resolve the war through nonviolence and sheer force of will, the girl in the *Love Will Prevail* video is killed while seeking to escape the violence. Although Zain asks how anyone could "murder an innocent child" and affirms that lives "won't be lost in vain," we see a soldier shoot the girl and kill her (Awakening Music [@Awakening-Music] 2013a).

As the girl collapses, blood oozes from her body and covers the white piano where Zain is sitting. Reinforcing the horrific scene are the clothes of hundreds of people laid out in circles surrounding Zain's piano. Even in this moment of clear injustice, however, Zain does not

13. For example, Zain appeared alongside Sinan Akçıl, a leading Turkish songwriter and producer, in *Gülmek sadaka* (Smiling Is Charity) a video produced by a Turkish media company (Netd Müzik 2018).

become enraged or blame anyone directly for the girl's death. We see neither the face nor the uniform of the solider who has killed the girl. In theory, the shooter could be from the Syrian government, from one of the many rebel groups, from the Islamic State, or from the many foreign forces that have participated in the Syrian Civil War. At a certain level, it does not matter to Zain who pulled the trigger: we all are responsible for not stopping a war in which little girls and countless others are killed in cold blood (Awakening Music [@AwakeningMusic] 2013a).

The violence and refugee crisis in Syria have had a profound impact on Zain and on many of his fans. Not only has he volunteered to aid Syrian refugees, but he has also held up the rebel Syrian flag at his concerts—even though he insisted to the *New York Times* in 2017 that he is "not into politics" (Marshall 2017). Both in person and on social media, Zain has also championed Erdoğan's aid to Syrians and to the Rohingya in a way he has done for no other leader, whether in Malaysia or elsewhere (Sani 2018). Strikingly, in 2014 Zain discussed meeting Erdoğan in person (Zain 2014). He congratulated Erdoğan's daughter on Twitter when she was married in 2016 (Zain 2016). He also hailed Turkey in 2017 as a "model for many Muslim countries—it is democratic, pluralist, and proud of its identity and heritage" (quoted in Sani 2018)—just as many Western analysts had concluded that the Turkish president was increasingly becoming an authoritarian leader.[14]

Zain sees support for Turkey's president and his family as "humanity" rather than "normal politics." "When you see these things," he told the *New York Times*, "I feel as a human and as an artist I have a responsibility to highlight what people are going through" (quoted in Marshall 2017). In this sense, his views are not outside the mainstream in Southeast Asia or elsewhere in the Muslim world, where support for Erdoğan remains robust.[15]

14. For example, see Simon Tidsdall's article "Recep Tayyip Erdoğan: A Dictator in All but Name Seeks Complete Control" (2018).

15. See Imran Khan's Tweet: "Congratulations to President Erdogan" (Khan 2018). One sees similar support for Erdoğan from Ahmed Bedier and other Muslim figures in the United States (Bedier 2018).

At the same time, Zain may recognize that highlighting "his responsibility" to support the Turkish president may not please all of his fans, especially in the West, where hostility to the Turkish president has been growing in recent years. It is worth noting that neither Awakening nor Zain made any reference to "Hasat vakti" on Facebook and other social media—a striking departure from other songs that are promoted weeks ahead of their release and days after they are available online. Zain also spoke about the video only to a handful of Turkish media outlets. Many stories elsewhere in the world were translations of the original English or Turkish stories.

Social Media, Social Movements, and Music

In *The Rise of the Network Society* (second edition, 2010), the Spanish sociologist Manuel Castells argues that advances in information technology and the proliferation of media have created "a world of uncontrolled, confusing change" that has compelled many people "to regroup around primary identities; religious, ethnic, territorial, [and] national" (3). Although Castells's book was first published in 1996, its ideas have gained in importance in recent years with the emergence of populist movements around the world, many of which are fueled by cultural, nationalist, or religious rage amplified by social media and men such as Anwar al-Awlaki (Bartlett 2018). In the eyes of many commentators and some industry leaders, such as Amazon's Jeff Bezos, these movements are extremely dangerous, bringing out the worst tribal instincts in men and women, old and young (Burch 2018; Stemm 2018).

By contrast, Zain and Awakening Media show that social media can also create social movements that are peaceful and embrace seemingly oppositional forces and peoples in every corner of the globe. Although Zain emerged as a singing star in Southeast Asia, he has won millions of fans in countries as different as Saudi Arabia, Singapore, South Africa, and even Castells's native Spain.[16] Today, Zain's

16. See *IOL* 2018 and Pérez 2018 as well as the Facebook page of the Maher Zain Saudi Arabia Fan Club (@MaherZainSaudiArabiaFanClub) at https://www

cultural and social presence is so strong that political leaders from Turkey to Malaysia have associated themselves with him and his music, hoping to benefit from his direct or implied endorsement. This takes us back to John Voll's coinage *glocal*, which combines *global* and *local* into one word to affirm the interconnectedness of global and local events as well as the need for analysts "to simultaneously view" figures such as Zain "through local and international lenses" (al-Saif and Ghabra 2016).

Awakening has responded to Zain's growing prominence and diversifying "glocal" fan base by having Zain produce songs in multiple languages besides Arabic and English, including Bahasa Malaysian, Mandarin, and Turkish. But even more interesting has been the desire of his fans around the world to make his music their own—a process vividly illustrated by their response to the #MZCover Campaign, where fans were asked to record a cover of any one of Zain's songs and upload their video to Zain's Facebook, Instagram, or Twitter account using the hashtag "#MZCover" (Awakening Music [@AwakeningRec] 2018). The campaign, which was launched in late October 2018 and is similar to AlKhudher's Dubsmash parody, has drawn an enthusiastic response. To date, fans have uploaded hundreds of their versions of "Assalamu alayka" and Zain's other songs in languages as diverse as Albanian, Arabic, Croatian, and Indonesian (Marie 2018).

These songs, which Zain has shared on his social media accounts and in a special video, show not only the intensity of his fans' reaction to his music but also something much deeper—namely, how social media can create new communities that transcend old boundaries while offering hope for the future of a world plagued by seemingly irreconcilable differences. This is, of course, a vision that Zain values. "I hope one day that as different nations and communities," he explained in 2018, "we can put our differences aside and live as one global family. That's my dream" (quoted in Sani 2018).

.facebook.com/pages/category/Musician-Band/Maher-Zain-Saudi-Arabia-Fan-Club -247864772017915/.

As analysts and scholars seek to better understand the Middle East and the Muslim world in the twenty-first century, they would be well advised to pay close attention to the lyrics sung by Zain and other Muslim artists, words that embody the aspirations of millions of Muslims. Zain and Awakening Music understand that Western culture has entered the consciousness of all the world's young and realize further that "love songs" can easily be transformed into sacred music, just as, once long ago, the deeply, humanly erotic "Song of Songs" was transformed into a poem about the soul and its longing for God.

For Zain, the road to a better world and to revolution is not to be found in angry politics or divisive rhetoric. Rather, it is embedded in the themes, structures, and chordal sounds of modern Western popular music that, in Zain's hands, has undergone a profound change of subject—one that he voiced in an interview about his legacy as an artist in 2015. His music, Zain predicted, will be more than a "creative pursuit," for it fundamentally challenges how the world looks at Muslims (Saeed 2015). Instead of reaffirming the vision of Islam promoted by Muslim terrorists or in mainstream media, he continued, his songs show Muslims as "normal people, and just like anyone else":[17] "we feel love, have families, and enjoy art" (Saeed 2015). "We," he insists, are "you," and you can feel that in the music we make. Indeed, in a contemporary world ever more defined by division and fear, such an ordinary vision of Muslims and their lives could have profound consequences.

References

Anadolu Agency (@AnadoluAgency). 2018. *Maher Zain'den Yeni Şarkısına Erdoğan'lı Klip*. YouTube video, June 1. At youtube.com/watch?v=mtKWWcg60qE.

17. Zain's wording echoes that of Sting's song "Russians" (1985), in which the British artist implies that the people of both the West and Russia have common sense and cherish their children. I thank my colleague Dr. Louis Haas for reminding me of this linkage.

Anisfitt22 (@Anisfitt22). 2015. *Humood Alkhudher Launching Album* Aseer Ahsan. YouTube video, July 22. At youtube.com/watch?v=hI40U-XxAR8.

Al-Arian, Abdullah. 2018. "Roundtable on Political Islam after the Arab Uprisings." *Maydan: Politics and Society*, May 2. At https://www.themaydan.com/2018/05/roundtable-political-islam-arab-uprisings/.

Awakening Music (@AwakeningMusic). 2009. *Maher Zain—Palestine Will Be Free*. YouTube video, Aug. 8. At youtube.com/watch?v=foSbqLi6U10.

———. 2010. *Maher Zain—Insha Allah*. YouTube video, May 1. At youtube.com/watch?v=KfXIF2Mm2Kc.

———. 2013a. *Maher Zain—Love Will Prevail, Official Music Video*. YouTube video, May 11. At youtube.com/watch?v=eoMJJCVBCgo.

———. 2013b. *Ramadan*. YouTube video, June 28. At youtube.com/watch?v=3G-t72JjRf0.

———. 2015. *Harris J—Salam alaikum*. YouTube video, Aug. 5. At youtube.com/watch?v=u_-McEvEGvI.

———. 2017. *Humood—Lughat al'Aalam*. YouTube video, Jan. 1. At youtube.com/watch?v=WtE2DRRJayg.

———. 2018. *Humood—Be Curious*. YouTube video, Mar. 13. At youtube.com/watch?v=4Aaj3-sMPPE.

Awakening Music (@AwakeningRec). 2018. "Join our #MZCover campaign now and show your #talent to the world! All you have to do is: https://instagram.com/p/BouDkA9n6Dz/." Twitter, Oct. 9, 2018, 9:55 a.m. At https://twitter.com/AwakeningRec/status/1049704927566712832.

Awakening Music (@Awakeningrecords). 2016. "Maher Zain is with Mesut Kurtis, Emre Moğulkoç, and Ahmet Kurtis in the studio in Istanbul cooking up some magic for Maher's third album #mz3rdalbum #MaherZain #AwakeningRecords." Facebook, Mar. 31. At https://www.facebook.com/awakeningrecords/posts/10153998902001772?comment_id=10154002112666772&comment_tracking=%7B%22tn%22%3A%22R0%22%7D.

Bartlett, Jamie. 2018. "Why Is Populism Booming? Today's Tech Is Partly to Blame." *Guardian*, Nov. 29. At https://www.theguardian.com/commentisfree/2018/nov/29/populism-tinder-politics-swipe-left-or-right-unthinkingly.

Bedier, Ahmed (@Bedier). 2018. "Congrats Turkey and President Recep Tayyip Erdoğan on winning the election." Twitter, June 24, 11:45 a.m. At https://twitter.com/bedier/status/1010957038808117249.

Berg, Carin. 2017. "The Soundtrack of Politics: A Case Study of Anashid in Hamas and Hezbollah." PhD diss., Univ. of Gothenburg.

Burch, Sean. 2018. "Amazon's Jeff Bezos: Social Media Inflames 'Identity Politics, Tribalism.'" *Wrap*, Oct. 15. At https://www.thewrap.com/jeff-bezos-social-media-makes-identity-politics-tribalism-worse/.

Castells, Manuel. 2010. *The Rise of the Network Society*. 2nd ed. Hoboken, NJ: Blackwell.

Daily News Egypt. 2010. "Fans Throng to Maher Zain's Album Debut Concert at AUC." Mar. 26. At https://dailynewsegypt.com/2010/03/26/fans-throng-to-maher-zains-album-debut-concert-at-auc/.

Daily Sabah. 2018. "Turkish TV Series *Ertuğrul* Could Be the Alternative to *Game of Thrones*, Reports Say." Feb. 23. At https://www.dailysabah.com/life/2018/02/23/turkish-tv-series-ertugrul-could-be-the-alternative-to-game-of-thrones-reports-say.

Foley, Sean. 2011. "Maher Zain's Hip but Pious Soundtrack to the Arab Spring." *Atlantic*, Aug. 11. At https://www.theatlantic.com/entertainment/archive/2011/08/maher-zains-hip-but-pious-soundtrack-to-the-arab-spring/243191/.

———. 2012. "Maher Zain, Technology, and Southeast Asia's Place in Modern Islam." At http://www.oxfordislamicstudies.com/Public/focus/essay1009_maher_zain.html.

———. 2014. "Can the Eastern–Western Ideology Be Reconciled through Music and the Power of Social Media?" *Verse69: The Beat of the Third Culture*, Mar. 11.

Habi, Eddino Abdul. 2016. "Global Star an Unknown at Home." *Straits Times*, Nov. 28. At https://www.straitstimes.com/lifestyle/entertainment/global-star-an-unknown-at-home.

IOL. 2018. "Islamic Music Superstar Maher Zain to Perform Live in Cape Town." July 26. At https://www.iol.co.za/entertainment/whats-on/cape-town/islamic-music-superstar-maher-zain-to-perform-live-in-cape-town-16259434.

Kamin, Azhariah. 2012. "Consciously Tuneful." *Star*, Apr. 18. At https://www.thestar.com.my/lifestyle/entertainment/music/news/2012/04/18/consciously-tuneful/.

Khan, Imran (@ImranKhanPTI). 2018. "Congratulations to President Erdogan on his electoral victory. Wishing his new term brings stability and prosperity for the people of Turkey." Twitter, June 24, 11:48 p.m. At https://twitter.com/ImranKhanPTI/status/1011139038210854912.

LeVine, Mark. 2008. *Heavy Metal Islam: Rock, Resistance, and the Struggle for the Soul of Islam*. New York: Three Rivers Press.

Malaysiakini. 2018. "Maher Zain dendangkan pujian buat Erdogan." June 5. At https://www.malaysiakini.com/hiburan/428459.

Marie, Mustafa. 2018. "Fans Perform Maher Zain's 'Al-salam alaik' in several languages." *Egypt Today*, Oct. 18. At http://www.egypttoday.com/Article/4/59152/Fans-perform-Maher-Zain-s-Al-Salam-Alaik-in-several.

Marshall, Alex. 2017. "On Tour with an Islamic Pop Icon Who Makes Fans Swoon." *New York Times*, Nov. 9. At https://www.nytimes.com/2017/11/09/arts/music/maher-zain-tour.html.

Netd Müzik (@Netd). 2018. *Sinan Akçıl—Maher Zain—Gülmek Sadaka*. YouTube video, July 12. At youtube.com/watch?v=q79C_g4IMIs.

Nex24.News. 2018. "Muslimischer Superstar Maher Zain veröffentlicht Song für Erdogan." June 3. At https://nex24.news/2018/06/muslimischer-superstar-maher-zain-veroeffentlicht-song-fuer-erdogan/.

OneFamily. 2017. "Press Release: Maher Zain Joins One Family as a Global Ambassador." June 9. At https://onefamily.org.uk/post/maher-zain-co-founds-digital-first-charity-one-family.

Pérez, Beatriz. 2018. "Un evento islámico atrae a unos 2.000 jóvenes al Palau de Congressos de Catalunya." *El Periódico*, Dec. 9. At https://www.elperiodico.com/es/barcelona/20181209/evento-islamico-islamic-relief-mil-jovenes-al-palau-congressos-de-catalunya-barcelona-7192303.

Pieslak, Jonathan. 2017. "A Musical Perspective on Jihad Anashid." In *Jihadi Culture: The Art and Social Practices of Militant Islamists*, edited by Thomas Hegghammer, 63–81. Cambridge: Cambridge Univ. Press.

"Raihan." 2006. In *Voices of Islam in Southeast Asia: A Contemporary Sourcebook*, edited by Greg Fealy and Virginia Hooker, 272, plate 11. Singapore: Institute of Southeast Asian Studies.

Rakyat Post. 2015. "'Kun Anta' Takes Malaysia by Storm Following Viral Dubsmash Video." June 9. At http://www.therakyatpost.com/life/2015/06/09/kun-anta-takes-malaysia-by-storm-following-viral-dubsmash-video/.

Saeed, Saeed. 2015. "Mawazine Sessions: Maher Zain's Mission to Inspire." *National*, June 29. At https://www.thenational.ae/arts-culture/mawazine-sessions-maher-zain-s-mission-to-inspire-1.106411.

Al-Saif, Bader Mousa, and Haneen Shafeeq Ghabra. 2016. "Higher Education and Contestation in the State of Kuwait after the Arab Spring: Identity Construction & Ideologies of Domination in the American University of Kuwait." In *Education and the Arab Spring: For Educators by Educators*, edited by Eid Mohamed, Hannah R. Gerber, and Slimane Aboulkacem, 97–114. Rotterdam: Sense.

Sani, Ahmet Esad. 2018. "Singing Star Maher Zain Releases New Song for Erdogan." Anadolu Agency, June 1. At https://www.aa.com.tr/en/culture-and-art/singing-star-maher-zain-releases-new-song-for-erdogan/1163015.

Saudi Gazette. 2013. "Al Jabr Electronic to Expand Haier Brand Share in Saudi Market." Dec. 12. At http://saudigazette.com.sa/article/28148/Al-Jabr-Electronic-to-expand-Haier-brand-share-in-Saudi-market.

Schewe, Eric. 2017. "How Cassette Tapes Helped Muslim Revivalism." *JSTOR Daily*, June 2. At https://daily.jstor.org/how-cassette-tapes-helped-muslim-revivalism/.

Seneviratne, Kalinga. 2012. *Countering MTV Influence in Indonesia and Malaysia*. Singapore: Institute for Southeast Asian Studies, 2012.

Siamdoust, Nahid. 2017. "Modern Iran in 8 Songs." *Typepad*, Stanford Univ. Press blog, May 2. At https://stanfordpress.typepad.com/blog/2017/05/modern-iran-in-8-songs.html.

Stemm, Jason. 2018. "Influence and Tribalism on Social Media." *Buzz Bin*, Sept. 17. At https://buzzbinpadillaco.com/influence-tribalism-social-media/.

Stjernholm, Simon. 2013. "Pro-violence and Anti-democratic Islamist Messages on the Internet." In *Pro-violence and Anti-democratic Messages on the Internet*, edited by Ewa Thorslund, 191–262. Stockholm: Swedish Media Council.

Tidsdall, Simon. 2018. "Recep Tayyip Erdoğan: A Dictator in All but Name Seeks Complete Control." *Guardian*, Apr. 19. At https://www.theguardian.com/world/2018/apr/19/recep-tayyip-erdogan-turkey-president-election-dictator-seeks-total-control.

TRT Arabi (@TRTArabi). 2018. *"Waqt al-Ḥiṣād" video klib jadīd lilmuğanninī Maher Zain' min ajal Turkiyā wa ar-Ra'is Erdogwan*. YouTube video, June 1. At youtube.com/watch?v=fxwgmMQ7lMo.

Wikipedia. n.d. "Recording Industry Association of Malaysia." At https://en.wikipedia.org/wiki/Recording_Industry_Association_of_Malaysia.

Yung-Hui, Lim. 2011. "Facebook Hits 70% Penetration Rate in Malaysia." *Forbes*, Dec. 20. At https://www.forbes.com/sites/limyunghui/2011/12/20/facebook-hits-70-penetration-rate-in-malaysia/#7b86cdd81c31.

Zain, Maher (@MaherZain). 2013a. "Love will prevail, by God it will! #Egypt #Syria #Palestine #Burma." Twitter, Aug. 9, 12:37 a.m. At https://twitter.com/MaherZain/status/365362535234826242.

———. 2013b. "'Love Will Prevail' is my new music video dedicated to Syria, and to all the oppressed people in Palestine." Twitter, May 11, 5:45 p.m. At https://twitter.com/MaherZain/status/333382306842697729.

———. 2014. "Congrats to PM #Erdogan on winning presidential elections. I had the honour of meeting him recently." Twitter, Aug. 10, 11:10 p.m. At https://twitter.com/MaherZain/status/498712983929749506.

———. 2016. "Congratulations to Sumeyye Erdogan & Selcuk Bayraktar on their blessed marriage." Twitter, May 15, 1:45 a.m. At https://twitter.com/MaherZain/status/731767436198842368.

———. 2018. "'Ya Nabi Salam Alayka' Passed 200 MILLION Views on YouTube." Facebook, Dec. 29. At https://www.facebook.com/watch/?v=323837921801216.

ZilzarLife. 2015. "Could Harris J Be the Muslim Justin Bieber, or the Younger Maher Zain?" Sept. 21. At http://zilzarlife.com/could-harris-j-be-the-muslim-justin-bieber-or-the-younger-maher-zain/.

Contributor Biographies

Index

Contributor Biographies

Abdullah al-Arian is associate professor of history at Georgetown University in Qatar. He is the author of *Answering the Call: Popular Islamic Activism in Sadat's Egypt* (2014). He is also the editor of the Critical Currents in Islam page on *Jadaliyya*.

Natana J. DeLong-Bas is associate professor of the practice of theology and Islamic civilization and societies at Boston College. Her books include *Shariah: What Everyone Needs to Know* (2018), *Islam: A Living Faith* (2018), *Wahhabi Islam: From Revival and Reform to Global Jihad* (rev. ed., 2008), and *Women in Muslim Family Law* (rev. ed., 2001). Editor in chief of *Oxford Bibliographies Online—Islamic Studies* and *The Oxford Encyclopedia of Islam and Women* (2013), she works on comparative theology, Saudi Arabia, women and gender, Islamic law, and the environment.

Tuve Buchmann Floden received his PhD in Islamic studies from Georgetown University in 2016. As an independent scholar, he focuses on the evolution of religious authority in modern Islam, particularly as seen through the use of modern media tools and the influence of popular preachers outside of the religious establishment. His publications include the Project on Middle East Political Science article "Defining the Media *D'ua* and Their Call to Action" (2017) and the curated bibliography "Muslim Television Preachers" for Oxford Bibliographies of Islamic Studies (2020).

Sean Foley is professor of history at Middle Tennessee State University. He is the author of *The Arab Gulf States: Beyond Oil and Islam* (2010) and *Changing Saudi Arabia: Art, Culture, and Society in the Kingdom* (2020). He has held Fulbright grants in Syria, Turkey, and Malaysia.

Shadi Hamid is senior fellow at the Brookings Institution and the author of *Islamic Exceptionalism: How the Struggle over Islam is Reshaping the World* (2016), which was shortlisted for the 2017 Lionel Gelber Prize for best book on foreign affairs. He is also coeditor most recently of *Rethinking Political Islam* (2017). His first book, *Temptations of Power: Islamists and Illiberal Democracy in a New Middle East* (2014), was named a *Foreign Affairs* Best Book of 2014.

Marcia Hermansen is director of the Islamic World Studies Program at Loyola University, Chicago, and professor in the Theology Department. Her numerous authored and coedited books include *Varieties of American Sufism* (2020), *Religion and Violence: Theological Reflections* (2017), *Islam, Religions, and Pluralism in Europe* (2016), and *Muslima Theology: The Voices of Muslim Women Theologians* (2013). Her translations include *Shāh Walī Allāh's Treatises on Islamic Law* (2011) and *The Conclusive Argument from God: Shāh Walī Allāh's* Ḥujjat Allāh al-bāligha (vol. 1, 1996). She writes on Islamic thought, Islam and Muslims in South Asia, Sufism, Muslims in America, and women and gender in Islam.

Albrecht Hofheinz is associate professor of Arab studies at the University of Oslo. His research interests include Sufism, Islamic reform movements and local history in the Sudan, Arabic manuscript cultures in Africa, and social media and sociocultural dynamics in the contemporary Arab world. His recent works include "Nextopia? Beyond Revolution 2.0" (2011); "Broken Walls: Challenges to Patriarchal Authority in the Eyes of Sudanese Social Media Actors" (2017); "The Islamic Eighteenth Century: A View from the Edge" (2018); and "Rāqī bi-akhlāqī: The Moral Turn—from Sufi Sheikhs to Facebook Groups?" (2019).

York Norman is professor of Middle Eastern and eastern European history at the State University of New York, Buffalo State. He focuses on twentieth-century Turkish political thought. His most recent book is *Celal Nuri: Young Turk Modernizer and Muslim Nationalist* (2021).

Knut S. Vikør is professor of the history of the Middle East and Muslim Africa at the University of Bergen, Norway. He has published on Saharan history (*The Oasis of Salt*, 1999), on Sufism in nineteenth-century Maghreb

(*Sufi and Scholar on the Desert Edge*, 1995), and on the history of Islamic law (*Between God and the Sultan*, 2005). He was formerly an editor of *Sudanic Africa: A Journal of Historical Sources*.

Shuang Wen earned her PhD from Georgetown University. Prior to joining New York University, Shanghai, as a clinical assistant professor of history, Wen held fellowships at the National University of Singapore and New York University, Abu Dhabi.

Jonathan Wyrtzen is associate professor of sociology and history at Yale University. His first book, *Making Morocco: Colonial Intervention and the Politics of Identity* (2015), won the Social Science History Association President's Book Award in 2016. He is currently completing a transregional reexamination of how the political order of the greater Middle East was unmade, reimagined, and reforged through the Long Great War (1911–34). His work focuses on state formation, nonstate forms of political organization, ethnicity, nationalism, religion, and sociopolitical action in the Middle East and North Africa.

Index